LILLIAN GISH

LILLIAN GISH

The Movies
Mr. Griffith
and Me

By
Lillian Gish
with Ann Pinchot

PRENTICE-HALL, INC., ENGLEWOOD CLIFFS, N.J.

Second printing......March, 1969

LILLIAN GISH   The Movies, Mr. Griffith, and Me
by Lillian Gish with Ann Pinchot

Library of Congress Catalog Card Number: 69-16169

Printed in the United States of America   T

Prentice-Hall International, Inc., London
Prentice-Hall of Australia, Pty. Ltd., Sydney
Prentice-Hall of Canada, Ltd., Toronto
Prentice-Hall of India Private Ltd., New Delhi
Prentice-Hall of Japan, Inc., Tokyo

To my mother who gave me love

To my sister who taught me to laugh

To my father who gave me insecurity

To D. W. Griffith who taught me it was

more fun to work than to play

❧ ACKNOWLEDGMENTS ❧

We owe a debt of gratitude to the Department of Film of the Museum of Modern Art for permission to delve through the D. W. Griffith files and to quote from his papers and Iris Barry's book on D. W. Griffith. We are especially grateful to Mrs. Eileen Bowser, the cataloguer of the D. W. Griffith Collection, to Mr. Willard Van Dyke, Mrs. Margereta Akermark, Mr. Arthur Steiger and Mr. Lucas Perez of the Department of Film who have all been so generous with their time and help to us. Our appreciation also to Mr. William K. Everson for allowing us to quote from his Griffith files, and to Mr. Paul Killiam for allowing us to quote from the Griffith autobiography. We are grateful also to Nell Dorr, Herb Sterne, Phyllis Forbes, Mae Marsh, Agnes Mitchell, and Evelyn Griffith Kunze who have been of such great assistance to us. To our editor Diane Giddis our deep thanks and blessings for guidance, understanding, and help.

Lillian Gish and Ann Pinchot

When she was a baby Lillian Gish had ash blond hair, very pale skin and a fragile body, according to the best recollection of her relatives. She has ash blond hair and a very pale skin today. Her body is so slender that people unacquainted with her might assume that she is still fragile—or at least frail. They could not be more mistaken. For Miss Lillian (as D. W. Griffith used to call her) exudes health and energy. A professional actress since she was five years old, she works whenever anyone offers her anything that seems suitable, and she is the one who never misses a performance.

When she went on location in 1967 in Africa to act in the film *The Comedians* many of the company succumbed to one or another tropical ague. But not Miss Lillian. She acted in the hot sun with no apparent inconvenience; she waited for the others to recover their health. She hopped over to Italy; she hopped back to the United States. She had hardly settled down in her apartment in New York before she started rehearsing in a new play, *I Never Sang for My Father,* in which she spent most of the season. After a long career in show business she is entitled to a little leisure; and her friends would be very happy if she took some because if she did they might have the pleasure of spending an evening with her. But the lady with the ash blond hair and the very pale skin and the erect, slender body is always in transit from America to Europe or Africa or from Fifty-seventh Street to Broadway; and the most her friends can snatch is a functional meal before that relentless evening performance.

Although Miss Lillian is the least pretentious and the least self-conscious of women, she is an American institution. Her life story is part of the American mythology. One of two daughters of a broken and impecunious family, she started earning her living when she was a child. When she began in the theatre actors were held in low social repute; and her mother, whose stage name was Mae Barnard, and she tried not to be too specific about their occupation when they visited relatives or made friends outside the profession. As a child performer she often had to dissimulate her age to escape the calamitous good intentions of the ominous "Gerry Society," which opposed child labor. As a child member of an ignoble profession she was thus in double jeopardy. In the second decade of the century when she began to act in films she faced another barrier. Stage actors looked down on film actors. Film actors were barred from respectable hotels in California. For the first fifteen or twenty years of her life Miss Lillian was under some sort of social cloud.

But she is fiercely respectable. She takes pride in ancestry; she is pleased that Zachary Taylor is a limb on her family tree. Although she has had very little formal education she is an exceptionally cultivated woman. Ever since she was a child she has been a ravenous reader in history, literature, drama and religion. She has been an Episcopalian most of her life. In private as well as in public she represents the best qualities of the American character. Economically she began at the bottom. As a civilized human being she has always been at the top.

In her capacities as both actress and woman there is something elusive about Miss Lillian. She was miscast as the amorous Marguerite Gautier in *The Lady of the Camellias* but she gave a shining, touching performance. For years I have tried to define the secret of the phenomenon of Lillian Gish. I think I know what makes her so magnificent. She has no vanity. She is not concerned with defining, exploiting or defending her reputation. She does not try to be smart or clever. In a play she is not concerned with what it does for her career; she is concerned with the group performance. Work comes first; she comes second.

It is characteristic of her that a large section of her autobiography is concerned with the life and career of D. W. Griffith, the great film pioneer, who taught her the art of the film and had a strong influence on her attitudes towards life. What she says about her acting in *The Birth of a Nation* and *Broken Blossoms* she offers, not as proof of her talent, but as evidence of his genius. She has always regarded herself as a learner.

Although Miss Lillian is not much interested in herself she is very much interested in other people and in what they do and think. That is why she has never been bored or immobilized. She began as a trouper; she is a trouper now.

BROOKS ATKINSON

Lillian Gish is a very considerable person. She is, furthermore, a lady. The word "lady" has become so outmoded as to seem archaic. Certain people do exist, however, to whom it truly applies, and Lillian is one of them. She is considerate and therefore good-mannered. Her values are good, her humor is good, and she has great good sense. All this excellence is flavored by a charming romanticism on one hand and an astringent sense of the practical on the other. These qualities are supported by a disciplined will, good health, and unflagging enthusiasm and energy, not only for her work but also for all the enjoyable things that life has to offer. Finally, she is and has always been a ravishingly beautiful woman.

Professionally she minds her own business, and film and theater gossip leaves her cold. She turns gently aside, without comment or reproof, from the failings and excesses of those who have attained more recent and inflated reputations. The prevalent sloth, bad manners, extravagance, exhibitionism, caprice and vanity of some stars she finds a curious but uninteresting phenomenon. If questioned about any particular example of bad behavior or egomania among her colleagues she will discuss only the talent of the person in question and the dangers to which such excesses expose it.

Lillian herself is not a vain person, although she believes that actors and actresses should guard their health and their appearance, the better to exercise their métier. Her early training and success as an idealized heroine incline her to cleanliness and prettiness, but she will follow most conscientiously the intentions of any director she respects. It must be admitted, however, that she is a little out of sympathy with the modern taste for comedy of stygian black and for drama that excludes the romantic in relationships in favor of the tortured, the twisted and the perverse.

As a professional she is impeccable. She loves her work and is always ready to tackle the daily responsibilities of whatever role, big or small, she has undertaken. Having contributed in no small degree to the early development of the art of film making under the aegis of D. W. Griffith, and having enjoyed several decades of great success as a film and stage star, she is nevertheless ready and eager to discuss the smallest detail and nuance of whatever role she now accepts.

In Dahomey, where we were filming *The Comedians,* I remember a day on which Lillian had a particularly difficult scene to play. The temperature was 130 degrees, and there was no shade—not a tree, not a house, not a café in which to take occasional refuge. Among the things that Lillian had to endure was being pushed in the face and thrown to the ground (a ground covered with sharp pebbles). As the sequence involved four cars, including a hearse from which a coffin had to be forcibly ejected, the work was slow, and the necessary detail of rehearsal considerable. Lillian remained calm, cool, and alert throughout the long day. Richard Burton, who was also in the scene, finally approached me and courteously suggested that the heat and excessive physical work might be too much for a lady of Lillian's delicacy and that perhaps we should stop work for the day. Naturally, I put the suggestion to Lillian. "Nonsense," she replied. "We are here to work, and we haven't completed the scene. Anyway you need the sun—and it will be just as hot tomorrow. I prefer to work until sundown." And that is exactly what she did. At 5:45 P.M. she finished the scene and gave a fine performance in it.

We all then drove back to headquarters. Lillian arrived at my villa

. xi .

later, looking fresh and radiant in a charming evening dress suitable to the climate, and we dined together. We discussed the theater, African politics, and the religious aspects of Graham Greene's literary work. At 11:30 she retired, saying that she was looking forward to meeting everyone on the set the next day—at 6:30 A.M. The evening demonstrated to me that a dedicated, disciplined actress is by no means inevitably a bore. Lillian would be equally at home with the Beatles and with the Archbishop of Canterbury. And they would equally appreciate her.

PETER GLENVILLE

☙ CONTENTS ☙

1

As I pressed my face against the train window, the rain seemed to cover it with tears. I wondered if it was raining on Dorothy's train, wherever Dorothy was. I wished Dorothy and Mother and I could be with one another all the time instead of only when the three of us were engaged by the same touring company. At such times we were overjoyed, for it meant that we could spend our days and nights together. But then we would have to separate again, and we might not see one another for a long time.

But Dorothy and I were luckier than other little girls. We didn't have to stay in one town and go to school—we were in different places nearly every day. We had our lessons in dressing rooms, stations, rented rooms. If we were all together, Mother would arrange the most interesting outings that combined lessons with sightseeing. Perhaps a schoolmaster in a little red schoolhouse might criticize this form of education, but Dorothy and I loved it. Mother always carried a history book under her arm so that she could read to us and answer our questions. In Massachusetts, she took us to Plymouth Rock, and we learned about the Pilgrims. Another time we went to Bunker Hill and Old North Church and heard about the American Revolution. Once, in Pennsylvania, she took us to Gettysburg, and, as we looked out on the gentle landscape where so many young soldiers rested in what Mr. Lincoln had called "hallowed ground," she told us about the Blues and the Grays. It all became very personal for us when she added that her father, Henry Clay McConnell, had been, at fourteen, a drummer boy in the Civil War. For the North, of course; he came from Ohio. Imagine Grandfather McConnell a drummer boy! On our next visit to his saddlery, we saw him in a different light.

Up north there were factories to visit. Detroit was particularly interesting. We saw from the beginning how an automobile was made, even though we had never ridden in one. And in Durham, North Carolina, we went by streetcar to see tobacco growing in the fields. Later, in the tobacco factory, a big, beautiful black woman stopped the machine and gave us a cigarette three yards long curled in a box. Another time we were shown how cotton was picked. Then Mother brought us to the cotton gin to watch the cotton made into cloth.

"These are gifts from God," Mother said, "and are provided by the earth for people who are intelligent enough to know what to do with them."

Sometimes Mother took us to the national cemeteries, and we looked for the names of our ancestors on tombstones. Among Mother's ancestors were English who came to America in 1632; the head of the family, Francis Barnard, decided to settle in Hadley, Massachusetts. His descendants intermarried with Scots, Frenchmen, and Irishmen. By the time Mother was born, the McConnells had migrated to Ohio. Mother's maternal grandfather was Samuel Robinson, a state senator and influential Ohio politician.

Our father was James Leigh Gish. When we were older, we learned that Professor J. I. Hamaker, who taught biology at Randolph-Macon College and whose mother was a Gish, was writing a book, *Mathias Gish of White Oaks*. The Professor traced the family back to 1733, when Mathias first settled in Lancaster County, Pennsylvania. When I asked him once if we had lowered the family standards by becoming actresses, he replied: "Oh, that's all right. I'm only bringing it up to the time of your grandmother, Diana Waltz Gish."

There were so many family names to remember: McConnell, Ward, Robinson, Taylor, Nims, Barnard, Waltz. Our Great-Aunt Carrie Robinson was always interested in the past, and she told us about our ancestor Zachary Taylor, the twelfth President of the United States. All those names were sometimes confusing.

Mother, for instance, was originally Mary Robinson McConnell, later Mrs. James Leigh Gish. When she first went on the stage, she did not want to disgrace her family by using their real names, so she took the name of Mae Barnard. Dorothy and I were usually billed as "Baby" Something or even as "Herself," much as a dog or cat would be identified on the program.

But the little girl whose face looked back at me from the train window knew who she was.

She was Lillian Diana Gish.

"Lillian has a sensitive nose," Mother often said.

Often when I travel a scent will wake me from a deep sleep more quickly than any sound. Countries, I've discovered, have distinctive smells; in France, particularly in Paris, it is the scent of chestnut trees. To me Rumania smells of burned wood, Yugoslavia of roasting coffee, Italy of oregano. But the smells of childhood linger longest in the memory, and Ohio is identified in my mind with the fragrance of fresh growing things in Aunt Emily's garden; of Grandmother Gish, whose perfume was sweet fresh milk; and of my friend Nell Becker, whose natural girl's healthy aroma was overpowered by the smells of developer and fixer from her father's darkroom. But mostly my nostrils remember the rich, pungent smells of Grandfather McConnell's harness-and-saddle shop. I am there once again in the deep, dark shop, with that magnificent horse—a splendid example of the taxidermist's art—standing in the front window surrounded by saddles, their high luster so painstakingly achieved by saddle soap and willing hands, their shiny stirrups and pommels gleaming in the murky light. Whenever I was allowed to visit the saddlery, Grandfather McConnell would lift me to the horse's back, and I would sit proud and straight in the saddle, my full starched skirts foaming over my thin legs. It was a game I dearly loved. Later, when it was necessary for me to learn to ride horseback, I was always comfortable in the saddle.

Mother and her sister, our Aunt Emily, were left motherless quite young. Their Aunt Carrie and Uncle Homer took Emily, and Mother remained with Grandfather McConnell. She was feminine and pretty, with a high, rounded forehead and delicate features. She was sensitive and took after her grandmother Emily Ward, the poet.

Our father, James Leigh Gish, clerked for a wholesale grocery firm in Springfield, Ohio. On a business trip to Urbana, he met Mother. He was handsome, his features regular, his eyes blue, his skin and hair even fairer than Mother's were. They were immediately attracted to each other and were married soon after. He was only twenty, and she was eighteen.

Father left his job and with his savings bought a small confectionery business in Springfield. The young couple was living with Grandmother Gish at the time of my birth, a little more than a year later. I was born with a caul, which Grandmother Gish said would bring me luck. My life did not begin with much promise, however; at three weeks I had an attack of membrane croup. When I was about a year old, Father decided that he would do better in the candy business in Dayton, and it was there that Dorothy was born. If Mother was anxious about my health, she must have been considerably cheered by her second born, who was, in the words of her adoring family, "a dimpled darling." Relatives who remembered us as babies have told me that I had ash blond hair, very pale skin, and a fragile body. Dorothy's curls were reddish blonde, and, although her skin was pale, she did not freckle as I did.

Memories of Mother and Father together are few. I do remember waking up one night to see them standing over my bed. They were evidently going to a party. Mother was in red satin with a long train, Father in a dark suit. They looked so beautiful that the image has not entirely faded from my memory even now. Father was gay and lively; he loved people and gatherings. Mother, with her taste and beauty, charmed everyone who met her. I believe they were happy then.

While we were still living with Grandmother Gish, I developed a habit that annoyed my father. Whenever a grownup left his chair,

I would crawl up on it. Father tried to break me of this habit, but it persisted. Finally, one day he turned me over his knee and proceeded to use a hairbrush on me. I did not take pain and humiliation in silence. Summoned by my screams, Grandma Gish hurried in.

"Leigh, you shouldn't do that," she chided him. "The child knows no better." She rescued me from my ignominious position, evicted Father from his chair, sat down, and put him over *her* knee. Then calmly and forcefully she applied the hairbrush to the same part of his anatomy. Poor Father!

Not that I was without mischief. I had a passion for Castoria, a medicine used as a panacea for children's ailments. Once when we were visiting Aunt Emily Mother saw me climb on a chair in the kitchen, reach for the Castoria bottle on the shelf, and take a mouthful. She said nothing then. But the next time I gagged over the liquid. I hastily restored the bottle to its place and never went for it again. Mother had substituted castor oil.

Father would sometimes take me for walks. We would stop for refreshment, not in an ice-cream parlor but in a saloon. My memories are of dark wood walls, sawdust floors, and the bitter smell of hops. He apparently liked to take me there and show me off. While he drank beer, I would sit on the bar and eat the free lunch—baked beans and sour pickles. I don't imagine that these visits pleased Mother, but it was not in her nature to criticize or nag. I remember being aware even then of her great calm. Perhaps I inherited it, for Mother said that as a child I would sit for hours in my little rocking chair, rocking my doll and staring out the window.

Father could never stay in one place for very long. Whether this restlessness was caused by a gypsy temperament or by a fear of being unable to fulfill his responsibilities was not clear to Mother. We moved from Dayton to Baltimore, where he went into partnership with a Mr. Edward Meixner, again in the candy business. But after two years of Baltimore Father again yearned for fresh horizons. Selling his share of the business to his partner, he set out to find the better life in New York City. Mother remained behind, working for Mr. Meixner. She had a flair for packaging, but unfortunately profits were not enough to support two families. Father sent her money but not enough. She decided to go to New York.

In New York Mother rented a flat on West Thirty-Ninth Street near Pennsylvania Station. She found a job as a demonstrator in a Brooklyn department store, bought furniture "on time," and rented a room to two young actresses. I cannot recall Father being with us immediately, but he was there for a time. I still remember his fair hair and golden beard. He had evidently lost his job, yet Mother managed. I marvel now at her strength. She was not twenty-five, yet she worked to support us, laundered and mended our clothes, and sewed until late in the night—all the while creating an atmosphere of serenity and love. She made all the clothes we wore. Dorothy and I played on the streets, sometimes joining other children, other times watching the organ grinder and his fascinating monkey.

Mother had bought some rather shoddy maple bedroom furniture, obligating herself to pay the furniture company $3 a week. A dark-browed individual known to us as "the Collector" appeared each week to pick up the money, which Mother left with Father. One day, when Dorothy and I were cutting out paper dolls in the dining room, a couple of men arrived and repossessed the bedroom pieces. Father had evidently taken the money and put it to other uses. He disappeared from our lives shortly afterward, although for the next few years he did appear at various times and places when we were on the road. Once, I remember, he was wearing a Van Dyke beard, a cape, and a flowing tie. Perhaps he thought that this theatrical attire would appeal to Mother. He would talk about coming back so that we could be a complete family again, but she would reply that she had tried it too many times to be fooled again. Sometimes he would threaten to take one or both of us with him. Our greatest fear was of being taken away from Mother. She gave us security, Father insecurity. As I grow older, I wonder which was more valuable to my growth. Insecurity was a great gift. I think it taught me to work as if everything depended on me and to pray as if everything depended on God. Somehow, through exposure to insecurity, you learn to do for yourself and not to count on the other fellow to do it for you. Wherever Mother was there was love, peace, and sympathy, yet without insecurity the blessings Mother offered might have left our characters weak and helpless.

One evening during one of those periods when Father was not with us, Dolores Lorne, a young actress, comforted Mother:

"Mary, you work for so little money. With your looks, you should be on the stage. I bet Proctor's could use you. With luck, you could do well—and educate your children properly."

That was how Mother became an actress. She found work as the ingenue in Proctor's Stock Company in New York for $15 a week. Evenings she tucked us into bed before going off to the theater. I can still vaguely see a small room with a table, chairs, and a mattress placed on the floor to protect us from bumps in case we fell out of bed. On matinee days she took us to her dressing room, where we played quietly while she was on stage.

Then one day an actress friend of hers, Alice Niles, came backstage and told Mother that she had been offered a good part in a touring company.

"The only hitch," she said, "is that I must find a little girl to play with me. What about Lillian? She's just the right age." I was five years old at the time.

Mother was reluctant at first, but Alice persisted. She pointed out that my salary would be $10 a week and that I could live on $3. The savings would certainly be enough to tide us over the summer when Proctor's did not operate. Besides, she promised, she would personally look after me; I would be safe with "Aunt" Alice. Her arguments finally prevailed.

It was, oddly enough, a great period for children in the theater. In most melodramas the heroine had a child or two or perhaps a little sister. Not much was demanded of the children; few of the roles were speaking parts of any consequence. Not long after I went on the road with my first play, Dorothy found her first acting job. Mother wrote me that Dolores Lorne had taken Dorothy to play Little Willie in *East Lynne*.

The Gish sisters were on the road.

. 7 .

❧ 2 ❧

Until the second decade of the twentieth century, many theatrical touring companies criss-crossed the country, playing mostly one-night stands. Stock companies were to be seen only in fair-sized cities; the touring companies were the major source of entertainment for rural America. Movies had arrived, but few small towns had movie houses. Isolated communities were hungry for any form of entertainment, particularly drama. Melodramas were especially popular. Audiences loved their action and suspense and sharply defined moral standards. Good was good, evil was evil, and no gradations existed to confuse the audience.

Risingsun was a pastoral village in northern Ohio, where professional road companies were booked regularly. The company was playing *In Convict's Stripes* the night that I made my debut, billed as Baby Lillian.

I had been carefully rehearsed before the performance: taught what to say, to speak loudly and distinctly, and to answer immediately. In the third act the scene was a stone quarry. To avenge himself on the leading lady, the villain had trapped her child and dynamited the quarry. The little girl was to be blown to bits. But from beyond the quarry the hero was to swing himself across the stage on a rope and grab the child just as a great explosion blew the whole place to pieces. As it was impossible to use an actual child, a dummy that looked like me was to be substituted; I would remain hidden behind a papier-mâché rock.

When we came to this scene in rehearsal, someone shouted "Boom," which signified the explosion. But on opening night, I was unprepared, hiding behind my rock, for a real explosion, a blast that shook the theater. I ran screaming off the stage in one direction, while the hero, clutching my counterpart, swung to safety in the other. The audience was delighted with this unexpected climax. I was found under the stage, hiding behind a box, and brought on stage to take my first curtain call, sitting on the hero's shoulder.

What a pity I was not old enough to appreciate the privilege: the leading man was Walter Huston.

Dorothy, meanwhile, had her own baptism in *East Lynne*. To play Little Willie, she was dressed as a boy. Although she was only four years old at the time, Dorothy considered wearing pants a form of punishment. "Aunt" Dolores had tried repeatedly to break her of the habit of picking out the stitches in the hem of her dress, without success. Finally, she warned Dorothy that the next time she did it she would be made to wear her "Willie" pants from the theater to their boardinghouse. Dorothy did pick out the hem again, and the threat was carried out. Even though the trousers were hidden under a coat, she wept with humiliation.

An accident in Fort Wayne, Indiana, proved a severer trial for me. One night, during a performance of *In Convict's Stripes*, a guard accidentally dropped his gun, and the discharge peppered my leg. The powder burns were painful. I ran off the stage to the dressing room. Fortunately, there was a doctor in the audience; he examined my leg and said that I could go through the last act. When I came on again, the audience broke into applause. After the final curtain, the doctor and I were led to the lobby, where I was placed in a deep chair. The doctor used long needles to pry out the buckshot. It hurt badly, for he used no anesthesia. But I had already been trained to conceal my private feelings in public. Pride helped me to survive without tears.

Grandfather McConnell read about the accident and sent Mother a clipping. No doubt some of the family considered it just retribution for Mother's calling.

There was a happy side to my accident though. Great Aunt Carrie and Uncle Homer Robinson also heard about it and sent me a little consolation gift, a fur neckpiece with its muff on a cord and a small pocketbook in the middle; it was of pale-beige lamb's wool. I loved it. It was worth every bit of my ordeal.

"Aunt" Alice, it turned out, was a vegetarian. I subsisted mostly on oatmeal and milk for 5 cents a serving. Often two portions made my dinner. I was grateful to her for looking after me.

As for Dorothy, she had a deep affection for her "aunt." Dolores Lorne was a Roman Catholic and always took Dorothy with her to church. At the end of the season, when we joined Mother in New York, Dorothy boasted to me that she was a Catholic.

"I don't care," I retorted. "I'm a vegetarian."

Despite our high hopes for financial stability, it was impossible for us to save enough from our combined salaries of $35 a week to stay in New York during summer until fall casting began. We had enough, however, to pay our fare to Massillon, Ohio, where we could live with Mother's sister, Aunt Emily, and Uncle Frank Cleaver. Uncle Frank was the window dresser at The Beehive, a big department store in Massillon. Aunt Emily, like Mother, was attractive, well groomed, and a meticulous housekeeper. The Cleavers accepted us warmly, with one suggestion from Aunt Emily: "Remember, if you tell anyone you're in the theater, the children won't be allowed to play with you."

To recall Massillon now is comforting. I see Dorothy, plump, merry, playing wildly with our cousins, who called her "Doatsie." I remember hauling grass to the chickens in a little red wagon and discovering the wonders of growing things, flowers to smell, and cherries to pick. And Sundays after church we met everyone we knew. By the end of the summer I could walk down the street and say, "How do you do," and people knew me.

Mother would not think of asking help from Aunt Emily and Uncle Frank. They were poor, but they lived the same life as did everyone around them. Mother paid our way by contributing staples to the family larder: barrels of flour, sugar, apples. She used the sewing machine to make our clothes for the coming winter, the little coats, hats, and dresses that aroused such admiration when we wore them.

I have often thought of the contrast between Mother's and Aunt Emily's lives. As the daughters of Grandfather McConnell, they should have, in the natural course of events, shared similar lives. Aunt Emily had her husband's devotion, a comfortable home, an appreciative family. Mother was completely on her own. In later years I once asked Mother why she had not married again.

"I wasn't sure another father would be good to you children," she said.

There are women who are primarily interested in men, and there are women who are essentially mothers. Mother was of the latter kind. She proved herself capable of being both parents to us with no equipment other than God-given wisdom. An attractive, feminine woman, she had her share of suitors, but she seems not to have taken any of them seriously.

Just before autumn, Mother, Dorothy, and I said goodbye to our relatives and friends and returned to New York to find jobs for the coming season. We went to agencies that specialized in children's roles. We had learned that if we came to the agency early and staked out our places on the bench near the door, a producer coming in to look for children for a new play would see us first. Dorothy and I would be there at 8:00 in the morning and would wait patiently for the managers, who usually arrived at 10:00. If by good fortune we managed to be chosen, we would be called into another room to audition for the manager. We always prayed to be in a company together, and our hopes were realized that fall when Mother, Dorothy, and I were hired for a touring company of *Her First False Step*.

Helen Ray was the star in this rousing melodrama. We played her children, and Mother had a small part.

Helen came to dinner with us some years later, when she was in *The Prescott Proposals* with Katherine Cornell. She still had a sweater that Mother had made for her during the run of *Her First False Step*.

"I had a long speech to read with Dorothy sitting on my lap," Helen told us, "but I couldn't keep her from looking at the audience. I knew how much she loved black jelly beans, so I put three on the table near us and told her she could have them later if she concentrated on looking at them. The trick worked for nearly every performance and saved my speech."

In the first act, Dorothy was brought in on Helen Ray's arms. I played the other child, barefoot in the snow, peddling newspapers. "Papers—World and Evening Journal!" I would cry. The "snow" consisted of bits of paper, which were swept up every night to be used again. Sometimes nails, bits of wood—once even a little dead mouse—would fall on me along with the paper flakes.

Her First False Step had plenty of action. In the second act there was a race through Hell Gate on a motorboat as the hero chased the villain, who had robbed a bank. The high point of the third act was a circus scene. To avenge himself on the mother, the villain threw one of her children—me—into the lions' den. The hero dived into the cage to rescue me. Mother was not too happy about my playing with lions, but I was pleased, for I liked animals, although I had never before seen a circus or met a lion personally.

Teddy and Jenny, the lions, and their trainer traveled with us. They were circus animals and had not been declawed. During rehearsals I learned that there was to be a fine screen of wire between us; it was invisible from a few feet away. Sometimes women in the audience would faint when the villain threw me into the cage—until the lion tamer, disguised as the hero, rushed in to save me. Then the screen would be pulled back, and the hero would chase the lions back and forth as the curtain fell.

During our first season a cub was born to Jenny. To us, the tawny little thing seemed an out-sized kitten, and we loved playing with it.

But, when it was a few weeks old, it was sent ahead of the company to publicize the play. Once it was put in the window of a shoe store, where it promptly used $38 worth of slippers as teething rings. At matinees the audience was invited to remain seated while Dorothy and I fed the cub's parents meat on long poles. We enjoyed meeting the audiences, and they made a great fuss over us.

Recently, a friend sent us an old scrapbook of Dorothy's early years. There is one photograph of her, with a big satin bow in her thick, curling, shoulder-length hair, a cluster of roses in her left hand, and tulle draped around her shoulders; her eyes are downcast, pensive and sweet. The effect is angelic, and the caption reads, "Little Dorothy, as Hope in *Her First False Step.*"

The following season, to cut expenses, the company took only one child. Dorothy stayed on with Mother, and I found a job as the sister in a play called *The Child Wife.* On one occasion, our troupes were playing in the same town. Our matinees were not on the same day, and I had a chance to be with Mother and Dorothy during their afternoon performances. Dorothy was then playing my former role. I could not bear to watch her in the circus scene. I rushed to the dressing room and put a pillow over my head, to shut out the sound of the lions' roars.

My fears were not groundless. We heard later that after the lions rejoined the circus, Jenny tore the arm off the trainer.

During the seasons that we were to roam the country, Mother and Dorothy were often in one company and I in another. I learned early to be self-sufficient and flexible. As our train sped past a hamlet, with the gates lowered and the warning bell clanging, I would see the little white church, the schoolhouse, the scattering of stores and houses, and I would tell myself how lucky I was to be on the road.

Our lives were divided between the theater and trains, which were our only means of transportation. No meals were served on the train, and we ate when we could. The jumps between towns were short. We usually slept in the daycoaches during the journey.

The trains took us to towns where we played for one night. Whenever we reached a new town, "Aunt" Alice would take me with her to rent a room in a second-class hotel or rooming house for about 50 cents for the day. The other ladies of the company, having deposited their heavy bags at the theater, would then come to call, stay for the entire day, and share the rent. They would lie crosswise on the bed and sleep or sew or, if the water was hot, do their laundry. I would curl up on a chair or go for a walk alone and watch the children of the town playing. We would give up the room before the evening performance and then take the next train out of town.

If there was a long wait in the depot a couple of men in the company would take off their overcoats and fold them into bedding for me. My bed was usually the sloping desk that was used for writing telegrams. Someone would stand guard to see that I did not roll off. If the waiting-room benches had armrests every two feet, I could slip under them, stretch full length, and go to sleep. I remember how unhappy we all were when I outgrew my makeshift sleeping quarters. After that I often napped on a stone floor, with papers underneath my body. Actors, like soldiers, can bed down anywhere. They learn to meet difficult situations or crises without complaint.

Once "Aunt" Alice and I were running across a small bridge in the early winter dawn to catch a train. I was carrying the small telescope bag that contained all my possessions. In my hurry to be ready, I had neglected to fasten the straps securely; they came undone, and my precious belongings tumbled into the fast-moving stream. Everything, including my beautiful little fur piece, was lost. "Aunt" Alice said that there was no time to recover it, as we would miss the train. I ran on. But it was a hard lesson for such a small child.

The problem of money was always with us. The company paid our train fares, but all other expenses were our own. As there was no Actors' Equity, players depended for survival on the success of productions and the honesty of producers. The stories I heard from older members of the company did much to sharpen my capacity for evaluating character. We learned to weigh each manager's reputation and the caliber of his productions. There were a few managers, like the late Charles Frohman, who never had contracts with their people. Mr. Frohman's word was enough. Unfortunately, we never had the pleasure of working for him. But sometimes even kindly, well-intentioned producers simply ran out of funds and left us stranded in mid-season far from New York. In order to survive, we would steal out of a hotel room or boardinghouse at night, leaving behind unpaid bills.

Because they were often forced to leave town without paying their bills, actors had low credit ratings. Few were welcome in first-class hotels. Helen Hayes told me that when, as a child, she traveled with John Drew and his company, he was taken into a first-class hotel but none of his cast was accepted there. When you were away from the theater, I soon learned, you did not mention your association with it.

Perhaps because of the insecurity of their lives, members of a troupe tended to blend into a warm affectionate unit when they were touring. By the time a company had been on the road a month, it was as close as a family, with no social difference between leading players and stagehands. We looked after one another in sickness and helped one another during hardship. If children were well behaved, they received affection and protection. Stagehands often read to us from our favorite books. I remember one carpenter knocking down a man for using offensive language in front of us.

When not traveling on Sundays we were sent to church. We liked that, for the churches were all different from one another. Mother's family was Episcopalian, and Dorothy and I were baptized and confirmed by Bishop Leonard of Cleveland, for whom some of our cousins were named. But Mother believed all religion was good and that any church was better than no church. In Catholic churches, we could not understand what was said, but all the bell ringing and popping up and down in the pews made the service exciting to young children.

Once, while walking alone, I saw a line of people filing into a church, so I joined them, only to find at the end of this line a wooden box inside of which lay the first dead person I had ever seen. Stifling a scream I ran out, and vowed never to stand in a church line again. Even listening to one of the actors read *Black Beauty* before the show that night could not erase that dead face from my mind. I wanted to ask why God made people dead. What was this mystery? But the "aunt" who looked after me for the tour was calling: "Hurry, dear. Get ready. Soon the curtain will be going up."

There was no time for somber thoughts.

Whenever Dorothy and I were in the same company with Mother, our favorite game was to go to the theater early, dress in Mother's clothes, and play house on stage while Mother sewed in the dressing room.

Being on the road must have been trying for Mother. The familiar well-ordered world of her girlhood was one of solid oak and mahogany, of fine linens and inherited silver, of a housekeeper and a hired man. But I don't think she suffered as much for herself as for us. We were often cold and hungry. It was dirt that we minded most— rooms encrusted with the soil of previous tenants, and bugs and cockroaches. If we were to stay in a room long enough, Mother would scour it. But once, when we were in a cold, shabby room with leaking walls and the smell of decay, I added to my nightly prayer, "Please God, don't let us wake up in the morning."

If we were in a town in the Midwest and heard of a church supper, Dorothy and I would pay our quarters to get in and stuff ourselves to the bursting point with food. The church members usually stared at us curiously; child actors were rare visitors to these suppers. In southern boardinghouses we indulged in fried chicken, candied yams, and rich, sticky pecan pie. Sometimes for an extra treat we would have a strand of chewy licorice or an orange on a stick, but these times were rare.

Mother told me that I was three years old when I made my first stage appearance, unexpectedly. Our Sunday school in Baltimore stuffed Christmas stockings for less fortunate children. That year Mother dressed eighty-six dolls. The Empty Stocking Club's distribution was held at Ford's Theater, with Nat Goodwin playing Santa Claus and Maxine Elliott helping to hand out gifts. Dressed in white, perched on Nat Goodwin's shoulder, I was part of the festivities.

Not more than three years later I was one of the underprivileged children on the receiving end.

We were playing in Detroit that Christmas. The stage entrance to the theater was always down an alley, and in Detroit we passed a large automobile showroom when we turned into the alley. When I came out after our Christmas matinee performance, I saw a Christmas tree in the showroom window and displayed beneath it all the things that I had asked of Santa Claus in a letter a week or so earlier: a sleigh; a little comb, brush, and mirror set; *Black Beauty;* and a fur piece almost like the one that I had lost. While I was standing there in awe, three strange men came out of the showroom.

"You're late, Lillian," they said. "Santa's been waiting for you." They led me inside and said the gifts were all mine. Oh, beautiful world, and how kind its people! Every time I play Detroit, I try to find out who those dear men were who, together with the stage-hands, actors, and actresses of our wonderful company, went to such trouble for an unknown child.

Another year Christmas fell on Sunday. Our company manager, a Mr. Schiller, who later became one of the heads of Metro-Goldwyn-Mayer, must have arranged for the company to travel by freight. We celebrated with a tiny Christmas tree in the caboose. It was a glorious surprise. The company gave us candy, nuts, two oranges apiece—an unheard-of luxury—stockings, hair ribbons and, best of all, a little sleigh big enough to hold both of us, which traveled that winter with the scenery and carried us to the hotel, theater, or depot, pulled by loving hands.

The only time Mother ever complained was when Dorothy wouldn't pick up her clothes. Taking good care of our clothes was important; we did not have many. Mother made us identical ward-robes—one coat, one good dress, and one everyday dress each. Her skill contributed much to our appearance. I remember how much the company admired the little black velveteen coats that she made for us.

Mother was always sewing for us but never for herself. One Easter we begged her to have a new dress. She finally bought herself some blue cloth and made a lovely Empire-style dress. Then she bought a hat frame and covered it with little roses from the dime store. She looked so pretty in them and planned to wear them Easter Sunday to church. Meanwhile, she hung them in the closet, and we went to bed, happy and excited.

It rained during the night, and the roof over the closet leaked. The next morning we discovered that the color from the roses had dripped down over Mother's lovely dress and stained it. It was ruined. What a tragedy it was. But it was Mother who comforted us. Always, I remember, Mother was the comforter.

She taught us to think for ourselves. Whenever we asked permission to do something, she never said "yes" or "no" but always "If you think it is the right thing to do." Sometimes this answer would exasperate me. As a youngster, I wanted to be told what to do, not to make important decisions alone.

A few years later, when I was an adolescent, I wrote an English theme about my mother. It expressed how I felt about the woman who was the most profound influence in my life.

The Face Most Familiar to Me

During the thirty-one winters that have passed over her dear head, she has learned to know life's vicissitudes. Instead of hardening her, they have made her a patient, sympathetic God-fearing woman, who seems to make the burdens of life easier for those around her. She is settled and reserved in manner, and she is to be distinguished by her low soft voice, which seems to go with her dignity of motherhood. She is of medium height and size. Her hair is of a golden brown, streaked with grey, and her large steel-grey eyes seem to see into the depths of everything. Her nose and chin are slightly pointed and her lips are closed in a way that suggests a smile. Her short, quick decisive step shows the magnanimity of her nature. It is my most sincere wish that I may grow up to be a counterpart of her.

Lillian Gish

Whenever Dorothy or I happened to travel alone, Mother would always pin a small button on our lapels. I used to think it was an ornament. People often stopped to talk to me, and I believed it was because they admired it. Later on I learned that the button was a Masonic emblem (Father was a 32nd-degree Mason) and that Mother hoped that fellow Masons would look after us.

Being with adults encouraged me to mature too early. I never really learned how to get along with young people of my own age. I could take care of my responsibilities, but I never learned how to play.

We made friends during those long tours on the road, although the nature of our work made it difficult to maintain friendships. Often friendships nurtured during a season on the road would languish after the cast separated. But such is the warmth and kindness of the profession that we could pick up after long intervals and continue as before. Even today I have friends who knew me as a child barnstorming through the country. Among our most durable and rewarding associations were those with a widow and her three children, who, like us, were child actors.

While we were in New York Mother had met Mrs. Charlotte Smith and her three children, and some time later our two families found that they could cut expenses by sharing a flat. Besides Mrs. Smith, there was Gladys, the older girl; Lottie, the middle one; and a dark, sturdy boy, Jack. We loved the Smiths, especially Gladys, who was like a little mother to us. There was never any question when she told us to do something. We did it. She would take us to the theater, where each of us would present his card, which bore the name of his most recent play, and say to the man at the box office: "Do you recognize professionals? We hear you have a very fine play with good actors. Perhaps we could learn from them."

The man would look at Gladys. "Yes, how many seats do you want?"

When Gladys said, "five, please," he would have to lean forward and look down, as some of the heads did not come as high as the box-office window. After climbing up to the gallery for our seats, Gladys would say, "Now you children listen carefully to the way they speak, and watch everything they do, as maybe someday we will play on Broadway."

Lottie, Jack, Dorothy, and I listened, not knowing that soon Gladys would be doing just that.

✤ 3 ✤

When I joined Mother and Dorothy in New York after *Her First False Step* and *The Child Wife* closed, Mother had saved enough money to open a candy-and-popcorn stand at the Fort George amusement grounds at the north end of Manhattan. While she was getting it ready, Dorothy and I posed for artists and photographers at $5 a day, but the work was not steady.

We had to take a room uptown, so the Smiths didn't join us, but they came often to visit us at Fort George. Mother hired a man to make the taffy. While he worked, the Smiths, Dorothy, and I would stand on boxes and call to the crowd to come and try the good candy and popcorn being made before their eyes. We took great delight in doing this.

"Where's Dorothy?" Mother asked one afternoon when the rest of us were perched on our boxes.

"I don't know," I said. "She was here a while ago; I didn't see her leave."

Mother looked around anxiously, but there was no sign of Dorothy. She hurried down the walk and, after a frantic search, finally spotted her younger daughter standing high up on the snake charmer's platform. Mother pushed her way through the admiring crowd and nearly fainted at what she saw: Dorothy had an enormous snake curled around her; the serpent nearly covered her small body. She was totally fearless and enjoying the awe and admiration of her audience.

That afternoon one unhappy little girl sat alone under the candy counter.

That summer Dorothy and I discovered the delights of potatoes Anna—sliced potatoes browned in butter in a large iron skillet. They became our passion; every spare nickel was spent on them. And the time we took from helping Mother was devoted to the pony track. Mr. Craemer, who had the pony concession, came to visit us many years later when we had left the theater for movies.

"How you could ride those ponies," he said. "With or without saddles, it didn't matter. On rainy days, when there was no business, I used to let you children exercise them. I can still see you racing around the wet track with your long blonde hair loose and flying behind you."

Once Dorothy's pony stumbled and fell. She went over his head and lay there in the mud. Mr. Craemer carried her into the small office and called Mother, and they summoned an ambulance.

At the hospital, they found that her arm had a compound fracture. Mother was with her, but evidently none of the people on the grounds could find me. Late that evening Mother came back to the park, looking frantically for me. She found me hidden behind the machinery of the merry-go-round. She took me in her arms and assured me that Dorothy would be all right. I had thought that Dorothy was dead, and I wanted to die too. Instead, I got a spanking for adding to Mother's anxiety.

In the autumn Mother signed the three of us for a play, *The Truth Teller,* with Maude Fealy, which was scheduled to open on Broadway. It never did. It was already mid-season when it failed on the road, and we were obliged to scurry about for jobs. I was chosen to dance in Sarah Bernhardt's company, which had just arrived from Europe.

I recall the Divine Sarah standing near me in the wings, waiting for the curtain to rise. My hair was very fair. Mother put it up in curlers every night, and when it was combed out the effect was like a nimbus around my face. Madame seemed attracted to my hair and would run her fingers through my curls. To my eyes, she was an apparition with her dead-white face, frizzed red hair, and eyes the color of the sea. She spoke in a singing voice, but the words were strange; I had never heard French before.

That production was the first in which I was required to dance rather than to act. It was confusing because I was accustomed to speaking lines. Certain things about the production impressed me, however. The floor from stage entrance to dressing rooms was spread with canvas to protect costumes. There was a maid backstage to press my costume before every performance. Discipline was rigid. When I came offstage, a maid took me by the hand, whisked me up the long flights to the dressing room, helped me change into street clothes, and promptly ejected me from the stage door. This brusqueness always disturbed me, for I was accustomed to the friendliness of our family-like companies.

When my part with Sarah Bernhardt ended, Mother, Dorothy, and I went on tour together in a melodrama, *At Duty's Call*. It proved to be a disaster. What we had always feared actually happened. We were stranded in an isolated southern town without our salaries or fares back to New York. That winter was, I suspect, the low point in our professional careers. Poor Mother, who had let us go hungry rather than borrow money, finally had to write to her father for a loan. Until then we had survived through our hard work and her thrift. The lessons of that ill-fated season, when we were cold, hungry, and discouraged, have lived on in my heart. People in stable professions—teachers, librarians, even clerks—were guaranteed weekly incomes. The financial fate of artists and actors was precarious. I absorbed Mother's philosophy: "If you can't pay cash, do without it. It will help you sleep better." For me, that was the Eleventh Commandment.

I can still remember the three of us in a cold, unfriendly room in a boardinghouse, with Mother trying to remain outwardly tranquil, and the visions it summoned up in my mind: Someday we would live in a house; there would be ample food and fine clothes, and she would never again have to worry. It was such experiences that shaped my character and my future.

That was also the season that Mother had her famous nightmare.

One night we were jolted awake by a scream, so wild and heartbroken that people in the house next to our boardinghouse were alarmed and telephoned the police that someone was being murdered. When the police arrived, Mother was laughing hysterically, which further aroused their suspicions. She explained to them that she had had a nightmare, probably caused by her supper, and they left. But poor Mother, who so disliked publicity, was mentioned in the papers. Even our Ohio relatives heard about her, but fortunately the press kept out one pertinent fact: that she was an actress.

That Christmas we learned who filled our stockings. Santa Claus was in symbol and fact our mother. Dorothy and I had hung stockings on either side of the double brass bed that we shared, and we awakened to see Mother filling the stockings with a few candies, nuts, a tangerine, and a bar of soap apiece. They were our only presents that holiday—except for surprise gifts from our first stage-door Johnnies. Two newsboys who evidently admired us presented us with a bottle of scent each. We thanked them shyly. Later, when we wanted to try out the cologne, Mother advised us against it. She said, "I'm afraid it will leave spots on your clothes."

Looking for a less visible place to use our gifts, we daubed the insides of our shoes. The cologne was evidently made of stronger stuff than we had suspected; our slippers developed a dreadful smell and fell apart. But we had tasted the delight of male admiration.

Finally, our luck changed. Mother and Dorothy were signed to go on tour with Fiske O'Hara, a successful producer, beginning a professional relationship that was to last three years. A playwright named Anne Nichols wrote a play for him each season. This arrangement ended, however, after O'Hara told Miss Nichols an amusing story of an Irish-Yiddish Romeo and Juliet. She later expanded the story into a play called *Abie's Irish Rose*. This fantastic success kept her so busy that she never found time to write another drama for Mr. O'Hara.

Mr. O'Hara acted in his own productions. He was a handsome Irishman with a romantic tenor voice, and he inspired dreams not only in the matinee audience but also in my little sister. Under his unwitting influence, Dorothy blossomed. Recently I unearthed a yellowed press clipping from that period, which says, "Miss Dorothy Gish, who plays the part of Gillie, is one of the daintiest and sweetest little actresses seen here in a long time, and her work is admirable." Another reviewer spoke of her "flirtatious eyes."

When Dorothy fell wildly in love with Mr. O'Hara she was seven years old, and he promised to wait for her. Dorothy was loath to let her adored one out of her sight. In one of his plays, she was to appear in the last act in her nightgown. Normally she stood in the wings waiting to go on. But sometimes in a small theater she could not see him from the wings. At stage right there was a fireplace, its logs lit by a red light bulb. One night she was so mesmerized by her hero that she crawled inside the fireplace and sat on the logs with the red light bulb under her.

Suddenly, during the love scene, the audience began to snicker. Mr. O'Hara quickly turned his back to the audience and looked down to check that his clothes were all right; then he glanced at Marie Quinn, his leading lady. Then he looked around the stage. There in the fireplace was Dorothy, dazed with love, watching her idol.

"Get the kid out of the fireplace," he roared.

Dorothy was nine years old when Mr. O'Hara married his leading lady. I was out with another company, but Mother wrote me: "I don't know what I'm going to do with Dorothy. Since the wedding she doesn't eat, just sits and daydreams. When I was dressing her for the second act, she fell right off the trunk while I was fixing her shoes."

In her final play for him, Dorothy had an entrance in the last act. On Christmas Eve Mr. O'Hara asked Mother to keep the door of their dressing room closed while he made a brief announcement to the audience: "We're changing this scene tonight and actually making it Christmas Eve, as a surprise to the child in our company. We will have a lighted tree on stage that she knows nothing about. I hope you will enjoy with us whatever happens."

Mother wrote me about it: "Dorothy went running onstage as usual, said her line, then saw the tree. She even stopped breathing, couldn't move or speak for a long time—then, bless her, she went right on with her lines after kissing Mr. O'Hara on the cheek. The years of training pay highest dividends in an emergency."

It had been drilled into us that when an audience pays to see a performance, it is entitled to the best performance you can give. Nothing in your personal life must interfere, neither fatigue, illness, nor anxiety—not even joy.

In those days most children were frightened by the bogeyman, but stage children were threatened with another menace. "If you don't behave, the Gerry Society will get you and put you in a big stone castle away from your mother," we were warned.

As the threat of being separated from Mother permanently was the ultimate in terror, I spent bad moments speculating about the dread Gerry Society and thinking how to elude its clutches. We were always having trouble with child-labor laws and with the well-meaning people who believed that minors should be protected from the evils of gainful employment. Few of us were aware of the original high-minded aims of the Society. It was founded in the last quarter of the nineteenth century by Elbridge Thomas Gerry, a New York lawyer who devoted himself to the protection of children working in factories and sweatshops. It was first known as "The New York Society for the Prevention of Cruelty to Children." No doubt the Gerry Society had a reason for existence in most areas of child labor. But its members seemed to single out theatrical children, who had busy, productive, and happy existences. Perhaps the Society thought that rescuing theatrical mites from their exploiting elders would bring the organization a good press. At any rate, we were always alerted to their presence in our vicinity. The Society was particularly active in the Chicago area, and we had to be prepared, which meant that we children, who had been taught to be truthful at all times, learned to lie. Mother was distressed about it, but there was no other choice. We managed to camouflage our immature bodies with long skirts, padding, and veils. I was ten years old when I made an appearance before a judge who accepted my high heels, full dress, and hair done in a Psyche knot as the appurtenances of a sixteen-year-old.

I remember once waiting anxiously outside a judge's chambers while Dorothy was being interrogated behind closed doors. She came out at last, shaking her head sadly. The old gentleman was very strange, she told Mother. He didn't know how many Commandments there were, so she had had to tell him.

We were fast approaching adolescence, and I was growing taller. Jobs were hard to find. When Maude Adams was casting for *Peter Pan*, I was taken to her dressing room at the Empire Theater for an interview. Miss Adams was such a little woman that it was decided to use a shorter child. Interestingly enough, years later when the play was to be filmed I was Sir James Barrie's choice for Peter.

Mother had saved enough money to open an ice-cream parlor in East St. Louis, near where her brother, Henry Clay McConnell, lived with his wife Rose and their son Clay. Eventually she sent for me to help her, and I joined her there. Dorothy was staying in Massillon. In a letter from East St. Louis to my dear friend Nell Becker, I asked: "How is my fat little sister? Does she seem to be satisfied? Bless her old fat heart, she is bad but I love her."

Poor Mother—the confectionery shop demanded all her time. The East St. Louis neighborhood, frequented by railroad men, was not exactly a spot in which to allow a young girl to roam around. The best solution, she decided, was to send me to a nearby convent, Ursuline Academy.

The convent, like the little time spent in Massillon, contributed much to my development. The peace and quiet and the protecting walls appealed to me. The convent's schedule did not seem demanding to me, accustomed as I was to discipline. The only thing that bothered me was the new hours; I had to be up by 5:30 in the morning. The food was simple and wholesome, the lessons interesting, particularly music and French. My natural hunger for knowledge, together with the awareness that Mother spent $20 a month to keep me there, made me an interested, dedicated student.

The sisters knew nothing of my stage experience. I never mentioned the stage, being fearful that if the sisters learned the truth I would be asked to leave. Even after I was chosen to appear in both a play and an opera at the convent, I thought I would like to be a nun. When I confided this ambition to my adored Sister Evaristo, she advised against it.

"No, my child," she said. "Now that I have seen you in our plays, I think the theater is where your future lies."

It was all I could do to refrain from confessing the truth. Perhaps she knew. But I kept silent, and later I learned that for her worldly advice to me Sister was made to do penance. But they were all such dear, dedicated women. I have since persuaded several non-Catholic mothers to leave their children in the sisters' charge, always with happy results.

School ended, I returned to Mother from Ursuline Academy, and Dorothy came on from Massillon. We were living with our Uncle Henry, Aunt Rose, and Cousin Clay and going over to East St. Louis each day to help in the candy shop. All was going well. Mother's little business was profitable, and we loved being with our relatives. It was a particularly happy time for Dorothy and me.

Adjoining Mother's sweet shop was a nickelodeon, and most of the time we were quite busy. Dorothy and I were supposed to stay in the shop, but when business was slack we would steal next door and trot into the hall.

One afternoon we took our places on the little wooden chairs and, sucking delicious oranges on a stick, waited impatiently. At last the lady player sounded the first chords on the piano, the projectionist turned his crank, the title flashed on the white sheet—*Lena and the Geese*—and we entered the world of fantasy.

Except for the faint whirr of the projector and the tinny notes of the piano, all was silent. We soon understood that we were in Holland. Lena, the peasant girl of the title, was pretty, with expressive eyes, a fetching smile, and masses of blonde curls. She looked familiar.

"Lillian, look!" Dorothy grabbed my arm. "There's Gladys Smith!"

It *was* our friend Gladys. Distracted by our discovery yet fascinated by the story, we sat there watching intently. What a satisfying film it was, calculated to move the heart and encourage the tear ducts. Like all our favorites, it was an American Biograph production. Although we were ignorant of his existence, we were already fervent admirers of the work of their director, David Wark Griffith. The film ran fifteen minutes, and after "The End" had flashed on and the screen was again merely a bedsheet we came blinking out into the sunlight and dashed into the candy shop with our news.

"Mother, guess who we saw acting in 'flickers'!" Dorothy couldn't contain her excitement. "Gladys. Gladys Smith!"

We finally nudged Mother into looking for herself, and she agreed it was indeed Gladys. "The Smiths must be having a difficult time of it to allow Gladys to appear in movies," she said with the formality of speech so characteristic of her. "We must look them up when we get to New York. It will be good to see them again."

At about that time I began to feel unusually tired. My fatigue was thought to be growing pains. But the day I collapsed in my room and could not even undress, my aunt called the doctor. My indisposition was more serious than growing pains: I had typhoid fever. The pattern of the sickness—recovery and relapse—took its toll of my constitution. My convalescence was slow. I was content to sit up, wrapped in shawls and with a glass of orange albumin at my side, and to look out the window. One thing troubled me, however; Mother was spending so much time with me. What about the shop?

They had withheld the shattering news from me: The nickelodeon had caught fire, and in the conflagration Mother's shop had been destroyed. There was no insurance. We were penniless again. It was back to Massillon for us, while Mother went to work in Springfield as a replacement for the manager of the confectionery and catering firm of Long's. We were at the bottom again, a familiar condition, but Mother would not allow us to be disheartened. She taught us to believe that every day was indeed a new beginning.

During those years we scarcely ever heard from Father. We never spoke of him, and I relegated thoughts of him to the attic of my

mind. But, when Mother received a letter from his brother Grant
Gish saying that Father was ill and confined to a sanitarium in Okla-
homa, we felt it my duty to go to him.

I was a seasoned traveler, but none of my experiences prepared
me for my first sight of Shawnee. The train pulled in after midnight.
The station was dark and unattended, and there was no one to meet
me. I stood there alone: directly across the track was a building lost
in darkness except for a downstairs light. I went in timidly. The old
man at the desk showed me to a room, and I stayed up the rest of
the night, too frightened to sleep. I prayed. The sisters of Ursuline
Academy would have been proud of me, I thought, as dawn finally
entered the window.

And after that frightening night I never did see my father. Uncle
Grant Gish told me that Father was too ill to stand a visit; perhaps
Uncle Grant was being kind to me, not wanting me to see my father
in an advanced stage of illness but to keep the memory of a younger,
more vigorous man. (Actually, he died about a year after.)

Uncle Grant invited me to stay with his family in Shawnee for a
visit. I accepted, and they sent me to the public school.

Uncle Grant was a railroad man and was away from home much
of the time, but his family treated me as one of its own. Shawnee was
not Massillon, but I accommodated myself to school—except for
mathematics—and a new set of friends and relatives. One of my
friends was an Indian girl whose family had a string of ponies and
who taught me to ride.

In the spring, I joined Mother in Springfield. Dorothy was at a
boarding school in Alderson, West Virginia. In June we picked her
up at the school, then visited our old friends the Meixners in Baltimore and Fiske O'Hara in his summer home in Connecticut.

Fiske O'Hara drove us to New York, where we rented rooms in a
boardinghouse on upper Central Park West and began to look for
jobs. We talked often about our friend Gladys Smith. Mother,
Dorothy, and I decided to call on her. We took for granted that
she could be found at the Biograph studio, whose address we found
in the Manhattan telephone directory.

The morning that we set out for the studio gave promise of a humid day, but Dorothy and I were cool in our full-skirted summer frocks and wide-brimmed leghorn hats. We took the trolley down to Fourteenth Street. Eleven east was a brownstone between Fifth Avenue and Union Square. We paused at the entrance to inspect the sign in the first-floor window: "American Mutoscope and Biograph Company." We went inside to find a winding staircase, to the right of which was a newly built partition with a window like a box office. A middle-aged man was sitting inside, whistling.

"Will you kindly let us see Gladys Smith?" Mother asked.

He looked puzzled. "No one works here by that name."

"Oh, yes!" Dorothy spoke up. "We saw her in one of your pictures called *Lena and the Geese!*"

"Oh, you mean 'Little Mary'? Wait a minute!" He disappeared in the rear and returned shortly. Our friend Gladys was with him. She seemed different, somewhat more grown up, except for her saucy expression and her hair, parted on the side and falling in ringlets to her shoulders. We greeted each other with hugs and kisses. Then, huddled on the bench, we listened while she brought us up to date. Although she was known in films as "Little Mary," not only Gladys but all the Smiths as well had changed their names. They were Pickfords now—Mary, Lottie, Jack, and Mrs. Pickford.

"Mr. Belasco thought it sounded better than Smith, and he changed it when I was in *The Warrens of Virginia,*" she explained.

"Mr. Belasco?" I said, awed. "We hope to see him soon. His manager William Dean is a friend of ours."

"I shall be in his new play," Gladys Smith–Mary Pickford said. We all beamed at one another.

"If you're to be in a play, how can you work in movies?" Dorothy wanted to know.

"Oh, they're great between stage jobs," our friend Mary replied. We were finding the transition in her name easy to accept. "I've been making films for three years, and all that time our family's been together. I'm earning more than I ever have before—much more!"

We gaped.

. 33 .

"And I've been offered twice what I'm making from another company," she added. "We have a nice apartment, and Mother has a car."

"A car!" Dorothy repeated. We were both thinking of our delight in the drive to New York City in Fiske O'Hara's automobile. Was it possible that these films could offer such grandiose salaries?

"You should try films," Mary suggested sagely. "You can always work in them while you're looking for a play. Now wait here, I'll find our director."

Just then a tall, slender man came down the stairs, singing in a fine baritone, "Là ci darem la mano, là mi dirai di sì."

"Oh, Mr. Griffith," Mary called.

"Yes, Mary."

"I'd like you to meet my old friends, Mrs. Gish and her daughters, Lillian and Dorothy."

That was the beginning.

Mary McConnell and James Leigh Gish, parents of the Gish sisters, shortly after their marriage.

Lillian and her mother.

Lillian and Dorothy wearing samples of their mother's exquisite needlework.

Early days in Massillon, Ohio. Lillian and her friend Nell Becker, later Nell Dorr.

Lillian and Dorothy as teen-age film favorites.

One of Lillian's favorite pictures of D. W. Griffith.

Nell Dorr's portrait of Lillian at fifteen.

"I remember one day in the early summer going through the gloomy old hall of the Biograph Studio," D. W. Griffith later wrote of that meeting, in notes for his autobiography, "when suddenly all gloom seemed to disappear. This change in atmosphere was caused by the presence of two young girls sitting side by side on a hall bench. They were blondish and were sitting affectionately close together. I am certain that I have never seen a prettier picture. . . . They were Lillian and Dorothy Gish. Lillian had an exquisite ethereal beauty. I only recently read Alexander Woollcott's comments on her Camille. 'But in the death bed scene, there was around Miss Gish a strange mystic light that was not made by any electrician.'

"As for Dorothy, she was just as pretty a picture in another manner; pert—saucy—the old mischief seemed to pop right out of her and yet with it all, she had a tender sweet charm."

I grope in the files of memory for my first impression of David Wark Griffith.

He looked so tall to my young eyes, yet he was two inches under six feet. He was imposing; he held himself like a king. Later I discovered that he could no more slouch than change the color of his blue eyes, which were hooded and deep-set. He was vigorous and masculine-looking. Under the wide-brimmed straw hat set on his head with a jaunty curve to the brim, his brown sideburns were rather long. His nose was prominent; his profile seemed to belong on a Roman coin, and he had the heavy lower lip and jaw of the Bourbons. It was an important face.

I grew tense under his gaze. He seemed to be dissecting us. What I did not know was that he needed two young girls for a movie he had in mind, which turned out to be *An Unseen Enemy*. As he came toward us, he changed his tune, singing in English, "She'll never bring them in, never bring them in."

I could not understand what he meant, but evidently Mary did. For, when he added in a teasing voice, "Mary, aren't you afraid to bring such pretty girls into the studio?" she retorted: "I'm not afraid of any little girls. Besides, they're my friends."

"Where are you from?" he asked me.

"The theater," I said, "but we come from Massillon."

"Massillyoon." It seemed to amuse him to mispronounce the name. "Well, I knew you were Yankees the minute I saw you." He smiled at Mother, as if it were a joke. Nothing in his voice gave away his background; it was simply a deep, resonant, beautiful voice. He asked Mother, "Can they act?"

Before she could answer, Dorothy interrupted with great comic dignity. "Sir, we are of the *legitimate* theater!"

"I don't mean just reading lines. We don't deal in words here." Aware of our confusion, he suggested, "Come up to the rehearsal hall, and I'll soon find out." He started up the stairs, then paused. "Miss Mary, will you please send Mr. Barrymore, Mr. Walthall, Mr. Booth, and Bobby up to me."

Leaving Mother downstairs, Dorothy and I followed him. We were frightened, yet we felt that the place could not be too sinister if our friend Gladys—Mary!—and a Barrymore were both involved. Mr. Griffith led us into a large chamber that might once have been a master bedroom. Soon several young men came in, and he introduced them to us: Henry Walthall, Lionel Barrymore, Elmer Booth, and the dark-haired boy we had met in the foyer, Bobby Harron.

"Gentlemen," he said in a courtly manner that we were to discover was characteristic. "These are the Gish sisters, Miss Lillian and Miss Dorothy. We will rehearse the story of two girls trapped in an isolated house while thieves are trying to get in and rob the safe." He stared at us. "You're not twins, are you? I can't tell you apart." He strode out of the room and returned with two ribbons, one red and the other blue: "Take off your black bows, and tie these on. Blue for Lillian, red for Dorothy. Now, Red, you hear a strange noise. Run to your sister. Blue, you're scared, too. Look toward me, where the camera is. Show your fear. You hear something. What is it? You're two frightened children, trapped in a lonely house by these brutes. They're in the next room." Mr. Griffith turned to one of the men: "Elmer, pry open a window. Climb into the house. Kick down the door to the room that holds the safe. You are mean! These girls are hiding thousands of dollars. Think of what *that* will buy! Let your avarice show—*Blue,* you hear the door breaking. You run in panic to bolt it—"

"What door?" I stammered.

"Right in front of you! I know there's no door, but pretend there is. Run to the telephone. Start to use it. No one answers. You realize the wires have been cut. Tell the camera what you feel. Fear—*more fear!* Look into the lens! Now you see a gun come through the hole as he knocks the stovepipe to the floor. Look scared, I tell you."

It was not difficult to obey. We were already practically paralyzed with fright.

"No, that's not enough! Girls, hold each other. Cower in the corner." Whereupon he pulled a real gun from his pocket and began chasing us around the room, shooting it off. We did not realize that he was aiming at the ceiling.

"He's gone mad!" I thought as we scurried around the room, looking frantically for an exit.

Suddenly the noise died. Mr. Griffith put away his gun. He was smiling, evidently pleased with the results. "That will make a wonderful scene," he said. "You have expressive bodies. I can use you. Do you want to work for me? Would you like to make the picture we just rehearsed?"

Wide-eyed, with our ears still ringing with the shots, we followed him downstairs. He was calm, but we were both badly shaken. On stage we would have known what was going to happen. We would have learned our lines; the burglars would perhaps have said "Bang, bang!" to indicate the shots. But here there was no script. Mr. Griffith seemed to be improvising; he was the only one who spoke.

"Well," I said, hesitating, "we'd want to talk to Mother first. And, actually, we are looking for parts on the stage."

"That's all right," he said. "I can't use you every day, so you'd still have plenty of time to call on agencies. Would you care to start work today as extras, sitting in a scene as part of an audience? I can use the three of you."

We asked Mother, who thanked him and said, "Yes."

"Bobby!" Mr. Griffith called to the boy.

"Follow him," he told us. "He'll show you where to go." Bobby led us through a door opening into a large room behind the staircase. Then he guided us to a corner that was screened off by a curtain and bare except for a couple of chairs and shelves. This, he informed us, was the ladies' dressing room. He gave us a stick of pale-yellow grease paint and cautioned us not to use rouge, except a little on our lips. "Red photographs black," he explained. "This is a modern story," he added, "so you can wear your own clothes. Only keep your hats off."

Made up, Mother, Dorothy, and I joined the group of actors who were to play the audience in that day's film. The room simulated a theater, but up front where the proscenium should have been there was only a man who kept a huge box—the camera—trained on the actors. The Cooper Hewitts, powerful mercury-vapor lamps hanging from the ceiling, gave off a pungent odor and a weird purple glow that transformed the audience into rows of corpses.

"Ladies and gentlemen," Mr. Griffith began. "You have just witnessed a magnificent performance on this stage. The final curtain is descending. You begin to applaud enthusiastically." He turned to the cameraman. "Ready, Billy?"

"Ready, Mr. Griffith."

"Camer-a-ah—" He rolled the word on his tongue. "Action!"

When the scene was over, the regular lights went on, and I inspected the studio. It was the parlor of the house, with a gallery above where, now that the shooting was finished, a carpenter hammered on a canvas set of a railroad station.

Such was our introduction to the Griffith style of directing.

As we all filed past a desk, someone gave each of us a blue voucher, which we then handed to the man in the partitioned booth in the office. He in turn gave us each $5. Five dollars! Fifteen dollars for the three of us for doing so little! And Mr. Griffith told Dorothy and me definitely to report back in the morning for the parts we had rehearsed.

Accompanied by Mother, we appeared promptly the next morning, feeling stiff and shy after that extraordinary session with Mr. Griffith. Bobby Harron greeted us warmly; he was also to act in the picture. We also met Mr. Bitzer, the cameraman, who said little, except to tell a rather innocuous joke once in a while.

Mr. Griffith had rehearsed *An Unseen Enemy* with other actresses, but after meeting us he decided we would be suitable for the leads and changed the plot just enough to fit us. In the morning he rushed us through more rehearsals. Then after lunch Dorothy and I picked out dresses from a rack of second-hand clothes reeking with fumigant and changed. Then we went into the studio, where the sets were in place, and started working.

When the first day's work was over, we rushed to the little window in the hall, wondering how large our checks would be. But again each one was for exactly $5. Five dollars a day was standard whether one played a lead or an extra; unless, of course, one was on weekly salary. Still, Dorothy and I earned $10 that day and $20 the following two days, a total, with our and Mother's first-day's pay, of $45 for four days, which was more than we had ever made in the theater. We left our names, asking to be called whenever there was work for us. Meanwhile, we would be looking for parts in a play.

"That Mr. Griffith," Mother said, "is such a nice man."

❦ 5 ❦

The "nice man" who directed us in our first movie that day—
and who was to change our lives radically—had traveled a long and
difficult route to the studio on East Fourteenth Street, a route that
originated in Crestwood, Kentucky, where David Wark Griffith was
born on January 23, 1875.

Mr. Griffith had a great sense of family; as he grew to know us,
he spoke to us often and with deep affection of his mother and with
endless pride of his father. Gradually we learned about his background and his people; and information I have gathered recently from
going over his files and the unpublished notes for his autobiography
has completed my knowledge of his life prior to the time of our
meeting.

Family, home, the South—these forces shaped the life of the man
who created the art of storytelling on film. The War Between the
States had been over for nearly a decade when he was born, but his
family lived in its grim shadow during all of his youth. The original
Griffith plantation, though not considered one of the great establish-
ments of the South, was nevertheless for years a social landmark in
Oldham County, Kentucky. It was burned and completely destroyed
by Union soldiers in the first year of the war. The gracious approach

to the house, its ruins, and the burned-out fields were overrun by wild shrubs, grass, and vines.

David was born in a small farmhouse that his father had built for the family after the war, near the old manor house. The only reminders of former glory were a few Negro families who, preferring the security of the known, lived in their shacks and helped to raise David and his six brothers and sisters.

David—when he was Mr. Griffith—once said to me, "I think the one person I loved most in my life was my father. I wonder if he cared anything about me particularly."

To everyone who knew him, Colonel Jacob Griffith was a vital, blustering, well-loved man. He was distinguished by his remarkable voice, which was rich and dramatic in tone and timbre.

At dusk, the Colonel would sit on the veranda looking out at the fields and tell the young David of the great battles of the Civil War. But often the Colonel went farther into the past, and, as he talked, young David's mind would be filled with heroic visions.

"You are descended from kings, David," the Colonel used to tell him, "the Apt-Griffith Kings of Wales."

David heard from his father that the first of their ancestors to migrate to America was Lord Brayinton. David's Great-Grandfather Salathiel fought in the American Revolution and afterward settled as a planter in Virginia. There David's father, Jacob Wark Griffith, was born.

Jacob was endowed with wanderlust and a thirst for adventure. The indolent life of the young southern aristocrat bored him. Before he was out of his teens he set out for Kentucky. There he studied medicine and even hung out a shingle in Floydsburg. But he soon abandoned the role of physician. He rode south, helping to conquer Santa Anna at Buena Vista with Zachary Taylor's outnumbered troops. (Zachary Taylor, incidentally, was one of my mother's ancestors.) When the Mexican War was over, Jacob married a southern girl, Mary Perkins Oglesby. She came from a distinguished Virginia family and was also related to the aristocratic Carters. But Jacob was evidently not yet content to settle down as a husband and father. Two years later he left his wife and children to take command as a captain-escort of a wagon team that left Missouri for California in the wake of the Gold Rush. He returned finally to Crestwood, situated just above the blue-grass belt, moved his family into the big house, took up in earnest the cultivation of his lands, and prospered. He was by then forty-five years old and the father of five children. He was elected to the Kentucky State Legislature and considered his soldiering days past. At the outbreak of the Civil War, however, he became a colonel in the Kentucky cavalry.

Years later his son David learned American history lessons at first hand. He heard about the firing at Fort Sumter and the beginning of the long and bloody war. The tragedy, the Colonel told him, was that the valiant men who had fought so heroically together in Mexico —Lee, McClellan, Grant—were divided in the Civil War. As enemies they marched on each other with great armies. Under the spell of his father's rhetoric, David could hear the thunder of Sherman's march to the sea and General Lee's tragic farewell to his troops.

"My father was a colonel under Stonewall Jackson," D. W. Griffith told me. "He was wounded five times. Once he was left for dead on the battlefield. He was virtually disemboweled. Fortunately, a surgeon nearby heard him moaning. The doctor sewed up the wounds, while my father bit down on the rim of his old campaign hat to keep from crying out.

"Later in the war, down in Tennessee, my father was scheduled to lead a cavalry charge. He was greatly troubled by a festering shoulder wound, but that didn't stop him. He was hit in the hip by a minié ball and was supposed to turn the command over to his subordinates. Then the bugle sounded. The cavalry was to charge. Father pulled himself up from his stretcher. He couldn't mount his horse, so he commandeered a horse and buggy and ordered a nearby soldier to help him into the buggy seat. Ignoring the pain in his leg, he urged the horse to the front of the column and in all of his bloody glory led the charge. His voice rose above the bugles as he bellowed, 'The wrath of God and Robert E. Lee upon the damned Yankees!' That's how he earned his nickname, 'Roaring Jake.' "

D. W. Griffith always glowed with pride when he retold this story.

When Mother, Dorothy, and I were with him in London during World War I, generals in the British War Office—all close students of American military history—recalled that Colonel Jacob Wark Griffith was the only soldier in history who had led a cavalry charge in a horse and buggy. D. W. was plainly more honored than if they had awarded him the Victoria Cross.

During the last days of the war Colonel Griffith and a small group of his men were elected to help President Jefferson Davis escape to the West. But a month after Lee's surrender to Grant at Appomattox, they were trapped at Irwinsville, Georgia. When Jacob was finally free to return home, he found it destroyed. He was able to build only a small farmhouse on the crest of the hill, and there in 1875 David was born. The Colonel served once more in the state legislature, but the circumstances of his life were different. The defeat of the South had brought financial hardship and moral despair in its wake. The only things left to the Colonel were his pride and his magnificent voice. Every Sunday night through the last years of his life, he gave readings for the family, neighbors, and friends who gathered in the farmhouse parlor. The Colonel read from the Bible or Shakespeare —or he and fellow veterans reminisced about the war, fighting the battles over again.

Though the presence of the Griffith children was obligatory, David at least never considered it a duty. Quiet, unobtrusive, often crouched under the table, but always near his adored father, he listened as drama and history unrolled in that sonorous voice. The stories fired his imagination and fostered pride in his heritage. He accepted legends and absorbed facts that were born again a generation later in his reconstruction of the South's tragedy, *The Birth of a Nation*.

He was a precocious youngster, already given to the use of words beyond the range of an average boy. The Colonel often tutored the boy, and his older sister Mattie also helped him with reading. He went to the country school, but it was Mattie, a teacher in a girls' academy, who made the process of learning a rich and exciting experience for him.

Often he played alone in the ruins of the big house, perhaps imagining the gracious days before the holocaust. He was already a loner by choice. The trivia of childhood evidently bored him.

His mother never allowed him to be called anything but "David." "Davy" was forbidden. In his autobiographical notes he says:

> She used to give me a little lunch basket and start me off to school with, 'Now David, remember who you are, and always keep in mind that your name means *Dearly Beloved.*' That was instilled in my mind. I remember one morning going to school and there were icicles on the trees, there was a branch particularly laden and gleaming and just as clearly as I can see a brick wall, I saw the face of Christ. I stopped and paused and said, 'My name is David and you know that means Dearly Beloved and I hope you may like me a little and I might be your dearly beloved because I love you and always have.' And then the sun perhaps changed a little on the icicles and the face disappeared, and until this day I often wonder if I might not have seen the face of Christ.

We who worked with D. W. Griffith later were aware of the mystical component in his nature. His vision seemed to stretch far beyond that of other men.

His first clear memories were of a beloved pet, a yellow sheepdog: "The dog was a cavalier dog like all of our family, whatever that means," D. W. wrote. "It generally means having a lot of ancestors on both sides and managing to escape being hanged. Also, like the rest of the family, the dog liked the ladies." It was the animal's duty to herd the flock of sheep. He was dependable and trustworthy until one day, in an excess of zeal, he mauled a sheep to death. David's father felt obliged to shoot the animal.

David accepted the decision without tears or pleading. He knew that when a sheepdog becomes a killer his useful days are over, yet he suffered deeply when the animal was killed. He was not allowed to bury the dog, although the animal had been his companion. "I asked what they did with him," he wrote, "but nobody told me."

I wonder if this experience left him with a sense of fear that if he loved too intensely his love would be taken from him. That he was always sensitive to rejection is evident to me from the early notes for his autobiography. He said that he was writing "this junk because I need the money and there are so many damn fools in the world that some of them are apt to read it." How carefully this off-hand statement helps him to insulate himself against critics!

As David grew older, he became aware of the plight of his debt-ridden family. Like their friends and neighbors the Griffiths were caught in the backwash of war, and their circumstances worsened. The war's end, like the general conduct of the war itself, had been noble. Men like "Roaring Jake" Griffith had looked with hope to President Lincoln. But Lincoln's assassination had wiped out their hopes.

When David was ten his father died. He accepted the loss stoically. But only then did the family learn that the Colonel had not only mortgaged his land but had also carried the mortgages at 10 per cent compound interest. All that was left was staggering debts. Mrs. Griffith gathered her brood and moved to a smaller farm, but ill luck dogged the family. The new farm failed to pay its way.

Finally, in despair, the Griffiths loaded their scant possessions onto a wagon and set off for Louisville, some twenty miles distant.

The boy welcomed the move. "We were going to live in the city," he wrote.

> No more back-breaking toil in the tobacco patch; no more yanking a two-horse plow around the row-end, no more struggle with obstinate cows; no more tediously long farm chores. We were going to the city—hooray! Hooray!
>
> We trundled right into the heart of the city of Louisville with our furniture piled atop the old two-horse wagon and I on top of the furniture.
>
> "Country jakes! Country jakes!" people shouted, laughing at us.

Louisville was a gay town. Young David was so captivated by the sights and sounds that he forgot the still-unresolved family hardships. The streets were thronged with colorful personalities who came to Louisville by riverboat—drummers, gamblers, minstrel men, and ragtime musicians, who brought a wonderful pulsating music from New Orleans. The city's six theaters were always booked solid with concerts, vaudeville, and theatrical troupes featuring such internationally famous figures as Helena Modjeska and Sarah Bernhardt.

When Julia Marlowe, queen of the American stage, played in *Romeo and Juliet* at Macauley's Theatre, young David occupied a 10-cent seat in the gallery. It requires no great imagination to picture the boy, leaning forward in his chair to catch every nuance of Marlowe's rich lute-like voice reciting Shakespeare's verse. As he joined in the ovation following the final curtain, he resolved to become the American Shakespeare. It was a goal that he was never to renounce.

He began to take singing lessons; his voice, so much like his father's, showed promise of depth and range. No doubt his interest in the opera originated during those two years. When he was a grown man he required few possessions, but, his secretary told me, he owned a magnificent library of operatic scores.

After he became old enough to work he held a succession of jobs. He was an errand clerk in a dry-goods store and a cub reporter on the Louisville *Courier*. But the work he cherished most was clerking in Flexner's bookstore. He spent hours hidden behind the stacks, his hungry mind absorbing the works of the contemporary writers, as well as all of Shakespeare and Dickens. Fortunately, old Mr. Flexner was a patient and kindly man.

"David," he would say, "I think it is wonderful that you should want to read all the books. But don't you think you should occasionally dust a little, too?"

He passionately admired Walt Whitman, whose deep love of country he shared. In later years I often heard him say that he would rather have written one page of *Leaves of Grass* than to have made all the movies for which he received world acclaim.

Edmund Rucker, an early friend of young David, describes him in those days as "tall, beaknosed, loose jointed." Mr. Rucker adds that David first appeared in Louisville wearing jeans that reached only to his ankles, red suspenders, and rawhide shoes and that he was badly in need of a haircut. He appeared stiff and hard to know. But the two boys often met at the library, and according to Rucker David already used big words and seemed greatly interested in history.

He had begun his apprenticeship as a writer, having roughed out a plot about the exiled Duke of Orléans, who, according to legend, had come to Kentucky and lived for a time somewhere along the Ohio River. Fired by the story, Edmund Rucker and David would explore the river's edge, searching for miles along the shore for what was alleged to have been the Duke's cabin. In his script David had the Duke fall in love with a Kentucky beauty and then renounce his love in favor of duty and return to the throne of France as King Louis Philippe. It is interesting to speculate on why this theme of an exiled princeling appealed so greatly to David and whether or not he saw a parallel between the restoration of the prince to his throne and the return of the Griffith clan to its original station. (When toward the end of the century he was touring the country as an actor, he used the name of David Brayinton during one engagement in memory of his ancestor Lord Brayinton.)

Someone had evidently told David that the way to write successful plays was to learn stagecraft and that the way to learn stagecraft was to act on the boards. This prospect appealed to David; like his father he had a strong theatrical strain. But his mother was horrified.

"The Griffith men have indulged in many things," she said, "but no one has fallen so low as to become an *actor.*"

In order to spare his mother embarrassment and to avoid tarnishing the family name, he changed his name from David Wark Griffith to Lawrence Griffith and went in search of an acting job.

None of the touring companies showed interest in the boy. At last, in despair, he found a place in an amateur group organized by two stage-struck quasi amateurs, a riverboat comedian and the local blacksmith. David Griffith's sole comment on his debut was brief: "Well, we escaped alive."

"We played one-night stands in small towns," he recalled about the troupe. "We were so bad that the audience usually got its money's worth out of heckling us. We seldom made enough to pay room rent, but the blacksmith usually solved that problem by making the landlord a member of the company and giving him a piece of the show. Before we broke up there were more landlords than actors in the troupe."

He was subsequently taken in by the Meffert Stock Company. It was a great opportunity, and David made the most of his part. In fact, his embroidery was so rich that, when, after the performance, he asked for a reaction, the company manager said dryly, "You are too grand for us."

At twenty-three David Wark Griffith was tall and lean, with a long handsome face. His chest was deep, his voice so compelling that it reverberated to the last row of the gallery. His voice teacher had told him that his voice was one of the most powerful he had ever heard; now the ambitious young actor made full use of it. For the next five years he toured the United States in road companies that offered bare subsistence or left him stranded in strange places. But he was learning his craft, and whenever a company folded he set about looking for another role.

"My education is still unfinished," he said with notable good humor.

Between jobs he worked at any chore to earn enough for food and shelter and a ticket back to the urban centers where shows were cast. During that period the variety of his jobs helped to give him insight into human behavior. He puddled ore in a steel mill. He picked hops in California with people whom he described as "thrifty plain people and operatic Italians who drank dago red and sang the sextet from *Lucia* while they picked." He worked aboard a lumber ship that traveled along the West Coast. At one time when he was penniless and without prospects, he hopped a freight, camped with hoboes, and lived on handouts. Finally, starved and frozen, he tramped the last few miles into Louisville, with his shoes wrapped in rags.

Failure did not deter him. These hardships developed his body and, as he told us later with great pride, gave him muscle. It was not in the nature of a Griffith to knuckle under to adversity.

Even the awareness of his mother's disappointment in his choice of profession served as a spur to his ambition. Conditions improved. He had a good year with Ada Gray's company on her farewell tour. That same year he played Abraham Lincoln with the Neill Alhambra Stock Company in Chicago; he then traveled west to appear in *Fedora* and later in *The Financier* and *Ramona*.

He often claimed that young women did not usually look on him with favor, but in San Francisco he met an attractive young actress named Linda Arvidson who responded warmly to his interest. They parted, however, when he was signed as a regular member of the famous Nance O'Neill Company. But during its leisurely tour of major cities on the way eastward Griffith apparently missed her. In Boston, where the company settled down for six weeks' run, Griffith wrote asking her to join him. She had been in San Francisco during the earthquake, and her safety was no doubt a source of deep concern to him.

In May she arrived, and they were married in the Old North Church.

Even in his youth, D. W. Griffith seemed an unlikely candidate for marriage. Something about him was larger than the conventional concept of marriage seemed to require. Yet he *was* married, and new responsibilities goaded old ambitions. To the trunk already stuffed with unsold manuscripts—full-length dramas, one-acters, short stories—he now added poetry. Even without any sales to encourage him his energy did not flag. When he was not writing, he was reading.

The theatrical season was dead when in June 1906 the young couple arrived in New York City. The Griffiths sublet a small apartment on West Fifty-Sixth Street and went in search of jobs for the fall. They were fortunate, and both were hired for the Reverend Thomas Dixon's Company, which had just completed a southern tour of Dixon's play about the Reconstruction, *The Clansman*. He was chosen to play the lead in another of Dixon's dramas, *The One Woman*, and she was to be an understudy.

While waiting for rehearsals to start, Griffith continued writing, a new play this time. He was also obliged to work at odd times for eating money, "scraping rust from the iron supports in the new subway for two dollars and a quarter per day." Feeling that he had to "keep up a front," he would steal out of the apartment to the alley and there put on his overalls before setting off for work.

And all during those humid summer months he completed his first three-act play. It was based on his West Coast experiences, and he called it *A Fool and a Girl*. It began its rounds among indifferent producers as the couple set out for Norfolk, Virginia, to appear in *The One Woman*. She was to be paid $35 a week and he $75, and this money would sustain them until his literary luck improved.

But their hopes failed to materialize. Griffith was fired after two months when an enterprising actor offered to play his part for half his salary. Naturally, Linda Arvidson was also let go.

They returned to New York, nearly penniless. On Christmas Day they made hamburgers to substitute for turkey.

Griffith played his part until after the meal, when, with coffee, he handed his young wife a slip of paper. It was a check! His play was sold! James K. Hackett, the producer, had bought *A Fool and a Girl*. David Griffith had achieved his dream; he was a playwright.

The advance of $1,000 seemed a fortune to the young couple. D. W. began to concentrate in earnest on his writing. Another success followed, a short story sold to *Cosmopolitan* magazine for $75. Then a poem was sold to *Leslie's Weekly* for $6.

The diversity of these sales was proof to him of the versatility of his talent, and he looked forward to the opening of his play.

A Fool and a Girl opened in Washington with Fannie Ward in the lead. It lasted a week in the capital and another week in Baltimore. Then it folded. Miserable and discouraged, the young Griffiths returned to New York once more, their funds exhausted. Griffith saw realistically that a free-lance writer's life, like that of an actor, was one of anguish and disappointment. For each success there were innumerable failures. The law of averages simply did not apply to the novice writer.

Yet the need to write, the hunger to have his words spoken on the stage, never weakened. As no acting jobs were immediately available, he continued to write. He began work on a drama of the American Revolution, to be called simply *War*. In preparation, he initiated a habit that was to be of enormous help to him later in researching *The Birth of a Nation, Intolerance,* and other historical dramas. He and his wife spent endless hours at the Astor Library, where, he says, "we copied soldiers' diaries and letters and read histories of the period."

Each day he devised fresh plots and variations on established plays. But to face each morning of writing meant also that he had to face the fact that he was a failure. He was as poor as he had been during his acting days, but he was no longer a vagabond; he was in his early thirties and married. The writer in him clung to his craft, but the mature man knew that other action was necessary.

🌿 6 🌿

In the tail end of the nineteenth century, a new phenomenon had captured the imagination of the American public. In places called "penny arcades," which were usually rented stores, people could see "moving pictures"—strips of film on assorted subjects—by dropping a penny into a slot and peering into a machine called the Kinetoscope. A few years after the Kinetoscope made its appearance, it was superseded by the Mutoscope, a peep-show machine owned by the American Mutoscope and Biograph Company, one of the leading motion picture companies. By 1896 film images were being projected on screens, usually in vaudeville houses. These early movies, which were mostly photographed vaudeville acts, were greeted enthusiastically. But the novelty was short-lived. By 1900 movies were the last act on the programs in the vaudeville theaters in which they were shown.

Movies seemed to have no future until, in the first year of the century, vaudeville actors struck for higher wages. Theater owners had no choice but to show movies exclusively. Film equipment was purchased in large quantities—until the end of the strike. Projection manufacturers, who had responded to the demand while it lasted, suddenly found themselves overstocked; theater owners were willing to sell their machines cheaply. The penny arcade owners, who had long wanted to show films on screens but had been unable to compete with the theater owners, now had an opportunity to buy the equipment at bargain prices.

Not only arcade owners but small-time entrepreneurs everywhere found a new and quick source of income. They rented unused stores, fitted them with projection machines, a screen, and some chairs, and charged a nickel admission. Called "nickelodeons," these new movie houses, cheap and accessible to everyone, enjoyed phenomenal success, and were established in small towns and large cities throughout the country.

The average program lasted thirty minutes and consisted of several short subjects, each running from 100 to 200 feet of film. The nickelodeons stayed open twelve hours a day. As the average film rental was about $15 a week and a well-situated nickelodeon could easily make $60 a day, the venture could be very profitable. Often the projectionist ran color slides with words of popular songs between shows. There were also suggestions on the audience's decorum and always the admonition, "Ladies, Please Remove Hats." Advertisements for local emporiums soon began to appear on the screen, adding to the owners' sources of income.

By 1908, there were already between 8,000 and 10,000 nickelodeons in the country. Originally dark and ill-smelling places, patronized in the cities by the poor and uneducated, the nickelodeons became cleaner and more well-appointed as they gained in popularity. But "respectable" people continued to look down on them and the movies that were shown in them. Stage actors called them "galloping tintypes," and considered working in them only slightly better than starving.

This was the situation when D. W. Griffith first became aware of the movies. He was walking down Fourteenth Street, worried and disheartened, when he noticed a line of customers before a nickelodeon. A few days later he was drinking coffee in a cheap restaurant called Three-Cent John's Eating Emporium. Seated across the bare table was a casual friend, an elderly actor who, because of his mournful expression, was known as "Gloomy Gus" Salter.

They exchanged hints on new theatrical prospects. "Why don't you go over and see Porter at the Edison Company?" Salter suggested. "He's usually good for a few days' work. Besides, he's always looking for stories for his motion pictures. And you're a writer."

Griffith regarded Salter indignantly. "I haven't reached the point where I have to work in films," he retorted.

"Gloomy Gus" shrugged. "Well, it's better than not eating."

On his way back to the rooming house where his wife was waiting for him, D. W. mulled over Salter's suggestion. Edwin S. Porter, who had begun as a cameraman for the Edison Company, had been experimenting with moving pictures. *The Life of an American Fireman,* which Porter released in 1903, depicted an event that, although staged, might actually have happened. Furthermore, by piecing his film shots and rearranging various action shots Porter had discovered the principles of editing. In *The Great Train Robbery* of the same year, he refined his technique. Longer and more complex in its editing than *Life of an American Fireman, The Great Train Robbery* was an immediate popular success. The result was a demand for films with stories, but there were no further developments in technique until the advent of David Wark Griffith.

Perhaps D. W. thought that, because films never gave billing to casts or writers, writing for pictures might not be too bad. It was better than letting his wife do without necessities. He told her of his plans.

"What an awful way to make a living," she said sadly. She too felt superior to this strange stepchild of a classic medium. "But I suppose it will have to do until something better comes along."

They went to work, Griffith pacing the floor as he dictated, his wife taking it all down on her typewriter. The next day, with a freshly written synopsis of *La Tosca* in hand, he went to the Edison Studios and offered Porter the scenario. Porter scanned it.

"It's not for us," Porter said, "but if you want to stick around, you can play the hero in the picture I'm about to make."

Thus casually David Wark Griffith made his entrance into the movies.

Porter's film was called *Rescued From an Eagle's Nest,* and Griffith played a woodsman who saved an infant from the eagle's claws. Griffith had hesitated before accepting the role, but Porter, accustomed to the reluctance of professional actors to work in the new medium, said, "No one will recognize you, if that's what worries you."

The salary was $5 a day, payable at the end of each day.

But Griffith's primary interest was still in the written word. As Edison was evidently well stocked with scripts, he decided to try other studios. Early in 1908 he approached The Biograph Company. His scripts pleased Wallace McCutcheon, the director, and soon he was disposing of a good many stories at the fabulous fee of $15 each. Among them were *Old Isaacs the Pawnbroker, Ostler Joe, At the Crossroads of Life,* and *The Music Master.*

That he considered the manufacture of movie scripts an unhappy compromise with his real goal is evident in an ironic entry in his autobiographical notes. The scripts he sold to Biograph were good, he said, because "most of them were borrowed from the very best authors." In those harsh times the only satisfaction was the security of a fairly regular income.

He also acted in some of the Biograph films. In his mid-thirties D. W. was a distinguished man who photographed strikingly even under the primitive conditions of the day. His wife was also acting at Biograph, using her professional name of Linda Arvidson. They played together in a capsule version of *When Knighthood Was in Flower,* and they kept their marriage secret, to avoid any criticism from other actors who might resent two Griffiths on one payroll.

Biograph was in serious difficulties about the time he came to work for the studio, D. W. once told me. This pioneer organization had produced a good many mutoscopes, which were a variation of Edison's kinetoscope. In a burst of optimism, the company branched out into films that told stories. But sales had recently dropped. Competition was fierce among the embryonic movie companies. Piracy was rampant. Unscrupulous rivals stole film prints, remade a few major scenes and coolly released the bastardized results as their own creations. Finally, Biograph found a way to block such blatant theft by putting the company's trademark—the initials "AB"—somewhere in each scene, on the doors, walls, or windows. Another problem involved constant lawsuits with Edison, who held the only patent on a particular camera.

Within its organization, Biograph had other problems, one of them being the need for a good director. Unlike Porter, who had begun his career behind the camera, Biograph's two cameramen—Arthur Marvin and Billy Bitzer—showed no ambition to direct. When one of the directors fell ill, Arthur Marvin suggested to his brother Henry N. Marvin, president of Biograph, that Griffith might be a prospect for a director. Griffith's scripts were lively and inventive, and he always gave more than was expected of him.

Griffith considered the new offer in silence. He finally shook his head. "Thank you, Mr. Marvin, but I don't think so."

"We'll pay you fifty dollars a week. And if you work out, a percentage of sales."

"*If* I work out," Griffith said wryly. "That's the catch. I'm making a pretty good living writing scenarios. Suppose I turn out to be a poor director and get fired? I'd be out of two jobs."

"That's the wrong way to look at it, Mr. Griffith. Films have a great future."

"Perhaps. But I don't know a thing about directing."

"You'll learn." Mr. Marvin sounded confident. "Let's keep it this way—should you fail as a director, I'll give you back your old job. Fair enough?"

"Fair enough. I'll try it."

Griffith had misgivings nonetheless. In the spring he had been offered a job in summer stock, but he had rejected it to continue writing scripts and occasionally to act in films. He had since wondered if he had made a mistake in turning down that offer. Then suddenly he was much too busy for introspection.

During two days in June Griffith directed his first movie. The film, about a child kidnapped by a band of gypsies, was called *The Adventures of Dollie*. Although Billy Bitzer was not the photographer on the film, he helped with the direction. Bitzer, who has left records of his sixteen-year association with Griffith, wrote of Griffith's directorial debut:

> The cameraman was the whole works at that time, responsible for about everything except the immediate handling of the actors. It was his say not only as to whether the light was bright enough but make-up, angles, rapidity of gestures, etc., besides having enough camera troubles of his own. . . . I agreed to help him [Griffith] in every way. He needed a canvas covering for a gypsy wagon. I would get that, in fact all the props. Also I offered to condense the script and lay out the opportunities it had so that he would be able to understand it. . . . He came to my house a few evenings later. He had been out looking for a suitable location, wanted a swift running stream quite close to a house. I had divided off half a dozen columns on the back of a laundry shirt-cardboard and headed the columns with titles—Drama, Comedy, Pathos, Pretty Scenes—and wrote in what I thought he should stress. . . . Judging the little I had caught from seeing his acting I didn't think he was going to be so hot. He was very grateful for this and some other tips I gave him.

"The night *The Adventures of Dollie* went into the can," Griffith himself recalled, "I went up on the roof of my cheap hotel to watch Halley's Comet flash across the sky. Down the street, gypsy fortunetellers were predicting a new era."

The ten-minute *Adventures of Dollie* was released in July 1908. Perhaps because Griffith was a reluctant director, *Dollie* scarcely deviated from the pattern established by Porter. But the film, which had cost $65 to make and was sold to film exchanges for nearly $100 a print, had a success greater than any previous Biograph production. The front office was elated.

Soon everyone wanted more films by the man responsible for *Dollie*. On the momentum of his first success, he turned out ten more pictures in a month. In August the front office gave him a year's contract guaranteeing him at least $100 a week.

Griffith had planned to concentrate on his own dramas after hours, but within a short time the demands of his new job precluded any hope of free time for himself. He started what was to remain his schedule during all his years as a movie maker: fourteen to sixteen hours of work each day, seven days a week. Soon he was either directing or supervising all Biograph films.

It was soon evident that Biograph's new director did not intend to blindly follow the established rules of film making. In one of his early projects, the story's climax depended on a circumstance that could not be shown by action alone.

"The audience must see that these two thieves are beginning to distrust each other," Griffith said.

"Why not use a balloon?" suggested Billy Bitzer, who was now working closely with Griffith. Thoughts at that time were always shown in double exposure, a "dream balloon" being inserted in a corner of the film.

"It's been done too often," Mr. Griffith said, impatient with what had already become a cliché. "Perhaps there's another way." He turned to a young actor standing nearby and suggested, "Let's see some distrust on your face."

The actor obliged.

"That's good!" Griffith exclaimed. "Everyone will understand it."

Billy Bitzer objected, as he was to do often when Griffith attempted something new: "But he's too far away from the camera. His expression won't show up on the film."

"Let's get closer to him then. Let's move the camera."

"Mr. Griffith, that's impossible! Believe me, you can't move the camera. You'll cut off his feet—and the background will be out of focus."

"Get it, Billy," Griffith ordered.

When it came time to film the scene, Billy shot it first from the normal distance. Then he moved the heavy camera much nearer to the actors. Although the performers' feet weren't visible in the second shot, it would be clear to the audience that the two thieves in the film were near a falling out.

After the rushes were viewed, Griffith was summoned to the front office. Henry Marvin was furious. "We pay for the whole actor, Mr. Griffith. We want to see *all* of him."

Griffith patiently explained the reason for this shot.

Marvin was not satisfied. He complained, "The background's fuzzy."

Griffith strode toward him. "Look at me Mr. Marvin," he said. "Do you see all of me? No! You see half of me, is that correct? Now, while you are looking at me, the door in back of me is indistinct, isn't it? Good Lord, Mr. Marvin, what I showed on the screen is something you and everyone else sees a thousand times a day—and you don't even know it!"

As he continued to make pictures, Griffith brought the camera closer and closer to the actors until he was taking close-ups of their faces. As a result of the close-up, the style of acting became less exaggerated, for the audience, seeing the actor's face, could read his expression and interpret the action for itself. Griffith also used close shots of objects to contribute to the development of the story.

Mr. Griffith then tried another experiment. He interrupted a scene with a visual comma; that is, he broke the scene into separate shots, showing one actor's face, another's reaction, then perhaps an object, thus giving depth and dimension to the moment. Later he would make sense of the assorted shots in the cutting room, giving them drama and continuity.

In October, after less than four months of picture making, he filmed an adaptation of *Enoch Arden,* renaming it *After Many Years.* The shipwrecked husband, finally rescued, comes home to find that his once-grieving wife has remarried. To show the wife's feelings as she thinks of her first husband, Mr. Griffith ordered the camera to close in on her face. Then, to make certain that the audience understood her thoughts, he switched to a scene of the husband on the desert island. He thus violated continuity of time and space.

Mr. Marvin thought Griffith had gone mad.

"You can't jump around like that," he said angrily. "It doesn't make sense! The audience will never understand it."

"Of course they will!" insisted Griffith. "Wait and see."

As with each Griffith invention, audiences not only understood it; they loved it.

The technique Griffith used in *After Many Years* was not entirely new. Nor was the close-up technically a Griffith discovery. Porter's *Life of an American Fireman* had contained a close shot of a fire alarm. Griffith's genius lay in his understanding of the interrelationships of separate shots, each contributing to clarity and pace, adding substance, mood, and emotion to the bare story outline.

In *Ramona* he further extended the film idiom by introducing the extreme long shot of distant horizons, used for atmosphere and later for panoramic action shots.

"I began to seek after atmosphere and effects and the clues to causes," he said later. "If I have had a measure of success, that effort was largely responsible, for it started me in the right direction."

Griffith also experimented with lighting. He disliked the flat sterile lighting that was then in use. In *Edgar Allan Poe, The Politician's Love Story, A Drunkard's Reformation,* and *Pippa Passes* he arranged for light to come from odd angles. He shot into the bright sun to obtain the effect of the rising sun; he photographed his cast by firelight. He was particularly captivated by the beauty of a scene when it was backlighted by the sun, which cast long, dramatic shadows in front of the actors. He was eager to capture that radiance on film.

"You can't do it!" Billy Bitzer and Arthur Marvin assured him emphatically. "Shoot into the sun, and the actors' faces will come out black on the screen!"

Bitzer and Marvin were capable cameramen, but their point of view was conventional and circumscribed. D. W. did not believe them. Surreptitiously he tried out his theory. They were right.

But it was not in his nature to write off an idea as a failure. A few weeks later, when he and his company were on location in Fort Lee, New Jersey, several actors joined him for lunch in a nearby restaurant. As they were eating, he suddenly noticed the dazzling effect of the sun as it created a halo over the men across the table from him. Yet their faces remained distinct. Why the clarity? Could the reflection of the white tablecloth cast light on their faces?

Back in the studio he experimented with white reflectors and found the answer. The new style aroused more complaints from the front office. His new technique was bad, he was told, because the actors appeared shadowy. But an influential man suddenly took his part. Jeremiah J. Kennedy, a vice-president of the Empire State Trust Company, which had a financial interest in Biograph, voiced his delight with the effects D. W. had achieved. "They look just like engravings, Mr. Griffith," he said. "Keep it up."

Mr. Kennedy was a collector of steel engravings.

For *Pippa Passes* Griffith had a sliding panel built into the wall of the set. Beyond it he mounted a powerful light. As Pippa lay sleeping on camera, the panel was lowered a crack, and the morning light Griffith had so adroitly created touched her face. She opened her eyes. The panel was lowered slowly, completely, until the room was flooded with light. Griffith had re-created the movements of the sun.

He ignored the complaints of Henry Marvin and continued to take plots from the classics. Primitive as they were, his twelve-minute versions of *The Taming of the Shrew* and *Resurrection* brought the film industry critical recognition. He also tackled social problems. Mr. Griffith was deeply sympathetic to the sufferings of the poor, to the injustices inflicted on them, and before he marked his first anniversary as a director he had used social problems as the themes of two fine pictures: *The Song of the Shirt* and *A Corner in Wheat.*

In 1909, almost a year after his first film, he elaborated the technique he had first used in *After Many Years.*

"I found," he said, "that pictures could carry not merely two but even three or four simultaneous threads of action without confusing the spectator."

In *The Lonely Villa,* which he made in the same year, a mother and her two children are trapped in a house by burglars. The heroine manages to telephone her husband. He rushes to the rescue. In a succession of short shots Griffith switches from the mother and her children to the burglars to the husband dashing homeward. As the film nears its climax, each shot becomes shorter. The tempo is thus increased and the suspense heightened. This device, which became known technically as "cross-cutting," became a staple in his directorial repertoire.

In *The Lonedale Operator,* which he filmed two years later, he refined the devices for building suspense. Blanche Sweet, as the heroine held captive in a railroad station, manages to tap out a telegraph message to her father and the man she loves, both of them railroad men. Inevitably, they rush to her rescue by engine. To increase suspense and to build up to the climax, Mr. Griffith again employed cross-cutting, switching from the girl to her sweetheart in ever-shortening intervals. Then he moved in even closer with a series of short, meaningful shots—to the smokestack, the screeching whistle, the turning wheels, the heart of the train that becomes a living creature in this race to save the girl. He thus created emotion out of motion.

Every refinement of technique proved costly, for it added to the length of the movie. Mr. Griffith was soon using every inch of film on a 1,000-foot reel. The front office was aghast. Mr. Marvin screamed that Griffith was ruining Biograph. The company officers hampered and impeded Griffith whenever he attempted something new, which was too often for their comfort. That his devices all proved extraordinarily successful did not change their attitude toward him. True, he made money for them, but they considered him extravagant and fanciful. Why experiment with a good thing when it made profits just as it was?

Their screams grew hysterical when Griffith presented them in 1911 with a movie in two cans—Biograph's first two-reel film. It was a remake of the *Enoch Arden* story, and it would barely fill a half-hour on today's television screen. But Biograph released it in two weekly installments. When audiences clamored to see the entire film at one screening, Griffith was vindicated. Again he was in the vanguard, and other companies soon followed his lead.

But Griffith was neither flattered nor happy, although directing did offer an outlet for his artistic sensibilities. In his dealings with the front office he was often frustrated. The obstinate blindness of the officials was an endless source of irritation to him.

Later that year he turned out a one-reel film with a southern setting. It was called *The Battle*. Blanche Sweet was The Girl, and Charles West was The Boy. Using the broad theme of a Civil War battle, he turned out a forceful and moving film. It was one of his first attempts at handling a large canvas, and his use of crowds was vivid and realistic.

Griffith also concerned himself with the technical side of film production. At that time, exhibitors, bedeviled by complaints of flickering films that gave spectators eyestrain, were faced with yet another problem—the mysterious streaks and smudges that appeared on film. The blotches were blamed on the camera, the film, and the chemicals used for developer, but all attempts to eliminate them failed.

Then one morning, as a cameraman started unpacking a fresh reel of film, Griffith handed him a pair of white gloves. "Perhaps the smudges are fingermarks," he suggested. He was right.

Except for a few rival producers, no one outside Biograph knew Griffith's name. But, although he was anonymous to the vast audience, the Griffith brand was on every Biograph film. Rivals copied his effects shamelessly, but the results never equaled his own. None had his range and versatility.

Of his efforts Griffith himself said, "I am not a genius. There are many directors who could make just as good pictures as I. But they will not stick at it, for it becomes very tiresome to go on directing day after day. But that is what one must do to learn, for none of us knows much about pictures. I know very little. By working, however, I hope to go on learning."

It didn't take long for filmgoers to appreciate the superiority of his films or rather of the films they knew only as Biograph's. As loyal Biograph fans grew familiar with the anonymous casts of Griffith's movies, they began to show tremendous interest in these faces. The most popular of these players was "Little Mary," whom we had known as Gladys Smith.

Mr. Griffith often retold the story of his first meeting with Mary Pickford. Bobby Harron, the office boy, told him that a young lady wanted to see him. She came in, small and fetching with thick gold curls.

"What can I do for you?" he asked.

"I thought I wouldn't mind acting in pictures for a while," she said. "That is, if the salary is satisfactory."

"Have you had any experience?" Mr. Griffith asked, amused at her condescension.

"I played two seasons with David Belasco."

"It so happens we need a type like you in our next picture. About salary—we pay $5 a day when you work."

"What!" She was a good little actress; her surprise sounded genuine. "I must have at least ten!"

Mr. Griffith shook his head.

"You must realize I'm an actress and an artist," she said. "I've had important parts on the real stage. I must have twenty-five a week guaranteed and extra when I work extra."

Mr. Griffith recognized a shrewd mind under those innocent curls. He promised to submit her proposal to the front office. She was hired on her terms, although, according to his private notes, several of the bosses thought her attractiveness overrated. But Mr. Griffith took her part and persuaded them to keep her. In less than ten years she was earning $10,000 a week, not with D. W. Griffith but with Adolph Zukor.

Mr. Griffith always wanted to pay his actors well, but he was often unable to get the money from Biograph. So he devised his own way of helping them. If an actor grew angry at the amount of work he had to do, D. W. would call him aside, explain he was powerless to pay the man what he deserved, and add, "Say, why don't you sell us a story plot?" Then Mr. Griffith would persuade Biograph to buy it for $15. Since the company needed plenty of story plots, it was possibe for a good many actors to make an extra amount each week. Sometimes even their wives would submit story ideas.

While Griffith was extending the range of his devices and broadening his choice of stories, he was also developing in his actors a highly effective, "natural" style of acting. "We are forced to develop a new technique of acting before the camera. People who come to me from the theater use the quick broad gestures and movements which they have employed on the stage. I am trying to develop realism in pictures by teaching the value of deliberation and repose."

This naturalness was the result of careful rehearsal, although he never used a scenario. But it was more than endless patience in rehearsals that distinguished him from other directors; his ability to find and detect talent was equally important. He began a personal crusade to enlist potentially good players, to prove to them the value of the new medium. I do not believe that he was instrumental in luring Lionel Barrymore to films, but he was gratified when Lionel became a Biograph regular. Lionel found films interesting. Perhaps because of his ambition to paint, composition and lighting fascinated him.

Griffith first met James Kirkwood, a popular stage star, at a club and persuaded him to become a film player. Kirkwood brought in Henry B. Walthall, who had been on stage with him in *The Great Divide*.

The caliber of most actors who applied for work did not satisfy Griffith. He knew from experience that the better-trained actors who were free were mostly scornful of films. Theatrical agencies were the logical source of competent actors. But, aware of the universal disdain of the film medium, Mr. Griffith lacked the courage to tap that resource.

Once, when he was in desperate need of a leading man, he loitered outside a theatrical agency, debating whether or not to go in and talk to the agent about his requirements. As he hesitated, a man emerged from the office. He was tall, youthful, and well built, and he carried himself well. That's the kind we need, Griffith thought, and followed him down the street.

"I beg your pardon, sir. Do you happen to be an actor?"

The young man paused—curious, amused, and no doubt impressed by Mr. Griffith. He answered, in a self-deprecating manner, "Well, some people say 'yes,' but most say 'no.' "

With some diffidence, Griffith introduced himself. He offered the young man a job, expecting a refusal. But to his surprise the fellow said, "How much do you pay?"

"Only $5 a day," Mr. Griffith replied, "but we're hoping soon to raise the ante."

"Cash?"

"You'll be paid in cash at the end of each day."

"You've got yourself a deal."

The young man's name was Arthur Johnson. The son of a well known Episcopalian minister, he was intelligent, well educated, personable, an altogether unusual man. He later admitted that it was Griffith's personality that won him over—as well as his promise of work at least two or three times a week.

There was an immediate rapport between the two men. They not only worked superbly together; they also became fast friends. Mr. Griffith used to say fondly of Johnson that he was "handsome, well educated, and lazy."

I never knew Johnson (he died suddenly, before I came to Biograph), but Mr. Griffith once told me, "He was one of the two people whom I had in my employ who actually refused a raise in salary."

Johnson, like all the other actors, was expected to supply his own wardrobe. It consisted of one dark-blue serge suit, which eventually became the most photographed outfit on the lot. D. W. told me, vastly amused, that it had been seen in at least twenty pictures! When he suggested that a new suit was in order, Arthur said indignantly: "What's wrong with this one? It's always been all right." That was the attitude toward fashion and possessions of the first matinee idol of the films.

Bobby Harron, the office boy, was sweeping the front steps one morning when a husky young man asked if there might be an opening for him.

"I can do anything," the man boasted. "I'm strong. I can handle props or run errands or act. Take your choice."

Just then Billy Bitzer, no flyweight himself, lumbered up the stairs. Bobby turned to him.

"Billy, this fellow wants a job."

"Anything doing?" the man asked.

"How should I know?" Billy answered and disappeared into the building.

"Wait a minute," Bobby said and went in search of D. W. The job applicant lingered outside, ready to depart; evidently rejection was a familiar experience. But Mr. Griffith, himself an advocate of rugged exercise, was pleased with him and immediately offered him a role in a slapstick comedy that he was directing. That was how Mack Sennett, later the father of the Keystone Cops comedies, found the opportunity to prove himself.

Sennett soon learned about Griffith's preferences in acting style. Once Griffith was directing a picture in which Sennett had a role. Sennett had not learned his part properly, and so when the scene was shot he kept his acting to a minimum. Later, to his astonishment, Griffith walked over, shook his hand warmly, and congratulated him.

"It was fine—just great!" said Griffith.

"But I didn't do anything," protested Sennett.

"Maybe that's why it was so good," Griffith said with a wry smile.

According to Sennett, he often supplied Mr. Griffith with an idea to fill a section of a film. He was obsessed with the notion of using policemen, and the prototype of the Keystone Cops appeared in a Griffith film. Later, when Sennett's Keystone Cops comedies became fantastically popular, Griffith was delighted with his protégé's success, but he still did not approve of holding up officers of the law to such ridicule.

Sennett would also manage to be in the projection room with Griffith and listen to his comments on the day's rushes. "He'd sit there in the semidarkness, that great mind of his at work like a precision machine," Sennett later told interviewers. "As the film unrolled, he'd give brisk orders. 'Cut that down' or 'Change that part,' 'No good' or 'We'll keep that.'

"Griffith was always talking about ways of doing things better, experimenting, trying new angles. He pointed out that writers used flashback technique, that portrait painters used the close-up technique. Some people have argued that Billy Bitzer should be given credit for these innovations. Not so. Bitzer may have carried out Griffith's orders and ideas with great skill, but it was the old master's creative brain that thought up those new techniques."

Sennett remembers that when he began to direct his own pictures he discussed most of his ideas with D. W. "Griffith, of course, was master of the drama, while my forte was comedy," Sennett has recalled. "But motivation, mood, and suspense are elements common to all kinds of entertainment."

Mr. Griffith would sometimes joke about the comedies Sennett was directing on the lot. "Well, do you feel funny today?" he would greet Sennett when they met each morning. Or "Got lots of laughs ready today?" Or "Your funny bone in shape today?"

Mr. Griffith also used to give Sennett useful tips. Once when Sennett had completed a picture on location at Fort Lee, New Jersey, Mr. Griffith happened to see his expense account. "Mack," he said, "let me give you a piece of advice. This expense account is too low. When you're on location, you can't afford to be cheap. Pay the policeman who helps you, the man whose front yard you use, the caterer who provides the cast with lunches a little more than you should. Then when you go back the next time you'll be more than welcome."

Sennett told many people that he followed this advice all the rest of his movie-making career and found it sound and profitable.

From what I've heard Mack Sennett admitted to being a brash, ambitious man when he first began to work with Mr. Griffith, and he was hungry to absorb whatever would help him. He soon discovered that, no matter how busy Mr. Griffith was, it was possible to talk to him if one was willing to walk. Mr. Griffith often walked home from the Biograph studio, either to his apartment on East Thirty-Seventh Street or later to the Claridge on Broadway and Forty-Fourth Street. Sennett managed to be at the door when Mr. Griffith was leaving for the day and casually fell into step with him. This became habitual.

What did they talk about?

"Mostly motion pictures—very little else," Sennett said. "I knew Griffith was the master, and I wanted to pump him as much as possible. We talked about acting techniques, problems of directors, costuming, lights, camera angles—almost everything there was to discuss about movie-making.

"I remember one time that Griffith explained to me the importance of getting suspense into a film. He had just worked out a suspenseful situation for the picture he was directing. I've forgotten which one it was, but it involved hanging a baby out of the window in a basket—with a rope tied to a door inside the building. The suspense lay in the fact that if someone opened the door the baby would fall.

" 'If the audience doesn't hang on every action or twist of plot, you've lost them,' Griffith said."

Like all members of the company, Sennett was loyal to Mr. Griffith. As a director for Biograph, his salary was $75 a week. Yet when Carl Laemmle offered him $275 he refused to leave Biograph.

"I could have used the money, but I was learning the motion-picture business from a master craftsman, and an increase in pay didn't mean a darned thing to me."

D. W. Griffith had come a long way in four short years. He had made more than 400 films and provided the new medium with a language all its own. He had almost single-handedly restored Biograph to solvency. From $50 a week his salary had jumped to $275 plus a percentage of every film sold. He had felt sufficiently proud of his achievement to sign his fourth contract with Biograph with his own name instead of "Lawrence Griffith."

For all his progress, however, his greatest accomplishments still lay in the future.

7

When Dorothy and I first met D. W. Griffith his new career had really just begun. Although we did not know it then, so had ours—in a different medium from the one we had known till then. Nor did we realize that for a long time our careers would be intertwined with that of the man who had so alarmed us with his wild behavior that first day.

The stage was our school, our home, our life. We had come to the movies only in the hope that they would feed and shelter us until we could return to the theater. We continued to seek work on the stage. We heard that David Belasco would need young actresses for his forthcoming production of *A Good Little Devil,* and Mr. William Dean, Mr. Belasco's manager and our old friend from touring days, arranged an interview with him. We felt very fortunate, for then as now there were hundreds of aspirants for each role.

We arrived at Mr. Belasco's office above the theater named for him. Mother, who encouraged our independence, did not accompany us.

Mr. Belasco was sitting behind his desk as we came timidly into the room. He was a handsome man with thick locks of white hair falling over his forehead. He wore a strange suit that resembled that of a clergyman.

It was midsummer, and the furniture was draped in white dust sheets and the shades drawn against the heat. No one spoke. I tried to avoid Mr. Belasco's stare by slipping behind Dorothy. I knew my obligation as the elder, but I was petrified. Dorothy moved in turn behind me. We continued shuffling behind each other until we were nearly out of the office. There was no immediate reaction from Mr. Belasco to this extraordinary exhibition.

"Thank you," he finally said, "for letting me see what you look like from the last row. Now come closer. I won't bite you."

We obeyed.

"I'm sorry I cannot use you both," he told us. "I need just one young actress." Then, pointing to me, he added: "But you can play the Golden Fairy. Would you like that?"

I could scarcely breathe. "Yes, sir. I love to fly."

"Have you ever tried it?" he asked.

"No, sir."

Whereupon he engaged me.

When we brought our news to Mother, she said, "We must go to the studio and ask Mary if this is the play she's to be in." We knew that she was to star in a Belasco production with Ernest Truex, and happily it turned out to be *A Good Little Devil*.

Meanwhile, as neither Mother nor Dorothy had a part for the fall season, we continued to count on Biograph for any work it could give us.

The day after we filmed *An Unseen Enemy* Mary Pickford telephoned to tell us that Mr. Griffith was pleased with the results. Being outspoken, she had evidently warned him that his manners were not understood by legitimate actresses. Thenceforth he called us Miss Lillian and Miss Dorothy, instead of Blue and Red, and he shot no more live ammunition over our heads.

Movie making was a strange, bewildering world, totally unlike any we had known. Yet everything about it was so fascinating that a ten- or twelve-hour working day would pass before we realized it.

There was never a script to be studied, no lines to be memorized. Everything seemed to spring spontaneously from Mr. Griffith's brain. He was the hub of all activity, coaxing, encouraging, challenging, directing. When the day's work was done for his cast, he continued to work through the night if necessary, editing the day's films and making plans for the next day.

The most important of his regulars was Gottlieb Wilhelm Bitzer, the cameraman. Billy, as everyone called him, was about forty years old, quiet and hard-working. He spoke little. Unlike Mr. Griffith, who was sensitive to every detail, Bitzer was absorbed in his camera work to the exclusion of everything else.

Three members of Griffith's staff were brought to the studio as teenagers by their parish priest because they needed jobs to help their families. Danny Grey became camera boy, assisting Bitzer; Jimmy Smith developed into Mr. Griffith's film cutter; and Bobby Harron, who started as an errand boy, was graduated to supporting roles.

Jimmy arrived early to start cutting film and stayed until late in the evening, while we were rehearsing. Billy arrived early, too, to set up his lights. At that time, his sole assistant was Danny Grey, who carried the heavy camera. Andy Reed was the head electrician. He spent hours lighting our faces while we stood there motionless, often for two or three hours at a time. There were young men to help move the lights. Everyone pitched in and helped with the general work.

The studio itself was a Victorian brownstone, solidly built and well laid out, originally the town house of a rich, self-indulgent bachelor. The ballroom—now the studio—had been the scene of lively balls and glamorous parties. Early in the twentieth century, the old New York families had deserted Fourteenth Street for the country atmosphere beyond Thirty-Fourth Street. By the time we knew it, the house and its environs had deteriorated. Before the American Mutoscope and Biograph Company leased it, a piano firm had struggled with the rent, and a tailor had occupied the basement, displaying lengths of men's suitings in the window.

But when we worked there the house was alive with movement; filled with people with strange painted faces, wearing odd costumes. They were actors who applied their own makeup, contrived their own costumes, often wrote their own stories (as Mary Pickford had done for *Lena and the Geese*), and fought for choice roles day after day, as a ceaseless stream of pictures poured out of the studio. They were not respected by some actors of the legitimate stage, but they brought to their work an excitement and spontaneity that did not exist anywhere else and has regrettably long since disappeared from most movies.

The hallways and dressing rooms were alive with conjecture.

"What's the new picture about?"

"Mae, dear, I've been rehearsing one scene all morning and I still don't know who's in it or what the complete story is."

"Well, you know Mr. Griffith!"

"How does this look? Wait—I'll tuck in the blouse."

"Did you see the papers this morning? That murder—"

"See it! I'm rehearsing it. We'll shoot it today and cut it tomorrow."

Dorothy and I were so wary of the whole business that first summer that we asked Mother to go with us to the studio each day. It was only after we were thrown together with the rest of the company on location and grew to know its members better that we began to feel at ease.

The studio called one morning to tell us that the company was going on location to the Delaware Water Gap for a week or ten days. There was work for us if we wished to come along—$5 a day and our living expenses paid. We were delighted to leave the city in the summer heat. Two films were planned: *Friends,* a story of a western mining company, and a contemporary piece, *The New York Hat,* written by a schoolgirl who signed her name A. Loos and was shortly to become Anita Loos, an important member of the company and Dorothy's and my close friend.

During our stay in the country the company lived in a small hotel, where the rooms were clean and simply furnished. After work we would meet at the local candy store for ice cream. One night we all decided to have a contest to see who could eat the most. The informality of the company was not shared by the director, however.

No one called him anything but Mr. Griffith or, among themselves, the Boss.

In recent years, Mr. Griffith had developed a kind of repertory company of young players, so that he would have access to heroes and heroines, character actors and children whenever he needed them. The group included Owen Moore, Elmer Booth, Donald Crisp, James Kirkwood, Edward Dillon, George Siegmann, Spottis-woode Aiken, George Nicholls, Harry Carey, Marshal Neilan, Kate Bruce, Claire McDowell, Florence Lawrence, Miriam Cooper, Fay Tincher, Alice Joyce, Mary Alden, Marion Leonard, and Hattie Delano. Because the cast members were mostly young and eager to prove themselves, there was a healthy rivalry among them, which Mr. Griffith encouraged. I heard from one of the men how Mr. Griffith had elevated Mae Marsh to the lead in *The Sands of Dee* over Mary Pickford and Blanche Sweet, who were the Biograph leading ladies at the time. The role called for a girl with long, flowing hair, which Mary especially and Blanche had in golden abundance. Mae's hair was not so long as theirs. Blanche's grandmother was at the studio the day the decision was made, and she uttered a sharp comment for Mr. Griffith's benefit. "I don't see how Mae's going to do it—she ain't got no hair!"

But Mae did it all the same, and Mary and Blanche were soon working even harder for the next big role.

Mr. Griffith had his reasons for promoting rivalry among us, but few took it with Mary Pickford's equanimity. There was a common wardrobe room with pipe racks for the clothes. The garments were second-hand or worse. An elderly man in the company combed second-hand stores and pawnshops for cheap clothes to be used as costumes. They had to be fumigated before we wore them. An actress would use a shirtwaist and skirt for one picture and the same skirt with a different blouse for another. The leading players always had first choice of costumes; the others used what was left over. After dressing, we were expected to show ourselves for Mr. Griffith's approval. One day, after he had seen and approved Mary's costume and she had walked off, I came forward. The entire cast was present. Mr. Griffith inspected my outfit and then said to Mary: "Look at your friend. She looks better than you do. Maybe I should let her play your part."

There was an embarrassed hush. Impulsively, I spoke up. "Mary, if this is a better costume, you take it, and let me wear yours."

She agreed. We were still in Mr. Griffith's presence, but that did not deter her. "I'll take it," she said, "but he's just trying to make me jealous. He always tries to do this." Once we were downstairs in the dressing room, she confided: "This is his way of creating rivalry. He thinks we'll all give better performances if we think someone else might get the part."

After I grew accustomed to working under Mr. Griffith and came to understand his ways, I was less nervous. Only once in those early days did I see his gentle good humor give way to anger. One of the girls, during a break in rehearsal, happened to say something about working in "flickers." He overheard the remark; anger flashed out of those hooded blue eyes.

"Never let me hear that word again in this studio," he commanded. "Just remember, you're no longer working in some second-rate theatrical company. What we do here today will be seen tomorrow by people all over America—people all over the world! Just remember that the next time you go before the camera!"

He strode away. Lionel Barrymore came over to me.

"Don't let it upset you, Lillian. It wasn't so long ago that D. W. himself used to talk scathingly of 'flickers' and 'galloping tintypes.' But now he has a vision. He really believes we're pioneering in a new art—a medium that can cross over barriers of language and culture. That's why he drives himself so hard.

"And you know, Lillian," he added, "I'm beginning to believe he's right."

As I would soon be going into rehearsals for *A Good Little Devil,* I told Mr. Griffith of my good fortune.

"How much is Belasco paying you?" he asked.

"Twenty-five dollars a week," I said proudly.

"Well, if you stay with me, I'll pay you $50 a week to be a permanent member of my company."

I did not know what to say to this grand offer.

"However," Mr. Griffith continued, "you'd be very foolish to take me up on it. The name Belasco alone is worth ten times my offer."

He did add that his offer would stand if I ever wanted to accept it. Furthermore, he would take Dorothy to California on a $15-a-week minimum guarantee, with $5 additional for each day she worked.

"I can't do more until she grows up," he said, "until I know how she's going to turn out."

We were all to separate again. Dorothy would go to California and share a room with Gertrude Bambrick, whom Mr. Griffith had discovered among the dancers in Gertrude Hoffman's company. She had come to the Biograph studio on the same day we had, and she and Dorothy had become good friends. Mother decided to return to Springfield, Ohio, to work with the Long Catering Company again. I would tour in *A Good Little Devil* and come to Broadway with it.

Rehearsals with Mr. Belasco were a new experience for me. Much time was spent on words rather than on action. My difficulty was with the word "apple"; it was important to make the audience in the gallery hear those two "p"s, which I had a tendency to swallow. It took weeks to perfect my enunciation. Next came the lighting; each of us had a baby spot, placed low, to light his face so that the audience could see the eyes. There was a new piece of direction; wherever I went, I seemed to hear, "Hit her with the baby!" The wires for flying were controlled by eighteen men backstage, and every wire had to be tried out before each performance. As I had professed a fondness for flying, I was chosen to do the testing, which meant I was required to come to the theater early before each performance.

Mary's understudy was a delicate, fair-haired little girl, who was later to be famous as a playwright, congresswoman, and diplomat— Clare Boothe Luce.

Mr. Griffith came to our opening in Philadelphia, bringing with him many of the Biograph players. After the performance, they came backstage with warm compliments and helpful suggestions. Mr.

Griffith was so interested in Mary and me and so proud of us that he came out to Baltimore, when we played there, to watch our performances again.

In Baltimore during the Christmas matinee I had an accident. In the second act, while the stage was darkened, I flew down from a great height to a five-foot wall, where I paused in the spotlight. After a moment, I was supposed to fly, protected by the wires, across the stage. This time, the wire came loose from the clasp on my back. I stepped off the wall—into space. The audience laughed. I was badly shaken, but my pride suffered even more. Picking myself off the floor, I ran to the dressing room. Mr. Belasco, who happened to be present that day, came in to comfort me and to learn whether or not I was hurt. He was very kind, and I assured him that I was all right, but was afraid I had spoiled his play.

All went well at the New York opening. *A Good Little Devil* was received favorably and settled down for a run. I rented a small room at the Marlton Hotel on Eighth Street just off Fifth Avenue for $8 a week and bought a little Sterno canned heat on which to warm my food. My diet was monotonous—mostly eggs, baked beans, and tea. I was determined to save $10 out of each week's salary to send to my mother.

The unbalanced diet combined with long working hours began to have its effect on my body. I grew thinner and more pallid. Mary said that I looked ethereal. She reminded me of the time that we had all lived together on the West Side and she was afraid to stay alone in the apartment with me because her mother had said I was "too good to live." Mr. Belasco was concerned about me; he took a paternalistic interest in his company, even paying the hotel bills, on tour, for the lesser players. He asked Mrs. Pickford to take me south for a couple of weeks, hoping that the sun and warmth would restore me to health. She was sorry not to oblige him, but her own children needed looking after. Finally, he offered to send me to California, where Mother had by then joined Dorothy; my understudy would play my part until I grew stronger. But it was apparent to everybody that he doubted that I would return. I thought he was being very kind, but later William Dean told me that he was afraid of a lawsuit because of the fall, which he thought had triggered my weakness. Such action never occurred to us; our family wouldn't know how to sue anyone.

It was a cold, bleak winter's day when I took the train at Pennsylvania Station. No one came with me to see me off. Then suddenly in the midst of a crowd of strangers I spied familiar faces—the men who handled the ropes backstage. They had come with their German band to give me a farewell serenade. They brought me little gifts: candies, nuts, magazines. And, as the brasses sounded and their ruddy faces beamed at me, I left for the West Coast in a flood of warm affection.

⚜ 8 ⚜

It was a five-day journey overland from New York City to Los Angeles. In contrast to bleak and blustery Manhattan, Los Angeles was warm and inviting that day in February 1913. The city smelled like a vast orange grove, and the abundance of roses offered a cheery welcome.

The climate was obviously agreeing with Mother. Dorothy was her usual bouncing self, full of amusing stories about film work. Mother was immediately concerned with my health. She hurried me off to a doctor. He told her: "Your daughter is badly run down. The tests show pernicious anemia."

His prescription for my recovery was simple: sunshine, rest, proper nutrition, and, for a tonic a California red wine called Zinfandel—two tumblers a day at lunch and dinner. He wanted me to drink the cheapest kind, at 50 cents a gallon. The taste was sour, particularly to my palate, which thrived on chocolate ice-cream sodas. But I soon regained my health, although I remained pale and underweight.

When I went to see Mr. Griffith, he put me to work on the same terms he had offered me in New York.

Although this was our first winter in California, Mr. Griffith and his company had spent the last three there. In New York, Mr. Griffith had often found the weather a handicap to production. Moreover, he needed a variety of backgrounds for his films, which eliminated New York as a year-round headquarters. After a visit, he had decided to make Los Angeles his winter quarters. Other film-makers had already discovered the virtues of the area. Los Angeles, then a residential city of about 300,000 people, had wide boulevards, churches and Spanish-style houses. Nearby were ocean and desert, snow-capped mountains and green valleys, Spanish missions and fruit farms. Although he was to spend much time there in the next few years, he was loath to call it his permanent quarters. He considered the climate marvelous for the body but bad for the mind and soul, and he always punctuated his stays with frequent trips.

He lived at the Alexandria Hotel, where Mack Sennett, his most devoted disciple, was also a resident. During the first year, according to Sennett, working quarters had been a vacant lot on Twelfth Street and Georgia, where Mr. Griffith had set up tents for dressing rooms.

Mary Pickford was not among the Biograph players in California my first year. She was still playing in *A Good Little Devil* when she and her mother discussed a new contract with Mr. Griffith. Mrs. Pickford had decided that Mary deserved at least $500 a week, which Mr. Griffith considered out of the question.

"Three hundred," Mr. Griffith countered. "That's the best I can do."

"You'll be sorry, Mr. Griffith," Mrs. Pickford said. "Mary can get five hundred."

He let Mary go. He had an ambivalent attitude toward his protégées. He helped them to achieve success, and when they wanted to leave he let them go without a restraining word. He was happy for them. His satisfaction at Mary's success—and later in that of Richard Barthelmess, Mae Marsh, and others—was genuine and spontaneous. He never clutched at anyone. He may have felt that as he had created so many stars, he could easily develop others. There would always be fresh talent to mold.

D. W. recruited his players from among professional actors or dancers who he felt had potential that he could help to realize. Mae Marsh and Bobby Harron were the exceptions, yet under his tutelage they both achieved stardom. His encouragement spurred actors to go beyond their limits. In some, he seemed to generate a spark that flickered and died when they left him. The Biograph repertory company proved a talent lode with which other studios could scarcely compete. Once you had worked with Mr. Griffith, other companies were always eager to hire you.

As for our darling Mary, she went on to another studio, and later Jesse Lasky, head of Paramount Famous Players, said that he would rather do business with a half-dozen bankers than with Mary and her mother. Mary did have a truly remarkable money sense. She never returned to work for Mr. Griffith, but a half-dozen years later, when she was the most popular film star in the world, she helped to form United Artists with Douglas Fairbanks, Charles Chaplin, and D. W. Griffith. As she invited Mr. Griffith to join them, there was clearly no rancor between them.

Mother took a small apartment for us only a block from the studio, so that we could walk to and from work. There were two rooms and a kitchen; Dorothy and I shared one room, and Mother used the other, which also served as dining and living room. The apartment had Murphy beds. There was a mirror on the wall, and when it was pulled down a bed was visible behind it and behind that a cupboard for hanging clothes.

Dorothy was already a promising comedienne, and Mother no longer had to work so hard; now she only occasionally came to work at the studio.

The Biograph studio on Pico Street was really nothing more than an open-air stage. Without walls or roof, it consisted solely of a large wooden floor built on the site of an abandoned streetcar barn. The shed nearby was sectioned off into dressing rooms, Mr. Griffith's office, and a one-rack costume department. We had only daylight to work in. When interiors were filmed, the set was unprotected from wind, and often while we were shooting scenes in the dining room the curtains and tablecloth would billow gently. Audiences must have thought it a drafty house. Because the whole process was so makeshift, Mr. Griffith's results seem all the more remarkable.

When it rained we all congregated in the rehearsal hall. There Mr. Griffith conducted rehearsals of not only his own current story but those of other directors as well. Often there were five or six stories in various stages of preparation. Mr. Griffith's powers of concentration were so great that he could watch a rehearsal, read notes, and talk to his staff at the same time. At times he would look at you without actually seeing you.

He had long legs and walked fast; during rehearsals he was everywhere. Sometimes he would make drastic plot changes; at other times he would suggest to an actor an odd walk, a curious mannerism, or some other bit of business to make the character interesting and individual.

Before a movie was filmed a player would often get a chance to rehearse each part in the film under his supervision. As casting was not decided on until shortly before filming, we were obliged to be familiar with all the roles we had rehearsed. This system taught us range and flexibility.

When we knew that Mr. Griffith was ready to announce his casting, our tension would grow. We would wait nervously to hear his choices. Often he would tell us in the most offhand way that we had parts. "Miss Gish," he might say, "have you gone to see about your costume?" Or "Mr. Walthall, you had better get measured for your uniform."

Mr. Griffith discouraged vanity in us. We were one big family, warmly united in a common goal. The films were important, not the players. If Mr. Griffith seemed to be playing chess with us, it was for an important purpose. Under his benevolent eye we came alive, stretching our talents in order to realize his conceptions.

Once the parts were awarded, the real work would begin. At the initial rehearsal Mr. Griffith would sit on a wooden kitchen chair, the actors fanning out in front of him, and, as he called out the plot, they would react, supplying in their own words whatever was appropriate for the scene.

As rehearsals continued, Mr. Griffith would move around us like a referee in the ring, circling, bending, walking up to an actor, staring over his great beak of a nose, then turning away. By the time that we had run through the story several times, he had viewed the action from every conceivable camera angle. Then he would begin to concentrate on characterization. Often we would run through a scene dozens of times before he achieved the desired effect. If we still failed, he would act out the scene himself with exaggerated gestures that he would later moderate in us.

He was a great showman. Once he was doing a mother's role, and raising his long face heavenward he cried out in anguish: "My son, my son—can you hear me there in heaven? Say that you hear me. Speak to me, my beloved son!"

The company was, as always, spellbound by his voice and manner. But a woman visitor on the set broke into laughter at the histrionics. Mr. Griffith smiled and said with a shrug, "Well, do it something like that, children." Then he sat down.

In rehearsals we were expected to visualize the props—furniture where none stood, windows in blank walls, doors where there was only space. Our physical movements became automatic and our emotions completely involved.

Most rehearsals were open—that is, the whole staff, actors, workmen, and the men from the laboratory were free to come and watch. Often there would be visitors on the set. Mr. Griffith loved the presence of an audience while his company rehearsed—and rehearsed so effectively that at the end of the scene, the onlookers would be in tears. Later, we learned to withhold, not to give as much as we would if the camera were operating. Film was expensive, and a scene was shot only once, so we conserved our strength for that one take.

When Mr. Griffith was hungry he would turn to us and say, "Hungry? Well, now you may eat."

During lunch he would help those who happened to be eating with him. If an actor did not know what to do with a character, if he was baffled and could not get insight, Mr. Griffith would say: "Well, haven't you seen someone like this in your life? Go find him. Go get an idea from someone, and bring it back to me, and let me see if it's any good. I can't think of everything! I'm writing the whole story.

. 85 .

You have only one character to worry about, so you try to round it out and make it real and whole!"

Often Mr. Griffith would leave a scene in the middle and be gone —no one knew where—for a half-hour or even two or three hours. He always returned with a quick, "Well, where were we?" Everyone would jump up, and rehearsals would continue. No one dreamed of objecting. The company worshiped him, and I once heard one of the character women murmur, "Master."

Sometimes these rehearsals continued until 10:00 or 11:00 at night, and the actors would grow tired and irritable. With a wonderful sense of timing the Boss would suddenly break into the scene, catch one of the girls in his arms, and twirl her around the room at a furious pace until the tension was dispelled in laughter and the cast went back to work.

But he always maintained discipline on the set. Whenever the tomfoolery threatened to get out of hand, he would say abruptly, "Let's stop kidding now. Let's get down to business," or *"Quiet!* We're working!"

I would often be called in to rehearse parts for the more experienced actresses, who would sit by and watch me to see how the story unfolded. They thus gained perspective on their roles. Afterward I was allowed to stay while the more experienced players took over. Changing places in this way proved to be beneficial both to the craftsman and the novice. I often saw the scene again in the darkroom, thus learning how to correct my mistakes and profiting by the skill of the others.

During that period Mr. Griffith once told me, "Try always to play with actors you consider your superiors; they will help you."

Jimmy Smith, the cutter, used to write down the sequence of events in the story to help him assemble the film when it came from the laboratory. He and Billy would also note the duration of each scene during rehearsal. These time sheets were extremely valuable in keeping a film from lagging. Mr. Griffith would call for one during filming.

"How long was this scene when we rehearsed it?" he'd ask. If a scene was longer than had been decided upon, we would tighten it.

If it was shorter, we would have to find what we had left out and use it.

"The main difference between a good and bad picture is timing and tempo," he would tell us.

Although Mr. Griffith had a tendency to exhort and exaggerate during rehearsals, he grew quiet when filming started. He usually put his head as close as possible to the lens to view the angle of each shot. Then he would sit down on his wooden chair and nervously twirl his ring or jingle a handful of coins in his pocket. He would shift the coins from one hand to the other. It later reminded me, after I had traveled through the Near East, of the amber prayer beads men there use to keep their hands occupied.

Sometimes he would suggest in that beautiful commanding voice: "Not so much, not so much. Less, less—simple, simple, *true*. Don't act it, feel it; feel it, don't act it." And then, "More, more, we need *more!*"

And we knew what *more* meant, just as we knew what *less* meant. As the scene unfolded, we were always fearful lest the camera catch us acting.

If the actors were especially good, he would relax in his chair, his smile benevolent, and say in that resonant voice: "Now, that's what I call acting! Did you see that, all of you? Did you learn something?"

He had various ways of coping when an actor could not project a mood. Once when Mary Pickford was still with the company he wanted her to register anger. But Mary was in a sunny mood; it was evident to him that the camera would not get the desired result. In the cast was a handsome young Irishman named Owen Moore. He was a good actor, but Mr. Griffith began to cast aspersions on both his acting and his character. Mary had a quick temper and great loyalty. She turned the torrent of her anger against Mr. Griffith.

"Shoot it, Billy," Mr. Griffith ordered.

Later he apologized to her. When he singled out this man for criticism he knew that Mary and Owen Moore were secretly engaged to be married.

Mr. Griffith's mind was constantly bubbling over with ideas. One morning, as we were sitting in the studio between takes, Lionel Barrymore stepped on an insect. I shuddered. Lionel said, "Lillian doesn't look as if she could hurt a cockroach."

Mr. Griffith laughed. "I don't believe she would." He paused. "You know, that might make a story. Miss Lillian, you play a young girl. You are living with your—" He looked around at the actors on the set and settled on Lionel. "Your grandfather, as played with flowing beard and his usual crustiness by Mr. Barrymore." (Lionel could play any character.)

"You have mice in the house," Mr. Griffith continued, "and you, a sweet innocent child, love them. But, unaware of your feelings, Mr. Barrymore has put out poison for them." He thus unraveled the plot, developing it as he went along. Then we began to improvise and to build character, working together until we had everything right—and a new film, *The Lady and the Mouse.*

Many times, if the shooting were going well, or the light was good, he wouldn't break for lunch but continue taking one scene after another. Sunlight often controlled his plans. If it looked as though a mist was forming or the light would dim later, he would keep going. We would often get so hungry we'd think we were going to collapse. Sometimes we had to play our most important scenes on empty stomachs.

We worked long hours every day, sometimes late into the night. We filmed all day if the weather permitted, rehearsed after the light failed, then watched rushes. But we never thought to complain. We considered it a privilege to work for Mr. Griffith. With him, we never felt we were working for a salary. He inspired in us his belief that we were involved in a medium that was powerful enough to influence the whole world.

The film industry's need was insatiable. No man alone could supply the heavy demand for new pictures. In addition to directing his own pictures, Mr. Griffith was training other directors and cameramen, as well as his actors. In those early days, I did not often have the opportunity to work with Mr. Griffith; it was a rare occasion when he chose me for a film.

I soon learned to be independent in expressing myself. When working with director Christy Cabanne, for example, I could make suggestions without fear. He was particularly pleased when I offered an idea for a scene. He had confidence in me, which gave me confidence in myself. I would sit in the cutting room later and discover for myself what was good and what was bad.

Later on, when Mr. Griffith learned of my interest, he said: "Well, she's got her own ideas. You might as well leave her alone because she'll do it her own way, anyway."

We also acted for W. S. Van Dyke, who later brought to the screen *The Thin Man* with William Powell and Myrna Loy; Elmer Clifton, who later made the film classic, *Down to the Sea in Ships* and promoted Clara Bow, later the "It" girl, to stardom; Raoul Walsh, whose future productions included *High Sierra;* Edward Dillon; Donald Crisp; Del Henderson, and Jack O'Brien.

When Dorothy and I first came to Mr. Griffith, he wanted to change our name—not because he anticipated that it would ever appear on a marquee but simply because he did not like its sound. "Geesh," he would say in an exaggerated manner. "Mees Geesh." He liked sweet names like Bessie Love. But Dorothy rebelled; in her childhood, she had acted under the name of Baby This or Baby That, she had been branded as Little Willie, and now she intended to remain Dorothy Gish. He gave in, but never stopped teasing us about it.

Not that names mattered. At first, legitimate actors had disguised their work in films by assuming other names; later, film starlets were rechristened with what studio chiefs and publicity men considered more appropriate names. Meanwhile, however, the audience was not aware of our identities. For young people whose images were seen everywhere, we were singularly anonymous.

Dorothy and I were in a transitional stage when we came to Mr. Griffith—no longer children and not yet young women. But he understood youth. Mae Marsh once said that he worshiped youth, and he was curiously young at heart. He had all the fey qualities of his Welsh forebears.

He also had a practical reason for surrounding himself with youthful players: The camera was heartless; it exaggerated. I remember John Barrymore's once saying, "If you stay in front of that camera long enough, it will not only show what you had for breakfast, but who your ancestors were."

Fortunately, I photographed "young." Billy Bitzer said that he could photograph me from any angle. But sometimes the harsh cameras made a fourteen-year-old seem an old hag. Children of fourteen and fifteen often played parts far beyond their experience or understanding.

Perhaps the youngest actor ever to suffer rejection was a three-week-old baby we needed for an interior shot. Rushed from an orphanage—there were at that time no laws against photographing infants—the little fellow was placed under the camera. Mr. Griffith took one look through the camera and sent the baby back to the institution with a note pinned to his diaper: "Please send us a young-looking baby. This one photographs like an old man."

Our California work schedule was similar to the one in New York. Four o'clock rising was not unusual during location trips. While it was still dark we would board the trolley car that would take us to the country. When we had leading parts we came by car, which the company hired. Mr. Griffith was driven by car too. I remember that he was always carefully dressed in a neat business suit, an immaculate white shirt, and a dark tie.

On location we did what was expected of us without fuss. One day I might have a leading role; the next day I could be working in the background, playing several small parts. Within a few hours I could be a village belle decked out in curls and ruffles; an Indian brave riding bareback on a wild pony, rushing to attack the belle's home; and a cowboy, my curls under a Stetson, racing to the belle's rescue. Doubles and stunt men were unknown.

I knew how to ride a horse backward and forward. Furthermore, youth and ignorance made me fearless. One day I was to play a scene in a careening runaway wagon. Bobby Burns, one of the famous Burns Brothers who had toured Europe with Buffalo Bill's Wild West Circus, was supposed to come to my rescue. As his horse thundered alongside the wildly swaying wagon, I leaped from it into his arms. He managed to catch me. But for a long breath it seemed as if we would all tumble to the ground. Then miraculously the horse regained its balance. Bobby Burns pulled in the reins, and we came to a stop. I thought it quite exciting—until I saw his face.

"That," he said hoarsely, "is the most dangerous thing I've ever done in my life."

Another time I was playing in a western opposite Raoul Walsh, one of our handsomest actors as well as directors. In the scene he and I and George Siegmann—a dear, gentle man who usually played villains—were to gallop past the camera on our steeds. One of the horses we were to use was wild and unmanageable, and everyone passed him up.

"I'll ride him," I offered.

We were supposed to go up the road and then turn around in order to pass the camera. My mount behaved as we went up the road, but once we had turned in the other direction, toward what he considered home, he took off like a wild creature. I could not stop him. We dashed past the camera and continued toward the woods. He meant to dislodge me under low-hanging tree branches and then to return to his stable. I was screaming. My shouts for help awakened Eagle Eye, a member of the company who was asleep in the bushes. He leaped up, caught the horse, and saved me.

Nonchalantly I slid off, found another animal, and went through the scene again.

Someone standing nearby remarked: "God looks after actors. They're his favorite children."

Chatsworth Park was the location where our westerns were usually filmed. It was called "the home of the rattlesnakes." Snakes were abundant there in spring, so each of us was supplied with a vial of antidote for snake bite. In one film I was to play a scene with snakes. Never having been on intimate terms with reptiles, I did not relish the prospect. But I rode out in the automobile with several snakes on my lap. I expected to find them cold and clammy, but they were surprisingly warm, even affectionate. They curled up and went to sleep in my lap. Later we played a very good scene together.

Mr. Griffith was afraid of snakes, so Del Henderson, who was quite a prankster, told him that he had hired a herpetologist to charm the reptiles and keep them out of Mr. Griffith's way. Only a man of Del's personality could have gotten away with that.

Mr. Griffith liked all other creatures. He had the most extraordinary results with animals; there must have been a hypnotic quality in his voice. He was on their wave length. In *Way Down East* he suggested the sleepy rural village with a shot of a kitten sitting on the porch of the country store. When he was ready to start filming, he made that kitten fall asleep.

"You should study these creatures if you want to know how to act," he suggested to us. "They can be understood around the world. They don't have to depend on a small set of western gestures that are foreign to most of the world to tell an audience what they're thinking. Look at that dog, jumping up and down, turning in circles, barking for his master. If only my actors could be as expressive."

After such remarks he would burst into song, usually an operatic aria, do a little shadowboxing by himself, or grab the nearest girl and dance a few lively steps. He always ended his lectures with a laugh. It made the atmosphere in our company such a happy one.

Mr. Griffith often went in search of his locations. Once he had found what he wanted he would send an assistant to ask about renting a front porch, a lawn, or an entrance—whatever was necessary for the film. Five or ten dollars was the usual sum offered in payment, and it was usually gladly accepted. Not many movies had yet been made, and people were delighted to have their properties used as locales. They would usually come out to watch the filming, and their comments were often painfully unflattering. We much preferred the bedlam of carpenters building sets at the studio to being out on the street watched by strangers who talked about us as we tried to concentrate on our scenes.

"Oh, isn't she a cutie?"

"I wonder if that's the man she's in love with?"

"If we hang around, maybe they'll play a love scene."

One of Mr. Griffith's assistants would try to silence them. "Please don't talk; we're going to take it."

But, if an assistant tried to silence them from a distance while the scene was being shot, they were apt to retort huffily, "Say, you don't own this street!"

Anxious to spare us any embarrassment or the danger of being molested, Mr. Griffith usually had some ex-prize fighters in our company.

But not all spectators were offensive. We had devoted followers too. There were always certain familiar faces among the watchers. We did not know who they were, but a small loyal band of them would find out where we were on location and track us down. Mr. Griffith was always pleasant and often joked with them.

Meanwhile, Dorothy and I were making friends on the lot, among them Blanche Sweet, who was without doubt the most beautiful girl on the lot. She was a genuine platinum blonde, with the most beautiful hands and feet I've ever seen on a human being, long and delicate like rose petals. We had adored her in many Biograph films. The first day she walked in when I was on the set my spine tingled, as if I had seen a ghost. My own reaction helped me to understand later how people felt when they saw me for the first time in the flesh off the screen. But in that early period it never occurred to any of us that we would be recognized. We did not for a moment believe that the shadows on the screen resembled us.

It took a while before we became friends with Mae Marsh, and the fault was ours. At the beginning we had thought ourselves superior because we had been trained in the theater. Mae had been a telephone operator. She came from a large Irish family, and the children were all attractive. None of them had ever been in the theater, but they did work in pictures. Her brother Oliver was a cameraman. Mae did not believe that she was much good as an actress; she was truly humble.

Mae was already in the company when Dorothy and I began working with Mr. Griffith. A short time before she had been visiting on the set with a cousin, and Mr. Griffith had noticed her. George Siegmann, who was Mr. Griffith's assistant as well as an actor, called her over. She was a slight, red-headed girl with freckles, awkward and shy. Siegmann told me of that meeting.

"Have you ever done anything in pictures?" Mr. Griffith asked her.

"No, sir, except one extra bit—and I wasn't very good at that."

"Would you like to be in pictures?"

"Yessir, but I don't think there's any chance."

"What's your name?"

"Mae Marsh. That's my cousin over there; *she*'s awfully good!"

"I know she is. Siegmann, have Miss Marsh wait. I want to rehearse that idea with her for *The Sands of Dee*. With Bobby Harron."

A week later Mae was playing the lead in the picture. The skinny little extra girl, who, when she first came to the studio, clasped her hands together so that people would not see the holes in her gloves, was a great success in that role. She did not remain an outsider for long. Her days as an ugly duckling were over.

She was an actress from the heart. Everyone adored her. They couldn't help it. Every quality she showed on the screen—innocence, bubbling youth, warmth, sheer goodness—was there in person too. When she was complimented she would exclaim, "Oh, I'm the cat's whiskers!" and giggle.

She had a quality of pathos in her acting that has never been equaled. When I first came on the lot she was playing all the parts I wanted. I later told her that she was the only actress of whom I was ever jealous. Not only did she play the parts I thought I could play, but she was better in them than I could have been. And that hurt.

Mr. Griffith was very fond of her. "Your talking and giggling make me forget my worries for a time," he told her.

Lillian (left) in a scene from one of her early films for Griffith, *The Musketeers of Pig Alley* (1912).   MUSEUM OF MODERN ART

Blanche Sweet (right) as Judith and Lillian as The Little Mother in Israel in Griffith's *Judith of Bethulia,* made in 1913 but not released till a year later.

Lillian and William Freeman as the lovesick sentry in *The Birth of a Nation* (1915).

Josephine Crowell as Mrs. Cameron, Henry B. Walthall as her son, The Little Colonel, and Lillian as the girl he loves in the famous hospital scene from *The Birth of a Nation*.

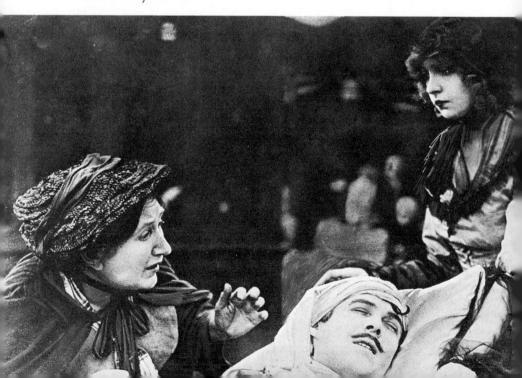

The freed slave Gus (Walter Lord), is seized by the Klan for attempting to rape Flora, The Little Dear One, and driving her to her death, in *The Birth of a Nation*.

The fabulous set of Babylon for *Intolerance* (1916).

Photographer Hendrick Sartov's first portrait of Lillian, who brought him to Griffith's attention.　　　　　PHOTO BY HOOVER ART CO.

Lillian as Elsie Stoneman, the young heroine of *The Birth of a Nation*.

Griffith in one of his famous wide-brimmed hats.

Family and friends: Mary Pickford, Mildred Harris, Mrs. Gish, Dorothy and Lillian.

Portrait of Lillian. PHOTO BY ABBÉ

🌿 9 🌿

I was hoping to get the lead in a new story, called *The Mothering Heart*. It was to be a two-reeler and would cost $1,800 to make, exclusive of salaries. *The Mothering Heart* was a chance to "play old," as we called acting parts beyond our years. The role was that of a thirty-year-old married woman. Mr. Griffith rehearsed me and then told me that I was too immature for it. It was a cruel disappointment. It seemed to me that I was never the right age—always either too young or too old. I discussed my plight with Dorothy, and we rushed out on a secret shopping expedition. At the next general rehearsal, my figure was considerably inflated with certain aids sold in the store's corset department.

"Mr. Griffith," I asked, "could I try the part just once again?"

He looked me up and down and said, puzzled, "Well, maybe you'll do."

In the scene I was to rehearse, the wife suffers jealousy when she sees her husband displaying interest in a cabaret dancer. She upbraids her husband on the way home, then decides to leave him.

As I rehearsed the scene, Mr. Griffith fed me the reactions of the injured wife: "You feel that you've been humiliated by your husband in public. You think that he doesn't love you any longer because you're carrying his child. You're afraid that he wants to get rid of you."

With his intense voice coaching me, I felt the heroine's agony.

After leaving her husband, the wife bears her child alone in a cottage. The infant dies. In her grief she wanders into the garden, picks up a stick, and beats the rose bushes until they are stripped bare.

This was Mr. Griffith's idea. He was justly famous for the bits of "business" that he injected into his films. Even when they were not really essential to the basic plot, they communicated emotions that he wanted to project. If an actor devised a good piece of "business" during rehearsals, Mr. Griffith would keep it in.

I won the role in *The Mothering Heart,* and it turned out to be a milestone in my career, primarily because, with two reels to work with, Mr. Griffith could concentrate more on the effects that he wanted and exercise more subtlety in his direction.

During the filming I worried that I was overplaying. But when I looked at the rushes during a lunch break, I asked Mr. Griffith why none of it showed on the screen. He explained: "The camera opens and shuts, opens and shuts with equal time—so half of everything you do isn't seen. Then take away the sound, and you lose another quarter. What's left on the screen is a quarter of what you felt or did—therefore, your expression must be four times as deep and true as it would be normally to come over with full effect to your audience."

He taught us that false emotions never move an audience, that you cannot make viewers cry with make-believe tears. "The first thing an actor needs is soul," he said. "The actor with soul feels his part; he is living his role, and the result is a good picture."

He showed great understanding of the tensions we built up in creating character and the often embarrassing physical aftermath. He told us about the great Sir Henry Irving, who always kept a bucket offstage for use when he got sick before a performance. Sir Henry's bucket was well known in England. He gave of himself so completely that he became physically ill. Mr. Griffith used this story to impress on us the importance of communicating deep emotion. Another example was Tommaso Salvini, who would become so involved in playing Othello that he would lift the man playing opposite him over his head and throw him to the ground. It was worth an actor's life, Mr. Griffith said, to play with Salvini.

He made it clear to us that acting required study. "No matter where you are, watch people," he told us. "Watch how they walk, how they move, how they turn around. If you're in a restaurant, watch them across the table or on the dance floor."

Whenever he saw some behavior pattern that intrigued him, he would use it at an appropriate moment in one of his pictures.

"Catch people off guard," he reminded us continually.

Sometimes, at the end of a shooting session, he would talk with those of us who remained to watch the rushes.

"Too many of us walk through life with blinders on our eyes. We see only what concerns us, instead of what goes on around us. Let's take a scene that is played again and again every day—one that we see and yet do not see. Let us imagine ourselves standing on a street corner. A pretty girl is waiting at the curb for a bus. A commonplace, undramatic event. Nearly every corner has a pretty girl waiting for a bus. But suppose we already know one fact—if the girl misses her bus, she'll be late for work. If she's late, she'll be fired. Let us begin then in the morning, when she comes awake abruptly in her room. We close in on the face of the clock to see the time. We watch her dressing with frantic haste. We see her drinking coffee. We show the hand holding the cup. It is trembling. We are becoming involved in the multitude of details which clothe every human event. When the girl leaves the house it is raining; she rushes back for an umbrella. Then we see her last-minute dash through the rain puddles for the bus. All of this, mind you, set against a montage of the hands of the clock moving and a backdrop of the office she is trying to reach. If we saw all this, we would be reliving our own tensions in similar circumstances, simply because we have been made to *see* it in all of its parts."

And he would repeat the familiar cry, "I am trying to make you *see!*"

To learn about human nature and to build our characterizations, we visited institutions normally closed to young people. At insane asylums, for example, we were escorted through wards by nurses or the doctors themselves. I particularly recall one place where I saw a man whom the nurses called "the Vegetable." If an attendant led him out to the garden, he would remain standing as he was left, often in a rigid, grotesque posture, arms extended or raised as if he were a tree. He would remain this way for hours at a time unless someone came for him. When he was placed on a chair, he would sit there until he drooped with exhaustion. One day I found him in the garden, stiff and unyielding, on a bench in the scalding noon sun. Another time, in a heavy rain, I saw him standing like a wood carving on the porch. He seemed to have no power or will of his own. Although there was nothing I could learn from his form of illness, it held a deep fascination for me.

Another patient whom I vividly recall was an eighteen-year-old Mexican girl. The first time I saw her she was chained to her bed, writhing and screaming for her dog. In time some of the patients began to feel at ease with me and would often begin to talk to me; the Mexican girl was one. She would catch my attention and ask, "How's Charlie Chaplin, how's Charlie Chaplin, how's Charlie Chaplin?" She repeated this question endlessly, like a wound-up mechanical toy. The nurses told me that she was a victim of syphilis but could be cured. I was never certain whether their prognosis was true or meant simply to cheer me.

I sympathized deeply with all the patients. They may have been aware of my compassion, for one day when the nurse left the ward for a moment a young woman shuffled over to me. She whispered: "I'm no more insane than you are. My relative put me in here for a purpose. Here's my mother's telephone number. Call her and tell her to come and get me. I'm unjustly confined."

She sounded completely rational. Her appeal touched me, and I took the number. Just then the doctor entered and looked at her shrewdly.

"Mary, why did you break the window this morning," he asked, "and then take the glass and cut your leg?"

She regarded him innocently. "But I had no pen. And I had to write with *something*."

Later, when I was faced in a film with a scene that required knowledge of insanity, I had seen enough of its physical manifestations to convey the necessary range of emotions.

During the filming of *The White Sister* many years afterward, I drew on my knowledge of epilepsy for one scene; it proved an effective way to register shock. Whenever I had doubts about the appropriate reactions to certain situations, I would consult an expert on the subject.

Mr. Griffith always emphasized that the way to tell a story was with one's body and facial expressions. "Expression without distortion," he always said. He meant, "Frown without frowning." Show disapproval without unsightly wrinkles. The only makeup he suggested was a golden tone, an idea he borrowed from Julia Marlowe, with whom he had acted and whom he admired tremendously.

I learned from him to use my body and face quite impersonally to create effects, much as a painter uses paint on canvas. Later on, when I worked with other directors, I would hang a mirror at the side of the camera, so that in a closeup I could see what effect I was producing.

Mr. Griffith kept constantly at his young players: "Let me see you walk with happiness. No, *not* gaiety, that's something else. That's better. Now, with sadness—*not* sorrow. Now—with comedy, tragedy, sickness, blindness. Now, let me see you run in all these ways. Some of you move like wooden Indians. Must I open a dancing school to teach you flexibility?"

He and I used to have a constant argument on one point. When I played a young girl, he used to have me hop around as if I had St. Vitus' Dance.

"Young girls don't do that," I complained.

"How else can I get the contrast between you and older people, if you don't jump around like a frisky puppy?" he asked. Then, imitating a young girl, he would get up and hop about, shaking his balding head as if it had a wig of curls. A stranger would have thought him mad.

We were encouraged to train our bodies for acrobatic pantomime, which was particularly useful when the camera was shooting from a distance. We were also called upon to perform the most dangerous stunts. None of us ever objected; it did not occur to us to object.

I studied fencing with a teacher named Aldo Nadi. He approved of my good eyesight and long legs and told me that in two years he could have me ready for the Olympics. But I was interested in fencing only as an adjunct to acting.

I also joined the Denishawn Dancing School, studying with Ruth St. Denis and Ted Shawn, whose pupils—among them Martha Graham—have since won acclaim for their great talents. Their large living room had been converted into a studio with mirrors and practice bars, and later, while Miss Ruth and Mr. Ted were on tour, Mother rented it so that we could practice early in the morning and late at night. Within a few years my body was to show the effects of all this discipline; it was as trained and responsive as that of a dancer or an athlete.

Mr. Griffith also encouraged us to take voice lessons to develop strength and proper breath control. His studio was certainly no training camp for weaklings; the working hours were unlimited, the demands unpredictable.

Under Mr. Griffith's tutelage, some of the younger girls of the company also had a small, impromptu class. Strindberg, Schopenhauer, Nietzsche—we read them all with earnest, patient concentration. We might not have absorbed all the ideas, but we tried awfully hard. I myself was seldom on the set without a book under my arm. During that time I developed an admiration for anyone who knew more than I did, and I must confess that the feeling is still part of me.

We also were expected to search for possible story material, reading everything in the public domain. We would find promising stories, change the locales, and use the characters and situations in our films.

Mr. Griffith urged us to mingle with audiences in movie theaters to observe their reactions. "It doesn't matter how *you* feel when you're playing," he said. "I'm not interested in that. I'm interested in what you make an audience feel. You may be crying or having hysterics, but if you're not making the audience feel that way, you're not any use to my story. Go to a movie house and watch the audience. If they're held by what you're doing, you've succeeded as an actress."

I have often sat in the balcony, staring at faces to measure the effect of a scene. More than once I've put my face directly in front of a spectator's face; instead of being distracted, I found, he would move his head aside in order not to miss a second of what was happening on the screen. Then I would know that I had achieved what I was striving for.

Mr. Griffith was at his most human and approachable during the Biograph years. He had more time to give us then. Although we were all respectful and never ventured an opinion unless asked, he was always open to suggestions. Often, after rehearsing a scene, he would ask Andy Reed, the electrician, or Shorty English, the property man, "Well, what do you think?"

They would tell him frankly, and he would listen. If the criticism seemed valid to him, he would appeal to the cast. "Andy says thus and so." Or "Shorty didn't believe it when you did that piece of business. Let's try it over."

He took a janitor's opinion as seriously as that of a critic. He wanted his films to please everyone. He listened as well as commanded, but he had no time to argue. "Just show me," he would say.

At that time he had no family nearby nor any personal ties; he and his wife Linda were no longer living together. Their marriage had disintegrated before Dorothy and I came to Biograph. Although they were separated, he did not file for divorce until 1935. It seems to me that no marriage could have survived his way of life. His energy was phenomenal; he took time off only to eat and sleep. If there was any man meant for bachelorhood, it was he.

But he enjoyed the devotion of the entire company, and he gave us his deep interest and love. I think he was in love with all his girls—or with the images of his heroines on the screen; I don't know which. Perhaps the answer lies in what he told me once as I was trying to shape the character of a young girl. "No," he said, after watching the first rehearsal. "It must be the essence of all girlhood, not just one girl. And she must have the wonder, curiosity, reserve, and trust of every girl everywhere."

The essence of virginity—purity and goodness, with nobility of mind, heart, soul, and body—is the stuff out of which, under his prompting, I created heroines. He made me understand that only governments and boundaries change, that the human race remains the same.

During that time I got to know a film from the time it was raw stock until it was shown to an audience.

Joe Aller, a Russian, handled the laboratory, which was situated on the studio lot. On his developing and printing of negatives rested the visual success of our scenes. He could lighten or darken the film. Often he worked through the night, and we would work along with him. He was supposed to sleep during the day, but sometimes he would wander over and watch the filming. Or Mr. Griffith would order, "Get Joe over here, and let him see the mood we're trying to get."

Joe showed me how film was developed in the "soup" and then left to dry on long wooden racks. Jimmy Smith, the cutter, taught me the arduous, eye-straining work of reading negatives and splicing and joining the finished print.

Often Mr. Griffith would say to me, "I'm too busy to leave here," nodding toward the set, "but you go back to the studio and help Jimmy."

If I had a morning off, I was sent to the darkroom to pick my rushes. Mr. Griffith seemed to have faith in my judgment. I used to fight to have more of me cut out of the film. I always thought an audience should be left wanting more rather than being surfeited with my image.

In those days we all worked closely with one another. Everything is different now. The men who work on developing film are far away from the studios. What was once warm and personal is now mechanical. In our time there was no class distinction, no nonsense like the later Hollywood caste system, in which those who earned $1,000 a week felt it beneath them to associate with those who earned only $500 a week. Actors, carpenters, darkroom men, wardrobe mistresses—when we gave a party they all came. One of my friends was Al Jennings, a part-time actor and a former gunfighter. Al was a case of the roughest being the gentlest. I have never seen kinder eyes, yet he had eleven notches on his gun though they may have been just for show. He taught me to draw and fire a gun, which he could do faster than the eye could follow. I am still a good shot; when later I played in *The Unforgiven,* John Huston, the director, was startled to find that I could fire faster than Burt Lancaster—thanks to my old friend Al Jennings.

What social life we had revolved around the people in the studio, for we knew no others. Our lives were circumspect and to an outsider probably quite dull. Dorothy and Bobby Harron sometimes went out together, but never for a late evening, as they were both expected in the studio early the next morning.

"Bobby started out as an office boy," Dorothy used to say proudly, "and gradually he developed into an actor, a leading man, and finally a star."

On the day that the local parish priest had brought Jimmy Smith, Danny Grey, and Bobby into the East Fourteenth Street studio looking for work, Bobby Harron was set for a future that neither he nor his family had anticipated.

Bobby was about fourteen then. He did odd jobs around the studio; whatever anyone wanted he knew where to find. He was Mr. Griffith's loyal and adoring shadow. D. W. was not a paternal type, but he behaved like a father toward Jimmy, Danny, and Bobby.

Bobby was young and serious, and something about him caught the heart. He was sensitive and poetic-looking, with the dark hair and eyes and fine bone structure of the black Irish. He was tall and slender, and when Mr. Griffith finally decided that he was ready to play leads, they had to add a mustache to his upper lip or lengthen his sideburns or have him wear a romantic cape—anything to give him age and dignity.

Bobby and Dorothy had been in love from the time that he was fifteen and she was thirteen. They would hold hands shyly. He never let her use any makeup, although it seemed to us that he always liked the girls who wore the most makeup. But he was Dorothy's love, and she did what he told her to.

Bobby came of a large family; he was the third of nine children, eight of whom were living. One day Dorothy and I took photographs of the family. When we showed them to Mr. Griffith, he came up with an idea of a film about a boy named Bobby who had been given a Brownie camera as a gift. Bobby would shoot pictures without discrimination. One of the snapshots would show his sister kissing her beau, with which he would blackmail her. For that period, it was a naughty story. Bobby Harron played the role of his namesake, and it was his first important part in a picture.

Bobby could play any role that Mr. Griffith gave him. Later an actor named Charlie Ray captured the public with a similar quality, but I never thought that his talent equaled Bobby's.

What I remember most about that hectic period is that Mother was finally free of money worries. Dorothy and I were assured of weekly salaries, not for only forty weeks of the year as in the theater but for fifty-two weeks. Mother was not a businesswoman by nature, but privation had taught her the value of money. From our childhood, Mother had saved a tenth of our earnings, and she continued this discipline. She taught us the difference between capital and income. "Don't mistake your salary for income," she warned us. "Should you break an arm or a leg, everything stops."

It was our habit to turn our checks over to her, and she kept them in a common account. As our salaries increased, she suggested that we live on 10 per cent of our earnings to build up a reserve. After the success of *The Birth of a Nation, Intolerance,* and *Broken Blossoms,* Mother arranged for a New York bank to look after us, and we have always had the good fortune to deal with bank officials who have taken a helpful interest in our welfare.

It was such a happy time for us! We were together; Mother made a warm, comfortable home for us. She was understanding and tactful. She knew how tired we often were after a day at the studio, and she would serve us dinner in bed. She never pried, but she was there, tranquil and loving, when we needed her.

The large rented house we were living in had a sleeping porch that we used at night. In California I slept outdoors whenever possible. Mr. Griffith evidently did not like the idea of the three of us being alone in that big house. He gave Mother a small pearl-handled revolver, a .22, for protection. None of us expected that she would ever have to use it. But one night, after I had already gone to bed and Mother had turned off her lamp, she heard strange sounds. She heard a window opening in the pantry; she saw the beam of a flashlight. All she could think of was her daughter lying unprotected on the porch. At the first sound, she had taken the revolver out of her bedside table. As she heard footsteps approaching, she cried, "You get out of here!" Without any more warning, she fired into the ceiling. The man fled.

During that time I began to suffer from headaches. I kept my indisposition to myself, but made an effort to track down its cause. The headaches, I discovered, usually started when I had a difficult scene coming up. Once I established the reason, I was able to overcome them.

During the late spring of 1913 rumors began to circulate that the boss was preparing a new film—four reels! He had never before made a film of that length. After swearing us to secrecy, he admitted that the rumors were true, but he was still cautious about giving details, even to us. He had learned through experience that if other studios heard of his ideas early enough, they would produce them before he could do so. "I am doing a dramatic story from the Bible," he said.

He had reserved two weeks for producing two films, but he ground one out in a single day and then launched into his greatest undertaking yet.

The film was *Judith of Bethulia,* which he adapted from a play by Thomas Bailey Aldrich, who in turn had taken it from the Book of Judith of the Apocrypha. It told the story of Nebuchadnezzar's general, Holofernes, who laid siege for forty days to the Israelite city of Bethulia. The beleaguered inhabitants, near starvation, were ready to surrender, when Judith, a young widow, conceived a bold plan. Dressed seductively, she stole into Holofernes' camp and caught his attention; after a wild night of feasting and revelry, the general finally fell into a drunken sleep, whereupon Judith drew out her sword and beheaded him. She brought the bloody trophy back to Bethulia with her and displayed it to the people. In the battle that followed, Holofernes' army was routed, and Bethulia was saved.

Blanche Sweet was cast as Judith and Henry Walthall as Holofernes. The secondary courtship between Nathan and Naomi was played by Bobby Harron and Mae Marsh. I was a "little mother in Israel" in a subplot, wandering through the city in the midst of the siege in search of food for my child.

We were surprised when the whole company was assigned to parts in the rehearsal of a single film. Directors became assistants for a few days, and everyone came to Chatsworth Park for the filming, sensing the importance of the event. Even Mother worked as an extra, although for her it turned out to be an unhappy experience. Her skin was delicate, and the desert sun, which was like a blast furnace in June, burned her badly, right through her dress.

People who knew Mr. Griffith believe that the success of foreign spectacles like *The Last Days of Pompeii* and *Quo Vadis?* spurred him on to attempt one himself, although he had seen neither of the imports. When *Judith* was finally released in 1914, critics considered it superior in every way to the imports. There is no doubt that the advent of the multireel film gave Mr. Griffith the determination to stretch his horizons. He had experimented as early as 1909 with a four-part story, *Pippa Passes,* but not on so immense a scale.

At Chatsworth Park Mr. Griffith built a street of Bethulia and a replica of the city walls. A tract was filled with pitched tents for Holofernes' campsite. A makeup man helped the extras, about fifty men, with their wigs, beards, and costumes. Some of the beards were made of curling crepe paper, and in the intense heat the crepe would sag and have to be refurbished. Blanche's costume was a crepe shift with a tiny pair of panties, which proved no protection during one scene in which she had to ride a horse sidesaddle. The shift was so snug that she wore the skin off her *derrière.*

It is odd what I remember of that ambitious production. The matter of lunch boxes, for instance. They cost a quarter apiece, and each contained a sandwich—thick white bread with only a sliver of filling, cheese mostly; perhaps a hard-boiled egg; a piece of fruit; and a half-pint of milk. I lived for so many years on those box lunches that to this day I cannot eat a sandwich.

Then there were the costumes. Each player was obliged to remember the details of his own costume, for there was no one to keep track of them for him. If he forgot, his job might be in jeopardy. And the problem of our hair was always with us. The California mist was rough on curls, so each night we put our hair up on "kid" curlers, which were our version of the hair rollers used today.

Gertrude Bambrick was in charge of the dancers, about twenty-five of them. Gertrude told me recently that she had taught Mr. Griffith how to dance. He loved to dance, and often when there was a break on the set he would turn to her and say, "Well, Miss Bambrick, how about a few steps?"

"At first," Gertrude said, "he didn't know his right foot from his left. But within six months he was a beautiful dancer. He never gave up on anything. He'd stick to it until he succeeded."

The advertisements later announced that *Judith of Bethulia* was the most expensive Biograph film ever produced. They went on to exaggerate the number of extras and the costliness of the sets, ignoring Mr. Griffith's talent for making much out of little. It is true, however, that *Judith* was more expensive and took longer to make than any other Griffith picture up to that time.

J. C. "Little" Epping, the company accountant, had the distasteful job of totaling daily expenditures and explaining them to the front office in New York. Mr. Epping was a small, bespectacled man with a perpetually worried expression. During the filming of *Judith,* he seemed daily to grow smaller and more harassed. As weeks passed and the company remained on location, he would appear repeatedly, mopping his brow.

"Mr. Griffith, may I see you for a minute?"

"Well, we're pretty busy right now."

"Afraid this can't wait, Mr. Griffith."

"All right; I'll be with you when I finish this scene."

A few minutes later, Mr. Griffith would join "Little" Epping for one of the many frantic conferences that often disrupted the shooting schedule.

Perhaps the money men had decided that it was dangerous to leave Griffith loose in the west. Probably the trouble began with the reports that "Little" Epping sent ahead. But that was his job—he was Biograph's "money censor"—so he couldn't be blamed.

After location shots were completed, the company packed up and returned to New York, where Mr. Griffith was to complete the film. On our return we found that Biograph had abandoned the studio on East Fourteenth Street for spacious quarters on 175th Street in the Bronx. There Mr. Griffith did the interior shots for *Judith*. The finished picture was the most eloquent support for his appeal for creative freedom. It showed what could be done when a master was allowed to exercise the full measure of his talent.

The front office, however, was horrified at the cost—$36,000 for one picture. It was incredible. The executives' fury was aggravated by the picture itself—its length, its depiction of the barbaric Holofernes, its gory beheading scene.

"They have no vision," Mr. Griffith told us bitterly. "They want to release *Judith* as *four* films instead of sending it out as one long picture and charging more for admission."

To compound the offense, while Griffith had been working on the Coast, the Biograph heads had decided to jump on the "feature" bandwagon anyway, to compete with foreign producers and the brash young Adolph Zukor, an independent exhibitor who had imported the French feature *Queen Elizabeth,* starring Sarah Bernhardt, and had formed a corporation called "Famous Players in Famous Plays" to produce movie versions of stage hits with well-known theater actors. In emulation of Zukor, Biograph had contracted with a theatrical firm, Klaw and Erlanger, to photograph its stage successes, using famous Broadway personalities. But Biograph had no intention of entrusting Mr. Griffith with the production of these features. They had engaged "stage experts" for that. They expected him to continue grinding out what he called "sausages"—one- and two-reel films made quickly and cheaply—at which he was expert. Terry Ramsaye, author of *A Million and One Nights,* once said, "When the situation calls for potboilers, Griffith is a fast cook." But Mr. Griffith was unsatisfied directing these movies. His vision could no longer be encompassed in one- and two-reel films. It was time to part company with Biograph.

While he was battling with the financial powers, they simply put *Judith* in the vault and did not release it for nearly a year. By that time foreign multireel films were being shown widely, and *Judith* was no longer a novelty. Still, when Biograph released it as a single film, it did prove that the future of films lay with features, made with greater expenditures of time, film, and money.

Even before the rumors began, we all had an unhappy feeling that Mr. Griffith would eventually be forced to break with Biograph. The front office was putting altogether too much pressure on him. None of us felt that we were working for Biograph. Our ties were with Mr. Griffith. As I remember, none of us had a contract with him; we simply worked for him. He would say to a player, "I'll give you . . ." and name a sum; he always kept his word. In those days we were continually being offered jobs by other companies, but Biograph was the top—thanks to Mr. Griffith—and one didn't descend from the peak just for money.

When we heard that he was leaving Biograph to go with another company, each of us fervently hoped to be taken along. One by one the actors would approach him and ask hesitantly, "What about me, Mr. Griffith?"

If the man was married and had responsibilities, Mr. Griffith might be reluctant to ask him to wait. "I don't know yet. It might be a few weeks—even months—before I'll be ready."

The company was buzzing with conjecture. It was said that Adolph Zukor had offered him $50,000 a year and that he had refused it. It was a period of uncertainty for all of us. Because Mr. Griffith was worried, we were worried too. We wondered if he was having trouble making new connections. But we trusted and believed in him. Once he made new contacts, we were sure, he would want his company with him.

It was during that period that Harry and Roy Aitken came into his life. The Aitken brothers had acquired five nickelodeons in the first decade of the twentieth century, thus forming one of the first movie chains in the country. The success of the new medium swept them up on the flood to riches. But they took a step beyond the nickelodeon to film distribution, where money and power were ultimately to rest. The film industry was not yet a decade old, and little had been done to make its products easily accessible to exhibitors. The few film producers in existence simply could not keep up with the demand. While the creative people were still groping to fashion a technique for this crude new form of communication, business stepped in and took ruthless control. In the race to keep their nickelodeons filled, the owners had to outbid one another for the newest films.

Harry and Roy Aitken shrewdly put their profits to work by opening a film exchange. It was the exchange that bought films from producing companies and rented them to exhibitors. The Aitken timing was superb, and they raked in profits. Within a month they were operating exchanges in Chicago, Milwaukee, and St. Louis. Within two years they had disposed of their chain of nickelodeons to devote all their energies to thirty-five film exchanges around the world.

Having made a fortune as distributors, the Aitkens were eager to produce films as well. Mr. Griffith wanted an alliance with a producing company that would allow him to exercise his talents. In October 1913 they joined forces. He became head of production for the Mutual Film Corporation, the distributing agency for the producing companies of Majestic and Reliance, also owned by the Aitken brothers, at the salary of $1,000 a week. He was also promised the right to make two films of his own a year.

"The new director of the Reliance and Majestic studios, Mr. Griffith, joins the Mutual companies at one of the largest salaries ever paid to a Motion Picture Director," wrote *Reel Life*.

Mr. Griffith took many of the Biograph directors with him. Though Dorothy and I had been offered contracts to remain with Biograph without Mr. Griffith, we never even considered the offers. Nor did others of his company, even though this loyalty meant going without work. Everyone wanted to stay with him—everyone except Billy Bitzer, who, incredibly, at first refused to go with Mr. Griffith. Billy later wrote:

> When Mr. Griffith decided to leave Biograph, I refused to join with him, although he offered to treble my salary. I didn't think the independent outfit he was going with could possibly stand the gaff of Mr. Griffith's spending of both film and money. Among the inducements Mr. Griffith pictured to me was one in which he said, "We will bury ourselves in hard work out at the coast for five years, and make the greatest pictures ever made, make a million dollars and retire, and then you can have all the time you want to fool around with your camera gadgets, etc., and I will settle down to write." Now I thought how can he be so sure of that when even now in the pictures we had . . . we never did know whether we had a best-seller until it went out?

But finally Billy was persuaded, and he, too, joined Mr. Griffith at Mutual.

Like many independents, Mutual had no studio in New York. Mr. Griffith hastily rented a loft near Union Square, improvised a studio, and went into immediate production on a five-reel film called *The Battle of the Sexes*. "This is a potboiler," he told us at the first rehearsal. The film took up the familiar theme of the philandering husband, the vamp, and the long-suffering wife. I played the couple's daughter.

It was important for Mr. Griffith to make a commercial film quickly and cheaply, in order to impress his new bosses and to raise money for the company. Speed was paramount. He put us and himself through a grueling pace. Mother, who seldom expressed herself on such matters, finally complained that I was getting no sleep. We were nearing the end of filming one day when Billy brought his lens close to my face. He frowned and stepped back. "Mr. Griffith, I can't shoot," he said. "Her eyes are too bloodshot."

Mr. Griffith sent me home for some sleep. A few hours later I was back at work.

The film was completed in five hectic days and nights. It accomplished its purpose of making money, thus starting the company off profitably.

Soon after making *The Battle of the Sexes* we heard that our Aunt Carrie Robinson had been stricken with cancer. Mother felt that she had to go to her. We were living in a furnished apartment on Riverside Drive, and she did not want us to be there alone. But her choice of a chaperone was rather odd: She asked Marshall Neilan, an actor in the company, to live there and look after us. Marshall had never before had two young girls as charges. He had quite a wild reputation, but his new responsibilities brought out unsuspected paternal instincts. He was very strict with us. When we obeyed his orders, he rewarded us by playing the piano—and he played beautifully. We were living a situation that could have made a successful Griffith film. We adored Marshall, and that year he married our dear friend Gertrude Bambrick. Later he directed some of Mary Pickford's best films.

When the weather in New York grew cold and blustery, Mr. Griffith was ready to take his small company back to the West Coast for what was to be the most crucial year of his career. According to Billy, they had to hock the film of *The Great Leap,* which W. Christy Cabanne had directed for Mutual, in order to pay the train fare back to Los Angeles.

Out on the Coast we were soon at work on *Home Sweet Home,* a film biography of John Howard Payne, the composer of the song by the same name. Henry Walthall played Payne; I was cast as his patient sweetheart. A large part of the picture was devoted to a series of subplots in which the song itself was the leading character, inspiring loves and saving marriages. Blanche Sweet played in one episode, Mae Marsh in another. Most of our company worked on this four-reeler; it was evidently Harry Aitken's idea to use nearly all the Griffith players in one film.

In the last reels of *Home Sweet Home,* Payne becomes a shameless sinner and dies in Egypt. His young love has died earlier while awaiting his return. D. W. sent Payne to hell for his wickedness— hell being rocks and smoke pots in Chatsworth Park—but the love of his sweetheart, who has become an angel, redeems him.

The scene in which Payne is brought from the smoking inferno up to heaven by his sweetheart was filmed in the studio. Henry Walthall and I, suspended by wires, were to be lifted up over the camera. But Mr. Griffith was dissatisfied with the scene. "When you fly them out over the top of the camera," he said, "the most prominent things are Wally's feet. That's no good."

There was a long discussion while Walthall and I, encased in leather harness, hung on the guide wires. Wally, a true southern gentleman, didn't raise his voice, didn't complain; he simply fainted and hung there limply. They took us down, then tried putting the camera on a little track on a platform, but nothing worked.

"Get them up again," called Mr. Griffith. "We'll have to fly them *away* from the camera, while we move it back."

So we flew backward into eternal bliss. Seen today, it is a very funny spectacle. The audiences of that period, however, wouldn't have dreamed of laughing.

In spite of its sentimentality, the film had vigorous characterizations and the usual Griffith technical skill.

Next he made *The Avenging Conscience,* with Henry Walthall, Blanche Sweet, and Mae Marsh. This film, two parts Edgar Allan Poe and one part D. W. Griffith, has been called the forerunner of the German psychological films like *Cabinet of Dr. Caligari.*

One of the films that Dorothy and I made for Majestic release was *The Rebellion of Kitty Belle.* Bobby Harron played with us in this film, and the advertisements refer to Dorothy and me as "Two Famous Sisters Seen Only in Majestics," and add, "Appearing for the first time together in a Majestic release." Majestic evidently had decided to use photographs of its players, for there is a photograph of me, with the note: "Lillian, who appears exclusively in Majestic releases and 'Griffith' specials, has been pronounced the most popular actress before the American Public." Dorothy's photograph is captioned, "The youngest comedienne of distinction in America, whose charming personality is to be found only in Majestic releases and 'Griffith' specials."

At that time Dorothy was being kept busy in a series of humorous pictures. She had an instinct for humor, a natural outgrowth of her spritely nature. She was a great deal like our father; when she arrived, the party began. Anita Loos reminded me recently that in those adolescent days Dorothy's humor leaned toward sight gags. She loved making herself ridiculous.

But she had an intuitive insight into human behavior. Usually she kept it pretty much to herself, but once, I remember, she said casually, "There are murderers and murderees." I realize now that for all her rollicking spirits she had a depth and perception that she carefully hid from us.

Dorothy was growing up; she was two inches over five feet tall and weighed 109 pounds. Her mischievous blue eyes, porcelain complexion, and fair hair made her irresistible. Everyone spoiled her.

"She's got no common sense," Mother often exclaimed. Often it fell on my shoulders to try to persuade Dorothy to do what Mother thought she should do. Dorothy was fiercely independent, and I think that her defiance of my suggestions was a healthy form of rebellion. For a while she was mentioned mainly as my little sister. According to a press release I found in her desk, "she rather resented this reflected glory." But after *The Mountain Rat,* a Majestic production, Dorothy became a personality in her own right. At that time, individual players were becoming well-known, and as their personalities developed the adoring public made them stars.

Mr. Griffith had his own ideas about stars.

"You want to be a star?" he once said to me. "It has nothing to do with my putting your name up in lights. First, you'll have to make pictures for at least ten years. And in every picture you'll have to be responsible not only for your role but for the scenes of everyone in the picture and the story itself. You'll be the first to arrive at the studio and the last to leave. Your private life—if you have any— must be like Caesar's wife: above reproach. One touch of scandal will be the end of you.

"Not until your name becomes a household word in every family —not only in America, but in the world, if the world feels it knows you and loves you—will you be a star in motion pictures," he finished.

At the end of that lecture, I decided that becoming a star meant too much hard work, that it was better simply to keep working in films until I could return to the theater, where I would not have to worry about my popularity in Europe, India, or China.

Although for those of us under the Griffith umbrella there was no star system—indeed, it was only after *The Birth of a Nation* that **Mr.** Griffith allowed our names to be used on programs—other studios already had rosters of young stars, and were bent on luring Griffith prodigies away from him whenever possible. But we remained steadfast, except for those he chose to send out into the world of his competitors.

❧ 10 ❧

Christmas found us in an apartment on Hope Street, where we had four rooms and a good kitchen. Mother invited Mr. Griffith, Donald Crisp, Bobby Harron, and several others who were without families for Christmas dinner. It was a true holiday for Dorothy and me; just being with Mother was a cause for rejoicing. Our guests arrived, all but Mr. Griffith. As the rich smells of holiday food filled the apartment we grew impatient.

"He can't be shopping," Mother said. "Everything's closed. He must still be working."

Mr. Griffith arrived by taxi at three o'clock, just as we were gathering around the big turkey that Mother had cooked. He held a large blue and white Chinese umbrella stand in his arms, filled with gifts for everyone—Oriental, naturally, as he'd been to Chinatown, the only place where shops were open. We were delighted with our earrings, fans, and all the other lovely things that he had brought.

Mr. Griffith was always a very generous man, but this quality was most conspicuous during the holidays. He was at his gayest when giving presents. He never had time to go shopping for Christmas gifts, so he would delegate Mother or someone like her to do it for him. He loved to surprise people with presents. He would pretend not to have brought anything, then slip a present in your coat pocket and perhaps innocently ask for your handkerchief or gloves. He loved to give pretty things to young people, and expensive trinkets or perhaps even fur coats to the older character women who could not afford such things. The character actresses all adored him, and he treated them with the courtesy of a southern gentleman. He kept some of them on the payroll simply to save them the humiliation of handouts.

One earlier Christmas, Dorothy was upset because her first fur coat had been stolen and she could not afford a replacement. It was a soft gray squirrel and she had looked fetching in it. On Christmas Day Mr. Griffith arrived as usual, carrying a box. He whispered to me: "Hide it; hang it up in the hall." I was as excited as if it had been for me. During dinner he said: "Oh, I'm cold, Dorothy. There's a draft in here. Will you go out in the hall and bring me the coat on the rack?"

Dorothy went out to the entrance hall. "Which one, Mr. Griffith?"

"That gray one, Dorothy."

Silence from the hall, while he beamed at us.

Then an ecstatic, "Oh, *Mister Griffith!*"

One day Mr. Griffith took Mother aside and told her: "My sister and my niece from Kentucky are coming to visit me for a few weeks. They don't know what a lonely time they'll have—unless you, Mrs. Gish, look after them." Mother was generally his personal shopper, and he added, "With your taste, perhaps you could get some clothes for Big Ruth—she's never been much interested in how she looks— and also Little Ruth will want something."

He gave Mother a wad of money to outfit them. In a few weeks, she was busy showing the sights to a pleasant, quiet woman who had the same cast of features as her brother. Little Ruth was his brother's daughter. We took the two Ruths shopping for clothes, and we enjoyed Little Ruth's excitement over the pretty things her Uncle David bought them. They stayed a few weeks and had a wonderful time. Meeting them gave us insight into another facet of his character. Until he married Evelyn Baldwin many years later, this was the nearest I ever saw him to a domestic mood.

He was a good, loving son, brother, and uncle. He had been deeply attached to his mother, whom he had supported until she died, a short time after Dorothy and I came to work for him. I dimly remember his going back to Kentucky for her funeral.

He also helped support most of the other members of his family. Among his papers, I found letters asking him for a new house or a new car; seldom was there a notation saying, "We saw your picture and enjoyed it." But he would never admit that people used him. I suppose he needed to be needed—and he was, by literally hundreds of people.

I believe one of the reasons that he felt so close to us was that we never asked him for anything. Consequently, he seemed to trust us more than he did most people.

His generosity extended to all who worked with him. "Sometimes he would call for extras to report, knowing full well that his shooting schedule precluded their use," Mack Sennett once said. "But it was his way of seeing that actors made a few dollars." At other times he would invite the extras to lunch with him. "He must have felt a good solid meal now and then would be welcomed," Sennett suggested. "He was once a hungry actor himself."

Whenever I knew of an actor who needed a job, I would ask Mr. Griffith to use him—and he always did. Ray Klune, who started with him as an office boy, finished high school and went on to college with Mr. Griffith's help.

He turned no one away. If anyone asked for a handout, Mr. Griffith would put his hand in his pocket, and whatever bill he came up with—a five, a ten, sometimes a twenty—he would hand over. If someone had a problem that could not be solved with cash, Mr. Griffith would ask one of his assistants to look after the person and help him.

When a projectionist ran film at night, he was paid for it. But, in addition, Mr. Griffith would pull a bill from his pocket, slip it into his hand, and thank him. It was usually $10 but often could be $20. He always expected to pay for what he wanted. He gave out of pride, mingled with appreciation.

Mae Marsh told me that he once paid the funeral expenses for a deaf little Italian voice teacher, though he had never met the man. She had told him how the neighbors were trying to take a collection and couldn't raise enough, so he asked her mother to attend to the arrangements, then paid for them.

One of his gifts to me was a fiery opal from Australia, which he had made up in a pendant. He himself never wore jewelry, except a ring with an Egyptian stone that Harriet Quimby, a woman flier and a friend of his, had given him. The ring could be used as a seal, to stamp letters, and also as a weapon. It could inflict injury in a fight.

Yet he could be inconsistent about money. I remember his making us take care of his tips, claiming he had no change. Years later, he would saunter through the rooms of my house in Beverly Hills, casually emptying the contents of all the cigarette boxes into his pockets.

"She has more money than I have, because she's working," he would say. "And besides, she doesn't smoke."

It amused him to pretend to be a pinchpenny. Once Mary Pickford told me that sometimes when he took her and her mother to dinner, he would say that he had no money on him, but that the Pickfords were so rich it couldn't matter to them if they paid the bill. So they always came prepared. He did it as a joke and they knew it and laughed at it.

Gift giving was one of his few extravagances. Mr. Griffith never wanted more than one or two rooms in a middle-class hotel, and never owned a house until late in his life, when he married Evelyn Baldwin and they bought a tiny house on Peck Drive in Beverly Hills. He ate and drank sparingly; I never saw him drink more than one glass of beer or one whiskey and soda with dinner. He always advised us to eat nourishing food but not to overeat. He often told me that I was the only one who didn't eat too much, although he knew of my weakness for ice cream.

He did smoke a good deal, however, although he never carried cigarettes. He would call out, "Give me a cigarette," and every man in the room would hold out a pack. He would look over the assortment and choose the brand he wanted. Then there would be a flurry of lighted matches. It was considered a great honor to have one's cigarette chosen. He would take a few puffs on the cigarette and then throw it away.

He had a great regard for his body and believed in keeping it healthy. He boxed every morning. Mack Sennett said that he also took a cold bath each morning, adding pails of chipped ice, delivered by the bellhop, to his bath water. He was very frightened of germs. He always worried about catching cold, perhaps because it was the only illness he seemed to know. The only times that I remember his actually being ill were when he had colds. He took great precautions against them. If you had a cold, you weren't allowed near him. He always kept doors closed and avoided drafts, particularly in automobiles. He didn't like having colds because, although they never stopped him from working, they made work an effort. When he had one, he would complain and swear about it, but he was never absent from work because of illness in all the years that I was with him.

His preoccupation with keeping fit was a concern with which I was particularly sympathetic. As a child I had been delicate and undernourished, but I had had a strong will to survive. I soon learned that in our profession if you were sick or tired, you simply kept quiet about it and did your work. To stand the strain of a fourteen-hour day six or seven days a week, you had to be in top physical condition. If a performer looked pale or run down, Mr. Griffith was apt to pass him by. I don't know how he happened to accept me, for I was the picture of frailty. Perhaps my work in the East Fourteenth Street studio had convinced him that I was hardy. Perhaps he was reassured because I was always on time, never complained of late hours, and never showed a sign of illness. The quality I had cultivated as a child on the road—what my friend Nell Dorr calls "Lillian's blinders"—helped me. I always concentrated on the job at hand and shut out everything else from my consciousness.

Once I brought a young girl, Lucille Langhanke, to Mr. Griffith's attention. She wanted to break into pictures, and I persuaded him to let me film a test of her. Afterward he explained to her in his courtly manner that there were no openings. But he told me privately: "She's beautiful but far too delicate. I don't believe she could stand the grind."

It's possible, however, that he was simply annoyed because I exposed over 1,000 feet of film testing Lucille. "Who do you think you are?" he demanded when he saw the test. Whatever the reason, Lucille didn't brood. Soon after, she became an outstanding player and changed her name to Mary Astor.

Mr. Griffith had almost a mania for cleanliness. He himself was always impeccably groomed, and he expected the young actresses on the lot to be equally immaculate. A female aspirant would lose out if she weren't scrupulously clean. Once, after an interview with a talented actress whom he had dismissed, he said exasperatedly, "She just doesn't *look* clean."

One morning Dorothy appeared at the studio wearing blue jeans, with her hair in kid curlers. He spoke to Mother about it, and Dorothy never repeated her mistake.

Mr. Griffith's emphasis on hygiene once had an unexpected consequence. Dorothy had been assigned to play the role of Kathy in *Old Heidelberg*. Her leading man was Wallace Reid, who was much older than she. John Emerson, an important man in the New York theater, was to direct it as his first film. When they were about to film the first love scene, he told Wallace to kiss Dorothy on the mouth.

"Oh, Mr. Emerson," she exclaimed. "We don't do such things in pictures."

"You're going to do it in this picture," Emerson said ominously. "How else are you going to play a love scene?"

"In films," she informed him, "we pretend to kiss. And with the camera at a distance, it seems that we do."

"Well, this time the camera is close and I want you to kiss him."

Not Dorothy. She turned and rushed off for "Daddy" Woods' office, with John Emerson in hot pursuit. Frank Woods, a kindly, white-haired man whom we all called "Daddy" Woods, was not only head of the story department but also judge in all our disputes.

"You know Mr. Griffith told us we must *never* kiss actors—it isn't healthy," she complained to him. "But Mr. Emerson doesn't seem to understand."

Mr. Emerson was furious. "How can I do a love story without a love scene?" he yelled.

The whole studio was interested in the dispute; it became a *cause célèbre*. Wally's wife heard about it. She called Mother and told her indignantly that her husband was perfectly healthy and that it certainly would not hurt Dorothy to kiss him. Finally Mr. Emerson won, and a tearful, rebellious Dorothy kissed Wallace Reid on the mouth before the camera.

D. W. Griffith was a proud man. We who knew him saw his pride as the pride of achievement. Strangers, to whom Mr. Griffith was an enigma, tended to misinterpret this trait as vanity.

Although he was reputed to be vain, he lacked the conceit to consider himself more than a director. Even later, when he wrote the stories for his twelve-reel films, such as *Hearts of the World,* he used a pseudonym. He held no exaggerated idea of his own importance. Unlike many American producers, he never criticized the European directors and producers. He had the highest regard for the Italians' camerawork, though he thought they lagged behind Americans in the telling of a story. He claimed later that America progressed faster in film making because of a four-year head start, during the time Europe was embroiled in World War I.

In going through his papers recently, I was startled to discover that he considered himself ugly. The truth is that he was striking and distinguished-looking. But apparently his failure as a leading man had confirmed his poor opinion of his looks. Looking back, I realize how much the size of his nose embarrassed him. At that time he avoided being photographed and seldom appeared in a news-reel. He did allow himself to be seen in films like *1776, or The Hessian Renegades,* perhaps because he considered the costume sufficient disguise.

He was in the habit of wearing wide-brimmed hats, not only for protection from the sun on location but also because he believed that they balanced his jutting nose and strong chin. But someone had warned him that hats were bad for the scalp, so he sliced off the tops in the hope that the sun's rays would halt the thinning of his hair. He used to sit, watching the filming, one leg crossed over the other knee, and unconsciously massage the top of his head. If there was a wind and his headgear felt insecure, he would calmly thread a shoelace through the brim and tie the ends together in a neat knot under his chin. But he affected none of the idiosyncrasies of the directors who made breeches and puttees symbols of the Hollywood director.

There was a suggestion of mystery about Mr. Griffith that has never been solved. He admired and loved women, yet he seemed afraid of them. He never saw a girl in his office without a third person present. He seemed concerned about his reputation. Perhaps he was simply protecting himself from blackmail. Hollywood was already filled with ambitious girls who would stop at nothing to get into films. Some unscrupulous young girls, having obtained an interview with a producer, would threaten to remove their clothes and accuse him of rape if he didn't promise them a role in a movie.

Mr. Griffith worried about the reputation of his youthful actresses as well, and sometimes lectured them on the dangers of venereal disease. "Women aren't made for promiscuity," he warned us. "If you're going to be promiscuous, you'll end up having some disease."

One of the films he made for Mutual was Paul Armstrong's sensational drama *The Escape,* which had to do with the horrors of syphilis. It was a daring topic for its time, and he handled it with power and taste. It was a better sermon for his innocent young actresses than any warning he could utter.

It was impossible to be neutral about Mr. Griffith. Like all men of great stature, he inspired both admiration and dislike. His secretary Agnes Wiener, who probably knew him as well as anyone did, thought that the reason Mr. Griffith was considered "odd" and "lonely" was that he was an intellectual giant among a tribe of pygmies. He had a vast knowledge of literature and music. Agnes told me that there were more than 1,000 classical records in his suite at the Alexandria Hotel.

But, if he seemed unlikable to those who did not know him, he inspired absolute devotion in the members of his company. In later years Billy Bitzer always said, "The happiest period of my whole life was my sixteen years with Mr. Griffith." We young actresses especially adored him, and he returned our affection. He enjoyed our company. Mae Marsh once told me:

"My first trip to New York—the 'Big City,' as he called it—I was to see all its wonders, and he arranged small parties to enjoy it with me. One Sunday, he took Gertrude Bambrick, Eddie Dillon, and me to Coney Island, and what a fine time we had!

"Although D. W. was much older than many of the young boys I dated in New York or California, he could sometimes act like a child. Once we took a hansom cab through Central Park. We were both singing at the top of our lungs when we were stopped by a policeman on horseback. He looked into the cab and asked, 'Lady, you all right?'

" 'Yes, officer,' I said. 'We are just rehearsing for the Met.' "

Often when we were filming outdoors, Mr. Griffith would take any of the young girls who happened to be nearby for a walk and point out nature's beauty.

"Some Sundays," Mae recalled, "when he didn't have anything better to do, he would drop by at our house for dinner, which my mother usually served midafternoon. After dinner, we would take a walk through the woods, which were at the top of the street, and, after resting a while and listening to the very interesting things he would talk about, we would have a foot race. D. W. almost always won."

He would often take us to the theater, especially the Yiddish theater and the Italian theater. He admired all the ethnic theaters, and we learned from them all.

Mr. Griffith disliked eating alone. He had a habit of moving around during a break in rehearsals and whispering to a select few, "Let's have lunch at Luchow's" or "Let's have dinner at the Astor." He loved his little secrets, and he would quietly invite a few members of the cast to a meal with the air of a medieval conspirator.

Mae Marsh told me, "Gertie Bambrick and I soon discovered that if we were late in taking off our makeup—while he was watching the previous day's rushes—then we all would be meeting at the front door of the studio, and he would ask us to dinner, sometimes alone but mostly with other actors, who also managed to linger behind and be included in the invitation."

Occasionally he would gather a group who liked to dance and would take us all to the Ship's Cafe in Hollywood for an evening of fun. Charlie Chaplin was often there with his own party, which always included an attractive girl. Mr. Griffith was by then a good dancer and never stopped until the music ceased or an early Sunday-morning call sent him home for sleep. Of all exercise he loved dancing most. There was rivalry among both men and women over who would be invited for these evenings.

It is easy to understand why Mr. Griffith inspired such enthusiasm in his staff. He had a commanding voice and a dramatic way with words. He was a great storyteller, and when he started to talk people would gather round; then he would start to shadow-box, and we all knew it was time to go back to work.

Yet for all his warmth and good spirits there was an air about him that forbade intimacy. In all the years that I worked with him I never called him anything but Mr. Griffith, and he called me Miss Lillian or Miss Gish. Although there was never any resemblance to a formal atmosphere in his studio, only with Billy Bitzer and Joe Aller did he relax enough to use first names. Dozens of times during the day we could hear his deep voice calling, "Billy, Billy!"

Even after Dorothy and I left Mr. Griffith, a certain formality remained with us. When Dorothy returned to the theater in the Depression years, she found it difficult to call the director by his first name, although she knew him well.

At the end of two weeks he said, "You don't like me, do you?"

"I don't know where you got that idea," she replied. "I do like you—very much."

"But you never call me by my first name."

"That's the way we were brought up," she explained.

"Mr. Griffith had an air about him that commanded respect," Mack Sennett recalled once. "Most of us called him Mr. Griffith. It seemed right that way. It was only after knowing him a couple of years that I began to call him D. W." Off the set Mr. Griffith kept pretty much to himself and never discussed his private affairs. "He was an extremely difficult man to know."

Yet he could be quite emotional. One night during our first summer with him, he took Dorothy and me to a New York restaurant. After dinner, as we were leaving, the orchestra began to play a sentimental tune of the day. He hummed softly in his beautiful voice, and his eyes misted over. He was so virile and robust that I would never have imagined that he could be touched so easily. But he was —and often, I later learned.

If an actor did a scene well, Mr. Griffith would hug him and say, often with tears in his eyes, "That's a darb!" "Darb" was one of his favorite words, though rather out of place in his usual flow of rhetoric.

After a hard, tense day, D. W. would find relaxation in quoting poetry or prose appropriate to the mood of the scenes that had just been filmed. Sometimes when a child was in a scene, he would pick the youngster up in his arms afterward and talk to him. He was good with children, and they adored him. He could get more from children than any director I've ever known. If he wanted them to cry, they cried. He would show them what he wanted and stimulate their imaginations.

He was unfailingly kind and sensitive, never more so than when he was auditioning actors. A Griffith tryout was comparable to one in the theater, tense and difficult both for those participating and for those watching. Mr. Griffith would talk to the actor, coach him, try to make him feel at ease. If the actor failed, Mr. Griffith was always gentle and tactful in dismissing him. He had known too much failure himself ever to reject anyone brutally.

Billy Bitzer wrote that in all their years together he never saw Mr. Griffith in a real temper more than a half-dozen times. If someone displeased him, he would reprove him in a gentle voice. He might say, "What were you thinking of?" and then pause. His gentle manner was more effective than anger. The culprit usually did better afterward.

Although he was unusually patient, he could get angry, and I learned to stay out of his way when an explosion took place. But there was often humor in his anger. I once heard him express his reaction to a well-known Broadway producer: "I've always had a rule in life that I don't discuss a bastard I don't like."

Once his temper was set off when a bit player wanted to leave the set on some trivial pretext. In that period each scene was shot just once, and Mr. Griffith gave the fellow three minutes to change his mind and stay. Mr. Griffith took out his watch and timed him. The man charged at Mr. Griffith, who defended himself and knocked the fellow out cold.

Mack Sennett once told some of the company what happened on location one day, when Sennett was still an actor.

"One of the actors began to use foul language. The Boss' southern blood came to a boil, and he told the man to cut it out because there were ladies present. The actor told Mr. Griffith to go to hell. One word led to another, and soon they were slugging it out, toe to toe. The fight never reached a decision because others on the set pulled them apart. But it gave all of us new respect for Griffith. We knew he was man enough to back up his opinions with his fists, if need be."

In general, Mr. Griffith avoided violence. If he had problems on the set, particularly on location, where strangers watched and sometimes caused trouble, he would behave with great courtesy. If his attitude was not enough to control the situation, he would draw a bill from his pocket and pay the fellow to leave.

"I wouldn't give him a dime," Billy once protested.

"The delay is costing us more than I gave him," Mr. Griffith replied.

Once, while his actors were changing into their costumes in an empty shack, a stranger came up to Mr. Griffith and said; "You the boss man?"

Mr. Griffith, anticipating trouble, pulled $5 from his roll and handed it to the man, asking at the same time, "Does this shack belong to you?"

"Oh, no, sir," the man answered. "I was just wonderin' how to get a job."

Billy often told friends that he thought Mr. Griffith believed that money could buy whatever he needed to make the filming go smoothly.

Although he always maintained his authority, Mr. Griffith was not above assisting with the physical labor that is often involved in film making. When the manual laborers had to build a shack for a set, Mr. Griffith would not be found on the sidelines supervising. He would pitch in and work beside the men with pick and shovel, even on a hot day. He made them feel that he wouldn't ask them to do what he wouldn't do himself. When he stopped, he would say, "You know, it makes you feel a whale of a lot cooler when you stop after a bit of exertion on a sultry day like this." Then he would hand a shovel to an actor standing nearby and say, "That's really so—try it." And soon all the men of the company would be helping.

Above all, Mr. Griffith was a film maker. Nothing came before his work. The people in his life had to conform to his style of living, which was dictated by his overriding purpose—to create films.

Agnes Wiener said that she had to be prepared to take dictation at any time of day or night. "I've taken notes on the backs of theater programs, paper sacks, newspapers, and napkins."

He usually signaled that a speech was coming on by saying: "Got a pencil? I want to dictate."

"I think," Agnes added, "that dictation was largely a means whereby he could organize his thoughts. After he dictated, I typed them up, double-spaced, and gave the notes to him. He never seemed to make use of the material. Just left it lying around until it disappeared."

One day he sent Agnes to the bank. He said, "They'll give you $4,000."

Agnes had never seen so much cash at one time. She slipped him the roll of bills, which he put in his pocket.

"Aren't you going to count it?" she asked.

"Haven't got time," he answered, going into the next room. A second later he peered back at her. "But I will—next time."

One morning he arrived on the lot, well-dressed as always, but wearing one brown shoe and one black shoe. It made him seem less Olympian to us but also revealed that his mind was always on his projects. He had a habit of walking away from whomever he happened to be talking to, as if his mind were still on the work he had left.

He let no one hamper the realization of his visions. As I came to

know Billy Bitzer better, I found that he didn't seem to take anything seriously. He was jolly and easygoing even in the midst of
pressures—an amusing relief for Mr. Griffith. But often he would
balk at Mr. Griffith's suggestions. Mr. Griffith, however, always obtained what he wanted in the end. He would see a scene in his mind
and ask Billy to translate it.

"But that's impossible, Mr. Griffith."

"Then we'll do it."

Mr. Griffith might want both the horses in the forefront and the
people in the distance in focus. Billy would tell him that it couldn't
be done. But Mr. Griffith would insist, and he would get the shot.

He was a zealot of a new and uncorrupted art. "Do you know,"
he would tell us, "we are playing to the world! What we film tomorrow will stir the hearts of the world—and they will understand
what we're saying. We've gone beyond Babel, beyond words. We've
found a universal language—a power that can make men brothers
and end war forever. Remember that. Remember that, when you
stand in front of a camera!"

To us, Mr. Griffith was the movie industry. It had been born in
his head.

🌿 11 🌿

One afternoon during the spring of 1914, while we were still working in California, Mr. Griffith took me aside on the set and said in an undertone, "After the others leave tonight, would you please stay."

Later, as some of the company drifted out, I realized that a similar message had been given to a few others. This procedure was typical of Mr. Griffith when he was planning a new film. He observed us with a smile, amused perhaps by our curiosity over the mystery that he had created.

I suspected what the meeting was about. A few days before, we had been having lunch at The White Kitchen, and I had noticed that his pockets were crammed with papers and pamphlets. My curiosity was aroused, but it would have been presumptuous of me to ask about them. With Mr. Griffith one did not ask; one only answered. Besides, I had learned that if I waited long enough he would tell me.

"I've bought a book by Thomas Dixon, called *The Clansman*. I'm going to use it to tell the truth about the War between the States. It hasn't been told accurately in history books. Only the winning side in a war ever gets to tell its story." He paused, watching the cluster of actors: Henry Walthall, Spottiswoode Aiken, Bobby Harron, Mae Marsh, Miriam Cooper, Elmer Clifton, George Siegmann, Walter Long, and me.

"The story concerns two families—the Stonemans from the North and the Camerons from the South." He added significantly, "I know I can trust you."

He swore us to secrecy, and to us his caution was understandable. Should his competitors learn of his new project, they would have films on the same subject completed before his work was released. He discussed his story plots freely only over lunch or dinner, often testing them out on me because I was close-mouthed and never repeated what anyone told me.

I heard later that "Daddy" Woods had called Mr. Griffith's attention to *The Clansman*. It had done well as a book and even better as a play, touring the country for five years. Mr. Griffith also drew on *The Leopard's Spots* for additional material for the new movie. Thomas Dixon, the author of both works, was a southerner who had been a college classmate of Woodrow Wilson. Mr. Griffith paid a $2,500 option for *The Clansman,* and it was agreed that Dixon was to receive $10,000 in all for the story, but when it came time to pay him no more money was available. In the end, he reluctantly agreed to accept instead of cash a 25 per cent interest in the picture, which resulted in the largest sum any author ever received for a motion-picture story. Dixon earned several million dollars as his share.

Mr. Griffith didn't need the Dixon book. His intention was to tell his version of the War between the States. But he evidently lacked the confidence to start production on a twelve-reel film without an established book as a basis for his story. After the film was completed and he had shown it to the so-called author, Dixon said: "This isn't my book at all." But Mr. Griffith was glad to use Dixon's name on the film as author, for, as he told me, "The public hates you if it thinks you wrote, directed, and produced the entire film yourself. It's the quickest way to make enemies."

After the first rehearsal, the pace increased. Mr. Griffith worked, as usual, without a script. But this time his pockets bulged with books, maps, and pamphlets, which he read during meals and the rare breaks in his hectic schedule. I rehearsed whatever part Mr.

Griffith wanted to see at the moment. My sister and I had been the last to join the company, and we naturally supposed that the major assignments would go to the older members of the group. For a while, it looked as if I would be no more than an extra. But during one rehearsal Blanche Sweet, who we suspected would play the romantic part of Elsie Stoneman, was missing. Mr. Griffith pointed to me.

"Come on, Miss Damnyankee, let's see what you can do with Elsie."

My thin figure was quite a contrast to Blanche's ripe, full form. Mr. Griffith had us rehearse the near-rape scene between Elsie and Silas Lynch, the power-drunk mulatto in the film. George Siegmann was playing Lynch in blackface. In this scene Lynch proposes to Elsie and, when she rebuffs him, forces his attentions on her. During the hysterical chase around the room, the hairpins flew out of my hair, which tumbled below my waist as Lynch held my fainting body in his arms. I was very blonde and fragile-looking. The contrast with the dark man evidently pleased Mr. Griffith, for he said in front of everyone, "Maybe she would be more effective than the more mature figure I had in mind."

He didn't tell us then, but I think the role was mine from that moment.

At first I didn't pay much attention to Mr. Griffith's concept of the film. His claim that history books falsified actual happenings struck me as most peculiar. At that time I was too naïve to think that history books would attempt to falsify anything. I've lived long enough now to know that the whole truth is never told in history texts. Only the people who lived through an era, who are the real participants in the drama as it occurs, know the truth. The people of each generation, it seems to me, are the most accurate historians of their time.

Soon sets were going up; costumes arrived; and mysterious crates, evidently filled with military equipment, were delivered. As we gradually became aware of the magnitude of the new project, we grew even more anxious than usual about being assigned roles in the film. All the young players wanted to prove their worth before it was too late. This distress from young girls in their teens may seem strange today, but the photography of that time aged one so drastically that we believed that by the time we reached eighteen we would be playing character roles.

When the final casting was announced, we learned that Ralph Lewis was to play the Honorable Austin Stoneman, the "uncrowned king of Capitol Hill." The character of Stoneman, a fiery political fanatic from the North, was patterned after the real-life Thaddeus Stevens, one of the legislators whose harsh policy toward the South wrecked President Lincoln's postwar plans.

Bobby Harron and Elmer Clifton were to play Stoneman's sons, and I was given the role of his daughter Elsie. Mary Alden was to be Stoneman's mulatto mistress Lydia Brown, whom Dixon described as "a woman of extraordinary animal beauty and the fiery temper of a leopardess."

George Siegmann was awarded the part of Silas Lynch, who, according to Dixon, was "a Negro of perhaps forty years, a man of charming features for a mulatto, who had evidently inherited the full physical characteristics of the Aryan, while his dark yellowish eyes beneath his heavy brows glowed with the brightness of the African jungle." Walter Long was to be the renegade Negro Gus, and Elmo Lincoln, a magnificent strong man who would later swing through the trees as Tarzan, played the Negro who attacks Wallace Reid, the stalwart blacksmith.

There were practically no Negro actors in California then and, as far as we knew, only a few in the East. Even in minstrel shows, the parts were usually played by whites in blackface. The only scenes in which actual Negroes appear in *The Birth of a Nation* are those in which the Stoneman boys, visiting the southern Camerons, are taken out to the plantation to see Negroes working in the cotton fields, and, later, in which blacks are shown dominating the postwar South Carolina legislature.

But one young Negro woman did play in the film—Madame Sul-Te-Wan. (We never did discover the origin of her name.) She was first employed to help us keep our dressing rooms clean at the studio. She was devoted to Mr. Griffith, and he in turn loved her. Later, when Madame was having financial difficulties, he sent her money to help herself and her small sons. She was one of the few friends near him when he died years later in Hollywood.

The faithful mammy was played by Jennie Lee, who also became a recipient of Mr. Griffith's generosity in later years. When she was taken ill, D. W. had Mae Marsh send her some money, saying that Jennie had been the inspiration for a story he had sold to a magazine and asking her to please accept half the payment.

Henry B. Walthall was a natural choice for the part of Ben Cameron, the "Little Colonel." He was a slight man, about five feet six, fine-boned, with the face of a poet and a dreamer. Indeed, when he played a part patterned on Edgar Allan Poe in *The Avenging Conscience,* he had resembled that romantic figure. Like Thomas Dixon and Mr. Griffith, Walthall came from the South. He had been born in Alabama and was proud that his father had fought the Union troops at Vicksburg. "Wally," as he was affectionately called, was everything in life that his "Little Colonel" was on the screen: dear, patient, lovable. His only fault was that he had no conception of time. Consequently, a man was hired for the purpose of getting him into makeup and to work on time for this film.

Mr. Griffith was fond of Wally, but Wally did cause him considerable anxiety. The bodyguard was assigned to Wally not only to get him on the set on time but also to keep him from imbibing too freely. On one occasion, Wally managed to give the guard the slip. He was finally traced to a hotel room, where he was found, not drinking, but simply exhausted and trying to get some sleep.

Wally was a bit too old—Mr. Griffith thought—to be playing opposite me, so Mr. Griffith tried to bridge the difference in our ages by having Wally keep a hat on during the filming.

The rest of the Cameron family was represented by Josephine Crowell and Spottiswoode Aiken as the parents; the dark-haired classic beauty, Miriam Cooper, as Ben's sister Margaret; Mae Marsh as the little sister Flora, all fluctuating emotions and the essence of girlhood; and André Beringer and Maxfield Stanley as the two younger Cameron brothers.

For President Lincoln, Mr. Griffith chose Joseph Henabery, a tall, thin man who could be made up to resemble Lincoln. The search for an appropriate Mary Todd Lincoln ended when he found a woman with an uncanny similarity to the First Lady working in wardrobe. Raoul Walsh was picked for the role of John Wilkes Booth. Members of Mr. Lincoln's Cabinet were chosen on the basis of facial resemblance to the historical characters. The other historical characters were re-created by Donald Crisp as General Grant, Howard Gaye as General Lee, and Sam de Grasse as Senator Sumner.

For the new film we naturally rehearsed longer than we had for any other film up to that time.

During his six years with Biograph, Mr. Griffith had taken strides toward his ultimate goal: filming his version of the Civil War. He had made a number of early pictures that touched on the War between the States. But it was soon obvious to everyone that this film was to be his most important statement yet. Billy Bitzer wrote of that time: "*The Birth of a Nation* changed D. W. Griffith's personality entirely. Where heretofore he was wont to refer in starting on a new picture to 'grinding out another sausage' and go at it lightly, his attitude in beginning on this one was all eagerness. He acted like here we have something worthwhile."

Although fact and legend were familiar to him, he did meticulous research for *The Birth.* The first half of *The Birth,* about the war itself, reflects his own point of view. I know that he also relied greatly on Harper's *Pictorial History of the Civil War,* Mathew Brady's *Civil War Photographs: Confederate and Union Veterans— Eyewitnesses on Location;* the Nicolay and Hay *Abraham Lincoln: A History;* and *The Soldier in Our Civil War: A Pictorial History of the Conflict 1861–1865.* For the second half, about Reconstruction, he consulted Thomas Dixon, and *A History of the American People* by Woodrow Wilson. President Wilson had taught history before going into politics, and Mr. Griffith had great respect for his erudition. For Klan material, he drew on a book called *Ku Klux Klan—Its Origin, Growth and Disbandment* by John C. Lester and D. L. Wilson. But he did not use the uniform that is worn by Klan members today. Instead he used the costumes that, according to Thomas Dixon, were worn by the earlier Klans—white and scarlet flowing robes with hood and mask to hide the features of rider and horse.

Brady's photographs were constantly consulted, and Mr. Griffith restaged many moments of history with complete fidelity to them. The photographs were used as guides for such scenes as Lee's surrender at Appomattox, the signing of the Emancipation Proclamation, and Sherman's march to the sea. He telegraphed a newspaper in Columbia, South Carolina, for photographs of the interior of the state capital, which held a majority of Negro representatives after the war, and constructed the legislative chamber according to the photographs.

The largest interior was Ford's Theater, the setting of the assassination scene, which was done in one day on the lot. So great was Mr. Griffith's obsession with authenticity that he unearthed a copy of *Our American Cousin,* which had been performed at Ford's Theater on the night of the assassination, and restaged parts of it. In the actual filming, as Raoul Walsh, gun ready, steals into the Presidential box, the lines being spoken on the replica of the stage are precisely those spoken at the fateful moment on the night of April 14, 1865. This fidelity to facts was an innovation in films.

Mr. Griffith knew the terrain of the battle fields, and he hired several Civil War veterans to scout locations similar to the original ones. After exploring the southern California country, they chose what later became the Universal lot for the countryside around Petersburg, Virginia, site of the last prolonged siege and final battle of the war.

He had studied maps of the major battles of the Civil War and, with the help of the veterans, laid out the battle fields. Trenches, breastworks, roads, brooks, and buildings were constructed to duplicate those of the actual battle fields. Troop movements were planned with the advice of the veterans and two men from West Point Military Academy. Civil War artillery was obtained from West Point and the Smithsonian Institution, for use when the camera was close.

Mr. Griffith also sent to the Smithsonian for historical records and then went over the documents with his advisers. But in the end he came to his own conclusions about historical facts. He would never take the opinion of only one man as final.

The street in Piedmont on which the Cameron house was located was complete with brick walks and hitching and lamp posts. A small set, it achieved scope from violated perspective—an old stage technique in which each successive house and street lamp is a little shorter, so that the setting seems to "recede" without actually taking up much space or requiring the use of expensive lumber.

We had no stage designer, only the modest genius of a carpenter, Frank Wortman, known as "Huck." Huck, a short, rather heavyset man in his forties, with friendly blue eyes and a weakness for chewing tobacco, didn't talk much, but listened intently to Mr. Griffith. Even before rehearsals started Mr. Griffith explained to him what he wanted in the way of sets. He would show Huck a photograph that he wanted copied, or point out changes to be made in the reproduction. They would decide how the sun would hit a particular building three, four, even five weeks from then.

Men during the Civil War era were rather small in stature (it was before the age of proper nutrition), so genuine uniforms could not be used by the later generation. Uniforms for *The Birth* were therefore made by a small struggling company, which has since become the famous Western Costume Company.

The Brady photographs also served as models for the soldiers' hair styles.

To absorb the spirit of the film, we came down with a case of history nearly as intense as Mr. Griffith's. At first, between making other films during the day and rehearsing *The Birth* at night, we had scant time for reading. But Mr. Griffith's interest was contagious, and we began to read about the period. Soon it was the only subject we talked about. Mr. Griffith didn't ask us to do this; it stemmed out of our own interest. We pored over photographs of the Civil War and *Godey's Ladies' Book,* a periodical of the nineteenth century, for costumes, hair styles, and postures. We had to rehearse how to sit and how to move in the hoop skirts of the day.

My costumes were specially made. One of them had a tiny derby with a high plume. When I saw it, I rebelled.

"The audience will laugh at me," I protested.

But Mr. Griffith insisted that I wear it. He wanted the audience to be amused. "It's a darb!" he said, smiling.

As always, sunlight controlled the shooting schedule. Preparations began at five or six in the morning. The actors rose at five in order to be ready at seven, when it was bright enough for filming. Important scenes were played in the hard noon sun. I remember that we used to beg to have our closeups taken just after dawn or before sunset, as the soft yellow glow was easier to work in and much more flattering. We continued to work—often without a break for lunch—until sundown.

At that time young actors were learning not only to act but also to direct. When they weren't acting, George Siegmann and Bobby Harron served as assistant directors. All the young people, in fact, were at Mr. Griffith's elbow to help in any way that he chose to use them.

To economize, Mr. Griffith used many of the actors in more than one role. Bobby Harron, for instance, might play my brother in the morning, and in the afternoon put on blackface and play a Negro. Madame Sul-Te-Wan played many small parts, with the help of various costumes. In the battle scenes several featured actors rode horses—but in the distance, well away from the camera. For many small roles, members of the company who happened to be working on other films came on the set of *The Birth* for a day or two.

The entire staff came on set to watch us, particularly Joe Aller and the men from the laboratory, so that they would know the effects that Mr. Griffith was seeking. This was of utmost importance, for each scene was shot only once. The only scene that was taken twice was the one in which Mae Marsh as the Little Sister leaps to her death from a cliff.

In those days there was no one to keep track of what an actor was wearing from scene to scene. He was obliged to remember for himself what he had worn and how his hair and makeup had looked in a previous scene. If he forgot, he was not used again. When the death scene was filmed, Mae forgot to tie the Confederate flag, which she'd been wearing in the previous scene, around her waist, and the scene had to be retaken. How we all envied her a second chance in a big moment!

In filming the battles, Mr. Griffith organized the action like a general. He stood at the top of a forty-foot tower, the commander-in-chief of both armies, his powerful voice, like Roarin' Jake's, thundering commands through a megaphone to his staff of assistants. Meetings were called before each major filmed sequence and a chain of command was developed from Mr. Griffith through his directors and their assistants. The last-in-command might have only four or five extras under him. These men, wearing uniforms and taking their places among the extras, also played parts in the film.

Griffith's camera was high on the platform looking down on the battle field, so that he could obtain a grand sweep of the action. This camera took the long shots. Hidden under bushes or in back of trees were cameras for closeups.

When the din of cannons, galloping horses, and charging men grew too great, no human voice, not even Mr. Griffith's, was powerful enough to be heard. Some of the extras were stationed as far as two miles from the camera. So a series of magnifying mirrors was used to flash signals to those actors working a great distance away. Each group of men had its number—one flash of the mirror for the first group, two for the second group, and so on. As group one started action, the mirror would flash a go-ahead to group two.

Care was taken to place the authentic old guns and the best horsemen in the first ranks. Other weapons, as well as poorer horsemen, were relegated to the background. Extras were painstakingly drilled in their parts until they knew when to charge, when to push cannons forward, when to fall.

Some of the artillery was loaded with real shells, and elaborate warnings were broadcast about their range of fire. Mr. Griffith's sense of order and control made it possible for the cast and extras to survive the broiling heat, pounding hoofs, naked bayonets, and exploding shells without a single injury. He was too thoughtful of the welfare of others to permit accidents.

In most war films it is difficult to distinguish between the enemies unless the film is in color and the two sides are wearing different-colored uniforms. But not in a Griffith movie. Mr. Griffith had the rare technical skill to keep each side distinct and clear cut. In *The Birth,* the Confederate army always entered from the left of the camera, the Union army from the right.

One day he said to Billy, "I want to show a whole army moving."

"What do you mean, a whole army?" Bitzer asked.

"Everyone we can muster."

"I'll have to move them back to get them all in view," Billy said. "They won't look much bigger than jackrabbits."

"That's all right. The audience will supply the details. Let's move up on this hill, Billy. Then we can shoot the whole valley and all the troops at once."

They never talked much, but they always seemed to understand each other. People around Mr. Griffith didn't bother him with idle talk.

When daylight disappeared, Mr. Griffith would order bonfires lit and film some amazing night scenes. Billy was pessimistic about the results; he kept insisting that they would be unsuccessful. But Mr. Griffith persisted. One big battle scene was filmed at night. The subtitle was to read, "It went on into the night." Nothing like it had ever been seen before. Those of us who had time were there—the women to watch, the men to help.

Although everything was carefully organized, whenever he saw a spontaneous gesture that looked good—like the soldier's leaning on his gun and looking at me during the hospital scene—he would call Billy over to film it.

In that scene, the wards were filled with wounded soldiers, and in the background nurses and orderlies attended their patients. In the doorway of the ward stood a Union sentry. As Elsie Stoneman, I was helping to entertain the wounded, singing and playing the banjo. The sentry watched me lovingly as I sang and then, after I had finished and was passing him, raised his hang-dog head and heaved a deep, love-sick sigh. The scene lasted only a minute, but it drew the biggest laugh of the film and became one of its best-remembered moments.

The scene came about in typical Griffith fashion. We players had no one to help us with our costumes. We had to carry our various changes to the set, as we could not afford the time to run back to our dressing rooms. Those period dresses, with their full skirts over hoops, were heavy. A kind young man who liked me helped me with my props and costumes. The young man, William Freeman, was playing the sentry, and he simply stood there, listening, as I sang. Seeing his expression, Mr. Griffith said to Bitzer, "Billy, get that picture on film right away." He knew that it would bring a laugh, which was needed to break the dramatic tension.

Since the release of *The Birth of a Nation,* I have often been asked by fans what happened to the sentry in the hospital. After *The Birth* was finished, I didn't see William Freeman again until the first World's Fair in New York. It was the day of the Fair's closing. I happened to be riding on a float for charity, and there, walking toward the float, was William Freeman. I recognized him immediately.

"My son is here," he said after we had greeted each other. "I would like you to meet him."

He disappeared into the crowd and returned shortly with a bright four-year-old, whom he proudly introduced to me. Then we said goodbye, and I haven't seen him since.

One morning, when we assembled for work as usual, Mr. Griffith was missing. This was unheard of. Nothing short of disaster had ever taken him away from the studio. Activity came to a standstill.

"Where's Mr. Griffith?" everyone asked. "Is he ill? Did someone die?"

But slowly one story gained strength, and by late morning the word was on everyone's lips. "Money. It must be money."

When Mr. Griffith finally appeared after lunch, he explained nothing. Instead he said wearily, "All right, let's get to work."

On payday, there were no checks for his company.

"There just isn't any money," Little Epping explained to us with a weak smile. "But give us a little more time, and we'll have the checks."

While Mr. Griffith was working for the Aitkens, Johannes Charlemagne Epping, whom we called "Little" Epping, was his financial shadow. If ever a man needed a business manager, it was David Wark Griffith. Mr. Epping, who had been Biograph's accountant and who went with Mr. Griffith when he moved to Mutual, was a good businessman. He was to make wise investments in the future and retire to Switzerland in 1925 a prosperous man. He tried to share his knowledge with his boss, but Mr. Griffith would not accept his advice. Mr. Griffith always insisted on managing his money himself, with disastrous results. He spent it unwisely, invested it foolishly, and sometimes squirreled it away and forgot all about it. But fortunately Mr. Epping did manage secretly to withhold funds from Mr. Griffith and to invest them as nonrevocable annuities, so that Mr. Griffith did not have to spend the last years of his life penniless. Yet Mr. Griffith seemed to consider Mr. Epping his adversary, someone to be outsmarted, instead of his protector and friend. Agnes Wiener remembers that he sometimes authorized days off for the actors with the warning, "Don't tell 'Little' Epping."

The day after Mr. Epping's announcement, Mother told me that she had offered Mr. Griffith help.

"Mr. Griffith, I'd like to buy into the picture," she said. "Three hundred dollars' worth."

"How much money do you have saved, Mrs. Gish?" he asked.

"Three hundred dollars."

"Mrs. Gish, I can't let you do it. You'd be taking too great a risk."

Had he allowed it, of course, she would have made hundreds of thousands of dollars.

We didn't receive our checks for several weeks, although we all knew that when Mr. Griffith got the money we would be paid. We continued to work every day, if not on *The Birth,* then on other pictures.

Mr. Griffith tried to make light of the situation.

"Come on, let's shoot this scene," he would say to the actors. "If we don't get it today, there's no money to make it tomorrow."

Although he joked, we knew how worried he was.

Harry Aitken, as president of the Mutual Film Company, had originally put up $25,000 for *The Birth,* but his directors, learning of the subject matter and the scope of the film, had panicked and demanded that the backing be withdrawn. Aitken had then raised the sum himself. But as the money dwindled perhaps Mr. Griffith was ashamed to ask Aitken for more, and felt obliged to raise the additional sum himself.

We heard from someone who had overheard him talking to "Little"

Epping that he had gone to see a Mr. Talley, the owner of a large moving-picture theater in Los Angeles. He didn't get the needed amount, so he went off to see department-store owners—in fact anyone who might conceivably lend him cash. Meanwhile, what little money there was had to go to the extras.

Then one day during that tense period a stranger appeared on the lot. Rumor spread that he was William Clune, owner of Clune's Auditorium, the largest theater in Los Angeles. (It is now the Philharmonic Auditorium.) Clune was proud of his theater and even prouder of his thirty-piece orchestra, which played in it.

For Clune's benefit, Mr. Griffith staged an impressive scene from the film, the marching of the Confederate soldiers down the street to war. Henry Walthall led the procession. Clune watched intently as Walthall passed on his charger; he saw the swinging rifles, the farewells of wives and mothers, and the flutter of stars and bars.

Mr. Griffith had been able to engage a small brass band to play "Dixie" as the procession marched along.

"That's not much of a band," Clune said, looking pained.

"No, it's not," D. W. agreed. "But think of how that tune would sound if your orchestra played it."

"I've got the best orchestra west of Mississippi," Clune boasted.

"Think of how 'Dixie' would sound in *your* auditorium with *your* orchestra!" Mr. Griffith repeated. "Why, you'd charm the audience right out of their seats! All we need is fifteen thousand more to finish the film. What do you say?"

"Well, that's quite a sum."

They walked out of earshot toward Mr. Griffith's office, and when they reappeared both men were beaming. After Clune's departure Mr. Griffith rounded up his staff.

"Let's start shooting right away. Clune may change his mind. And for heaven's sake send that band away."

Mr. Griffith was back in production.

Once again, he was working against time. Clune's money meant that he could go on with the film, but not without watching his expenditures. To demonstrate that he was being frugal he walked around with a hole in his shoe, declaring to us that he wouldn't "buy new shoes until we start getting money back at the box office."

Even Mr. Clune's contribution proved not to be enough. Before production was completed, Mr. Griffith had to call upon his friends for money to complete the film.

In going through Mr. Griffith's papers recently, I came across some "facts" about *The Birth of a Nation* that read like most press releases of that day. Robert Edgar Long, in his soft-cover book *David Wark Griffith: A Brief Sketch of His Career,* published in 1920, suggests that professors of history from at least a half-dozen universities were called upon for facts and figures, so that no errors would mar the film's authenticity. He says that Mr. Griffith had plans to shoot some 5,000 scenes; to use 18,000 men as soldiers; to make 18,000 Union and Confederate uniforms for these men; to hire 3,000 horses; to build entire cities and destroy them by fire; to buy real shells that cost $10 apiece in order to re-enact the greatest battle of the Civil War; and to select fragments from about 500 separate musical compositions to synchronize perfectly with various scenes. Many scenes, he says, were photographed from fifteen to twenty times before Mr. Griffith was pleased with the results. He adds that the scene of Lincoln's assassination was rehearsed at least twenty times before it was actually filmed.

I know that in later years Mr. Griffith himself was prone to exaggerations that were a press agent's dream. Perhaps he too believed that these gross overstatements and inaccuracies would enhance the film's prestige.

It seems to me, however, that the truth is a much finer tribute to Mr. Griffith's skill. In the battle scenes there were never more than 300 to 500 extras. By starting with a closeup and then moving the camera back from the scene, which gave the illusion of depth and distance, and by having the same soldiers run around quickly to make a second entrance, Mr. Griffith created the impression of big armies. In the battles, clouds of smoke rising from the thickets gave the illusion of many soldiers camouflaged by the woods, although in actuality there were only a few.

The scene of Sherman's march to the sea opened with an iris shot

—a small area in the upper left-hand corner of a black screen—of a mother holding her weeping children amid the ruins of a burned-out house. Slowly the iris opened wider to reveal a great panorama— troops, wagons, fires, and beyond, in the distance, Atlanta burning. Atlanta was actually a model, superimposed on the film.

The entire industry, always intensely curious about Mr. Griffith, was speculating about this new film. What was that crazy man Griffith up to? He was using the full repertoire of his earlier experiments and adding new ones. He tinted film to achieve dramatic results and to create mood. In the battle scene at Petersburg, the shots of Union and Confederate troops rushing in to replace the dead and wounded are tinted red, and the subtitle reads "In the red lane of death others take their places." And, at the climax of the film, there were the thrilling rides of the Klan. These rides were beautifully handled—first, the signal riders galloping to give warning; then, one by one and two by two, the galloping hordes merging into a white hooded mass, their peaked helmets and fiery crosses making them resemble knights of a crusade.

Before the filming of this scene Mr. Griffith decided to try a new kind of shot. He had a hole dug in the road directly in the path of the horsemen. There he placed Billy and the camera, and obtained shots of the horses approaching and galloping right over the camera, so that the audience could see the pounding hoofs. This shot has since become standard, but then it was the first time it had been done, and the effect was spectacular. Billy came through safely, and so did his precious camera, as Mr. Griffith must have known it would. He would never have taken a chance with a camera; it was far too costly.

Among the obstacles that cropped up during the filming was a lack of muslin needed for Klan uniforms. There was also a shortage of horses for battle scenes. Both were war scarcities. When the war in Europe broke out, the Allies were rounding up horses and shipping them to France. Mr. Griffith found himself in competition with French, English, Russian, and Italian agents, all in search of horses. Acting as his own agent, he was obliged to rent horses at higher prices from a dealer in the West.

We had outstanding riders like the Burns Brothers, who led the Klan riders and supervised any scene involving horses. Henry Walthall was a superb horseman, as were some of the other actors. The cowboy and circus riders beneath the Ku Klux sheets did a superb job. In the mob scenes they reared their horses until clouds mushroomed, but not one of them was hurt.

What I liked most about working on *The Birth* was the horses. I could always borrow a horse from the set, and during my lunch hour I would canter off alone to the hills.

I saw everything that Mr. Griffith put on film. My role in *The Birth* required about three weeks' work, but I was on call during the whole time that it was being filmed. I was in the studio every day— working on other films, being available for the next scene if needed, making myself useful in any way that was required.

My dressing room was just across the hall from the darkroom, where Jimmy Smith and Joe Aller worked. Whenever I had a few minutes I would join them, watching them develop the film and cut it. I would view the day's rushes and tell Jimmy my reactions to them. I saw the effects that Mr. Griffith obtained with his views of marching men, the ride of the Klan, the horrors of war. Watching these snatches of film was like trying to read a book whose pages had been shuffled. There was neither order nor continuity. Here was a touching bit from a scene with Mae; there was a long shot of a battle. It made me realize the job that Mr. Griffith had ahead of him after the filming was done.

The shooting was completed in nine weeks, but Mr. Griffith spent more than three months on cutting, editing and working on the musical score. I still remember how hard he worked on other films during the day and then at night on *The Birth*. Of all his pictures up to that time, none was more beset with difficulties. Without his spirit and faith, it might never have been completed.

🌿 12 🌿

The first run-through of the complete film was to be shown to most of the cast that evening, and we gathered in the small projection room. I was already familiar with the film, having seen all the rushes. But I was swept along with the others as the story unfolded. The film ran for two hours and forty-five minutes, and when the lights came on we all sat in stunned silence. As I glanced over my shoulder, I noticed that Mr. Griffith was still in his seat. When they could control their emotions everyone gathered around him with praise and gratitude for having been part of it.

There are unforgettable moments in all Griffith films, scenes that are etched forever in the minds of the spectators. *The Birth of a Nation* had many such moments. Among them was the scene of the homecoming of Ben Cameron, the Little Colonel. He is returning, gaunt and ragged from the war. As he walks slowly down the main street of Piedmont, there is not a soul to recognize him. Flora, the Little Sister, has been reduced to wearing a burlap dress, which she has decorated with "Southern ermine," bits of cotton streaked with soot from the fireplace. As the family sees him approaching, Flora motions excitedly that he has grown a mustache. She runs to the door to meet him. Smiling sadly, he picks a bit of cotton off her dress, and they go into each other's arms. As they walk into the house together, the audience sees only the mother's arms slipping around her son's shoulders. With the musical background Mr. Griffith chose for the scene, it is enormously touching.

Later Ben warns his family not to leave the house. (Under the leadership of Austin Stoneman, the Negroes are intimidating the whites.) But the water supply is low, and, carrying a bucket, Flora runs out to the spring. She spots a chipmunk and runs into the woods after it. Gus, the Negro, sees her and tries to head her off. Terrified, she races toward the cliff. She tells Gus that if he comes any nearer she will jump. He approaches, and she leaps from the cliff.

When Ben comes home, he finds her missing, and goes out in search of her. When he sees Gus's cap in the woods, his fears are heightened. He discovers the little girl at the bottom of the cliff in great agony. Her death in his arms, together with the homecoming, established Mae Marsh as a fine emotional actress.

In 1926 Mr. Griffith sent Mae a telegram from New York: "Just saw a rerun of *The Birth* the charwomen are now mopping up the aisles of the tears the audience shed watching your unforgettably beautiful performance. God bless you always."

Years later—in the 1940s—Mr. Griffith claimed that Walthall's Little Colonel was the greatest male performance in the history of films.

Like many southerners, Mr. Griffith had great love and admiration for Abraham Lincoln. In all scenes in which the President appears, the treatment of his character is tender and sympathetic. In one scene Elsie Stoneman takes Mrs. Cameron to meet Lincoln; she is seeking Ben's release from the prison hospital. President Lincoln kindly grants it. He is portrayed as equally gentle with northerners and southerners.

Many years later, when Carl Sandburg brought me his last four volumes on Lincoln, he said, "I think you will find the first two especially interesting, because I tried to put into them the same American flavor and spirit that Griffith got in *The Birth of a Nation.*"

When I repeated this remark to D. W., he was flattered and delighted.

Mr. Griffith's genius was never more apparent than in the battle scenes. Long shots showed the immense field of battle and, seemingly, thousands of men; the stirring charges; and then suddenly, the hand-to-hand combat at the breastworks. Many years later the critic James Agee was to write: "The most beautiful single shot I have seen in any movie is the battle charge. I have heard it praised for its realism, and that is deserved; but it is also far beyond realism. It seems to me to be a perfect realization of a collective dream of what the Civil War was like . . ."

"Far into the night, the battle rages," announces the subtitle, and audiences saw chains of belching cannon and small arms fire flaring across the field in the night.

The battle ends. "War's peace," reads the subtitle, and we see a still shot of a trench littered with the corpses of soldiers, then a shattering picture of a dead man's arm raised above the heap in silent, frozen appeal.

Other scenes were equally effective. When, many years later, *Gone with the Wind* depicted the carnage of war with a shot of masses of wounded and dying men in a makeshift hospital in a railroad station, Mr. Griffith commented wryly, "Chaplin said I got the same effect with a closeup of a few corpses."

The author of *Gone with the Wind*, Margaret Mitchell, herself saw *The Birth of a Nation* no fewer than twelve times. Compared to *The Birth, Gone with the Wind* seems to me to resemble a pretty musical version of the Civil War. By contrast, *The Birth* is like a documentary of that war, conveying the agony of a nation being torn apart. Mr. Griffith was telling in film language a story that transcended that of a handful of people to dramatize a point of view that nearly wrecked the Union. Involved in the issue of slavery was a way of life that split the Union long before the advent of war. He believed that it was impossible for the North to understand the South's point of view on slavery or for the North to present an accurate and impartial account of the South's role in the Civil War. It was this point of view that he so triumphantly presented on the screen.

The Birth of a Nation was revolutionary in many respects, not the least of which was its use of music. It was not the first movie to have an orchestral score, but it was the first to exploit the full dramatic and expressive possibilities of music.

Mr. Griffith had always been singularly conscious of the importance of music in conjunction with a movie. He brought to the screen the first original scores for pictures. "Watch a film run in silence," he would say, "and then watch it again with eyes and ears. The music sets the mood for what your eye sees; it guides your emotions; it is the emotional framework for visual pictures."

He often worked for weeks with musicians to find music that would match each character and situation. (Contrary to all reports, however, he never had music on the set during the filming, because he thought that it would be distracting. The one exception was for comedy; Dorothy was allowed music between scenes to put her in a gay mood.) But the score for *The Birth* was the longest and the most ambitious yet. Each actor had his individual theme. I was called in to hear several pieces of music, and helped choose one for myself that was also Mr. Griffith's choice. It was called "The Sweetest Bunch of Lilacs" and later achieved a different kind of fame as the theme song for the radio team of Amos 'n' Andy.

Mr. Griffith had engaged Joseph Carl Breil to do the score for *The Birth;* it was to be based on nineteenth-century music. Mr. Breil would play bits and pieces, and he and Mr. Griffith would then decide on how they were to be used. The thrilling ride of the Klan, for example, was accompanied by Edvard Grieg's "In the Hall of the Mountain King."

The two men had many disagreements over the scoring of the film. "If I ever kill anyone," Mr. Griffith once said, "it won't be an actor but a musician." The greatest dispute was over the Klan call, which was taken from "The Ride of the Valkyries" by Richard Wagner. Mr. Griffith wanted a slight change in the notes. Mr. Breil fought against making it.

"You can't tamper with Wagner!" he protested. "It's never been done!"

This music wasn't *primarily* music, Mr. Griffith explained. It was music for motion pictures. Even Giulio Gatti-Casazza, General Director of the Metropolitan Opera, agreed that the change was fine. Finally Mr. Breil agreed to it.

Mr. Griffith was the first director to include the name of the man who was responsible for the musical score in the list of film credits.

The Clansman, as it was originally called, opened at Clune's Auditorium in Los Angeles on February 8, 1915, with a forty-piece symphony orchestra and a large chorus. The audience was profoundly affected by the film. After the final shot, a vision of Christ superimposed on a scene of flowering fields and happy children at play, everyone rose and cheered wildly. *The Clansman* ran for seven months at Clune's.

Two days after its opening in Los Angeles, William de Mille wrote to Samuel Goldwyn:

> I heard rumors that the film cost nearly $100,000. This means, of course, that even though it is a hit, which it probably will be, it cannot possibly make any money. It would have to gross over a quarter of a million for Griffith to get his cost back and, as you know, that just isn't being done. Remember how mad Biograph was with Griffith when he made *Judith of Bethulia* and how much money that lost, even though it was only a four reeler? So I suppose you're right when you say there is no advantage in leading if the cost of leadership makes commercial success impossible. *The Clansman* certainly establishes Griffith as a leader and it does seem too bad that such magnificent effort is doomed to financial failure.

He should have remembered that D. W. was always doing things that "just weren't being done."

As for the cost of *The Birth,* it amounted to $61,000. Another $30,000 was spent for exploitation, advertisements, and making duplicate prints. As the film's popularity became worldwide, the negative soon wore out; there was only one, each scene having been shot only once. Duplicate prints were made from other prints and were pirated in many countries. But I am certain about the actual cost of the film. I never forgot it because Mr. Griffith told it to me several times. It struck me as an enormous sum at that time, like millions. Now it seems such a small amount for such a magnificent achievement.

The Birth of a Nation influenced Mr. Griffith to shoot scenes more than once. Today, of course, it is common practice to take a scene several times. I know of a Shakespearean tragedy that required eighty-six takes for one scene. We never took anywhere near that number. Before shooting Mr. Griffith would rehearse endlessly, and the people working with him were trained craftsmen who knew what was expected of them.

Before its opening in New York, Mr. Griffith took the film to the White House, where it was shown in the East Room to President Wilson, his family, members of his Cabinet, and their wives and daughters. Mr. Griffith was eager for the President's reaction; he respected Woodrow Wilson as a historian and had at that time a high regard for him as President.

After watching the film, the President sat quietly for some minutes. Then he said, "It is like writing history in lightning, and it's all too true."

This statement was used by Mr. Griffith in publicity.

On the following evening, another private showing was given before the Chief Justice Edward D. White and the Associate Justices of the Supreme Court, the diplomatic corps, and a specially invited audience of 500 guests. The impact of *The Birth* on them was no less, evidently, than it had been on the President.

After Mr. Griffith ran the film for Thomas Dixon, the author exclaimed, "That isn't my story at all. It isn't *The Clansman*. It could be called anything else."

"Would you mind," Mr. Griffith asked, "if I call it *The Birth of a Nation?*"

"Certainly not," Dixon replied, "it sounds like a more appropriate name for the story you have told."

William de Mille's dour prediction that *The Birth of a Nation* could not possibly make $250,000 simply reflected the state of the movie industry at that time. No one could conceive of multimillion-dollar profits because no one before D. W. Griffith had realized the potential power of the movies.

When the film began its official run at the Liberty Theatre in New York on March 3, 1915, it was called *The Birth of a Nation*. It was the first motion picture to run for more than two hours, with an eight-minute intermission between the sections on the War and Reconstruction. It was the first film to be shown twice a day in a legitimate theater at theater prices. As few in the industry believed that audiences would pay $2 for a movie admission—a nickel was still the standard rate, with the top price a quarter—Mr. Griffith and the Aitkens had had to form their own company, the Epoch Producing Corporation, to distribute the film.

The audience at the Liberty was totally unprepared for the emotional impact of the film. Dorothy Dix reported in the *New York Journal:* "I believed that the silent drama could never touch the emotions very deeply . . . *The Birth of a Nation* disproves this. Here is a war play the like of which has never been presented on any stage before . . . that worked the audience into a perfect frenzy."

Tributes to the film were legion: "A new epoch in the art is reached"; "the spectators actually rise from their seats and burst into cheers"; "it's worth $5.00 a seat"; "produced by a genius"; "biggest"; "greatest"; "most profound."

Such tributes are still coming today and increasing in number as Mr. Griffith's stature comes to be appreciated by the new generation. I remember particularly James Agee's comment, written after Mr. Griffith's death. *"The Birth of a Nation,"* he wrote, "is equal to the best work that has ever been done in this country. And among moving pictures it is alone, not necessarily as 'the greatest'—whatever that means—but as the one great epic, tragic film."

Mr. Griffith wrote me not long after the opening, suggesting that Mother and I come to New York. On our arrival, he took me to the theater and watched, mesmerized, as the audience laughed, wept, and finally rose in an overwhelming ovation. I followed him into the box office. It was gratifying to sit there on a high stool and listen to the ticket sellers announce that no seats were available for weeks.

Lines outside the box office were blocks long. Mr. Griffith, of course, was elated.

"Have you ever seen anything like it, Miss Lillian?"

"Never, Mr. Griffith."

No one ever had.

I think the proof that Mr. Griffith himself had no idea what a sensation *The Birth* was going to be was the fact that while he was cutting the film and arranging the musical score for it, he was also making a small film to be called *The Mother and the Law*, which was to follow *The Birth*.

The Birth recouped its cost in the first two months of its run at the Liberty, and ran for forty-four consecutive weeks there, a record that was then unsurpassed. Crowds were so large that four other theaters booked the film at the same admission price. By the end of 1915 the gross receipts in New York City alone were $3.75 million. *The Birth* ran almost a year in Boston and Chicago. Then it toured the other important cities in the United States. At times there were twenty-eight companies on tour in the United States and also in Europe, South Africa, and Australia. The touring companies traveled in a style suitable perhaps to a large circus. In Arkansas, the *Hot Springs Sentinel* reported, "The Griffith drama comes here with a baggage equipment of two sixty-foot cars, a complete staff, including mechanical experts and a stage crew, and a large symphonic orchestra regularly carried on tour—a company of fifty people altogether." In some towns the movie played to three and four times the population, proof that it was drawing people in droves and that a good many were seeing it more than once.

In the first two years of its life, *The Birth of a Nation* played to an audience of 25 million people. In the South the movie ran continuously for twelve years. In 1924 it was revived at the Auditorium in Chicago, where it broke all records for that house. Three years earlier it had played nationally at popular prices, and it ran throughout the country for a full ten years.

Then in 1931 a new print was made with a synchronized musical score and sound effects. This version is the one used in theaters today. But unfortunately the synchronized score is only a tinny echo of Mr.

Griffith's original. Despite claims that it is "uncut and uncensored," three whole reels have been eliminated, for what reason I cannot fathom, as these cuts weaken the impact of the film and reduce many scenes to gibberish.

The Birth of a Nation has become the all-time money maker in film history. There have been so many black-market prints in circulation that no one will ever know its true gross. A man closely associated with the business side of the film once told me that the total box office take was much more than $100 million.

Perhaps as remarkable as its gross profits are the personal fortunes The Birth provided for many people. When I returned to Hollywood after an absence of several years, during which I made The White Sister and Romola abroad, my new boss, Louis B. Mayer, a founder of Metro-Goldwyn-Mayer and one of the most powerful men in Hollywood, met me at the train station.

"I want to thank you," he said, "for starting me on the road to success."

"What do you mean?" I asked, for I had never met him before.

"Well," Mr. Mayer said, "in 1915, when The Birth of a Nation was released, I was running a group of theaters in Haverhill, Massachusetts, where I'd started out with a nickelodeon. When The Birth came along, I pawned everything I owned—my house, my insurance, even my wife's wedding ring—just to get the New England states' rights. Since then, everything's been very pleasant. If it hadn't been for D. W. Griffith, The Birth, and you, I'd still be in Haverhill."

In those days, rights to distribute films in each state were sold outright, once the road shows had completed their tours. All profits then went to the owner of the rights, who showed the film in his own theaters and then sold the rights to show it to other exhibitors.

Investors also profited enormously. The Aitkens made a fortune. Mr. Clune, who already had a $15,000 investment, obtained the California rights and made a great deal of money. John Barry, a friend of Mr. Griffith, who had helped find backing for the film and had taken his commission in stock, accumulated a return of 700 per cent in two years.

Twenty-five years later, when I was traveling in upper Egypt, a messenger handed me a note from a gentleman. It read, "May I meet the lady who almost made me a millionaire?" The man introduced himself, saying that he was one of those whom Mr. Griffith had asked for a loan of $5,000. Had he given it, he would have made millions on his small investment.

Because of *The Birth of a Nation,* the movies, which had been a struggling new art form, were suddenly transformed into a multi-million-dollar industry. Control began to shift from directors operating on shoestrings to businessmen. The formula story came into being. The motto was, "Do only what has already proved successful, and keep on doing it." Most films were just another product coming off the assembly lines like cars.

Although we did not know it then, an era had ended.

From the beginning, *The Birth of a Nation* encountered extraordinary censorship and protests, as well as praise. A host of important liberals assailed the film for alleged prejudice and race baiting.

Oswald Garrison Villard, a grandson of the early abolitionist, attacked the film in *The Nation* as "a deliberate attempt to humiliate ten million American citizens and portray them as nothing but beasts."

Jane Addams of Hull House said that she was "painfully exercised over the exhibition."

Mr. Griffith was accused in a five-column newspaper article by historian Albert Bushnell Hart of having "made a mockery of the Union victory in our Civil War."

The Boston branch of the National Association for the Advancement of Colored People distributed widely a pamphlet called "Fighting a Vicious Film; A Record of Protest against *The Birth of a Nation.*" As proof that President Wilson repudiated the remark he had made after viewing *The Birth,* the pamphlet cited a letter from the President's secretary:

The White House
Washington, April 28, 1915

My dear Mr. Thacher:—

Replying to your letter and enclosure, I beg to say that it is true that *The Birth of a Nation* was produced before the

President and his family at the White House, but the President was entirely unaware of the nature of the play before it was presented and has at no time expressed his approbation of it. Its exhibition at the White House was a courtesy extended to an old acquaintance.

Sincerely yours,
(signed)   J. M. Tumulty
Secretary to the President

Part of the early success of *The Birth* may have arisen from the immediate raging controversy it incited. Everyone wanted to see the film that the N.A.A.C.P. and the Booker T. Washington clubs were trying to have outlawed. Fist fights and picket lines occurred at many premieres of the film. The opening at Clune's had nearly been halted by rumors of a race riot. Extra police stood guard around the theater just in case. The same thing happened in New York. Two weeks before the film's showing in Boston, birthplace of the abolitionist movement, it was assailed from rostrum, pulpit, and classroom (though many history teachers brought their classes to see it). When it opened at the Tremont Theater, 5,000 Negroes marched on the state capitol building demanding that the film be banned. Outside the Forrest Theater in Philadelphia fights and rioting broke out between 500 policemen and 3,000 Negroes. War news in the papers gave way to stories of this violence. Cities all over the country clamored to see the film.

In answer to a particularly virulent newspaper attack on *The Birth*, Thomas Dixon, on April 7, wrote a letter to the editor that said in part:

> . . . In answer to your editorial attack yesterday on *The Birth of a Nation* as author of the book and play on which the larger film drama is based, I accept the full moral responsibility for its purpose and its effect on an audience.
>
> We submitted *The Birth of a Nation* to a jury of three clergymen in New York—the Reverend Thomas B. Gregory, Universalist; the Reverend Charles H. Parkhurst, D.D., Presbyterian, and the Reverend John Talbot Smith, D.D., Roman

Catholic editor of *The Columbian,* organ of the Knights of Columbus.

They did not suggest a single change or cut but fully agreed with the high praise given by the dramatic critic of *The Globe.* They declare in substance that the play in its final impression on the audience does six things:

1. It unites in common sympathy and love all sections of our country.
2. It teaches our boys the history of our nation in a way that makes them know the priceless inheritance our fathers gave us through the sacrifices of Civil War and Reconstruction.
3. It tends to prevent the lowering of the standard of our citizenship by its mixture with Negro blood.
4. It shows the horror and futility of war as a method of settling civic principles.
5. It reaffirms Lincoln's solution of the Negro problem as a possible guide to our future and glorifies his character as the noblest example of American democracy.
6. It gives Daniel Webster for the first time his place in American history as the inspiring creator of the modern nation we know today.

I am not attacking the Negro of today. I am recording faithfully the history of 50 years ago. I portray three Negroes faithful unto death to every trust and two vicious Negroes misled by white scoundrels. Is it a crime to paint a bad black man, seeing we have so many white ones?

Thomas Dixon

The Reverend Mr. Dixon offered a reward of $5,000 to the National Board of Censorship and to any member of the Negroid Intermarriage Society if they could find "a single essential error in the book or film version of *The Birth of a Nation."*

Ugly attacks of violence flared up wherever the film was shown and have continued to this day. In May 1921 a protest demonstration was staged during a revival in New York. In Chicago the picture was first shown under a permanent injunction restraining the police from interfering after the management had agreed not to admit children under eighteen. When the picture was revived in 1924, there were still legal problems. A producer close to Mr. Griffith has recalled that the late Harold Ickes was hired by the city to prosecute two of the jury trials. After he had berated the film in the courtroom, Ickes allegedly said behind his hand, "That's the best picture I ever saw in my life." As late as 1952 the film was banned in Baltimore, but it was finally shown there despite a barrage of protests.

Mr. Griffith reacted to the violence and censorship with astonishment, shock, and sorrow. Not even he had realized the full power of the film he had created, a film that raised the threat of legislation for national censorship. Then slowly his reaction turned to anger. His personal crusade to protect his films began with *The Birth* and lasted until his death. Over the years twelve suits were brought against him and *The Birth,* and he won them all. I know that, no matter what film we were working on, if he heard that opposition to *The Birth* was developing, he would stop work, hurry to the city in question, and fight the accusations. In 1920 he almost single-handedly defeated a film-censorship bill before the Virginia legislature. He fought by way of newspapers, magazines, and speeches. He wrote, published, and distributed a pamphlet entitled "The Rise and Fall of Free Speech in America." He purposely refused to copyright it, making it available to anyone who wanted to reprint it:

> Today the censorship of moving pictures, throughout the entire country, is seriously hampering the growth of the art. Had intelligent opposition to censorship been employed when it first made itself manifest it could easily have been overcome. But the pygmy child of that day has grown to be, not merely a man, but a giant, and I tell you who read this, whether you will or not, he is a giant whose forces of evil are so strong that he threatens that priceless heritage of our nation—freedom of expression.
>
> The right of free speech has cost centuries upon centuries of untold suffering and agonies; it has cost rivers of blood; it has taken as its toll uncounted fields littered with the car-

casses of human beings—all this that there might come to live and survive that wonderful thing, the power of free speech. . . .

The integrity of free speech and publication was *not* . . . *attacked* seriously in this country until the arrival of the *motion picture,* when this new art was seized by the powers of intolerance as an excuse for an assault on our liberties.

The motion picture is a medium of expression as clean and decent as any mankind has ever discovered. A people that would allow the suppression of this form of speech would unquestionably submit to the suppression of that which we all consider so highly, the printing press.

And yet we find all through the country, among all classes of people, the idea that the motion picture should be censored.

Mr. Griffith's defense of *The Birth* was based on the story he told: "Of whatever excesses or outrages the blacks may be guilty, these they commit as blind and misguided, if violent, pawns of their satanic new white masters from the North." But of an attack on race or on the Negro race as such, Mr. Griffith insisted, there is no hint, no scene or sign. The villain in the film is not Silas Lynch but Austin Stoneman, whose violent hatred of the South and hypocritical treatment of Negroes are obvious.

To support his view of the Reconstruction and the Ku Klux Klan, Mr. Griffith cited the various documents that he had consulted before filming. He produced records of the House of Representatives and Supreme Court of South Carolina to back up his depiction of the Negroes who controlled the legislature there. To substantiate scenes of Negro violence, he cited records from high courts throughout the South. He also defended his right under the guarantees of the Constitution to offer a view of the Civil War as he saw it. He admitted freely that it was a Southern point of view.

Of all the criticisms, the one from which Mr. Griffith suffered the most was the accusation that he was against Negroes. "To say that is like saying that I am against children, as they were our children, whom we loved and cared for all our lives." Mr. Griffith had grown up with Negroes on the farm, and as a baby he had had a Negro mammy. He always treated Negroes with great affection, and they in turn loved him. Being a Southerner, he could communicate with them, and they liked to be around him because he was amusing. When some of them turned against him after the showing of *The Birth,* he was deeply wounded.

To the charge that important Negro roles were played by whites, Mr. Griffith replied that there were scarcely any Negro actors on the Coast and that there had been no money to bring them from New York. Besides, Mr. Griffith was accustomed to working with actors he had trained.

If he were alive today, I feel certain that Mr. Griffith would have done a film of affirmation about the Negro. In fact, shortly before his death we talked about doing such a film. He believed that the Negro had made great strides since the end of slavery, when a million white men had died to help set them free. He said that the white man had taken centuries to attain the intellectual and spiritual powers that many Negro citizens had achieved in a few decades. He believed that no other race in the history of mankind had advanced so far so quickly.

Mr. Griffith was incapable of prejudice against any group. Two years after the uproar over *The Birth,* when he agreed, at the behest of British and French officials, to make propaganda films, he was obliged to portray all Germans as loathsome. This troubled him, for he never believed that there were marked differences among people. Regardless of background, he felt, they were all children of God.

In the midst of these battles, Mr. Griffith began work on an answer to his critics in the medium he had created. "The world is too full of 'Think as I think or be damned,' " he told me. "What the censors are doing has been done time and time again in the history of mankind."

Throughout his conversation, his speeches, even his pamphlet, one word recurred—"intolerance."

✣ 13 ✣

The word "intolerance" became the title and the theme of his new film. Many writers have expressed the belief that Mr. Griffith realized the great harm that he had done by producing *The Birth of a Nation* and that *Intolerance* was his apology for it. Such statements are completely untrue. He did not consider his film harmful at all. He told what he believed to be the truth about the Civil War, as he had heard it from those who had lived through the conflict. He had no reason to apologize for his film. *Intolerance,* on the contrary, was his way of answering those who, in his view, were the bigots.

He said to me: "I've always said I would rebuild Babylon for you. Now I'm going to do it, and make it part of a new story I have planned, showing man's inhumanity to man for the last 2,500 years."

Mr. Griffith intended to tell the story of Belshazzar, the young King of Babylon, and the destruction of his kingdom. The fall of Babylon, as Mr. Griffith saw it, was brought about by the scheming of the high priests, who, fearing the introduction of new religious ideas, betrayed the city to Cyrus, Emperor of the Persians. He intended to merge this story with three others: the betrayal of Jesus, ending with the Crucifixion; the betrayal of the Huguenots on the Eve of St. Bartholomew in 1572, when 50,000 Protestants were

. 165 .

massacred in Paris; and the struggle between capital and labor in the modern United States, which was the theme of *The Mother and the Law,* the film Mr. Griffith had been working on while editing *The Birth.* The story was based on reports from a Federal industrial commission on the shooting of nineteen strikers by the militia of a chemical manufacturer, and on the records of a murder case that was then capturing headlines. The plot centers around the fate of a laborer (the Boy, played by Bobby Harron), who is forced out of work because of a strike, brought on because his employer has cut wages in order to contribute to some "false charity." Later the Boy becomes a criminal, is framed by a gangster (the Musketeer of the Slums), and is sent to prison. The same "reform" organization that in effect has robbed him of his job now takes his child away from his wife (the Dear One, played by Mae Marsh) to raise it "properly." Released from prison, the Boy arrives home to witness a struggle between his unwilling wife and the lecherous Musketeer. The Boy takes on the Musketeer, and in the struggle the gangster is killed— not by the Boy but by the gangster's mistress, who has been hiding outside the window, jealously spying on her lover. She throws her gun into the room and flees. In the confusion, the Boy picks up the weapon, and the police arrest him for murder. The climax comes with his wife's last-minute attempt to have him pardoned.

The film was completed shortly after *The Birth* was released. When Mr. Griffith ran *The Mother and the Law,* we all agreed with him that the film was too small in theme and execution to follow *The Birth.* Mr. Griffith was in the awkward position of having to surpass himself. Yet he could not afford to discard *The Mother and the Law.*

Later, after he had completed the three period episodes, the modern story looked even smaller and old-fashioned by comparison, so he redid it completely, strengthening its drama to make up for its lack of visual appeal. It was a stroke of good fortune for the cast of *The Mother,* which was thus given the opportunity to better its performances.

Because the four stories were so widely separated in time and geography, Mr. Griffith decided to tie the episodes together with an image of the Eternal Mother rocking the cradle, accompanied by Walt Whitman's line, "Out of the cradle, endlessly rocking." Mr. Griffith loved Whitman; he could quote pages of his poetry. I shared his admiration; from the time I learned to read, Whitman had been my favorite American poet.

The film was to open with this image, which would be repeated to introduce each of the four currents. The first subtitle would read, "A golden thread binds the four stories—a fairy girl with sunlit hair—her hand on the cradle of humanity—eternally rocking—." That was my role.

While Mr. Griffith was working on *Intolerance,* he was also producing films for a new organization, the Triangle Film Corporation, which had been formed in July 1915 by Harry Aitken, with Mr. Griffith as vice-president. "Triangle" referred to three top directors— D. W. Griffith, Mack Sennett, and Thomas Ince—who worked independently in their own studios. Sennett, who had launched Charlie Chaplin and the Keystone Cops, continued to make comedies. Ince concentrated on drama. Mr. Griffith made both.

During this period, a typical day might start with a story conference with "Daddy" Woods, head of the scenario department. Then, between work on *Intolerance,* Mr. Griffith would supervise in detail the rehearsals, shooting, and editing of films made by his assistants. Late into the night he would watch the daily rushes and lay out the next day's schedule. He also gave outlines of original scenarios for a number of Triangle films under one of his many pseudonyms—Granville Warwick. One of these, *Diane of the Follies,* gave me the rare opportunity to play a vamp. Naturally, I was happy not to be playing another "Gaga-baby," a term we gave to sweet-little-girl roles, which were actually difficult to do. It took more effort to play one of them and hold an audience's interest than it did to portray ten wicked women.

In addition to all these activities, Mr. Griffith was involved in promotion of *The Birth of a Nation.* He often spoke at the openings of his film.

He was also often called upon to defend *The Birth* against censorship or to argue against some bill coming up in Congress that he thought might hurt the future of films. At such times he spoke eloquently. He talked to governors and senators; he addressed state legislatures. It was time-consuming, but he was the dean of films and the one man to whom the industry turned whenever a harmful bill was raised. He was glad to be its spokesman.

Mr. Griffith hurled himself into the making of *Intolerance* with incredible energy and concentration. Again he did all the research himself, although he often discussed the source material with "Daddy" Woods. His encyclopedic mind had always filled me with awe, but the knowledge he called on during the filming of *Intolerance* was simply staggering.

Once again everyone became absorbed in history—Babylonian, French, and, of course, biblical. One of the dancers in *Intolerance* was Carmel Meyers, whose father, Rabbi Meyers, helped with the biblical research. Mr. Griffith knew the Bible well, but it was his habit to use people as a sounding board. He talked to all of us, and we often came up with sound ideas.

As always, Mr. Griffith worked without a script. We all helped compose the subtitles.

Although my part was small, I was much more involved in *Intolerance* than in the other pictures I was making. Most of the pictures I acted in at that time are vague in my memory, but *Intolerance* remains vivid. I read no other books but those dealing with the various periods of history portrayed in the movie.

Research was no chore for me. I was particularly fascinated by Catherine de Medici, married to a man who disliked her but fathered her nine children in nine years. She later had several of her own sons killed in her lust for power. I was too young and unworldly then to understand or accept her actions. When I expressed myself to Mr. Griffith, he said: "Don't judge. Just be thankful it isn't you committing some black deed. Always remember this, Miss Lillian—circumstances make people what they are. Everyone is capable of the lowest and the highest. The same potentialities are in us all—only circumstances make the difference."

For this film he had almost unlimited funds, for after the great success of *The Birth of a Nation* it was easy to find backers for the new film. Nor was he obliged to rely on ingenious effects to suggest size and significance. Where formerly he had suggested thousands of extras, through his skill alone, he now actually hired that many for *Intolerance*.

A small village of shacks and tents on a vacant lot across the street from our studio provided housing for construction workers and extras. Railroad tracks were laid to reach the huge main gate to the walled city of Babylon. Freight cars from two railways brought in food and building supplies, as well as horses and elephants. Mr. Griffith raised the pay of extras to $2 a day plus a 60-cent free lunch, which was a new high for the industry.

Once again, he was conferring with Huck Wortman on the sets for the new picture. Huck would listen, ask a few questions about measurements, occasionally spit out a stream of tobacco juice, shake his head once or twice doubtfully, then walk away with a preoccupied expression. He, Mr. Griffith, and Billy Bitzer determined where the light would fall at various hours of the day during the coming months, and Huck's crew of 700 men began the construction of sets on a tightly guarded location on Sunset Boulevard, with Mr. Griffith supervising every detail. The sets were constructed without the benefit of a single architectural plan; the only blueprints were in Mr. Griffith's head.

A few weeks later, passers-by halted and stared in disbelief. Above them rose a huge network of scaffolding. Gradually in the following days the outline of an immense walled city took shape, reaching skyward until the extraordinary set was visible for miles around.

The immense, opulent Babylonian set was unlike anything that had ever been constructed for movies. The walls enclosing the court of Belshazzar were over 200 feet high. The court, which was approached by numerous steps, was flanked by two colonnades supporting columns fifty feet high, each column in turn supporting a great statue of the elephant god erect on his hind legs. Behind the court were towers and ramparts 200 feet high, their crests planted with flowering shrubs and trees to represent the famed hanging gardens. The set was studded with rows of rosettes, rich entablatures, huge torchères, finials, tiled fretwork, and bas-reliefs of winged deities, lions, and bulls.

The east wall of the Babylon set was three-quarters of a mile away from the main camera. The tops of the walls were as wide as roads, enough for two chariots to pass each other at top speed. At one point during the filming, as Del Henderson was driving one of the chariots on the wall, he had trouble with the horses. Mr. Griffith shouted to him: "Get out of there. Get out before you're killed!"

Del shouted back, "How can I get out?"

Riding those chariots was not easy. In order to hold his balance, the driver had to brace his knees against the front, and his knees would get rubbed raw.

In addition to the Babylonian court, the Medici court and the cobble-stoned streets of sixteenth-century Paris were built. The great Medici throne room was constructed with magnificent wall tapestries, brocaded curtains, glittering candelabra, and a great columned dais supporting a canopy of the most intricate mosaics.

As the sets grew in magnitude, Allan Dwan, one of the assistant directors on *Intolerance,* as well as director for many of the other films being made at the studio, said to Mr. Griffith: "You've bitten off one hell of a chunk. How are you going to get actors to dominate all this magnificence?"

"If it's good," Mr. Griffith answered with a wry smile, "you'll be doing it yourself next year."

Mr. Griffith designed and was responsible for many of the costumes. He worked particularly hard on the Babylonian ones. Whenever there was a break in his schedule, he would have the players model the costumes. If he had fifteen minutes after lunch before he was due back on the set or a little time in the evening, he would say to one of his acting company: "Get into that costume. I want to see it."

Then he would call in Billy Bitzer or "Daddy" Woods or whoever happened to be nearby and ask: "What do you think? Do you like this headdress? Is it too high—too dark, perhaps? How will it photograph?"

In the Babylonian period young girls went into the Temple of

Sacred Fire, and as their contribution to the love goddess Ishtar each one gave herself to a man who came to the temple to worship. Mr. Griffith wanted to show these young virgins in costumes that would be seductive yet in no way offensive. All the young girls—among them Mildred Harris, who was to be Charlie Chaplin's first wife—were dressed in floating chiffons and photographed in a fountain, not dancing but moving rhythmically and sensually to music. Some of the scenes were shot through veiling or fountain sprays to add to the erotic yet poetic effect.

He was equally concerned with the men's costumes. I remember that the men who wore false beards used to push their beards up onto their foreheads when they became unbearably hot.

"Get those beards off your forehead!" Mr. Griffith would call out, not in anger but in amusement. Often the men pushed their wigs down like eyeshades, and again he would remind them to put their hair back in place.

Mr. Griffith wanted the main characters in the Babylonian episode to be larger than life. Walter Paget, who played the young king, although he was well over six feet tall, was made to look taller with built-up shoes. George Siegmann, who played Cyrus the Persian conqueror, was a big man too, and his height was also exaggerated with built-up shoes. There were no Adler elevated shoes in those days; Mr. Griffith had to create his own. Cyrus' tall headdress added even further to George's height.

Seena Owen, a beautiful girl, played the Princess Beloved of the king. Unlike the usual Griffith heroine, she was a full-blown young woman, a type that would appeal to the Eastern taste. She, too, wore high heels. But when she was made up and in costume, Mr. Griffith felt that something was lacking.

"Her body is important and handsome enough," he said, "but her eyes—."

Seena had lovely blue eyes, but he wanted them to look supernatural. "How can I make them look twice their size?" he wondered. Then, calling in the wigmaker, he asked if it would be possible to paste lashes around her eyes.

Seena explained to me once how the lashes were made. The wigmaker wove human hair through the warp of the thinnest gauze in a strip twenty-four inches long. He cut off two tiny pieces from the end and fastened them to her eyelids with spirit gum. Each day as she needed them, she cut off two more small strips. Those were the first false eyelashes.

One morning she arrived at the studio with her eyes swollen nearly shut. The studio was in a turmoil. What had they done to Seena? Would she be blind? Doctors were summoned, and they told us that her eyelids had been irritated by the weight of the false lashes. Fortunately, Mr. Griffith had already shot the important scenes with her, and he ordered her not to use the lashes again. In a few days she was back at work in the great banquet scene.

To heighten the tragedy of the fall of Babylon, Mr. Griffith created the story of the Mountain Girl, who falls in love with the King and tries to save him. A Brooklyn girl, Constance Talmadge, played the part. A natural comedienne, she was the youngest of the three Talmadge girls—Norma and Natalie were the other two—who, guided by their staunch mother, were to achieve film fame. Constance's carefree, fun-loving nature made her the pet of the studio.

Mr. Griffith wanted Constance's costume to look as if it were made of whatever stuff would be available to her in her mountain lair. The homespun fabric was rough and the weather hot, and during the long delays between shots Constance sometimes took off the pads that made her figure more womanly. Often by the time she was called before the camera, she had forgotten them completely.

"If you please, Miss Constance," Mr. Griffith would say, "half of your figure is missing again. Do you think I want a lopsided heroine?"

She would forget where she had left the pads, and we would all go in search of Constance's figure.

During that time, Mr. Griffith brought over Sir Herbert Beerbohm Tree and Constance Collier, two of England's outstanding stage stars, to do a film version of *Macbeth* for one of his young directors. Sir Herbert and Miss Collier also appeared briefly in *Intolerance*. Sir Herbert brought with him his strangely beautiful and poetic daughter,

Iris. They were players Dorothy and I had known about in our childhood, and we were completely awed at meeting them.

When Mr. Griffith first told me that the English actors were coming, I said with a wistful sigh, "It must be wonderful to be a great actor."

When their first rehearsal was scheduled, all of us young players gathered on the sidelines, sitting on the floor to watch them. Now, I thought, we'll learn how to act! At that time we had no ears. Words were used, but we scarcely heard them, as we were trained only to see with the eyes of the camera. We were startled to see two figures standing in one spot while only their mouths moved.

The next few minutes were excruciating. Sir Herbert and Constance Collier were aware that films were silent, but that was the extent of their knowledge. They stood before us speaking Shakespeare's words—a cardinal sin, as it was hardly Mr. Griffith's plan to put the entire film in one long subtitle. Their exaggerated gestures and grimaces, though quite appropriate for the stage, were painfully overdone for the intimacy of the camera.

Mr. Griffith had too much respect for Sir Herbert to cause him embarrassment. He decided that it would be better for the actor to see for himself the difference between theater and films. Once they had seen their first rushes, the English actors realized their failure.

"Mr. Griffith," Sir Herbert began after rehearsals one evening, "do you think you could teach me something about this new medium?"

Mr. Griffith smiled and motioned him to a chair. Like a schoolboy, Sir Herbert sat through the rehearsal of another film, watching us and trying to learn how to be articulate without words. He remained in Hollywood and gradually learned the technique of acting for silent films.

As work on *Intolerance* progressed, I noticed a short man with a face of stone and a monocle, who played a Pharisee in the biblical story. Mr. Griffith mentioned that he had been an extra in *The Birth*. He looked so strange, with his bullet head, that the girls were afraid of him and would cross the street to avoid meeting him, even though they knew that he was married to our wardrobe mistress. He took his acting career seriously and was also one of Mr. Griffith's assistant directors. During the filming of another movie, I saw him break into tears when the part for which he had rehearsed was given to another actor. Mr. Griffith put his arms around the man and restored his composure with a few encouraging words. After that spectacle, the girls were not afraid of him anymore. Not many years later, Erich von Stroheim became world-famous, both as an actor and as a director.

Another performer who played a minor part in *Intolerance* was Douglas Fairbanks, a handsome, swashbuckling actor whom Mr. Griffith had persuaded to leave Broadway. Mr. Griffith believed in Doug but had to do a good deal of work with him before he was ready for films. D. W. told me: "He has such verve. We can use his body."

Mr. Griffith was not averse, once in a while, to playing a joke. One of the funniest moments of Douglas' introduction to the movies never appeared on film. He and Allan Dwan were on a studio stage discussing a western that they planned to make. Douglas was in cowboy chaps with two six-shooters at his belt. Suddenly a lion padded onto the stage, sniffed, and scowled, showing his fangs. With a yelp both men took off for a nearby shed.

Seconds later Mr. Griffith walked on stage, grabbed the lion by its mane, and led it away, saying softly, "Come kitty . . . good kitty."

As he and the beast passed the shed where Dwan, ex-Notre Dame football coach, and Fairbanks, swashbuckler, were hiding, Mr. Griffith halted and called out in his deep voice: "Don't be afraid, boys. I won't let him hurt you."

Mr. Griffith had already used the lion in *Intolerance* and knew him to be tame.

Two major scenes highlighted the Babylonian episode—the feast of Belshazzar and the fall of the city to Cyrus. For the feast, more than 4,000 extras in costume filled the immense court and its ramparts. Hundreds of dancers, led by Gertrude Bambrick, opened the great feast. Three bands, placed strategically about the quarter-mile set, played for the dancers. Among the Denishawn-trained dancers was Carol Dempster, who was later to appear in films as a Griffith heroine.

Mr. Griffith was no longer satisfied with the technique he had used in directing *The Birth* crowd scenes. As in *The Birth,* he used a megaphone to reach his lieutenants in the field and worked out a set of signals, this time with his megaphone, for the others, who were half a mile away. But for this film he decided against directing from a stationary tower. He wanted the camera to record every detail of the fantastic scene, so he installed Billy in a balloon that could be raised or lowered. But the wind played havoc with Billy's attempts to keep within the limits of the set, so Mr. Griffith came up with another idea. He put the camera on a rope-manipulated elevator—with a platform large enough to hold himself, Billy, and me sitting with feet hanging over to take up less room—and placed the entire contraption on tracks that ran deep into the set.

This forerunner of the modern camera crane enabled Mr. Griffith to create one of the most fabulous effects ever filmed. Having perfected the closeup and set a standard for crowd scenes, he now fused the two techniques. At the opening of Belshazzar's feast, the camera was a quarter-mile from the end of the great court. It started to move toward the set, then glided slowly down over the heads of the extras and dancing girls, then moved forward again to halt before a miniature chariot drawn by two white doves and holding a white rose—a gift from the King to the Princess Beloved, who sat at the other end of the table. Fantastic in conception, the shot was also a tribute to Billy's skill, for throughout the long swooping ride on the crane, he had managed to keep his camera in perfect focus from the enormous expanses of the entire set to the petals on the rose.

Billy was called "Eagle Eye" because his camera could see far beyond the range of the human eye. In a later scene, during which the King drives his chariot on top of the wall surrounding the city, one sees from a mile away the busy life of the city. The distant city, as well as the foreground action of the King in his chariot, is in focus. Yet this vista was not superimposed, as audiences might think; one camera photographed both scenes.

For the siege of Babylon, one of the largest scenes ever staged, Mr. Griffith filled the screen with mass shots of Cyrus' army. During the shooting of this sequence, word went out that Mr. Griffith would pay an additional $5 to any extra who would jump off the wall. There were nets below to catch the jumpers, of course. When the camera began grinding again, all the extras started leaping from the parapets.

"Stop those crazy fools!" Mr. Griffith ordered. "I haven't enough nets—or enough money."

There were always ambulances, a nurse, and a doctor on the set, but apart from minor injuries no mishaps or casualties occurred. Credit for this extraordinary safety record goes to Mr. Griffith, who had everything so well organized that no one became excited or confused about what was expected of him.

During the shooting of the mass scenes, everyone on the lot, including actors from other productions, blended into the mob. After all, this looked like an important "first" by the director who was by then God of Hollywood.

Next in magnitude came the court scenes in the palace of Catherine de Medici. It was there that Mr. Griffith used ceiling shots for the first time. Sets generally do not have ceilings, but Mr. Griffith wanted to show the magnificent ceiling of the throne room and had Billy shoot up at it. This technique later won acclaim for Orson Welles in *Citizen Kane,* long after Mr. Griffith had discarded shooting from the floor.

In the biblical episode, the stone temples and narrow roads of Cana and Galilee, which Huck Wortman carefully recreated three miles west of the studio, were completely authentic. Nearly four decades after *Intolerance* was made, my sister Dorothy and I visited Jerusalem, and I experienced one of those strange moments of *déjà vu.* Then I realized that Mr. Griffith had built the city on a back lot in California. For the rest of the trip, as I passed the Garden of Olives and the Sorrowful Way, I kept expecting to see him, with floppy hat and megaphone, directing at the end of some dusty street.

As production continued and costs soared, Mr. Griffith's backers became alarmed. Finally they refused to advance any more money.

Mr. Griffith, with a gesture that was to become habitual, bought out their shares, going into debt to do so. Whenever money became scarce, he would simply mortgage another piece of *The Birth*. I know of no other reason to explain why he had nothing left of that film's tremendous profits when he died.

Intolerance is reputed to have cost $1.9 million in the end. It was the costliest production up to that time and for many years after.

My role as the Eternal Mother took less than an hour to film. Nevertheless, I was closer to *Intolerance* than anyone else except Billy Bitzer and Jimmy Smith, the cutter. I felt that there was more of me in this picture than in any other I had ever played in. Perhaps because I wasn't acting a long role, Mr. Griffith took me into his confidence as never before, talking over scenes before he filmed them, having me watch all the rushes, even accepting some of my ideas. He sent me to the darkroom to pick the best takes and to help Jimmy with the cutting. At night, as I watched the day's rushes, I saw the film take shape and marveled at what Mr. Griffith was creating.

Every week overwhelming effects poured from the darkroom. Some of the scenes were shot in startling shapes: triangles; diamonds; diagonals; frieze-like panels that blocked out all but a long thin strip of the film; and semicircles that opened like fans. In the shots of the virgins in the Temple of Sacred Fire, the impression of sensual motion was reinforced by having the camera turn from left to right and back again, and also by having the screen frame close in, then move out, then in again. Small iris shots opened to reveal huge panoramas. Other shots contained double and triple exposures. There were huge closeups of only the lower half of Miriam Cooper's face or of only Margery Wilson's eyes.

The lighting effects were equally dramatic. The contrasts extended from Babylon under a brilliant glaring sun to the darkened backstreets of Paris, where moonlight washed the cobblestones. Mr. Griffith used tinted film for parts of each story, to intensify emotional impact. Night scenes were blue; the Babylonian night battle scenes were red; the French court was amber. But the principal source of light was the sun. For the shot of me at the cradle, the set was darkened, and sunlight poured through a hole in the roof. Perhaps his extensive use of sunlight suggested to his mind the subtitle of the film, *A Sun Play of the Ages*.

The intricate interweaving of plots in *Intolerance* and its astounding length, which began to run into hundreds of reels, demanded the concentration and decision making that could have gone into thirty or forty films. Yet Mr. Griffith continued to work without notes or script, and, in the months it took to make that gigantic film, he continued to supervise other films that Triangle produced. With the burden of so many smaller films, Mr. Griffith took more than twenty months to complete *Intolerance*. Left free, he could no doubt have finished it in six.

The true power and magnificence of *Intolerance* came not from its size but from the cutting and editing of the negative. Mr. Griffith worked on every foot of film, slicing each scene to the core of its drama, joining the sequences in amazing harmony. The picture began with the modern story; then, after a transitional shot of me rocking the cradle, the camera moved back through centuries to focus on the massive gate of Babylon, then wandered through the gate into the crowded alleyways. Once the stories were all introduced, time spent on each segment was shorter. The scenes gained momentum, as the camera shifted freely from the modern factory to the wedding at Cana, from the parapets of Babylon to the Medici court. Each story was in itself a miracle of parallel action and cross-cutting. In the swift, overpowering climax, the four stories mingled in "one mighty river of emotion," to use his own words, as short, staccato shots from each story exploded across the screen: the Mountain Girl racing to warn King Belshazzar; the first bloodletting in Paris; the Dear One hurrying to obtain a pardon for her innocent husband; Christ on the road to Calvary. At the breathless climax some of the shots were mere flashes, each hardly perceived, as the succession of pictures pelted the viewer: the fall of Babylon, the Crucifixion, the massacre, the Boy saved from the scaffold seconds before the trap was to be sprung.

Like all Mr. Griffith's films, *Intolerance* was rich in unforgettable moments: the closeup of Mae Marsh's anguished hands as she hears her husband's death sentence; the knives in the hands of the executioners, ready to cut the ropes that will plunge the young husband to his death; the death of the Mountain Girl; Cyrus' warriors galloping toward Babylon; the tiny chariot witth its white doves.

Never had Mr. Griffith's technique been so fresh and resourceful. Again and again the film leaves the viewer with an after-image that does not fade but continues to intrigue the mind, keeping alive the emotions he experienced originally in seeing the film. Mr. Griffith could arouse a sense of horror in the viewer and then make him weep with tenderness. In *Intolerance* his genius reached its fullest expression.

When Mr. Griffith finished editing *Intolerance,* it ran approximately eight hours. He planned to exhibit it in two parts, each a four-hour section, on two consecutive nights.

The dimensions of this film have never been equaled. When the exhibitors who were going to show *Intolerance* heard of its length they refused to handle it, and by that time they were in a position to dictate what they would or would not book. Although Mr. Griffith had ignored similar objections when he introduced the two-, four-, five-, and twelve-reel films, this time, unfortunately, he listened.

He was advised to cut the film to one evening's entertainment. He should have ignored the advice. His own instinct was right. Success or failure, *Intolerance* was his monument, the measure of the man himself. But the exhibitors won. The public was never shown *Intolerance* in its entirety.

"Intolerance must succeed!" he said to me one evening as he was cutting the film again in obedience to the exhibitors' demands. The film was down to two and a half hours and much too tight. I had been so closely involved in the cutting and editing of the film that I was apprehensive over the result. How could he tell four stories of such magnitude in so brief a time?

Intolerance opened at the Liberty Theatre in New York on September 5, 1916. It was accompanied by an orchestra from the Metropolitan Opera. Nervously Mr. Griffith and all of us awaited the verdict of the public and critics. As with *The Birth,* the praise was overwhelming. First-night audiences stood up to applaud the master and his masterpiece.

Film Daily said: "Stupendous, tremendous, revolutionary, intense, thrilling, and then you can throw away the old typewriter and give up with the dictionary because you can't find adjectives enough. Mr. Griffith has put on the screen what is, without question, the most stirring human expression that has ever been presented to the world."

Everywhere respected critics and writers lauded the film. We were elated.

Yet something went wrong. In the first four months at the Liberty, *Intolerance* outdid the box-office record of *The Birth*. Then attendance began to fall off. It ran for five months in New York, but in the last weeks it was obvious to us all that the film was failing. In other cities it was the same story—a first surge of attendance, then a drop to almost nothing.

"I don't know where to go or where to turn since my great failure," Mr. Griffith wrote to me. He told me sadly of wandering through darkened theaters, barking his shins on empty seats.

Eventually the film was withdrawn. It is one of the few pictures that has never had a second run in most neighborhood houses. It had not nearly begun to pay for itself. With what funds he had, Mr. Griffith started to pay off his million-dollar debt. It took him years.

Many reasons have been advanced for the failure of the film. *Film Daily,* though praising the picture, had added that "the hardest thing the audience had to swallow was the revolutionary construction employed by Mr. Griffith in building four separate stories."

Variety said that the film was "so diffuse in the sequence of its incidents that the development is at times hard to follow." Audiences found the climax particularly bewildering. In the shortened version, the film's images fell on them like spent buckshot, without force or direction. I think it is important to remember that the world never saw *Intolerance* as Mr. Griffith wanted it seen. I believe that, had he shown the film in two four-hour screenings as he had planned, it would have been successful.

But there were other reasons for the failure. He should have left the details of other productions to his assistants, who were competent enough. He should have finished *Intolerance* as quickly as possible to keep down the costs. And he should have given his players the kind of publicity and exploitation that was by then starting in the industry. Had he done so, their pulling power might have made up the deficit of the film and a good deal more beside.

Stars had become important. Although Mary Pickford had left him long before and was making millions for other studios, Mr. Griffith was nevertheless surrounded by some of the best-known faces in the world and by a good many others who would become famous within the next few years. His films were the training ground for future stars.

The original print of *The Birth* had carried no screen credits, although Mr. Griffith's name appeared in both credits and subtitles. It was not until the critics' demands to know the names of the players became too great to ignore that the list of players was released. Yet *Intolerance* too carried no credits for the actors. The same policy was followed on all the films made under his assistants during the months it took him to make *Intolerance*. Without exploitation of the top leads as "stars," as was the custom in other studios, these films were only moderately successful.

But Mr. Griffith was not interested in promoting stars. In fact, he never even made attempts to keep them. Mae Marsh received $35 a week while making *The Birth* and $85 a week for *Intolerance*.

"After *Intolerance,* I signed with Mr. Samuel Goldfish [sic], who offered me $2,500 a week for the first year and $3,500 for the second year," Mae wrote me. The newly formed Goldwyn Pictures Corporation felt that as a "name" she was worth it.

After Blanche Sweet had played the lead—anonymously—in *Judith of Bethulia,* the Lasky Company offered her a contract starting at $500 a week. She went to Mr. Griffith and asked his advice.

He spoke very softly: "I think it's an excellent opportunity for you, one that will advance your career. If I were you, I'd take it."

Blanche was astonished and deeply hurt. Later she told me: "I felt like a child breaking away from its parent. He had given me all the love and knowledge and philosophy he could. He was proud of me."

She was unable to understand Mr. Griffith's attitude. He sent players off with good wishes and followed their future careers with great admiration. I don't think it ever occurred to him that he too might profit from them, as others were about to do.

Another factor in *Intolerance*'s unpopularity was its timing. In 1916 and early 1917 the country was preparing for war. The papers were filled with war headlines. Yet here was a picture that preached peace and tolerance. It was the antithesis of what people were then interested in. As the country grew more and more war-conscious, *Intolerance* was censored and barred in many cities. Before the film was released Mr. Griffith had said: "Wilson kept us out of war. I would rather have him re-elected than have *Intolerance* a success."

"Be careful what you wish for," I answered. "You may get it."

In the years since the "failure" of *Intolerance*, I have lived to see its elemental power affirmed. All teachers of film that I have ever talked to, and numerous critics as well, have said that *Intolerance* is the greatest film ever made. "History seems to pour like a cataract across the screen," Iris Barry, first curator of the Museum of Modern Art's Film Library, has said of it. And the Babylonian scenes inspired generous praise from the University of Oxford's great Assyriologist, Archibald Henry Sayce.

Its influence has since been felt in every country. Sergei Eisenstein, the great Russian director, acknowledged that *Intolerance* had become the one basic textbook for the entire Soviet film industry. The film ran continuously in Russia for ten years; it made millions, though not a cent reached Mr. Griffith. In 1922 a delegation from Moscow called on Mr. Griffith and extended to him an invitation from Lenin himself to come to Russia and take charge of all the country's film production. From the theme of *Intolerance*, Lenin had inferred that Mr. Griffith must be a Communist, particularly in view of the modern story, with its battle between capital and labor. Mr. Griffith declined the invitation. Although the film depicted the merciless treatment labor suffered at the hands of capitalists, Mr. Griffith himself was an aristocrat who never forgot his father's reminder that the Griffiths were descended from kings. Sects, parties, politics meant little to him. He cut through the surface to the inner core of humanity—the brotherhood of man.

Theodore Huff, Professor of American Film History at New York University, called *Intolerance* "the greatest motion picture ever produced. In its original form and properly presented, it is a masterpiece of creative conception and execution which ranks with such works of art as Beethoven's Ninth Symphony, Rembrandt's 'Descent from the Cross,' Da Vinci's 'Mona Lisa,' the sculptures of the Parthenon, or with works of literature such as Tolstoy's *War and Peace,* the poetry of Walt Whitman or Shakespeare's *Hamlet."*

To me, *Intolerance* recalls Mr. Griffith's words: "We have gone beyond Babel, beyond words. We have found a universal language, a power that can make men brothers and end war forever. Remember that! Remember that when you stand in front of a camera!"

14

Just before the United States entered World War I, Mr. Griffith decided to sail for London. *The Birth of a Nation* was already playing there, a great success at Drury Lane Theatre, which never before had opened its doors to motion pictures. Now *Intolerance* was to open there, and Mr. Griffith wanted to see that it was properly handled. It was a great honor for his films to be presented at Drury Lane, and it helped to relieve some of the depression he was feeling over the fate of *Intolerance*. He was forty-one years old when the film was released, and, although none of us was aware of it, he had reached the apex of his career. He was still to make great pictures, but he would be harassed by debts till the end of his life.

Before leaving for England Mr. Griffith severed his ties with Triangle and signed a contract with Artcraft, Adolph Zukor's company that produced for Famous Players-Lasky, which was to put up some of the money for his next film. Now, with the Boss 6,000 miles away, the company was disbanded, and directors and actors went their separate ways. Mr. Griffith asked Billy Bitzer, Bobby Harron, Dorothy and me, and a few others not to take jobs until he knew his future plans. The day he bade us goodbye he gave Mother and me a package wrapped in old newspapers, not even tied with string.

"This is all I have in the world," he said. "Will you keep it safe until I return?"

Impressed by his trust in us, we rented our first safety-deposit box, where the package remained until Mother could safely put it into his hands on his return. To this day I don't know what was in that bundle, but I suspect that it was cash and bonds.

Before its opening at Drury Lane *Intolerance* was shown at Buckingham Palace for the King and Queen and royal family. When it opened, it was enthusiastically received by both critics and public. Many prominent Britishers—Winston Churchill, David Lloyd George, Lord Beaverbrook, Sir James Barrie, H. G. Wells—praised it highly. Yet, despite the accolades, *Intolerance* ran only eight weeks in London. As in the United States, Mr. Griffith's sermon on peace and brotherhood ran counter to the temper of the British people at the time. Still, for Mr. Griffith it was a personal triumph, and he never ceased to talk to us about it for years to come.

Later we learned that he had been summoned to No. 10 Downing Street by the Prime Minister, Lloyd George, who told him that he had the greatest power in his hands for the control of men's minds that the world had ever seen. Mr. Griffith told me that Lloyd George had added, "I want you to go to work for France and England and make up America's mind to go to war with us."

The talk ended with the understanding that in exchange for partial financing and carte blanche to film anywhere in France or England, Mr. Griffith would undertake to make a propaganda film. Both governments would cooperate with troops, artillery, people—whatever would be needed to produce the film.

It was a fortunate offer for Mr. Griffith. He was at loose ends. Before *Intolerance* he had always known exactly what he was going to do next. But after *Intolerance* he was slow to make a decision, and when he did he would worry about whether he was right or wrong.

A devoted student of Napoleon's career, he had told me once: "Napoleon's downfall didn't come at Waterloo but on the day he lost the ability to make a quick decision. Decide—and decide quickly. Even if you're wrong, it's better that way."

When we were in Paris later that summer and Mr. Griffith took us on an all-night walk through the city, we went to the tomb of Napoleon. He spoke then of Napoleon's dreaming too big a dream for one man. "Perhaps I was dreaming too big a dream when I conceived *Intolerance*," he said. "I was reaching out—stretching beyond my talents. I was trying to say something to influence the whole world. Maybe it's not possible to reach out and speak with a message of compassion for the entire world. I should have confined myself to America and the English-speaking people—or to the Western world."

The United States declared war on Germany on April 6, 1917. The news was shattering to us. With Mr. Griffith, we had truly believed that President Wilson would keep us out of war. It was a time of innocence that must be difficult for young people today to comprehend. We were a simple, kindly, naïve people—about to receive a lesson in international diplomacy. In August 1914, when Germany invaded Belgium, our official policy had been neutrality. But a year later, after the British ship *Lusitania* was torpedoed and 114 Americans had been killed, it became increasingly difficult to maintain our position of neutrality. Finally, when the Germans initiated unrestricted submarine warfare, the United States entered the war. Yet many Americans were ambivalent in their feelings toward Germany, for many of them were of German heritage. A German name—as Billy Bitzer was to discover—could be a source of embarrassment.

Mr. Griffith cabled us that the State Department was arranging passage on the next boat for Mother and me. Meanwhile, he went up to the front to see the war at first hand.

The State Department arranged passage for us on the *St. Louis*, the first camouflaged ship to leave the United States after our declaration of war. We went with the first contingent of doctors and nurses from Presbyterian Hospital. For three days we zigzagged through the dangerous Atlantic without escort. All the nurses were ordered to sleep on deck with their life belts on. Mother and I had rubber suits with weighted feet and packets of emergency rations that would enable us to survive in the water for two weeks if the ship was torpedoed. We were the only civilians on board and felt grateful that we could sleep through the night in our cabin.

When we arrived in London, we found Mr. Griffith in great form. Over dinner the first night, he told us that our government would be sending Dorothy, Billy Bitzer, and Bobby Harron on the next big sailing. He then outlined his story for *Hearts of the World,* the propaganda film he was planning. The plot revolved around the lives of a group of individuals in a French village as it changed hands in the course of the war. Now that the United States was in the war, the purpose of the film would be to intensify the people's fighting mood. It seemed strange that Mr. Griffith, who had so fervently supported President Wilson because of his promise to keep us out of the war, should now be involved in a film to sell war.

Dorothy, Bobby, and Billy sailed for Europe on May 28 on the *Baltic,* a British ship. As the crossing on our smaller ship had taken ten days, we didn't expect that their crossing would take any longer. We did know that they were traveling in convoy with some very important person, and we feared that their ship might be a target for attack.

When it was time for the *Baltic* to dock, we went to Liverpool and waited and waited. The ninth day passed, the tenth, the eleventh, the twelfth. Mother was hollow-eyed from sleeplessness and sick with worry.

Dorothy later told me: "Originally, I wasn't supposed to go abroad, as you know. Mr. Griffith wanted other actresses for the part he had in mind. But they were afraid of the submarines, and as a last resort he took me. There was a lot of red tape involved in getting my passport. I went alone to the New York Immigration Office, and on the last day I was told in conference by an official in a hush-hush atmosphere that I would be sailing on the *Baltic.*

"This information scared the wits out of me. I thought that if the officials were telling me, then lots of people must be in on the secret, spies included, and we'd surely be sunk.

"But it seemed like a perfectly normal sailing. On board, I met the mother of Ivor Novello [who later acted in Mr. Griffith's *The*

White Rose] and she looked after me. I guess she knew I was frightened, never having been on an ocean voyage before.

"When we got out to the Ambrose Light, the sea was choppy. There had been no uniformed personnel on the pier when we left. And now tugs came up to the ship and men in uniform, carrying knapsacks, climbed aboard into the hold of the ship. The tugs were bouncing around on the waves like cork, and I couldn't bear to watch for long—I was afraid the soldiers would be crushed to death."

Two days out at sea General J. J. Pershing made an appearance, wearing civilian clothes. The women passengers rushed at him, and Dorothy felt sorry for the poor man. He was quite handsome and charming to everyone. One day when she was sitting on deck, he came by and said to her, "You've been avoiding me."

"No, General, I haven't," she answered, "but everyone else is after you."

"I know you," he continued, "because, when I was on the Mexican border, I saw your pictures." He then mentioned some of Dorothy's comedies. He was evidently referring to the time when he was leading the expedition against Pancho Villa.

"Tell me something about film making," he said. "In newsreels I get so uncomfortable I become self-conscious."

"We have a cameraman aboard, and we have film," Dorothy said. "Why don't we go up on deck some afternoon and practice shooting film of you? I'll talk to you, and you can answer me naturally."

General Pershing agreed, and they spent a pleasant afternoon filming on board. Dorothy later wondered what became of the film.

"Having Billy Bitzer aboard created suspicion wherever he went," Dorothy recalled, "because of his German name. When we arrived in England, we were all searched. A friend of mine had given me a bottle of holy water and a scapular medal, and I accepted her gifts gratefully, even though we are Episcopalian. When the inspectors in England came across the holy water, they were puzzled. Apparently, my explanations weren't reassuring enough, for they took the bottle away. Perhaps they thought it contained TNT.

"One evening there was entertainment on shipboard. General

. 189 .

Pershing told some anecdotes. Madame Novello sat down at the piano and announced she was going to sing a song which her son had just composed. Whereupon she launched into the warm sentimental notes of 'Keep the Home Fires Burning.'

"A convoy was supposed to meet us once we were in the danger zone, but we didn't rendezvous at the exact time, and for a day and a night we were without convoy. We were nervous because the moon was as bright as the sun.

"Altogether we were thirteen days at sea. When we arrived in Liverpool, a crack Welsh regiment came down to the ship to meet General Pershing. They had a goat—evidently their mascot—which had been groomed and barbered for the occasion. When a general came off the ship, even the goat stood at attention."

Finally, on that thirteenth day, two pale, anxious females kissed an excited Dorothy as she greeted us with the news that General Pershing and his staff were on board and had come to take over the American command.

We all stayed at the Savoy, where the staff took a personal interest in us. We had a sitting room and a bedroom on either side overlooking the Thames Embankment. We used the living room for rehearsals, as all the English studios were closed. We mapped out the scenes, and Billy timed them as best he could, with the four of us—Dorothy, me, Bobby, and Mother—playing all the parts.

Mr. Griffith loved England and its people. While he was there he made friends with many members of the aristocracy and was often invited to the great houses of England, among them Lord Beaverbrook's. Lady Paget, widow of the former Ambassador to the Court of Vienna, offered her estate to Mr. Griffith as a location. Mr. Griffith directed some of the most distinguished extras ever to appear in motion pictures: King George V and Queen Mary, Queen Mother Alexandra, Princess Bibesco of Romania, Lady Lavery, and Lady Diana Manners.

I later heard Lord Beaverbrook speak gratefully of Mr. Griffith's gaiety. They all needed it during that time, he said.

Mr. Griffith usually brought the latest gossip back to us at the hotel, and we listened like wide-eyed children.

Lillian in the great Griffith war film *Hearts of the World* (1918).

Lillian and Robert Harron in *Hearts of the World*.

Dorothy as the enchanting Little Disturber in *Hearts of the World*.

The formation of United Artists Corporation (1919), with Charlie Chaplin signing, Griffith and Mary Pickford at left, and Douglas Fairbanks at right.

Lillian, Richard Barthelmess, and Dorothy; Dick played leading man for both sisters.

Lillian and Robert Harron in *True Heart Susie* (1919), one of the rural poems that Griffith directed after World War I.

Lillian and Robert Harron in *True Heart Susie.*

Lillian as Lucy, the Girl, and Donald Crisp as Battling Burrows, her sadistic father, in Griffith's *Broken Blossoms* (1919).

Lillian in *Broken Blossoms*.

"That fellow Churchill!" he exclaimed. "Just as the talk becomes interesting, he gets me in a corner and starts telling me a story that he wants to sell me."

"Are they any good?" I asked.

"They're all right but no better than mine," he answered.

Lloyd George had suggested to Mr. Griffith, "Put him to work writing, Griffith. It will keep him out of mischief. Every time we let him out of our sight, he gets us into trouble." This conversation took place not long after the disastrous Dardanelles campaign.

Mr. Griffith told us that Lloyd George had teased him about the mediocrity of the American mind, whereupon he retorted that the Americans could only build on what the English had originally sent us.

While he was away one weekend Mother, Dorothy, and I explored London. One afternoon Mother paused to admire a Pekingese puppy in a store window. Seeing her and no doubt recognizing a kind face, the proprietress came out and begged Mother to give the little creature a home. A new law prohibited more than a certain number of dogs to a family, and the puppy would probably have to be destroyed. When Mother asked us if we would like a tiny Peke, we both exclaimed "no!" We would be leaving England for France shortly, and the journey ahead would be too strenuous for a little dog. Besides, we had always said that we weren't going to turn into old ladies who made fools of themselves over lapdogs. After we had registered our objections, Mother promptly brought him home, and Chu Chin Chow became part of an adoring family for the next twenty-one years. Mr. Griffith put Chu in his pocket when we went to Westminster Abbey, and Chu slept through the service with only one audible snore during prayer.

During a stroll we saw Queen Mother Alexandra riding through the streets in her carriage. It was her birthday. Everyone on the street either wore or carried a rose, and as she drove by the people tossed their flowers into her carriage. By the time she passed us she was sitting in a bower of pale-pink roses. It was a romantic image that is still vivid in my mind. She looked as we imagined that a queen should look.

Much of our time away from Mr. Griffith was spent on research, for we were to play French girls, and by the time we reached France it would be too late to start creating characters.

"I'm not going to introduce you to anyone here," Mr. Griffith told us. "I want you to spend every minute away from rehearsals learning to be better actresses."

He sent us to Victoria and Waterloo stations, where the soldiers embarked on the first leg of the journey to France. We saw the farewells, the last waves, and, for those left behind, the lonely walk out of the station. Even more shattering was the succession of casualties, the paraplegics, the amputees. London, unlike Paris, allowed its severely wounded into the city. (I am told, however, that the English kept their worst cases out of large cities during World War II.) At first, we made the mistake of taking Mother with us on these trips. But she would come home shaking and hysterical from such heartbreaking sights.

"It's only in wartime that emotions are off guard," Mr. Griffith said. "You want to be actresses, but you've never lived. You don't know what life is all about." He added grimly: "I hope you may never again have such an opportunity. But since it's here, I don't want you to miss it."

We were constantly alert for mannerisms, gestures, facial expressions that we could use. Once Mr. Griffith and I were walking in Whitechapel looking at people; we often found characters right out of Dickens there. We saw an Oliver Twist and were about to speak to the little fellow when Mr. Griffith grabbed my arm. He had spotted a girl with a remarkable shoulder-swinging walk.

"Oh, where is your sister? That's just the walk for Dorothy. Can you show her? We must use that walk—it's a darb!"

For an hour we followed the girl and then rushed back to demonstrate the walk to Dorothy. It was loose and from the shoulder, rather defiant and carefree. It became part of Dorothy's character as the Little Disturber in *Hearts of the World*.

Soon after Dorothy arrived in London a man from the post office came to our rooms to deliver a package. He mentioned that antiaircraft-gun practice was scheduled for 11:00 that morning and told us not to be alarmed when we heard the guns firing on top of the next building—the Hotel Cecil. As he was talking, we heard the firing begin.

"That's odd," he said, looking at his watch. "They've started ahead of time."

Just then Mr. Griffith appeared. "It's an air raid," he exclaimed. The floor waiter came in then and told us that if we went to the end of the corridor we could see the raid in progress. It was London's first daylight aerial bombardment. We saw the planes coming up over the Thames River in the distance. Soon they were nearing us, flying in perfect fan formation, and so low that we felt we could hit them with a stone. All antiaircraft guns were turned on them. Shrapnel was bursting all around, but the sight was so overwhelming that no one was able to move. The planes flew over the Houses of Parliament, where we thought they would surely drop their bombs. We held our breath; they broke formation and turned back. We rushed down the hall to another window, where we saw them going higher and higher and finally disappearing; we heard the bombing in the distance.

"They've hit somewhere," Mr. Griffith said. "Let's follow them."

He bribed a taxi to take us to Whitechapel, where bombs had exploded. Traffic was thick; everyone was curious about this first air raid. Bombs had ripped open a large section of the slums. Ragged children with knives dug up bits of shrapnel for souvenirs. We paused before a shattered building, now all rubble and acrid smoke. Women stood on the sidewalk, sobbing. Men with frozen faces clawed through the ruins looking for the bodies of victims.

"What was here?" I asked a bystander. "What building was this?"

He turned a tear-stained face to me. "It was a school. They were flying so high the bombs went through to the kindergarten before they exploded."

Mr. Griffith was crying too. "This is what war is," he said. "Not the parades and the conference tables—but children killed, lives destroyed." He shook his head and turned away.

The next day we learned that ninety-six children had been killed in that building.

We lived through many raids in London, including the first night bombings. No siren alarm system had yet been devised. Instead, as planes approached, policemen pedaled through the streets on their bicycles, blowing whistles and shouting: "Please—take cover. Take cover, please."

London was blacked out from the time we arrived. One evening at about 11:00 we were in our rooms—Mother in bed, Dorothy in the bathroom, and I combing my hair. It was about ten days after the first daylight bombardment. Without warning, there was a terrific noise. Mother sat up; Dorothy rushed out. The hotel lights went out. We groped our way to the windows and drew back the draperies. The Germans had dropped a bomb on a tramcar outside our windows on the Thames Embankment. It was a beautiful moonlit night. The silence was audible for a moment, then it was broken by the cries of the wounded.

Dorothy and I hurried Mother into the hall. I then rushed back to get Chu Chin Chow, who was hiding under the bed in terror, and ran out again. A woman in the suite next to us dashed out, went back for her jewel case, came back with it, and promptly fainted. Pearls, diamonds, emeralds, and rubies spilled all over the carpet, where they were all later found.

We went downstairs to find a safer place until the bombing stopped. We gathered in a spacious room where people were having dinner. A bomb fell nearby, and I overheard a young officer remark casually to his dinner partner, "Rawther noisy tonight, isn't it?"

An American woman huddled near us. She told us that she had been a survivor of the *Lusitania* sinking and had been rescued after clinging for hours to a deck chair in the water. She said that she didn't know which was worse—torpedoes at sea or raids on land.

The same night, I believe, bombs fell on nearby John Street, where James M. Barrie and George Bernard Shaw had apartments. An experimental theater was also hit, as was the Charing Cross Hospital. Dorothy and I got dressed at 4:00 in the morning. The concussion of the bombs had shattered windows, and pulverized glass lay like snow over the streets. We heard one old lady, deep in her cups, calling the German planes "devils" as she shook her fist at the sky. That was the harshest word we heard against the foe while we were in Europe.

There are incidents etched in my mind that evoke Dickens' London. Once we saw a large coal cart being pulled through the streets by a big dray horse. Women and children walked behind it, their aprons outstretched to catch bits of coal that bounced out of the cart.

And all the while the English endured the ordeal without complaint. "You can never lick such a people," Mr. Griffith said, shaking his head in admiration.

Dorothy and I went to Nathan's, the well-known theatrical costumers in London. In our enthusiasm, we dragged Mr. Griffith over to show him our discoveries. We exclaimed over the materials—how they would *move*. We always needed fabrics that would look heavy but wouldn't hamper us in walking or running. And the lovely rags! To my joy, Mr. Griffith allowed me to send three trunkloads of these "poor" clothes back to America. Anyone can make a new dress, but worn clothes, real rags, are rare. I still own some of these "cotton-stocking part" clothes.

Clarkson the wigmaker—affectionately called Willie—fashioned wigs for us. He worked with such intensity over his masterpieces that he would be wet with perspiration at the end of the fitting, while we listened, rapt, to his stories of the theater.

For my role in the film, I was to wear a short, blonde wig and many pads, even around my waist, to make me look like a strong peasant girl. Dorothy had a black wig to frame her face. Bobby Harron had sideburns, a small mustache, a loose tie, and a flowing cape. With his dark eyes, he looked very much the poetic French youth, his character in the film. Mother had several costumes, as she was to play background characters. There were so few of us that we all doubled in parts.

Mr. Griffith had toured the countryside looking for locations before we arrived in England. He wanted backgrounds that resembled France. The battle and other scenes of destruction would later actually be filmed in France. He finally chose the villages of Sheer and Broadway, and for a few weeks we stayed at the inn where Shakespeare was said to have written *A Midsummer Night's Dream.*

With us was a darling seventeen-year-old English boy, whom Mother promptly added to her brood. He had an original mind and a sense of theater. In one scene the French girl I was playing packed her possessions and left home just a few minutes ahead of the approaching Germans. This young actor was supposed to help me by pushing the loaded wheelbarrow down the street. At his own suggestion the boy pushed the wheelbarrow toward the camera instead of away from it. I am sure that if Mr. Griffith had not been so preoccupied with such a responsible assignment, he would have perceived the boy's extraordinary talent. The boy was Noël Coward, and this film was his first.

A short time ago, when Noel was in America to mark the publication of a book of short stories, we were reminiscing about that time. Noel remembered how kind Mother had been to him, how she saw to it that he didn't feel himself an outsider in our company. Years after, whenever Noel was in the United States, he made it a point to visit Mother, who was by then an invalid.

At last the time came for us to leave for Paris. It was the summer of 1917, and Paris was out of bounds, closed even to our soldiers on leave. Mr. Griffith took us to the American Embassy in London to apply for visas for our journey across the Channel. We were kept waiting. Finally a messenger came out. Mr. Griffith jumped up and was about to speak when the man said, "Are these the Gish girls from Massillon, Ohio?"

"Yes," Mother said, "they are."

"Well, then, will you kindly come into Mr. Skinner's office?"

We left the astonished Mr. Griffith and went into the private office. Robert Skinner, who was later to be Minister to Turkey, greeted us warmly. His wife had taught us at Trinity Church Sunday School while we were staying with Aunt Emily in Massillon. The problem, he told us, was not with our visas but with Wilhelm Gottlieb Bitzer's. At that time everyone of German heritage was suspect. The clerk told Mr. Griffith firmly, "We're sorry; we cannot accommodate you with Mr. Bitzer's visa."

When Mr. Griffith realized that he wasn't going to be able to bring Billy to France, he said to him, "Oh, why did your mother christen you Wilhelm Gottlieb?"

Although Billy never did receive permission to cross the Channel, Mr. Griffith was impressed by our acquaintance with Mr. Skinner. "Well, praise be to Massillon!" he exclaimed, and never mispronounced it again, not even in jest.

Mother accompanied us to France, determined to follow us even to the front. "There are only three members left of our family," she said resolutely, "and if one of us is going to die, all of us are going to die together."

Because of mines, we were turned back on the first, second, and third attempts to cross the Channel. Finally, on the fourth try, our little ship made it. Although Dorothy and I were both seasick, Mother wasn't afflicted, being too busy looking after others.

We arrived in Paris at midnight. There had been an air raid while we were on the train to Paris, and all the lights were out. A cab found its way through the moonlit streets to the Grand Hotel. Mother was exhausted after our dangerous journey, but Dorothy and I were too excited to be tired or frightened.

Mr. Griffith said to Bobby Harron, Dorothy, and me: "Now children, if you wish, I will show you what the most beautiful city in the world looks like with only the moon above it. You may never get another chance. When you come here in future years, the lights will be on, God willing."

The four of us set out, to the sound of constant bombardment in the distance. The eternal cannonading was to become a part of our lives during our stay. Air raids in London were sudden and frightening—silence first, then the bombardment, with noise that seemed to shatter our eardrums, and then silence again. In Paris, in contrast to London, the sound of war never ceased. But we found it reassuring—it meant that the French guns were between us and the enemy. In fact, we became so habituated to it that silence would have shocked us.

That night, however, the horrors of war seemed far away. We were young and in Paris, and Paris in the dark was beautiful. We walked until the lovely dawn bathed the city, along the Seine where Notre

. 197 .

Dame suddenly loomed up, down the avenues and boulevards, across the bridges, past the great monuments and fountains. And all the while Mr. Griffith beamed at us like a happy father.

Returning to the hotel, we found Mother trying to order breakfast. But her English and the waiter's French had no meeting ground. When I gave everybody's order in French, Mother, Dorothy, Mr. Griffith, and Bobby burst into laughter. It was just like one of those ads back home: Everybody laughed when I sat down at the piano.

But I had been studying French in secret, preparing myself for such an emergency. Everything I ordered arrived—to the surprise of everyone, especially me. I was looked upon with new respect by my mother and sister.

Mother took us to the great couturiers of the day—Poiret, Worth, and Lanvin—where we daringly ordered our first *haute couture* gowns. Mother's knowledge of fine fabrics and workmanship guided us in our selection. We weren't on salary then, but Mr. Griffith advanced us enough money to pay for the clothes.

A distinguished Frenchman was assigned as an interpreter to Mr. Griffith, and a charming white-haired gentlewoman was engaged as a companion for us. She was shocked that Mother allowed us to see all the French plays we wanted to see, especially one play that we planned to attend that was definitely not for young women. When she expressed her surprise, Mother reassured her. "Don't worry," Mother said optimistically, "they won't understand it."

Somewhat appeased by Mother's assurance that our French was too inadequate for us to comprehend the play, Madame accompanied us to the theater and translated the dialogue for us. But I understood enough to know that her translation was far removed from the words being spoken on the stage.

Madame did not understand what we were doing in France; she reasoned that if we were not of royal blood then we must be connected with someone high in our government, as Paris was then out of bounds to all but the most important war personnel. In fact, all the Frenchmen with whom we came in contact during this period treated us with deference on the same assumption.

No one knew what happened to us on the days we disappeared from the hotel. We were shooting up front and had to maintain complete secrecy. The credentials Mr. Griffith carried from Downing Street permitting him to go to the front lines were the envy of all war correspondents. The front wasn't far from Paris in those days. We went through the East Gate in two cars—one with Mr. Griffith, in a uniform of sorts, and his French soldier-cameraman for outdoor shots; the other with Bobby dressed as a French private, Dorothy and me with coats over our costumes and Mother. Although Mother was not in any of these scenes, she would never let us go without her.

We headed north to Senlis and then east. We passed ruined towns and abandoned trenches, bleak markers of the former battle lines. I remember the odd feeling I had seeing a coffee pot perched on top of a pile of rubble, the sole evidence that a house had once stood on the spot. Closer to the front, we saw acres of woodland and orchard scorched by shellfire. I have never forgotten the look of amazement on the faces of the soldiers we passed. What were three females doing up front? they seemed to ask.

Our first location was a village that had been destroyed when the Germans were advancing on Paris. We worked quickly, intensely, quietly—with no shouting from Mr. Griffith, only hurried tense orders, followed at once with precision by the three of us. The casualty list was high in the vicinity at that time.

After finishing, we moved to a dugout for a fast bite of lunch, which we had brought with us. Then we went up closer to the front for more scenes. We were in range of the long-distance guns. Shells and shrapnel fell close enough to make us nervous.

Whenever Mr. Griffith had scenes with us, he would shoot them and then escort us back to Paris. Otherwise he would go out to the front alone. This routine went on for weeks.

"Those salvoes you heard were part of a creeping barrage," he explained one night over dinner. We had been filming on a dangerous location earlier in the day. "The area just ahead of the trenches was being shelled, clearing the way for soldiers to advance. Then it swept forward across enemy positions." He added grimly that "sometimes a barrage was dropped on our own trenches, which were supposed to be already empty—just to make certain our troops were moving ahead."

I realize now that we were sent where even nurses weren't allowed to go. Nurses weren't expendable. Over the months we all became highly nervous and lost weight. Dorothy and I later recovered from the ordeal, but Mother never did. She had already gone through a great deal of stress and anxiety. She suffered a serious case of shell shock; she trembled so badly that she couldn't hold a cup in her hand without spilling its contents. This shock led to other ailments and contributed, I believe, to her early death.

One night, after we had been waiting anxiously, Mr. Griffith returned to the hotel, shaken and ashen-faced. "We were to meet some soldiers at the edge of the forest," he told us. "But just as we started out, the Germans stepped up the attack. We jumped into an old pillbox. We were hit. Two of our guides were killed. Then, across the woods, we saw the men we were supposed to meet. They were heading for the pillbox when a spray of shrapnel stopped them. We yelled at them to stay under cover. They couldn't hear us. They got up again—started running. Then six or seven shells landed right on top of them." He paused, his voice weary and heartsick. "When the smoke cleared, there was no sign of them. They were obliterated."

During the six months we were overseas Mr. Griffith made a film record of every type of armament and equipment used at the front. For once he was spared the task of research. He could film battle scenes as history staged them. He photographed actual infantry charges, men horribly wounded, men dying; the mud, the trenches, the machines of destruction. It was truly "history written in lightning."

Although the British War Office had subsidized the film, Mr. Griffith, because of his inability to keep track of his expenses, was actually out of pocket thousands of dollars by the end of the filming. But he didn't mention his indebtedness.

Because Mr. Griffith filmed all our scenes first, we weren't in a vulnerable position for long. Nevertheless, the work drained us. We were glad when he told us that we were going home.

Our ship bound for home had six eight-inch guns to protect us from the enemy. We awakened one morning to the sound of gunfire. Rushing into our life suits, we hurried on deck—to discover another boat nearby. It hadn't answered our signal to hoist its flag. Fearing it was an enemy boat shielding a submarine, our ship had opened fire across its bow. Our captain said the boat had put on its brakes so fast it skidded in the water. Up went a Scandinavian flag, and all hands on both ships waved friendly white handkerchiefs.

By late November 1917, we were back in the old studio at Hollywood and Sunset. Sets were built, the other roles were cast, and the company began rehearsing for the remaining scenes of *Hearts of the World*. Mr. Griffith immediately put us on a day-and-night schedule.

We all worked until midnight on Christmas Eve and all day Christmas. It was nearly New Year's Eve before Dorothy and I had a chance to open the presents under the tree that Mother had trimmed for us. We had been too immersed in the film to care about anything else. This picture was our contribution to the war effort, and we wanted it finished and released before the war ended.

Hearts of the World had its premiere at Clune's in March 1918 and opened a few weeks later in New York. The advertisements for the film carried the slogan, *Do You Want to Go to France?*, which I had suggested while we were discussing the exploitation. At that time, strangely enough, everyone was trying to get over there.

Hearts of the World enjoyed great success until the Armistice, when people lost interest in war films. The film inflamed audiences. Its depiction of German brutality bordered on the absurd. Whenever a German came near me, he beat me or kicked me. I remember particularly one scene in which I was badly beaten by a German soldier.

In the evening as I was taking my bath, Mother came in to scrub my back.

"Lillian, what in the world are those welts?" Mother exclaimed, dismayed.

Even though I had been padded during the shooting of the scene, the beating had still left marks.

I don't believe that Mr. Griffith ever forgave himself for making *Hearts of the World*. "War is the villain," he repeated, "not any particular people."

(In the 1920s, Mr. Griffith returned to Germany and made *Isn't Life Wonderful?* which was in effect an apology to the people whom he felt he had harmed in the earlier film. It was, in my opinion, a charming film, the best of the pictures Mr. Griffith made after I left him. It received a good press.)

Although it was Mr. Griffith's original intention to make only one war film, he had brought back enough footage—86,000 feet—to warrant doing three more. One of these was *The Great Love,* no prints of which now exist. Another was *The Greatest Thing in Life,* one of Mr. Griffith's best films and one of his most neglected. This film has also disappeared. Its theme was his favorite, the brotherhood of man. Treating the question of black and white in a new and daring way, it told the story of a prejudiced Southern officer who finds himself in the same shell hole with a Negro private. When he is hit the Negro rescues him, and in doing so is himself fatally wounded. As the Negro is dying, he cries for his mother, and the white man, pretending to be his mother, kisses him on the lips. It was a dramatic and touching scene, during which audiences sat tense and quiet.

When the film was completed, Mr. Griffith needed a title for it. One day I was lunching on cheese sandwiches and a malted milk with Mr. Griffith and Harry Carr, who was then head of our "idea" department. As the theme of the film was love, I suggested *The Greatest Thing in Life* as a title.

"That's it!" they both agreed.

In the future, whenever they were stymied about any problem, they would say, "Order her a malted and a cheese sandwich."

When I recall the long, stimulating hours we spent discussing ideas or promotion for a Griffith production, I find it rather sad to see that today the practice of having director and actor work together on creative publicity is no longer followed. In the Griffith days I helped to write story and subtitles, as well as ads. Now everything is departmentalized. An actress doesn't have to concern herself with the script. She memorizes her lines, goes to the studio, and says them. Somebody there dresses her hair. Somebody else makes up her face. In a film I made not long ago there were four people to help me prepare for my scenes: One did my face; another my neck, arms, and hands; another my hair; and the fourth dressed me.

The last of Mr. Griffith's war films was *The Girl Who Stayed at*

Home, of which *Film Daily* said, "D. W. Griffith's name will overcome a bad story." The writer added, interestingly enough, "It would be wise to emphasize Robert Harron, George Fawcett and two finds, Carol Dempster and Clarine Seymour, in advance publicity."

These young actresses had joined our growing company. Both were to become Griffith leading ladies. Clarine Seymour, a dark-haired, lovable little beauty who had great talent, won an instant response from audiences. Of the two, Carol Dempster, who had danced in *Intolerance,* seemed the more ambitious.

Of Mr. Griffith's war films, the late Francis Trevelyan Miller, the author and historian, said: "Hereafter history must be divided into four epochs—the stone age, the bronze age, the age of the printed page and the film age. You are the first of the great cinema historians."

Most war films after the Armistice were poorly received. People believed that war had been ended for all time. They wanted to forget about blood and havoc and sacrifices. They wanted to have fun. Although the reviews of *The Great Love* and *The Greatest Thing in Life* were favorable, people were looking to the future.

❧ 15 ❧

After Dorothy and I returned to Los Angeles, our salaries were raised. I was earning $500 a week. Mother rented a small house with a tennis court and a sleeping porch that Dorothy and I could use. We were working inside the studios most of the time, and we needed fresh air. Mother's shell shock had subsided, and we hoped that there would be no recurrence of her illness. The only lingering effect on Dorothy of our experiences abroad was an extreme sensitivity to noise. She complained that the blasting of the new subway reminded her of the bombings.

Dorothy's Little Disturber in *Hearts of the World* was an enormous success. She stole the film with her comic face and movements. No one was more pleased than I, because I had persuaded Mr. Griffith to use her rather than Constance Talmadge, who was his original choice.

Bobby Harron was still her only love. It was a childlike love affair, but I think they had unspoken dreams of marrying. As for me, I was in love with pictures and the man who created them—though not in the way that Dorothy loved Bobby. Mr. Griffith was the least domestic person I ever knew; I couldn't imagine him married to anyone. He had more interest in work than in private life. He liked his relatives and was usually generous with them, but he didn't want them near for long. He always looked uncomfortable in a house— out of place, caged in. The only surroundings in which he seemed comfortable were the studio, a hotel dining room, a lobby. He told me many times that he was trying to persuade his wife to divorce him. I secretly hoped that she would not; I felt sure that he would make an impossible husband were he to remarry.

Work was also the most important thing in my life. Other actors had lively parties about which we were to hear later, but our lives outside the studio were unexciting and circumspect. When I went to a party given by someone from the studio, it wasn't much fun for me. I have a sensitive nose and long hair, and smoke seems to be attracted to my head. So I either had to hang my head out a window or go home and wash my hair.

The Hollywood of *Sunset Boulevard* was never part of our lives. Mr. Griffith's players simply had no time to get into mischief even if they had wanted to. As the film industry grew, however, its occasional scandals provoked national debates on morality. Mr. Griffith was right in warning us to avoid scandal. The American public read avidly of the tragedy of Wallace Reid—the former kissing partner of our reluctant Dorothy—who died of drug addiction. Film personalities were targets for gossip and speculation.

Fans were avid for the intimate details of their lives, and writers began to spin those fabrications that would become known as "press releases." Filmgoers took a possessive interest in their stars and re-acted like righteous parents to news of filmdom's moral dereliction. The climate of the country was puritanical, and judgment of film stars was harsh and unforgiving.

That fame and money shook the inner balance of young players is understandable. Without discipline it was impossible for them to keep a hold on reality. We heard talk of fantastic mansions, custom-made cars, fabulous jewels, and wild parties. It was all far removed from our world, where a date ended at 10:00 because one was expected on the set, fresh and rested, at 8:00 the next morning.

One morning Mr. Griffith was driving me to our location for the day's filming when we passed a billboard advertising *The Greatest Thing in Life*. There was a huge picture of me on the billboard.

"That should be my picture, not yours," Mr. Griffith said. "It's my film."

I was looking out the window when he spoke, and I laughed, thinking he was joking. But, when I turned toward him, there was no smile on his face. In the silence that followed, I realized that he actually meant what he had said. I was puzzled. This was totally unlike the D. W. I knew. If he had felt this way before, there had been no sign of it, for he had never been petty or cruel.

The picture on the billboard was a still shot taken by Hendrick Sartov, and I wondered if that might be the source of his anger. Sartov had been my discovery. He was the portrait photographer to whom I had gone for still pictures for *Hearts of the World*. The portraits were most flattering. Naturally, I had shown them to D. W. and Billy Bitzer.

"Look at these. Why can't you make me look like that on the screen?" I said.

"Quite something," Mr. Griffith said tersely. Perhaps he didn't like my implied criticism of Billy. He added, as though speaking to a child, "Well, since you're so smart, get the photographer, and let him make you look like that."

"Oh, may I?"

"Certainly. But you'll have to do it on Sunday. We're too busy during the week."

I returned to Sartov's portrait studio and asked if he would like to work in motion pictures.

"I don't know anything about it," he said, "but I'm willing to try."

I arranged for him to be at the studio on a Sunday, and Billy promised to work with him.

Sartov was to take shots of me for *The Greatest Thing in Life*. He moved around, checking angles, setting up lights. Billy was most cooperative. Two big "heads" were taken of me, to be inserted into the film later. When we saw the rushes, we realized that they were special. Mr. Griffith thought them superior to any he and Billy had photographed. When they were shown on the screen at Clune's, the audience murmured "ah!" and then burst into applause.

Sartov had a job at the Hollywood Art Studio at the time, but shortly after he signed a contract with Mr. Griffith as a special-effects man, and went on to become a photographer on his films.

Mr. Griffith's contract with Adolph Zukor's Artcraft had called for six pictures to be released through Famous Players-Lasky, or Paramount, as it came to be known. He was to receive $250,000 when he delivered each negative and a large percentage of the earnings. Although Mr. Griffith retained ownership of *Hearts of the World,* the six films he produced after it belonged to Paramount.

In January 1919 it was announced that Mary Pickford, Douglas Fairbanks, Charlie Chaplin, and D. W. Griffith, possibly the greatest powerhouse of box-office talent in Hollywood at that time, had formed their own producing-distributing company, United Artists. They would direct and supervise their own productions, and the company would distribute and exhibit them. Their aim was to escape the restrictions imposed by the front office and to keep for themselves the profits their films made. Each was to release four pictures a year.

Not long afterward and before his last three pictures were made for Artcraft, Mr. Griffith signed with First National to make three pictures at $285,000 apiece. He was counting on the profits of these films to finance those for the new company.

For Zukor he quickly made *A Romance of Happy Valley,* a rural comedy with Bobby Harron and me, based in part on Mr. Griffith's own life. It was set in Kentucky, his own birthplace, and told the story of a youth who leaves home, makes a fortune in the big city, and returns to distribute largess to his needy family. In this film he vividly recreated the camp meetings of the Southern revivalists. When he directed these scenes for the film, a bystander said, "If that man had gone into the ministry instead of motion pictures, he would have become another Dwight Moody."

For years, no copy of *A Romance of Happy Valley* could be found, and we were convinced that the film was lost. But Eileen Bowser recently discovered it in Russia, and by a series of "trades" she managed to bring it to the Department of Film of the Museum of Modern Art in New York.

It was a simple film, with a quality of innocence, of life seen through the eyes of the young. A review in the June 2, 1919, issue of *The New York Times* remarked that Mr. Griffith "has brought meaningful humanity to the screen, more nearly pure, less mixed with artificiality than it has been in a motion picture play, except in other works of Mr. Griffith's, next to the best of which, considering its pretensions, it holds its own."

His next rural poem was *True Heart Susie,* a variation on *David Copperfield,* made in the spring of 1919. It is the story of Susie, a "plain and simple" country girl who is too naïve and forthright to scheme for a husband.

I played the part of Susie. Mr. Griffith wanted Susie, like Cinderella, to be regarded by the audience as plain at first. In most scenes, I wore a shapeless long dress covered with a pinafore and a small, humorous hat pulled down squarely across my forehead. Other details conveyed Susie's character. I held my arms rigidly at my sides. As I tagged after William, the boy Susie loves, I walked with little, quick, determined steps. In one scene, Susie, though a timid girl, gives a mischievous smile that suggests another, hidden side of her. At the end, as she and the boy walk up the road away from the viewer, she gives a quick joyous kick of her foot.

Of this performance Eileen Bowser said: "Her skillful acting makes the sentimental story genuinely moving . . . and as the naïve but faithful Susie, she grows in stature from a funny, happy adolescent to a dignified woman. . . . Of all Griffith's leading women, Lillian Gish alone could have risen above the cloying sweetness of the role."

Each of the rural films was sympathetically received by reviewers, simply because Mr. Griffith had made them. But obviously they were expecting more from him, and I suspected that he was expecting more from himself.

Traveling about the world later, I found that *True Heart Susie* was one of Griffith's most respected films. I was pleasantly surprised to learn that it was included in the film library at Buckingham Palace and the favorite of Queen Mother Alexandra.

By that time Mr. Griffith was no longer really directing me. He told a friend, "I give her the outline of what I hope to accomplish and let her work it out in her own way."

I was happy working for D. W. He didn't restrict me, he allowed me to be creative, and he listened to me. Of that period, Eileen Bowser has written, "The next few years might be called 'the Gish period' in Griffith's career, with Lillian Gish playing the lead in one film after another, continuously growing in stature as an actress."

"And then," Dorothy usually finished the story, "I slammed the door on a million dollars."

She always told the story with humorous pride, but it was quite true. After *Hearts of the World,* Paramount came to Mr. Griffith and told him that the company wanted to sign one of the Gish girls to a contract. He discussed it with me. I then talked it over with Mother, and we decided that it would be best for Dorothy to take the contract. She was then a Griffith player, but by the terms of the new contract to be made with Paramount and Mr. Griffith she would star in seven films that would earn her a total of a million dollars.

Mother didn't go with Dorothy to the conference at which the contract was to be discussed, thinking it would be good for her to handle it on her own. Dorothy attended the conference, listened politely, and then just as politely said "no."

When she reported her response to us, I asked startled, "Why did you turn it down?"

"A million dollars—at my age," Dorothy replied blithely. "Why, it would have ruined me."

Instead she began work on a series of comedies produced by Mr. Griffith and directed by Elmer Clifton, Chet Withey, F. Richard Jones, and others. They were known as the Dorothy Gish Artcraft Series and were highly successful.

Her costar in many of them was Richard Barthelmess, who had the most beautiful face of any man who ever went before a camera.

Richard's mother was an actress, who had taught the Russian star Alla Nazimova to speak English. Nazimova had given him a bit part in a picture. When Dorothy saw him in the film, she said, "I want him for my pictures."

Dorothy had an instinct for picking potential stars. She discovered another young man, slender and dark-haired, and had him cast as a gigolo in one of her pictures, *Out of Luck*. In one scene the gigolo was supposed to be making love in a café to a rich woman. Mr. Griffith came over to watch rehearsals and was pleased with the young man's performance. As he often did, he suggested a bit of "business" for the scene. The gigolo is sitting beside the woman, who is wearing pearls. As she turns her head to watch the dancers, he picks up her strand of pearls, singles one out, and tests it with his teeth to see if it is real. It was a perfect touch for the character and has since been copied many times with equal success.

While Dorothy was making this film, Mr. Griffith was rehearsing a Western called *Scarlet Days* about a Mexican bandit at the time of the Gold Rush. Dorothy thought her discovery would make a better Latin than Richard Barthelmess, who was to play the lead. When she expressed her opinion to Mr. Griffith, he shook his head. "I agree with you, Dorothy. But women are apt to find him too foreign-looking."

It was a strange miscalculation for him to make.

Dorothy couldn't use the young man again because he took so long to dress and her pictures had to be turned out quickly. But Rudolph Valentino went on to play the lead in *The Four Horsemen of the Apocalypse* and became the idol of women everywhere.

"Well, I was wrong in that," Mr. Griffith admitted to me. "Now they apparently like these foreign fellows. I thought they only liked the American type. Maybe they're changing."

When we knew him, Valentino was simple, unpretentious, very much the Italian gentleman. Bobby Harron brought him into the group because he was shy and a newcomer. Dorothy, Bobby, Rudolph, and I, along with other friends, would go riding together. Rudolph rode well; his two great loves were horses and dancing. He had many talents; he designed riding clothes for Dorothy and me, and

. 211 .

he was a good cook. Often on our return from an evening canter, he would go into our kitchen and cook spaghetti for us.

Dorothy's constant companion at that time was Constance Talmadge, who was as vivacious and outgoing as Dorothy. When she came into a room, people would smile in anticipation of her antics. A friend once described them as "two young puppies, standing on their hind legs, wagging their front paws at each other."

Mr. Griffith used to call them "brainless" on the set. "Dorothy hasn't got a brain in her head," he would say affectionately, "and the same goes for Constance. Come here—you two brainless ones!" Dorothy and Constance, knowing that he loved them, would ignore his gibes and continue to clown.

The two girls were inseparable. Constance spent so much time at our house that Mrs. Talmadge packed a valise of her clothes and sent them to us. "No use keeping her clothes," she told Mother, "since she's never here."

When we were discussing our early friends once, Dorothy recalled that Constance, even in adolescence, was beautiful—tall, with expressive brown eyes heavily outlined with dark lashes. "She used them shamelessly to get her way, particularly with Mr. Griffith."

Dorothy had developed a sudden interest in baseball at the time *Intolerance* was being made. A friend had taken her to a baseball game, and they had sat so far up in the bleachers that the whole game seemed to be in pantomime. When there was an argument between two players and the umpire, the behavior of the players, gesticulating wildly, and the response of the umpire, shaking his finger at them, struck Dorothy as hilariously funny. After this introduction to the game, she became a staunch fan.

Connie shared her interest in the sport. "While Connie was working in *Intolerance*," Dorothy told me, "I often had the afternoon off. Usually Connie would ask me in the morning, 'Where are you going today?' and I'd tell her to a ball game. She would brighten. 'Maybe I could go too,' she'd say, and of course nothing could have pleased me more.

"If Mr. Griffith was shooting a scene she wasn't in or if she were about to be made up for a scene to be filmed later on in the afternoon, she'd approach him and announce: 'I feel *terrible!* I don't know *how* I'm going to work today.'

"Mr. Griffith would say, 'Well, I'll shoot around you.'

"And off we'd trot to the ball game.

"I don't think anyone else could have got away with it, but Connie did.

"Nobody ever caught her in any of her little fibs, and I used to envy her talent for changing the truth to please herself. Had I lied, even small white lies, I'd have been caught. But not Connie."

Dorothy was always frank with D. W. and said precisely what she thought, which was not the best approach with him. I had learned to be more tactful; if I had a suggestion, I would often preface it by saying, "Do you remember, Mr. Griffith, the other day you said . . ."

During this period, Dorothy and I wrote character sketches of each other for *Stage* magazine. I wrote of her:

> She is a criticism of all the things I am not. When I look at her, I always miss in myself the qualities that I was born without and that, I daresay, I should have been much happier with. She is laughter, even on the cloudy days of life; nothing bothers her or saddens her or concerns her lastingly. Trouble gives only an evanescent shadow to her eyes and is banished with a shrug of a shoulder.
>
> Work to her, however, is play. Had she been born a boy, she would, I feel certain, have smeared her face with brown butternut oil and gone 'round the world with a hurdy-gurdy, waking up sleepy old people behind closed windows. She takes nothing seriously but her mother, her meals and her dog.
>
> I envy this dear darling Dorothy with all my heart, for she is the side of me that God left out. Her funny stories, her delight in sitting on men's hats, her ability to interest herself in a hundred and one people in whom she has not the slightest interest, her talent for quick and warm friendships, her philosophy of silver linings—why was I denied these?
>
> I surely take no pleasure in being the rather melancholy

person I am. I, too, would like to believe in all the lovely rainbows in which Dorothy believes. I, too, would surely be happy to find some day that hard work was not hard work at all but just a charming pastime. Unfortunately for me, however, a Klieg light is just a Klieg light and not the English moon.

All my life I have wanted to play happily as she does, only to find myself bad at playing. As a little girl, I wasn't much good at playing and I find that, try as I will, I don't play very convincingly today.

When Dorothy goes in swimming, she splashes the ocean into a beautifully gala muss; I just go in swimming. When she dances, there is no tomorrow; when I dance the trombone always stubbornly reminds me of a director in a bad mood. When she goes to a party, the party becomes a party; when I go to one, I'm afraid it very often stops being a party. And I don't like it. I want to be like she is.

I am not unhappy. I simply am not gay. It must have rained on the evening I was born, and it seems arbitrarily to have kept on raining in my heart ever since. She, as I once heard a girl described in a play, is like "a bright flag flying in the breeze."

The world to her is a big picnic with a great merry-go-round and lots of popcorn and wonderful balloons. All music, even the worst, seems so beautiful to her. All people amuse her. She even has fun getting her feet wet. I have fun too, but it is only the joy I get out of apparently never-ending work—and what kind of fun, I'd like to ask, is that?

And Dorothy wrote equally frankly of me:

The tradition which has grown up around Lillian seems to be that she is a shy helpless bit of fragility, drifting around in a sweet gentle daze. If she's really like that, "maybe I'm wrong" as the Two Blackbirds are fond of saying.

It's perfectly possible that I am wrong. I have a growing suspicion that two people can live for years in close proximity and never understand each other. I must confess that Lillian's idea of me, revealed every now and then, certainly differs startlingly from my own idea of myself. Perhaps we're both

wrong—and right. As in the Pirandello play, "Right you are—
if you think you are."

At any rate, the popular conception of Lillian as soft and
dreamy makes me think a little of the "gag" used too often
in the comic strips. A hat lies upon the sidewalk; some person
kicks it enthusiastically and finds to his astonishment and pain
that there is hidden inside it a brick or a flatiron.

Anyone who has tried kicking Lillian has discovered the
solidity of that resistance. Life has stubbed its toe, often and
often, trying to disorganize her stability. She remains steadfast, unshaken, imperturbable.

How I envy her the singleness of purpose, the inde-
fatigability, the unabating seriousness which have taken her
straight to the heights she has reached and will carry her on
and on! Nothing really matters to her except her work and
her career. She has little time or patience for anything or anybody unrelated to her work. Her eyes are fixed on her goal;
her ears are attuned only to the voice of her duty. If she misses
some of the beautiful shyer souls that require a patient search,
of which the reward is only a flash, perhaps, of beauty—why,
that is the sacrifice she must make and she makes it willingly,
almost scornfully. That is why she is where she is today.

She is blessed with a constitution that can respond to any
demand. Long after I am ready to be hauled off on a shutter,
she, apparently so frail, can go on tirelessly, unruffled, cool and
calm. That exquisite complexion of hers, that lovely lineless
face—these she owes to her serenity, her unfailing poise. What
a priceless combination for an artist! Unswerving ambition,
deep seriousness of purpose, and not a nerve in her body!

I wish with all my heart that I could see my life so clearly,
so wholly, so free from confusion and march with such firm
vigor toward achievement. Mother and I tease her at times
about her remorseless activity. One of our pet names for her
is The Iron Horse. A favorite family joke of ours is to the
effect that "we hope neither of us dies while Lillian is doing a
picture." We laugh—but we admire.

Don't think she has no lighter moments. There are a number of persons whose minds or personalities she respects, and
she finds great happiness in their company. In literature and

the theater, she demands the best, and gets it. She will not spare a moment for a book or a play until she has made sure it is worthy, and thus she eliminates all waste motion.

She is to me a never-ending source of astonishment and admiration. And I never cease to wonder at my luck in having for my sister the woman who, more than any other woman in America, possesses all the qualities of true greatness.

☙ 16 ❧

In the fall of 1918, Mary Pickford and Douglas Fairbanks had brought to D. W.'s attention Thomas Burke's collection of short stories, *Limehouse Nights.*

"There's a great story in it called 'The Chink and the Child,'" Doug told Mr. Griffith. "You could make a wonderful picture of it."

Set in the misty gloom of London's Limehouse district, it told of three ill-fated characters: Battling Burrows, a sadistic prize fighter; his twelve-year-old daughter Lucy, whom he brutally beats whenever he is drunk or angry; and an idealistic Chinese, Cheng Huan, a poet who had come to England during World War I to bring the peace of Buddha to the warring West. One day, after a terrible beating from Burrows, Lucy escapes from her locked room and crawls, bleeding badly and half crazed with pain and terror, into the street. Cheng finds her and carries her to his room, cleans her wounds, dresses her in silken robes, and puts her on a couch with a doll. A spy brings the news to Burrows, and he, suspecting something "unnacherel," storms out to find Lucy. He breaks into Cheng's room while the Chinese is absent and drags Lucy home. The terrified girl breaks away from him and locks herself in a closet. Burrows finally breaks down the door and beats his child to death. When Cheng finds Lucy gone, he hurries to the boxer's rooms, kills Burrows, and returns carrying the body of his "broken blossom" through the shadowy alleys of Limehouse to his own room. There, before a little altar, he puts a knife through his heart.

Shortly after reading it, Mr. Griffith told me that he was going to film the story with me in the role of Lucy. I objected. I didn't want to play a twelve-year-old.

"I'm too tall, Mr. Griffith," I told him. "You find an eight- or nine-year-old—she'll look twelve on the screen anyway—and I'll work with her and help her with the scenes. Besides," I added truthfully, "I don't feel well."

It was the first time I had ever complained, and Mr. Griffith brushed it aside.

"You go up to Wardrobe and see Mrs. Jones. Find something to make you look the part. You know well enough no eight-year-old can play those scenes at the end, when her father drags her home and beats her to death."

I crawled up to the room where our costumes were fixed. "Mrs. Jones," I said to the wardrobe mistress, "I feel awful."

"You've most likely got a cold," she said.

I asked her to adjust the fit of the dress that I had bought in London for *Hearts of the World*. As I had worn it under a coat in that film, I could wear it again for the new picture. Then I decided to walk home, hoping that the exercise would make me feel better.

I soon realized that the walk home might be more than I could manage. I felt weak and dizzy. There were no benches on the street where I could rest, and several times I had to lie down—under bushes, behind a privet fence, any place out of sight of passers-by— to regain enough strength to continue. My journey home took four hours. I managed to get into the house just before dark and literally crawled up the back stairs so that no one would see me. I collapsed on the bed, where Mother found me. She hurriedly called a doctor. By the time he arrived, I was delirious, with a temperature of 106 degrees. The doctor told Mother that I had Spanish influenza, which was then sweeping the country. In that epidemic more people lost their lives than were killed in the war. Coffins could not be made fast enough; in many sections the dead were buried in mass graves.

At our little studio five died, including Tessie Harron, Bobby's sister, who was terrified when she realized that she had the disease. I wasn't frightened; I was too sick to care.

It was impossible to find a nurse at that time. Mother worried about Dorothy. Dorothy wanted to catch the virus so that she wouldn't have to leave home. She would come into my room, lean over my sick bed, and breathe deeply. Finally, Mother sent her to the Talmadges, but she herself stayed home to nurse me. Fortunately, she soon found a fine nurse to relieve her.

One morning in November, after the fever had abated, I thought I was delirious again, for I heard bells ringing, whistles blowing, cars sounding their horns. But Mother brought the good news that the war was over.

From that moment on, I started to improve—perhaps because, having seen the war at first hand, I had been even more disturbed by it than most people. Then too, letters poured in from my friends and relatives, as well as messages from the studio that everyone was praying for my recovery. D. W. sent word that neither he nor anyone had been able to work properly since my illness.

Feeling loved and needed, I made a quick recovery. Still wearing a medical mask, I reported for work and began rehearsing Lucy. Dick Barthelmess was to play Cheng. In order to give a Chinese cast to his features, he wore a tight rubber band under his black Chinese cap. He managed to look Oriental without the use of obvious makeup. Donald Crisp, a big burly man, was chosen for the part of Battling Burrows.

As usual, we worked long hours. It was the worst time to be working so hard, for the epidemic still had not subsided. Mr. Griffith's almost neurotic fear of germs was particularly acute at that time. Nothing could keep him from his work, but throughout the shooting he forced me to wear my face mask whenever I was off camera. And he was careful not to come within ten feet of me.

One day we were rehearsing the scene in which Lucy's father throws a spoon at her, just to see her jump. He then complains that she never smiles. Without thinking I pushed up the corners of my mouth with two fingers.

Mr. Griffith, who was sitting across the hall from us, jumped up.

"Hold it! That's great! I've never seen a gesture like it. We'll use it all through the picture." He even forgot not to come near me in his excitement. "When did you think that up, Miss Gish?"

"I didn't, Mr. Griffith; it just happened," I answered, not knowing that this gesture was to become a kind of trademark for me around the world.

The scene of the terrified child alone in the closet could probably not be filmed today. To watch Lucy's hysteria was excruciating enough in a silent picture; a sound track would have made it unbearable. When we filmed it I played the scene with complete lack of restraint, turning around and around like a tortured animal. When I finished, there was a hush in the studio.

Mr. Griffith finally whispered, "My God, why didn't you warn me you were going to do that?"

Donald Crisp was directing a film at Paramount, so all his scenes were shot at night and on Sundays. The little thin dress that I wore was inadequate protection against the cold winter nights. Dorothy announced, "If Mr. Griffith works my sister to death, I'll get a gun and shoot him."

To simulate the night fog of London, they used a fine spray of water and carried smoke pots through the drizzle. These scenes were later justly praised for their beauty.

The Chink and the Child was completed in eighteen days and nights.

In rehearsals we had timed the film so perfectly that, when it was first cut and put together, it was only 200 feet over. There were no retakes. Several weeks later Jimmy Smith, who was cutting the film, said to me: "What's the matter with the Boss? I can't get him to look at the picture. Why doesn't he get it ready?"

I asked Mr. Griffith why he hadn't seen it.

"I can't look at the damn thing; it depresses me so," he said. "Why did I ever do a story like that? It will drive the audience out of the theater, providing you can persuade them to come in and look. I was a fool to do such a story."

But as he began to work on the cutting, writing titles and working on the score with the composer, Louis F. Gottschalk, he began to appreciate its poetic quality and finally with great pride took it to Paramount.

Adolph Zukor's reaction was explosive.

"You bring me a picture like this and want money for it? You may as well put your hand in my pocket and steal it. Everybody in it dies. It isn't commercial."

Mr. Griffith stalked out. He came back in a few days with $250,000 and threw it on Zukor's desk: "Here is the money. And here is the contract signing it over to me. Now you give me my negative and print."

He never told me where he obtained the money, but I assume it was from a bank, as his signature at that time was good enough to borrow on and interest rates were not high.

It was agreed that *Broken Blossoms,* as the film was now called, would be distributed by United Artists as its first release.

For its New York opening, Mr. Griffith leased the George M. Cohan Theatre on Broadway and Forty-second Street. Before the opening he decided to film, on the stage of the theater, a prologue of Carol Dempster dancing. One day he ran the film at the theater during the dance rehearsal. The stage lights that he had ordered for the dance prologue were on while the film was being shown, and blue and gold lights were accidentally thrown onto the screen. The effect was startling, and Mr. Griffith incorporated the results into the final movie, by having sections of the film tinted in the laboratory.

Mother and I happened to be watching the screening that day. When the curtain came down, we heard the most awful noises back-stage—shouts and screams and the sound of furniture being smashed. We rushed back to find Morris Gest, Mr. Belasco's son-in-law, breaking chairs, kicking props, and yelling at the top of his voice that this was the greatest so-and-so thing Broadway had ever seen. And instead of a $3 admission, people should pay $300 to get in!

His enthusiasm was both frightening and thrilling.

"Mr. Gest, if you feel that way," Mr. Griffith said, "will you handle the picture for us?"

Mr. Gest smiled. "It would be a privilege, Mr. Griffith."

Broken Blossoms opened in New York on May 13, 1919. Although Mr. Griffith had started production on it in the winter of 1918, his refusal to look at it for so long had delayed its release. The audience was deeply moved. The reviews exceeded in praise any picture I was ever in. One New York paper reported, "One can think only of the classics, and of the masterly paintings remembered through the ages; so exquisite, so fragile, so beautifully and fragrantly poetic is *Broken Blossoms.*" Another said that this film ought to be the Bible in the hand of every director making films in the future. The New York *Call* wrote: "He has far exceeded the power of the written word. It would be impossible for the greatest master of language to picture the emotions as Griffith has perpetuated them." No picture up to that time had received such worldwide critical praise.

Edward Wagenknecht, Professor of English at Boston University, wrote, "But so far as the players are concerned, *Broken Blossoms* is Lillian's film first of all, and the deep sincerity of her terror and passion seem all the more moving and remarkable for always being conceived and projected as the terror and passion of a child."

Richard Barthelmess also received raves for his sensitive portrayal of Cheng.

Broken Blossoms set a new style with its moody lighting and soft-focus photography. It influenced film makers all over the world, especially German, French, and Russian directors.

Though *Broken Blossoms* was a shorter film—an hour and twenty minutes—than Mr. Griffith's epics, people were willing to pay $3 a seat to see it, a record for that time. All Griffith pictures were compared to *The Birth of a Nation* when it came to making money. Whenever his other productions didn't achieve those fantastic profits, the trade deemed them failures. But *Broken Blossoms* was a tremendous success, and proved that a film didn't have to have a chase or a rescue or a happy ending to hold an audience.

Back in California Mr. Griffith hastily filmed the first of the three pictures that he had contracted to make for First National, *The Greatest Question.* Then in the fall of 1919 he moved his entire company to Mamaroneck, New York, where he had bought an estate.

The estate, which he intended to convert into a studio, was located on Orienta Point, a great peninsula of land jutting out into Long Island Sound and surrounded by a sea wall of rocks and glorious old trees with branches chained together to withstand the sweeping winter winds. It had a pier from which one could swim. Mr. Griffith added a big stage and a projection room to the house and remodeled the old mansion to accommodate offices and dressing rooms for his players. The magnificent old dining room, which was at least thirty feet square, became a rehearsal room. The butler's pantry was turned into an office for Agnes Wiener, his secretary. There was no kitchen in the big house; the studio restaurant was in a separate building. Mr. Griffith had a cottage built near the beach for his private dwelling. None of the people at the studio ever saw the inside of that cottage. He brought with him from California a Japanese couple, who lived in the cottage with him. The husband was his chauffeur, on duty day and night. "D. W. didn't have any home life," Agnes told me, "and he didn't give his staff much chance at a home life either."

He stayed at the Claridge Hotel in New York while he was waiting for the studio to be finished and rehearsed his company there. One day he called me at the Commodore, where Mother, Dorothy, and I were staying until we found a suitable house in Mamaroneck, and asked me to have dinner with him. Over our meal at the Claridge he said suddenly, "I don't want to break up a happy family, but how would you like to direct Dorothy's next picture?"

I stared at him, dumbfounded.

"You know as much as I do about making pictures," he went on. "If you work with Dorothy, it would free her director, Elmer Clifton, to help me in Florida." He was planning to film the exteriors of his two remaining pictures for First National there. While he was gone, he added, he hoped that I would also supervise the completion of the studio. Why he wanted to leave such an enormous job to an inexperienced girl is still beyond my comprehension.

I had always believed that Dorothy's gaiety and humor had never been completely captured on film. Perhaps I could do it after all, I thought. When I mentioned it to Dorothy, she was agreeable.

In the search for a story, Dorothy happened on a magazine cartoon that intrigued her. A husband complains to his wife that she is so dowdy that no one ever notices her. She is furious with him. She'll show him who's unattractive! So she tells him to follow her down the street. She walks ahead and makes faces, both enticing and comic, at every man who passes her. Naturally, each one turns around to look at her. We wrote an entire story around this absurd situation.

Dorothy found a handsome leading man from the theater, James Rennie. Before Mr. Griffith left, he saw the rehearsals and liked them. We wanted Dorothy Parker, whom we considered witty, to do the subtitles, and he agreed. Luckily she accepted and made her screen-writing debut with us. I remember one subtitle that she wrote for a scene in which Jim Rennie was in a barber shop having his nails done: "The divinity that shapes our ends."

When Mr. Griffith left for Florida, he took most of the staff with him. In addition to preparing for the film, I was obliged to see to the completion of the studio.

I also had to have miles of telegraph poles laid before the heavy wires needed for the extra load of lights could be hung, as well as having the sets built—all under the pressure of time, which is the most expensive commodity in a production. In New York I selected all the furniture and props for the sets that Huck Wortman was building. Not wanting to shake his confidence in me, I gave the dimensions for our large drawing room set myself, but they turned out to be all wrong. When our cameraman couldn't photograph the entire room without shooting over the back wall, he threw a tantrum, tearing his hair and yelling. The war had affected his nerves, and handling him was another problem.

It was late November and we had no heat. The weather turned so cold that we couldn't photograph our actors indoors without photographing their breaths. It looked as if they were smoking at each other. We hurriedly transferred to a small studio in New Rochelle while a furnace large enough to heat the new studio was installed.

Dorothy also presented difficulties. She had her own ideas; I had mine. Finally I got her interested in our new leading man, rehearsing their love scenes over and over, so that she would leave me alone. Had I known it would result in an unsuccessful marriage some months later, I wouldn't have done it.

Mae Marsh's younger sister Mildred was playing a secondary role. Mildred was tall, slim, pretty. Dorothy was petite and round. I planned one scene that would include Dorothy as the bride and Mildred as her bridesmaid. The contrast between the two girls was so charming that I wanted them to come down the stairs together. But Dorothy was furious with me. She wanted to descend the staircase alone. I persuaded her to let me shoot it both ways, and when she saw the rushes she agreed that what I wanted was right.

I couldn't sleep at night or even rest for worrying about all my problems.

Meanwhile, headlines proclaimed that Mr. Griffith was missing after he and his company of twenty had sailed on the yacht *The Grey Duck* from Miami for Nassau on a Wednesday morning. Planes and a coast-guard cutter took up the search and on the third day found them all waiting helplessly in a cove. This episode didn't help my state of mind.

I had been allowed a $50,000 budget, but my money was running low. I knew it was imperative to complete the picture in order to save on salaries extended over the holidays. Our last scenes were scheduled for two days before Christmas. They were to be taken atop a Fifth Avenue bus, as Dorothy looked down on a passing car that carried her husband and another woman. Then I discovered that in order to make films on the streets of New York, a permit was required. It would take several days to obtain a permit. Time was short. The alternative was running the risk of going to jail.

"Will you take the chance?" I asked my company.

"Yes!" they agreed.

We went ahead. As we turned onto Fifth Avenue at Fifty-seventh Street, heading south, a policeman looked up at me standing by the camera, raised his hand to stop me—and looked again. Suddenly he put his fingers to his mouth, pushed up the corners in the smile I had made familiar in *Broken Blossoms,* and pointed to me as if to say, "Am I right?"

"Yes," I nodded.

He really smiled then and nodded back, "Go ahead."

The picture—called *Remodeling Her Husband*—was finished Christmas week. We brought it in for $58,000, and it turned out to be the second biggest money maker of all Dorothy's films for Paramount. Mr. Griffith was later generous enough to say that the first two reels were as good as anything he had ever done. But I knew he was only being kind.

After my experience with *Remodeling Her Husband,* I was cured of any desire to make films. I had acquired a new respect for directors. Now I understand why they think every inch of film is theirs. Mr. Griffith's resentment at seeing my picture on the billboard for *The Greatest Thing in Life* became clearer to me.

When the company came back from Florida, the studio was in perfect condition for them to take their interior shots. Mr. Griffith finished the two films quickly.

When I asked him why he had left me with such chaos to contend with, he laughed. "I knew the men would work harder and faster to help a girl. I'm no fool."

"I think it was unfair," I retorted. "I never want to direct another film."

"Why shouldn't you? You know as much about making pictures as I do, and you know more about acting for them than anyone else."

I thought that he was teasing me until I read in one of his interviews that he had said the same thing to the press.

About that time Mother leased an old house that Stanford White had designed, in Mamaroneck. Every room had a fireplace. There was a spacious porch and an acre of beautiful landscaping. We loved it. We who had used trolleys for so long now had three cars in the garage—a big Cadillac, Dorothy's sports roadster, and a small Ford for the staff. We brought from the Coast our wonderful chauffeur-handyman, Harry Sabata. Our cook, Anna, was skinny, energetic, and highly resourceful. One morning before dawn I came down to the kitchen and found Anna at the range, holding an umbrella over her head while she cooked bacon. The leaking roof wouldn't deter her from making a hearty breakfast for me. It reminded me of my trouping days, when I had sat on a train holding an umbrella over my head to keep from being rained on. Anna, knowing how important the morning meal was for me, would prepare pancakes and fried apples or bacon and eggs and toast and coffee. She knew that I might not get another bite for eight or nine hours.

Ice cream remained a passion with Dorothy and me. When Dorothy was working in pictures and later in plays, her first request on coming home was always for a dish of homemade ice cream. If there was none, she would be terribly upset and shout, "I'm leaving home!" Usually our freezers were stocked with quarts and half-gallons of Anna's ice cream, packed in ice and salt, as protection against this threat.

Mr. Griffith had achieved artistic independence, but in the process he had contracted even greater financial obligations. The expense of setting up with United Artists and building his new studio was enormous. We learned later that the profits from Dorothy's pictures helped to make the studio possible. As usual, Mr. Griffith was vague about money, and it was easy to believe that all was well. The truth was that when he first started work on the Mamaroneck studio, he had sent off an urgent wire to "Little" Epping, who was en route to California on the 20th Century Limited: "Account of drain in building studio will need profit from *Romance Happy Valley* here as soon as due." That film had been released nine months before, and with the money he planned to "unmortgage" several of Dorothy's pictures and in turn to free their profits to pay his mounting construction and salary costs.

Although *Broken Blossoms* had made a profit, the films Mr. Griffith directed for First National—*The Greatest Question, The Idol Dancer,* and *The Love Flower*—were not successful. The cost of picture making had risen so high that even without other debts he was always courting complete ruin.

Many times, Agnes Wiener remembers, he would announce to the whole staff on Friday night, "I'm sorry but everyone here will have to be laid off, beginning next week." Then he would single out certain players and tell them privately: "I didn't mean you. I want you to come back on Monday." It was his way of keeping his overhead down, yet his old carelessness with money and his generosity continued.

☙ 17 ❧

After *The Love Flower,* Mr. Griffith made a film version of a play, *Romance,* with Doris Keane, which was not profitable. It was important that his next picture make money. For an enormous sum— $165,000—he bought a stage melodrama, *Way Down East.* The purchase price was over twice the entire cost of *The Birth of a Nation.* For the first time in his life he hired a young playwright, Anthony Paul Kelly, to do a script.

We all thought privately that Mr. Griffith had lost his mind. *Way Down East* was a horse-and-buggy melodrama, familiar on the rural circuit for more than twenty years. We didn't believe it would ever succeed. As I read the play I could hardly keep from laughing. I was to play the role of Anna Moore, a country girl who is tricked into a mock marriage by a city playboy and abandoned when she becomes pregnant. After bearing her child, who dies, Anna finds work on a farm. The farmer's son, played by Dick Barthelmess, falls in love with her. Unfortunately, the playboy owns the farm next door. Eventually Anna's secret is revealed to the stern farmer. True to tradition, the farmer raises his hand toward the door. Out Anna goes— straight into a blizzard. She stumbles through the snow to the river and out onto the ice floes, where she faints, unaware that the floes are breaking up as they head for a steep waterfall. At the last moment, the farmer's son comes after her. He leaps from floe to floe and scoops her to safety just as the ice teeters on the brink of the falls. Naturally they are married and everything ends happily.

After I had read the play I wondered how I was going to make Anna convincing. I knew that the whole story depended on my making her plausible. As Mr. Griffith had no other contracts in the future to count on and so much of his money was already invested in the script, this film had to succeed.

Daily rehearsals began in a big room at the Claridge Hotel, where Mr. Griffith auditioned many of the best theater actors, who were now eager to appear in a film of D. W. Griffith's. Lowell Sherman, handsome and urbane, was chosen for the role of the villainous playboy, Lennox Sanderson. He later went on to a long, successful career as an actor and film director. Clarine Seymour was to play Katie, the girl whom the squire had chosen as a bride for his son David. Burr McIntosh was to be Squire Bartlett. Mr. McIntosh had once been the editor of a magazine, and he remembered that as children Dorothy and I had posed for photographs for him. He was always apologizing for having to treat me so cruelly in the film. Norma Shearer, then unknown, was an extra in the barn-dance sequence.

Kate Bruce, a character actress whom we all loved and a member of Mr. Griffith's company, was given the role of Squire Bartlett's wife. At first Mr. Griffith didn't want to use her. He liked Brucie, but she had a habit of forgetting how she had looked or which costume she had worn in a previous scene. "I can't use her," Mr. Griffith told me firmly, "unless you'll remember for her." I promised I would. (Now a film actor doesn't have to worry about such matters; photographs of him and his props are taken for every scene.)

Brucie had a gentle, well-modeled face. Mr. Griffith always made his character people beautiful. During the shooting of the film, he told Billy not to pay so much attention to me but to concentrate on photographing Brucie to advantage. "She's the mother," he would say, "and I want her to look lovely."

During our seventh week of rehearsals, Mr. Kelly brought in his completed script, for which he was paid $10,000. But the only thing that Mr. Griffith finally used from the script was a piece of business with the gloves I was wearing. Anna, the poor country cousin, arrives to visit her rich relatives. The butler takes her bags and coat. Her cousin wants to help her take off her gloves, but they are attached to elastic and snap back. Mr. Griffith later said that the laughter this unfailingly drew was worth the price of Kelly's script.

We rehearsed tirelessly for eight weeks, twice as long as we rehearse plays today. We also worked on our costumes for the film.

"Anna is from the country," I said to D. W., "but I don't want her to be quaint or funny. I just want her clothes not to be noticed. I want her to be more important than whatever she has on." He agreed with me. We hoped we were making timeless films, and we would always try to dress his heroines in a classical way. I was conscious of style, as most young women are, but I knew that if my costumes were in style one year they would be out of style five or ten years later. For this film we tried again for that timeless quality in Anna's clothes. For the sequence of the ball given by Anna's rich cousins, Mr. Griffith had Lucille of New York send out all her models for that year. Mrs. Morgan Belmont, a socialite who played a role in the film, wore these styles, but they were dated soon after. My evening dress by Henri Bendel was cut on classic Greek lines. It wasn't in style then, and it wouldn't be in style now, but it has never been out of style.

The farm scenes and the interior scenes were filmed on the studio lot. We filmed the baptism of Anna's child at night in a corner of the studio, with the baby's real father looking on. Anna is alone; the doctor has given up hope for her child. She resolves to baptize the infant herself. The baby was asleep and, as we didn't want to wake him, I barely whispered the words "In the name of the Father and of the Son and the Holy Ghost . . ." as I touched the tiny temples.

There was only the sound of the turning camera. Then I heard a thud. The baby's father had slumped to the floor in a faint. D. W. was crying. He waved his hand in front of his face to signify that he couldn't talk. When he regained control of himself, he took me in his arms and said simply, "Thank you."

Mr. Griffith intended to shoot all the exterior scenes outdoors, including the blizzard. He wouldn't be satisfied with the fake fury of a studio storm. He took out insurance that there would be a blizzard before a certain date. It was the first time, I believe, that a producer insured himself against vagaries of the weather. He also wanted each of his principal players insured for a million dollars. Four doctors examined us for three days. They found Dick Barthelmess suffering from sinus trouble. Clarine Seymour had an ailment. (Tragically, she died of intestinal complications later on during the filming of the winter scenes. Mr. Griffith had to find a substitute for her, and he chose a young dancer, Mary Hay, who resembled Clarine from a distance.)

Finally, I was the sole player Mr. Griffith's insurance brokers were willing to insure, perhaps because a short time before Mother had had both Dorothy and me examined for the New York Life Insurance Company, and they had written her a letter of congratulation on the health of her daughters. Before that, everyone had been considerate of me, particularly as I was going to be exposed to the elements wearing only a little wool dress. After the policy came through, it was taken for granted that I could take care of myself.

For the climax of the movie, where Anna was to be driven out into the blizzard, stumble onto the river's ice, and faint, I tried to get into condition early with exercise, walks in winter gales, and cold baths.

Our house was near the studio, and I was to report for work at any hour that snow started to fall, as we had both day and night scenes to film. It was a late but severe winter; even Long Island Sound was frozen over. I slept with one eye open, waiting for the blizzard. Winter dragged on and was almost over, and still those important scenes hadn't been filmed.

The blizzard finally struck in March. Drifts eight feet high swallowed the studio. The trees on Orienta Point lashed the sky and groaned, as the chains that held them together were stretched taut. Mr. Griffith, Billy, the staff, and the assistant directors stood with their backs to the gale, bundled up in coats, mufflers, hats, and gloves. To hold the camera upright, three men lay on the ground, gripping the tripod legs. A small fire burned directly beneath the camera to keep the oil from freezing.

Again and again, I struggled through the storm. Once I fainted—and it wasn't in the script. I was hauled to the studio on a sled, thawed out with hot tea, and then brought back to the blizzard, where the others were waiting. We filmed all day and all night, stopping only to eat standing near a bonfire. We never went inside, even for a short warmup. The torture of returning to the cold wasn't worth the temporary warmth. The blizzard never slackened. At one point, the camera froze. There was an excruciating delay as the men, huddled against the wind, tried to get another fire started. At one time my face was caked with a crust of ice and snow, and icicles like little spikes formed on my eyelashes, making it difficult to keep my eyes open.

Above the howling storm, Mr. Griffith shouted: "Billy, move in! Get that face! That face—*get that face!*"

"I will," Billy shouted, "if the oil doesn't freeze in the camera!"

We lost several members of our crew from pneumonia as the result of exposure. Though he worked with his back to the wind whenever possible, Mr. Griffith's face froze. A trained nurse was at his side for the rest of the blizzard and the winter scenes.

The scenes on and around the ice were filmed at White River Junction, Vermont, where the White River and the Connecticut flowed side by side. The ice was thick; it had to be either sawed or dynamited, so that there would be floes for each day's filming. The temperature never rose above zero during the three weeks we worked there.

For the scene in which Anna faints on the ice floe, I thought of a piece of business and suggested it to Mr. Griffith, who agreed it was a fine idea. (I was always having bright ideas and suffering for them.) I suggested that my hand and my hair trail in the water as I lay on the floe that was drifting toward the falls. Mr. Griffith was delighted with the effect.

After a while, my hair froze, and I felt as if my hand were in a flame. To this day, it aches if I am out in the cold for very long. When the sequence was finally finished, I had been on a slab of ice at least twenty times a day for three weeks. In between takes, one of the men would throw a coat around me, and I would warm myself briefly at a fire.

This kind of dedication probably seems foolish today, but it wasn't unusual then. Those of us who worked with Mr. Griffith were completely committed to the picture we were making. No sacrifice was too great to get the film right, to get it accurate, true, and perfect. We weren't important in our minds; only the picture was. Mr. Griffith felt the same way; it was his picture, not he, that counted.

Dick Barthelmess had only a short time before been a sophomore at nearby Dartmouth College. His old schoolmates thought it would be exciting to watch a film being made before their eyes and came to visit. They didn't stay long; the subzero weather drove them indoors.

The scene of Anna's rescue from the falls was all too realistically re-created. Mr. Griffith was directing Dick from a bridge over the river, but the noise of the falls drowned out his directions. Dick, a slight young man, was hampered by the heavy raccoon coat and spiked boots he had to wear. As I headed toward the falls on my slab of ice, Mr. Griffith shouted to Dick that he was moving too slowly, but Dick couldn't hear him. The people on the banks were also yelling frantically. As Dick ran toward me he became excited, leaped and landed on a piece of ice that was too small. He sank into the water, climbed back out, finally lifted me in his arms as I was about to go over, and ran like mad to shore.

Years later when Dick and I were reminiscing, he said: "I wonder why we went through with it. We could have been killed. There isn't enough money in the world to pay me to do it today." But we weren't doing it for money.

That is why it was a shock to me when for the first time in my memory Mr. Griffith settled for less than the truth. We were about to shoot the scene in the little log cabin where Dick takes me following the rescue. Mr. Griffith told me to get ready. I looked and felt half dead after the river scene. My hair was wet and stringy, my face nearly frozen. "I'm ready," I said.

"Yes, but the climax is over. The audience will want to see you

Dorothy with James Rennie (left), whom she later married, and an unknown player in *Flying Pat* (1920).

Griffith directing Lillian on the ice in *Way Down East* (1920). Billy Bitzer (left) is shooting, while assistant director Herbert Sutch looks on.

Griffith directing Lillian in *Way Down East*.

The famous confrontation scene in *Way Down East*. The Squire sends Lillian out into the blizzard. From left to right: Burr McIntosh, Kate Bruce, Vivia Ogden, Lowell Sherman, Lillian, Mary Hay, Creighton Hale, George Neville, Richard Barthelmess, Edgar Nelson.

Lillian on the ice floe in *Way Down East*. After three weeks of rehearsal for this scene, she claimed that her arm felt like an icicle.

look beautiful again. Go put on fresh makeup, and comb your hair."

I almost never presumed to argue with Mr. Griffith, but this time I rebelled.

"Mr. Griffith, it won't look right after what I've gone through."

"Don't tell me how to make motion pictures," he said angrily. "Hurry up, and do as you're told! This picture has to make money! Now go and make yourself pretty!"

I obeyed. But in the scene it is evident to those who know me that I was awfully mad at some one!

Before they could be released, our pictures had to pass the scrutiny of the censor board of every state. One scene, in which Anna bears her child, was so realistic that D. W. was afraid it would never pass the censors. We had developed a plan for outwitting censors. Before a preview Mr. Griffith would ask the members of the censor board to lunch with us. During the meal we would try to discover what their main interests were. Later, as the film was being run and the "censorable" scene approached, we would bring up the censors' pet subject and divert their attention until the scene was safely passed. My greatest triumph as the censor's Delilah came in Pennsylvania, a state that did not then permit showing even a picture of a woman knitting little garments.

Before the New York opening of *Way Down East,* another tragedy occurred within the company.

Bobby Harron was then living in Los Angeles with his parents in a house that he had bought for them. He was twenty-six years old and was becoming a finer actor with each picture. He had turned down many offers in order to remain with Mr. Griffith, to whom he was intensely loyal. Although he hadn't played a part in *Way Down East,* he had come east for our premiere.

The night before the premiere, the light from his telephone flashed on the hotel switchboard.

"I've shot myself," he gasped. "Send for a doctor."

He was taken by ambulance to Bellevue Hospital, where his old childhood friend, Father McQuird, found him. As Bobby came out of a coma briefly, the priest said: "My boy, there is One who knows the truth. Tell me, tell Father McQuird, was it accidental? Or did you—"

"Oh, Father McQuird, I swear to you, I never dreamed of the other thing," Bobby said weakly.

He had bought the pistol from a man who needed money. He had put the gun in the pocket of his dinner jacket and forgot about it. Then, as he took his dinner clothes from the trunk, the gun had fallen to the floor and gone off.

Bobby died in Bellevue of what was reported as an accidental gunshot wound. Mr. Griffith arranged all the details of the funeral. Bobby's mother was summoned to New York shortly after the accident, but she didn't learn of his death until she and her daughter Agnes arrived in New York. There was no one to meet Mrs. Harron and Agnes, and, as I was closest to them, Mr. Griffith had delegated me to give them the sad news. I had never had to tell anyone about a death, so I enlisted the help of a friend, a priest, who accompanied me to the station, and we brought Mrs. Harron back to our house in Mamaroneck.

Dorothy was in Europe with Mother at the time, on a trip with Mrs. Talmadge and Constance. When she heard the news she was crushed with grief.

Way Down East was the big success that we had all hoped it would be. Mr. Griffith had transformed a crude melodrama into a compelling masterpiece. His picture of rural America was nostalgic and realistic, and the last-minute rescue on the ice was a miracle of camera work and cutting.

Way Down East played for more than a year on Broadway at legitimate theater prices and was enthusiastically received all over the United States and abroad, although in France audiences couldn't understand why Anna was punished for having a baby. The film ultimately made more money than any other Griffith film except *The Birth of a Nation.*

"Lillian Gish's acting in this film," William K. Everson later wrote, "was perhaps her very best for Griffith. This is not to denigrate her performances in prior Griffith films but this was the first real Gish vehicle for Griffith, and the first in which her big dramatic scenes were not subdued by the overall story and the stress on melodrama."

⚜ 18 ⚜

Dorothy was seeing a lot of James Rennie, her leading man in the picture I had directed. She, Jim, Constance Talmadge, and John Pialoglou, a young Greek, were a constant foursome.

Dorothy recalled that most men who courted the irrepressible Constance wanted to marry her, but John did not. Evidently his lack of interest in marriage intrigued her. A man who loved her yet refused to propose—that was a challenge.

One night Dorothy asked me, all innocence, if I had heard any rumors about her and Jim.

I had. "Is it true?" I asked.

Dorothy nodded.

When John finally proposed to Constance, they were all lunching together, and she persuaded Dorothy to make it a double wedding. Connie and John and Dorothy and Jim motored up to Greenwich, Connecticut, and were married that afternoon—the day after Christmas, 1920.

I believe that if Connie had not influenced Dorothy she would never have married Jim. She was young, giddy, and had no serious thoughts at the time.

When Mother heard the news, she couldn't believe that Dorothy had taken such an important step without consulting her.

After the wedding, Dorothy showed no inclination to leave home. Finally, Mother packed her clothes and sent them over to Jim's apartment.

"You belong with your husband," she said.

Dorothy burst into tears. "If I'd thought you would put me out, I wouldn't have married." She made us promise that we would all rent a house together in the country in three months.

Mother and I grew to love Jim. His father, a Scottish-Canadian doctor, was a robust individual who wore kilts until he was eighty. Jim's mother was a lovely, cultivated woman. The Rennies hadn't met Dorothy before the marriage. Later Jim's sister Mary told me that they thought Dorothy completely charming and that they all loved her, particularly Jim's mother. Dorothy adored them too and always had a photograph of Mrs. Rennie near her. Charlotte, Jim's older sister, became Dorothy's secretary.

Mary Rennie recalls the time that a writer friend of hers went on the set to interview Dorothy. She found Dorothy delightful and completely unassuming. "There's nothing very exciting to write about me," Dorothy told the interviewer. Then, nodding toward Jim, she added, "But there's a young man—talk to him."

Jim was a lot like Mr. Griffith. When he had had a drink, he would talk endlessly about Shakespeare and the Bible, which endeared him to D. W. They became good friends.

After *Way Down East* Mr. Griffith made his next picture, *Dream Street,* without me. Perhaps he was tired of using me, or perhaps he thought I was becoming too independent. My salary was by then quite high. At any rate Albert Grey, who was Mr. Griffith's brother and general manager (his name was different because Mr. Griffith thought it wiser not to let it be known that his manager was his brother), told me that the Frohman Amusement Company wanted to make a picture with me. To me the name Frohman meant the distinguished theater producer Charles Frohman. But Albert Grey told me that it was the producer's brother who had made the offer and advised me to accept. I didn't know then that this was just to take me off the Griffith payroll. When I left Mr. Griffith, many of his people came with me. We were halfway through the film, *World Shadows,* when the Frohman company collapsed. It was a calamity for me, as I felt responsible for those who had come with me.

Dream Street, which was released in April 1921, was distinguished primarily for its attempt to use synchronized sound, seven years before the arrival of talking pictures. The process, an invention of O. E. Kellum, involved recordings of dialogue and music synchronized with the picture by means of a device attached to the projector. The experiment was crude and only partially successful, and was abandoned after the initial showing of the film.

Mr. Griffith decided against experimenting further with sound. "It puts us back to Babel," he said. "Do you realize how few people in the world speak English? If we make pictures that talk, we can't send them around the world. That's suicide."

After he had finished *Dream Street,* Mr. Griffith asked me to come back. He announced that he was going to make Goethe's *Faust* and that I was to play Marguerite. I was filled with misgivings. I did some research and discovered that *Faust* had never been a financial success in the United States. At first I said nothing. D. W. had taught us all a lesson with *Way Down East.*

Harry Carr was my close friend and confidant. He was a wise older man, and a true friend of D. W. I confided my doubts to him. He agreed with me. "It'll just be another opportunity for D. W. to get up on a soap box and preach to people," he said. "What he needs is a money maker."

Perhaps I should not have interfered but kept still and played in *Faust,* which was done beautifully four years later in Germany, although the American public failed to respond to it. But a few days later I went to D. W. with my statistics. He heard me out with a frown.

"All that may be true," he said, "but *Faust* is a classic. I can make it into a great film."

"Well," I said, as tactfully as I could, "I suppose it's a chance to preach a great moral."

"What is this, a conspiracy?" he asked. "Harry Carr said almost the same thing to me yesterday. Do you have a better idea?"

I had just read a play even older than *Way Down East*. It was a melodrama of two orphans, one of whom was blind. I mentioned it to Mr. Griffith.

He said, "You only want me to make the story because there's a part in it for Dorothy."

"No, I've traced audience reaction to it," I said and told him what I had learned. *The Two Orphans* had played successfully in forty languages. It had a long record of popularity. In downtown New York in the 1920s there was a German theater, a Chinese theater, a Jewish theater, and an Italian theater. The Italian theater was playing *The Two Orphans* that week. I took D. W. down to see it, and even though neither of us could understand Italian its dramatic possibilities were obvious. In it was an actor called Frank Puglia, who was to play the crippled Pierre in the film. Mr. Griffith was impressed by the play and decided to film it.

The original story told of the efforts of two young girls—the blind Louise, whom Dorothy played, and Henriette, my role—to find each other after being separated early in the play. D. W. recognized that the material did not have sufficient scope, so he transposed the story to the time of the French Revolution. This gave him an opportunity to add mob scenes, duels, executions, thundering horses and cannons, and a last-minute rescue at the guillotine to the pathos of the original story.

As he had for *The Birth* and *Intolerance*, D. W. plunged into research. His main source was Thomas Carlyle's *French Revolution*, but he also drew on Hippolyte Taine, François Guizot, and Abbott. He consulted our friend Louis Allard, Professor of French at Harvard University, and the Marquis de Polignac. Endless details were researched, including the way Robespierre walked and the songs that were sung at the time.

D. W. liked to talk about the research that his idol, Charles Dickens, had put into *A Tale of Two Cities*. He told us that when Dickens had written to Thomas Carlyle for advice on research for the French Revolution, the Scottish historian had piled a horsecart high with the reference books he had used for his monumental work and then had them dumped in Dickens' front yard. Perhaps even

Carlyle would have been impressed with the mass of material D. W. absorbed for *The Two Orphans.*

Mr. Griffith constructed replicas of the Palais Royale, Nôtre Dame, Versailles, and the Bastille that were completely authentic. The room in the Palais Royale where the king appears is an exact replica in dimensions, decorations, paintings, and all other details of the grand salon of the actual palace. The coach in which the orphans ride was modeled exactly after the famous old Normandy coach that traveled daily to the gates of Paris.

For *Orphans* Mr. Griffith again had a designer do the costumes, but for my taste they were too much in the fashion of the time. I went to Herman Tappé and told him my ideas, and the two of us worked out Dorothy's and my costumes for *Orphans.* All the other costumes were duplicates of those worn in the Revolutionary period.

We began rehearsals upstairs at the Forty-fourth Street Theater, where *Way Down East* was still playing to capacity. Although *Orphans* ultimately cost more to produce than *Way Down East,* Mr. Griffith watched his expenditures closely on this production. Once we filmed a mob scene when there was no sunlight, although sun and shadow were necessary for effective mob scenes. We never went back to shoot it a second time; Mr. Griffith couldn't spare the money.

Billy Bitzer and Hendrick Sartov were the cameramen on *Orphans.* Sartov had helped with the photography on *Way Down East* and photographed all of *Dream Street.* I heard that Billy was becoming embittered by Sartov's rising influence. During the filming of *Orphans,* his resentment of Sartov became apparent. Once when D. W. asked the two of them to work together on a problem, Billy bristled and refused to help. Another time when Sartov asked him for advice, Billy snapped, "Why should I help you take my job away?"

Then one day, as we were scheduled to shoot a major scene, Billy failed to appear. D. W. waited for a time and then motioned Sartov to start shooting. Billy was never again the sole cameraman on a Griffith production. After helping with the photography on Mr. Griffith's *America* three years later, he left the company. D. W. brought him back to Hollywood again in 1927, but the relationship did not last. Billy had begun to drink heavily, and eventually he drifted to the sidelines of the industry. In the early 1930s he contributed a few articles to film trade magazines, and, when the Depression hit the picture industry, he found employment on a W.P.A. film project. Afterward he went to work as an adviser to the newly founded Museum of Modern Art Film Library. He died in 1944.

Joseph Schildkraut was my leading man in *Orphans*. He played the part of a young French nobleman and was very striking in his white wig. (Dorothy said he was prettier than she was.) But he was so self-conscious during our love scene together that they had to take it three times. Later a critic on the New York *Mail* wrote of it, "There is a love scene that is the classic of all screen love passages, a delicately beautiful episode."

Twice during the making of *Orphans*, I disagreed with D. W. The first time was during rehearsals. I felt that one particular scene lacked the intensity that the situation demanded. It was at the base of the guillotine, when Henriette meets her blind sister.

He could always tell when I was dissatisfied. "You don't seem pleased, Miss Gish," he said.

I shook my head. "Mr. Griffith, I've seen scenes as good as this in other pictures."

"Oh? In that case, what would you suggest?"

"Well, I'd like to do it less casually—with the greater depth of emotion she would feel at such a moment."

I then played the scene my way. When I finished, I was almost afraid to look at Mr. Griffith.

Without a word, he walked up to me, sank to one knee, and kissed my hand before the company. "Thank you," he said.

The second time that I disagreed with him was when we were watching the final cut of the film. I told him I thought he had drawn the climax out too long. He was quite peeved and told me that I had forced him to do so by acting too intensely at the climax of the first act.

"You carried that climax so high," he said, "I can't top it." I lost that battle.

Orphans of the Storm, as the film was called, opened December 28, 1921, in Boston and on January 3, 1922, at the Apollo Theater

Lillian in *Orphans of the Storm* (1922).

Lillian and Dorothy in *Orphans of the Storm;* Dorothy played the blind sister.

Lillian at the guillotine in *Orphans of the Storm,* a superb example of Griffith's technique of creating suspense.

Dorothy, Griffith, and Lillian leaving the White House after a screening of *Orphans of the Storm*. They were guests of President Harding.

in New York City. The critics welcomed it as one of D. W.'s best films. The picture contained no outstanding innovations but was instead a kind of showcase for all the brilliant techniques he had developed, mastered, and brought to unrivaled peaks. The sequences of the storming of the Bastille and the last-minute rescue of Henriette at the guillotine recalled the ride of the Klan in *The Birth of a Nation* and the climax of the modern story in *Intolerance*.

One critic commented: "A great work of art. It has the sweep of *The Birth of a Nation*, the remarkable tragic drive of *Broken Blossoms*, the terrific melodramatic appeal of *Way Down East*, and a warning written in fire and spoken in thunder for all Americans to heed."

"*Orphans of the Storm*," D. W. wrote in a synopsis of the film, "is great anti-Bolshevik propaganda. It shows more vividly than any book of history can tell, that the tyranny of kings and nobles is hard to bear but that the tyranny of the maddened mob under the blood lusting rulers is intolerable."

My performance as Henriette was well received. The New York *Herald* said, "She has a way of reaching right in and straining at one's heartstrings." Dorothy drew almost as much acclaim for her portrayal of the blind Louise as she had for her Little Disturber in *Hearts of the World*.

Mr. Griffith told Dorothy and me that he was going to show *Orphans of the Storm* at the White House and that we were to go with him. The prospect of a visit with the President of the United States was both thrilling and frightening. Poor Dorothy was sick from the moment we received the invitation. We drove with Mr. Griffith to the White House. After a brief wait, we were ushered into a splendid room. Dorothy, as was her habit, lingered behind me. The President approached, white-haired and nobly proportioned. To our awed young eyes, Warren G. Harding looked more like a President than Mr. Wilson. He was like a Roman statue carved out of marble.

He held out his arms to me and said "Darling!" Then he greeted Dorothy with equal warmth, and from that moment on we felt at ease.

The first day of our visit was spent entirely at the White House. We had lunch with the President and Mrs. Harding. Twice during our visit Mrs. Harding gave us beautiful flowers that she had picked from their greenhouses.

We opened *Orphans of the Storm* in Washington that night. The next day we were invited to what was said to be the unofficial White House—Mrs. Evelyn Walsh MacLean's magnificent home. We were happy to see Mrs. MacLean again; we had met her once before when she had visited the studio at Mamaroneck with Tallulah Bankhead during the making of *Way Down East*. Before dinner we met Harry Dougherty, the Attorney General, who was soon to become notorious in connection with the Teapot Dome scandal. He was standing in the drawing room, cigar thrust at an angle in his mouth, a derby on his head, and he was swaying.

Mr. Griffith was the center of attention, and he was flattered that Washington turned out to honor him. The city was kind to us too, and our hotel rooms were filled with flowers. Mother was at the hospital in New York during that time, recuperating from surgery. Mrs. Harding gave us each a big box of flowers to take back to her.

When it was released, *Orphans of the Storm* caused riots in France, as *The Birth* had in America.

The New York Times reported on September 17, 1922, that the Griffith film had provoked the anger of Parisians:

> A disturbance was caused last night at a boulevard motion picture house during the first production of D. W. Griffith's film, *Orphans of the Storm*. Although it was actually started by a handful of young Royalists whose ire was aroused by the manner in which the ancient regime was depicted, it apparently had a wider significance than a mere demonstration by a few hot-headed, unbalanced youths. Their angry protest was supported by almost the whole body of spectators . . . the reason being the American producer's idea of conditions under the old monarchy profoundly offends French pride and self respect. . . . "It is inadmissible that a foreigner should take upon himself thus to travesty an epoch whose faults and quali-

ties we know better than he. And one must ask what the censors were thinking of to allow a film which denotes so unfriendly a spirit toward French history."

When he was informed that hostile demonstrations had accompanied the Paris showing of *Orphans of the Storm,* Mr. Griffith was amazed. In defense of the picture, he said, "If there are any grounds for complaint on the part of the French people, they are to be found in *A Tale of Two Cities,* and the complaint should have been lodged long ago against Mr. Charles Dickens, from whose famous novel the incidents of the picture largely were drawn."

Orphans of the Storm was Mr. Griffith's last big success at the box office. But, although it made money, it did not make as much as it should have. Mr. Griffith decided to show it on a road-show basis, as he had done so successfully with *Way Down East.* But the road shows were improperly managed by his brother Albert, and losses were incurred. Furthermore, the system of showing the film in legitimate theaters bypassed the neighborhood theaters, which were sprouting up all over the country. And the enormous publicity costs for the film drove profits down.

Prior to the film's release, First National Exhibitors, a company for which Mr. Griffith had once worked, had released an Italian version of *The Two Orphans* and had sold it to exhibitors as "the production with a million dollars' worth of publicity behind it." They did not mention that it was Mr. Griffith's publicity.

Shortly after *Orphans* was released, Mr. Griffith called me to his office. I went, eager to learn what film he was planning next and whether or not I would have a part in it.

"You know as much about the high cost of making pictures as I do," he said. "With all the expenses I have, I can't afford to pay you what you're worth."

I read his mind in an instant, remembering Mary Pickford, Blanche Sweet, Mae Marsh—all the stars he had created and then sent on their way.

"You should go out on your own. Your name is of as much value as mine with the public, and I think in your own interest you ought to capitalize on it while you can."

Thus, in the most friendly way, an artistic and business association of many years was broken off as casually as it had begun.

After *Orphans of the Storm* Mr. Griffith made *One Exciting Night,* the first screen murder mystery, with Carol Dempster and Henry Hull. It was a prototype for W. S. Van Dyke's *Thin Man* series, combining crime and suspense with comedy, but it was not the hit D. W. needed. His next film, *The White Rose,* for which Mae Marsh had come back to him, led F. J. Smith to comment in *Photoplay,* "Somehow he seems to us to be a great man living within a circle of isolation, surrounded by minor advisers, genius out of touch with the world. . . ."

In *The White Rose* Mae was superb, even though she was afraid that a flapper role would not suit her. It was the last film she and Mr. Griffith did together. In spite of its pictorial beauty and lyricism, it was not a success.

After *Orphans of the Storm* Mr. Griffith wanted to do a film with a heroic conception. Among his ideas was a film devoted to the history of the world, "for promoting the League of Nations." He negotiated with H. G. Wells for the script, but nothing came of the plan.

In 1923, D. W. saw Al Jolson's act in New York and offered to make a film with him. Jolson agreed, but he was afraid that the intense lighting on the set might melt his blackface makeup. Mr. Griffith promised to eliminate that problem and the two shook hands on the deal.

On a Monday afternoon a few weeks later, Jolson arrived at Mamaroneck for his screen tests. Mr. Griffith led him to the front lawn of the studio estate. The singer looked around in amazement. D. W. had built an entire open air stage, complete with outdoor sets and the most modern equipment.

"It's all for you," he told Jolson proudly. "We're ready to start shooting next week. Why don't you drop back here on Thursday for a look at the tests? Then we'll start rehearsals on Monday."

Jolson did appear on Thursday. Flashing his famous smile, he was ushered into the projection room. Jolson, watching himself for the first time on film, sat through the test in complete silence. When the lights went on again, the Griffith staff saw that his smile had given way to a scowl.

Monday came, but not Jolson. He couldn't be found. Mr. Griffith learned that he was on a boat that had sailed for Europe.

D. W. was shocked and amazed that anyone would go back on his word. He had never signed us to a contract; a shake of the hand was his bond, and he had dealt that way with Jolson. Now he was left with an outdoor stage that had cost nearly $100,000, and the people he had hired for the production.

"I don't understand it," he said later. "The boy"—as he called Jolson—"didn't appear unhappy over it at all. When Jolson walked out and left for Europe, however, it finally dawned, even through my thick head, that he might have been discouraged."

After I left D. W. I heard that the money *Orphans* earned had to go to pay off the debts of his corporation. At the time of *Orphans,* his finances were already hopelessly entangled. Frequently during the shooting of *Orphans,* we had waited on the set all day for him to return from a trip into New York, where he was frantically trying to round up financial backing.

Way Down East temporarily eased the search. But in 1921 he was foolish enough to mortgage the negative of that film, plus *Dream Street* and the yet unfinished *Orphans* and all the money they were to earn, in return for a loan of $340,000. Eight months later he borrowed $267,000 to make his next film, *One Exciting Night.* A half-year afterward he borrowed $650,000 for *The White Rose,* and nine months later he borrowed another half-million to complete the picture he was working on—*America.* In less than a year, he obtained two more loans of $250,000 each, for a grand total of $2.25 million. This utter lack of common sense in his business dealings was to spell doom to his talents.

❦ 19 ❦

I had been speculating about what I should do now that I was on my own. I had long thought of making a picture abroad. My trip to England and France during the war had convinced me that films should, whenever possible, be made in the actual locations of their stories. But nothing presented itself to me, and I was too concerned with Mother's health to make a search. Mother had developed a goiter and had to undergo surgery at the Presbyterian Hospital in New York. My financial obligations were great at the time, and I wrote to my friend Nell, "My next picture, if all goes well, will be made by myself, so if it makes money I may get some of it."

Richard Barthelmess had left Mr. Griffith to go with Inspiration Pictures. He came to show Mr. Griffith and me the results of what he had been doing while we were making *Orphans of the Storm.* When we finished looking at *Tol'able David,* the film he had made with director Henry King, we were bursting with pride and admiration for him. It was a beautiful film, and Dick surpassed himself in it. Mr. Griffith held Dick in his arms and told him, with tears in his eyes, how proud he was.

Later Dick said to me, "This is a little company, just starting—why don't you come with us?"

"I'd certainly like to meet them, if you think they would be interested," I said.

I met Charles H. Duell and Boyce Smith, heads of Inspiration Pictures, and their director Henry King. Duell, a member of an old New York family, was a lawyer interested in making pictures. I was impressed by their apparent eagerness to do fine films.

That summer I read a novel, *The White Sister,* which years before had been made into a play for Viola Allen. It was a love story about an Italian girl, Angela, who is separated from her lover, a young Italian nobleman and army officer, when he goes to Africa with his company and is believed to have been killed. The girl becomes a lay sister in a convent, and, when she has despaired of ever seeing her lover again, she takes her final vows and becomes a nun. Then the officer, who has been a prisoner for years, returns. He wants his loved one back and finally, in desperation, kidnaps her. In the book she renounces her vows, and all ends happily.

What particularly appealed to me about the story was the dramatic ceremony in which the nun becomes a bride of the Church. It had never been re-created on stage or screen. Then, as now, it was not easy to find new material. I decided that the story would make an interesting film. I signed to go to Italy to make the picture for very little salary and a gross percentage of the profits after double the cost of the negative had been returned to the producer.

The White Sister would be the first modern religious story to be filmed, and the big companies refused to handle its distribution. "People get religion free on Sundays; you can't make them pay for it during the week," they told us.

But I was determined to make the film. "I'll tour it in a tent if I have to," I said.

Before we sailed I had dinner with Mr. Griffith and told him the story of *The White Sister.*

"I only wish mine was as good. I'm planning to do a story based on the American Revolution," he said.

"It sounds exciting," I said. "It ought to be another *Birth of a Nation,* if you can get the audience to accept those wigs on the men."

At that time costume pictures were not popular, though *Orphans* had been an exception.

Inspiration Pictures bought twenty-four tickets for passage on a boat bound for Italy, but we had only twenty-three passengers scheduled. Everyone was on a talent hunt for an actor to play the Italian prince in the film. Finally the photographer James Abbé said that he had been to see Henry Miller and Ruth Chatterton in a play, *La Tendresse,* and that there was a young Englishman in the cast who would be just right. Henry King and I saw the play, and afterward went backstage and asked the young actor if he would make a test for us the next morning. Once we had run the test we knew our search was over. Ronald Colman was perfect for the part.

I sent Henry Miller, who was the producer as well as the star, a note explaining our predicament, and that gracious gentleman, knowing what an opportunity it was for Mr. Colman, let him sail with us forty-eight hours later.

I had asked Agnes Wiener to go with us.

Agnes wrote recently:

> I was thrilled at the opportunity. It was "between pictures" for the Griffith Company and I asked for leave and was given it so I could go with Lillian. But one of the studio personnel whose nose was perhaps out of joint told me Mr. Griffith wasn't pleased that I was so ready to desert the Griffith studio for new fields. I felt terrible. On a Sunday morning, when I knew Mr. Griffith would be working on the stage at the studio with Billy Bitzer on some comera effects he was striving for, I took a train up to Mamaroneck and talked with Mr. Griffith. I told him what I'd heard and that I wouldn't leave although a trip to Europe was appealing. If he had something coming up that would require whatever help I could give him, I would stay. Never will I forget how that great kindly man put his arms around my shoulders and told me that if I thought he would stand in the way of such an adventure, I should be on my knees in church on that Sunday morning! When the Italian liner sailed, I had in my stateroom the largest basket of flowers on the entire ship and a hand-scrawled note from D. W. Griffith himself.

On the *S. S. Providence,* the little ship that took us to Naples, we arranged to use a small upper deck for rehearsals while we were at sea.

I had left Mother in New York under the care of a nurse, and an old friend of my aunt from Massillon, Mrs. Marie Kratsch—or Petty, as I called her—came with me as my chaperone.

No American film company had ever been to Italy. We had been told that we would find a studio completely equipped. Instead, when we arrived in Rome we found a bare studio with only two klieg lights —the only ones in Italy. At once, a man was put on a night train for Germany to buy and ship us enough equipment for the production.

Meanwhile, we rehearsed and began searching for locations. In Italy, we discovered, power was held by three groups, Mussolini and his party, the Vatican, and the King and his followers. Some good angel had put us on the boat with Monsignor Bonzano, who was on his way to the Vatican to be made a cardinal. He had learned that we were planning to do a Catholic story and promised us help from the Church for our film. It was destiny that he was on that boat. Without him we could not have made our picture. Officials of the Church advised us on every religious scene, to ensure its authenticity, and arranged for me to visit more than thirty cloistered orders before I decided on the one that we would use for *The White Sister*—the Order of Lourdes.

I learned from the nuns how to walk and move in the heavy habit, and how to use my hands. Their serenity is reflected in their every gesture. I was given the privilege of seeing before dawn several ceremonies of the taking of the veil, the marriage to the Church. And our entire company was invited to the Vatican when Monsignor Bonzano received the red hat.

I have never forgotten the color and pageantry of the elevation of a cardinal. It took place at dawn, and all ambassadors to the Holy See attended in full regalia. Two of our actors, Barney Sherry and Charles Lane, were more than six feet tall, white-haired, and so distinguished-looking in their white ties and tails that they were mistaken for ambassadors and taken in with the highest in the Church. They held up their heads as they passed us but managed to wink.

Lillian at the time of her last pictures with Griffith.

Griffith demonstrating his rapport with animals.

Lillian and Ronald Colman in Rome during the filming of *The White Sister* (1923).

Lillian as the sensitive young girl who becomes a nun in *The White Sister*.

Portrait of Lillian in her M.G.M. years.

Cardinal Bonzano must have been greatly loved, for tears flowed as he received his honor.

When we were filming in Rome, the atmosphere was spiritual. Years later, when Helen Hayes and Clark Gable were making a new version of *The White Sister,* Helen called me long-distance. She was dissatisfied with the rushes. Clark was a good actor, but he was subtly wrong for the part. She asked me how, in our original film version, we had achieved certain effects.

"How is it on the set between scenes?" I asked her.

"Oh, you know, the usual stories and jokes," Helen replied.

"Then you're not going to get it," I was obliged to tell her. "You cannot set up a camera and take a picture of faith."

We used the Villa d'Este as the convent and built beautiful interiors at the studio, so beautiful that I would have liked to live in them. The workmen had a love for their work, and the sets reflected it. Those early weeks in Rome exploring that magnificent city are among my happiest memories. I visited the churches and everywhere I left candles burning for Mother's recovery.

We all loved Italy and her people and wondered how they would respond to us. In the beginning, they did not want to work for us. But finally they came, reluctantly, thinking at first that we were crazy, because we never stopped working. Then they began to see the results and became our loyal friends.

Our studio was on the outskirts of Rome, and from my dressing room I could see the dome of St. Peter's in the distance. We usually ate our lunch at the caretaker's house, and the food was simple but delicious. Italian bread, sardines or cheese, and a glass of wine made a perfect meal. I wanted to be among the Italians, not only because I was sympathetic to them but also for the sake of the character I was portraying. I wanted to know Rome and the people of the country as Angela would know them.

Transportation was something of a problem during filming of the early portions of the story. When anyone was needed, a note was found to be faster than the telephone. Luckily we hired our fleet of automobiles from a close friend of Mussolini, and through the offices of the charming Count Carlo di Frasso we were allowed to photograph the royal hunt. The quiet approach of Charles Duell, Henry King, and the rest of our company opened many doors that were later closed to others.

The whole company was living in two hotels on the Via Veneto, the Excelsior and the Majestic. It was soon apparent to all of us that the Colmans were having personal problems. Once Thelma Colman ran down the hotel corridor crying: "He's dead! He's dead!" Some of the company ran in to find Ronnie on the floor.

When he came to, he said, "I must have fallen and hit my head."

Later the Colmans had a bitter quarrel at a company party. That finished their stormy marriage.

Ronnie looked like an aristocrat; he could make you believe that he was a prince. But he had all the reserve of an English gentleman. To get him to play with the passion and abandon necessary for the kidnapping scene, Henry King plied him with whisky. Ronnie actually said "damn" during the scene! It was a great surprise to all of us. We had to work all night to finish the scene, and the next day he couldn't remember what had happened.

Although the ending in the book had been a happy one, we decided that a tragic end would be better for the picture. We couldn't expect to hold the sympathy of audiences if a half-hour after our heroine had taken solemn vows she repudiated them. Instead, there was a volcanic eruption, causing a flood, and the officer was drowned. We went to Mt. Vesuvius to shoot some of the volcano scenes.

While I was in Naples I was told that my hotel room had once been occupied by Eleonora Duse. I had never seen Duse and very much longed to. Then my chance came; she was to play in a D'Annunzio drama at the Constanta Theater in Rome when we returned.

Henry King and his wife, Petty Kratsch, and I went to see her. The theater wasn't half filled. The house lights were not dimmed when the curtain went up, so that many in the audience did not stop reading their newspapers when Duse came on stage. At the final curtain she received a solitary wreath of white flowers, slightly wilting, that looked like a funeral wreath. I came to the theater every possible night during her run, and we were to have met. But I was told that she was ill and thought it best not to disturb her.

She remained a legend to me. A year later, when she made her final appearance in the United States, I saw her in New York. She opened at the Metropolitan Opera House in Ibsen's *The Lady from the Sea*. Every seat was taken; even the orchestra pit was covered and chairs placed there. Morris Gest arranged for me to have a chair near the prompter's box so that I could see at close range. Duse came on stage. She swayed, as if she were about to faint. Then something mystical took place. There was thundering applause as the audience stood up and sent its strength to her. She absorbed it, seemed to grow taller, and went on to fill that huge theater with magic.

One of my treasures is a souvenir of Duse. When she died, a wreath of white roses from the King of Italy was placed on her bier. One of my friends, John Regan, obtained a rosebud from it, placed it in a small carved box with a reproduction of Botticelli's "The Three Graces," and sent it to me. For a long time I kept it on the little table by my bed.

To film the ceremony of the taking of the veil, we worked all day and through the night until the next morning—twenty-five hours without stopping. Then I was allowed two and a half hours' rest before working again until 11:00 that night. Then Petty Kratsch and I motored through the night to Florence, where I inspected some of the costumes and sets, already partly arranged for, which we would be using the following year for our next film, *Romola*.

I had wanted to do *Romeo and Juliet* in the original Italian setting, but a letter from home informed me that the exhibitors protested that "Mr." Shakespeare's name kept people out of the theaters. A relative of our producer's suggested *Romola*, the George Eliot novel, and, although I had misgivings about the story's appeal, I had agreed to make the film in Florence the following winter.

On the boat sailing from Cherbourg to New York, I went to bed and slept around the clock. Nobody worked harder than motion-picture actors in those days. I was drained. *The White Sister* was my film; I had been completely involved in it. The producers had faith in my judgment, and I knew that I had to justify that faith.

We returned to New York to cut our film and set it to music. No company wanted to release it. *The White Sister* was to open at the

Forty-fourth Street Theater in New York on September 5, 1923. Mother was in a sanitarium outside the city, but she sent me a telegram: "Mother wishes you all success possible in your new picture. I know you will be sweet and dear in it."

Nell Dorr remembers the afternoon before the premiere. She was in the living room of my suite at the Vanderbilt Hotel. The rooms were banked with flowers from friends, business associates, and fans. Telegrams were pouring in, and the telephone and doorbell were jangling without interruption. Nell says that she was managing, but not very well. She was flustered and growing more nervous by the minute.

One telephone caller insisted, "It is most urgent that I speak with Miss Gish." Nell hesitated and then decided it would be best to check with me.

"I opened the door to the bedroom," Nell recalls, "and there you were stretched out on the bed and sound asleep."

Nell couldn't understand how I could sleep in the middle of all that clamor. I told her that it was a matter of concentration. At the start of my career, when we were on location or even on the set, I was often painfully self-conscious, particularly in love scenes. I found it impossible to shut out completely the presence of outsiders. So I devised a method of improving my concentration. I would put a salt cellar on the mantel, stare at it, and then, shutting my eyes, call up a picture of it in my mind. If other thoughts intruded, I blocked them out. At first, a minute seemed a long time to hold only that image in my mind, but gradually I increased it to two minutes and longer. Eventually, I could blot out the noise around me.

"This gift of concentration, which Lillian so painstakingly developed, has always filled me with great admiration," Nell has said. "During a time of my life when I was filled with anxieties about my family and found the nights long, gloomy, and filled with apprehension, Lillian would say: 'Now Nell, you must sleep. You will fritter away your health unless you sleep. Your mind can't hold two images at the same time,' she would add, 'so see yourself falling asleep.'

"And, you know, she was right."

The White Sister was an instant success. After its opening Nicholas

Schenck, Eastern head of Metro-Goldwyn-Mayer, relented and consented to distribute the film. Henry King was obliged to return to Italy to make preparations for filming *Romola* in Florence; he left me in New York to cut *The White Sister* from the twelve reels it had been when it opened to nine for later release in theaters all over the country.

I took the film to Mamaroneck to screen it for D. W. He predicted that a rush of religious films would follow its success, and not long after he was proved right.

✹ 20 ✹

After D. W. saw *The White Sister* he invited me to Mamaroneck to see his latest film, *America,* an epic study of the early colonies and the Revolution. Apart from a few scenes, the film was a heartbreaking disappointment. Time and again the film seemed to verge on the mastery one expected from Mr. Griffith, only to sink back into the commonplace.

Slowly the sad truth emerged. There was no one left among his staff to say "no" once in a while. He needed the gently abrasive minds and personalities of those who had once been close to him. He had thrived on the tactful suggestion, the quiet hint that some other director had done as well, that a better effect could be found. Secretly he knew that he needed this help. His constant questioning and his endless appeals for advice had been his way of admitting it. As scene after scene in *America* fell short of its promise, I could almost hear his deep voice ring out, as it had in the Biograph Studio: "Well, what do you think of it? What would *you* do?" Perhaps he no longer sought opinions. Or perhaps he was surrounded by people who did not want to incur his displeasure.

In any case, when the preview was over, D. W. immediately started small talk. He may have sensed what I was thinking, but to my relief he did not ask me what I thought of the film. I couldn't have told him.

Later, I heard reports that *America* was failing at the box office. Eileen Bowser has since written, "After years of distribution, reissue and sale of stock footage *America* earned back its cost, but it never was very profitable—possibly because its historical detail and educational spirit were at odds with the Jazz Age in which it was produced."

D. W. had been forced to mortgage the first half of his picture in order to make the second. He had received a half-million dollars, at 6 per cent interest, but it was far from enough. Even when the film was completed, he owed six months' salary to nearly everyone in the company. As meager receipts trickled in after the release of *America*, D. W. must have known that he could not continue at his Mamaroneck studio.

In July 1924 Adolph Zukor announced that D. W. had joined Paramount's staff of directors. Behind the headlines and the publicity releases I sensed the real story. D. W. had lost his gamble for independence.

He made one last independent picture before joining Paramount. When Zukor's announcement was released, D. W. was in Europe filming *Isn't Life Wonderful,* about the aftermath of war in Germany. The film showed how war brutalizes people. It was a story of starving children, helpless refugees, the multitude of personal tragedies that war brings to both victor and vanquished. It was the only picture he made after I left him that I thought worthy of him. Honest, moving, but grim, the film found scant audiences in America. It lost money. Shortly after, D. W. went to work at the Paramount Studios in Astoria, New York.

I returned to Italy to film *Romola,* my second picture for Inspiration. *Romola,* set in Renaissance Italy, was a good story, but it failed somehow to arouse my enthusiasm for anything but the beauty of its period. I would play Romola; Dorothy was to have the role of Tessa; Ronald Colman was Carlo Bucelline; and William Powell, a newcomer from the theater, was to play Tito, the villain. We had planned to film all of it against the background of Florence, but the telephone poles, streetcar tracks, and other signs of modernity made that impossible, so in our studio on the outskirts of the city we erected our own fifteenth-century Florence. We brought from Rome many of the people who had worked on *The White Sister,* and added an even greater number of Florentines.

Mother, who was well enough to come with us, was captivated by the skills of the Italian needlewomen, and she bought rare laces and dozens of hand-embroidered linens, many of which I still have. I remember how concerned she was about the poor of the city. She wanted at Christmas to arrange for the distribution of turkeys but found it wasn't feasible, since none of them had stoves for cooking. In the end, she distributed money.

Work kept us confined—work and constant rain. But we made progress. The Italian workmen were superb. We could rely on them to build a replica of anything from a great church to a banquet hall.

One of the most difficult scenes was that in which Tito throws Tessa into the Arno. Dorothy simply would not drown. Mother and I were watching with binoculars from a window in the Grand Hotel while the scene was being filmed. The Arno was dirty and filled with debris. When they pushed Dorothy's head down, her other end popped up. Although she could not swim, she could not submerge either, being small-boned and plump. Finally they gave up.

Henry King, the director, was called away after production was completed, so I was left with the final cutting of the film, which still lacked the scene of Tessa's death. So we went to the waters off Mamaroneck to drown Dorothy. An expert diver was there to pull her under. It was late October and very chilly, Dorothy had a bad chest cold, and to top it all off she was terrified of the water. We insisted that she take a drink before going into the water—she hadn't touched strong liquor since the age of three, when I had had the measles and she had taken my medicine. After she drowned successfully, we made her run up and down in her wet clothes to get her circulation going. She was over her cold the next day.

Romola was released by Metro-Goldwyn-Mayer, with a premiere at the George M. Cohan Theatre in New York on December 1, 1924, and five days later at Sid Grauman's new Chinese Theater in Los Angeles.

Mother, Dorothy, and I went west for the opening. As the train pulled into the station, we wondered what convention was being held there, for it was packed with people wearing big red badges. As the train slowed down, I noticed our names printed on those badges. Dorothy started to shake, Mother looked frightened, and I was speechless, wondering why we had not been warned. As we stepped down from the platform, there were Louis B. Mayer, King Vidor, Sid Grauman, and a number of other directors and producers. Mother, mistaking Irving Thalberg for an office boy, gave him our baggage checks. (Irving smiled and took them, saying he was always being mistaken for his own office boy.) We were quite overcome by the warmth of their greeting. Our tears turned to laughter when we learned that the Los Angeles Fire Department was to head our parade through town. At the Ambassador we found our dear friend Mary Pickford waiting for us in a flower-filled drawing room.

In general I liked making pictures but not the notoriety and publicity surrounding them. I had attended some Griffith openings, but I never really enjoyed the experience. The only time I had a personal press agent was when I later hired Richard Mitchell to keep my name out of the papers without hurting anyone's feelings, which was not easy. I wanted my career to last, and I thought that if I were constantly in the papers people would grow tired of me. But this was the first time I experienced the fantasy of a Hollywood premiere. I scarcely ate or slept during the five-day visit.

Although *Romola* did well, I never thought the drama matched the splendor of its fifteenth-century backgrounds. Douglas Fairbanks maintained that it was the most beautiful picture ever made, but I found it too slow-paced.

Giavonni Poggi, then director of the Uffizi Gallery in Florence, said of it: "In the film *Romola* the costumes, the principals and the ensembles seem to have been studied with the greatest possible care. Bravo for the beautiful work of Inspiration Pictures." And Firmin Gemier, director of the Odéon National Theater, Paris, wrote: "I must tell you how marvelous I think *Romola* is. Your reconstruction of the golden age of Florence gave me one of the greatest surprises of my life. It is a glorious moment from an epoch in which all true artists, all people of culture, all those who have loved and thought passionately, would like to have lived."

During that time, two sculptors, Dimitri Dirujinski and Boris Lorski, modeled busts of me. Nicolai Fechin did a portrait of me as Romola that was bought by the Chicago Art Institute. When I was in that city playing in *Life with Father,* it was hanging in the Goodman Theater.

I had been seeing a great deal of Charles Duell, who was my lawyer, producer, and financial adviser. He also suggested that he become the executor of my estate. I often signed papers that he brought me, relying on his word that they were for my benefit. But I began to have the uncomfortable feeling that he was taking over my life.

Looking back at that period, I realize that he thought of me as a valuable piece of real estate with the lease about to run out. I had never needed a lawyer before. I was not accustomed to contracts. I had worked with Mr. Griffith, whose word was his bond. Now I was being pressured to sign new contracts, to change existing ones. I began to have misgivings; something told me to beware.

Under the terms of my contract with him, the Duell company was obligated to make only one picture with me and had the right to terminate the contract on sixty days' notice, whereas I could be held to making twenty-eight pictures if the producers so desired. Those terms did not seem fair to me.

After *Romola* was finished, I received a diamond ring from Duell, but it was charged to the company as a gift for finishing the picture. And before long I returned it to him. A short time later, when he seemed deep in financial problems, he proposed to me.

He wrote me a number of persuasive letters.

In one, he tried to convince me that marriage would be to our mutual advantage, almost as if it were a business arrangement to be entered into. He made great plans for our future together: we would set up headquarters in Rome, then embark on a round-the-world cruise the following year. (This seemed to be his way of declaring his independence of Hollywood.) He also suggested that he might go into politics; an idea that he thought I should consider as well. Wasn't all this, he asked me, a good tip to take?

It was not a good tip. Duell asked me to assign my share of the profits from *The White Sister* to him. I realized that I was in trouble, but I did not know to whom I should turn. Not to D. W.; he was equally helpless when it came to legal matters. But the previous year in Rome I had met Senator Hiram Johnson, his wife, and his son Jack. The Johnsons had treated me as an adopted daughter and had told me to call them if ever I needed help. I wrote to them of my troubles, and they suggested a law firm to take care of my interests. Accordingly I decided to go to Chadbourne, Stanchfield, and Levy and to consult them about my predicament.

When I told Duell, he said, "If you do that, I will ruin you."

"How can you ruin me?"

"I can say whatever I wish about you, and they will believe me. You are only a motion-picture actress, while I am in the Social Register."

If I had not been so startled by his threat, I would have thought it was something out of an old melodrama.

In a letter written some time later, he suggested that I shouldn't worry even if the percentages on *The White Sister* stopped briefly, as I would soon be getting my full salary on our next picture. He warned me that it would be to my advantage to agree without further fuss; otherwise, the consequences would be disastrous. The result of any conflict, he implied, would be to hurt us both in the industry.

There is something in my New England and Pennsylvania Dutch blood that made this the wrong thing to say to me.

On January 31, 1925, The New York *Morning Telegraph* reported:

A serious breach in the business relations of Lillian Gish and Charles Duell, her lawyer, trustee, adviser and employer, was forecast yesterday, when Charles H. Duell, Incorporated, filed a summons and complaint asking an injunction to restrain the star from appearing with any other company and asking that she be made to fulfill her contract with the Duell organization. . . .

When questioned about the injunction proceedings brought by Charles H. Duell, Jr.'s personal company against Miss Lillian Gish, the latter's attorney, Messrs. Chadbourne, Stanchfield and Levy said, "This latest move is part of a design to force Miss Gish to support Mr. Duell. The experiences of Richard Barthelmess and Henry King are only repeated in Miss Gish's experience with Mr. Duell. Each of these outstanding artists has found it impossible to live under his business arrangements. Miss Gish's situation discloses, in our opinion, the worst condition of the three.

"Mr. Duell assumed to act as her lawyer, her trustee, her manager and at the same time to contract with her as the executive head of a company to produce her pictures.

"She started with a fairly intelligent contract. It was between her and Inspiration Pictures, Inc., a highly responsible first class corporation. Her work was done faithfully and well. And yet, after two years, during which Mr. Duell constantly whittled down her rights and, from time to time, took first this and then that advantage of her . . . she suddenly finds herself ostensibly yoked to Mr. Duell's personal company. So Inspiration Pictures, Inc. is entirely relieved from obligation. . . .

"Acting in his dual capacity, he apparently hoped to bind her to him for a period of years under an arrangement by which he would share the fruits of her artistic efforts without any danger of liability to him whatsoever.

" 'Heads I win and tails you lose' is not yet recognized as a basis for legal agreement.

"The injustice of this design is apparent when it was known that Mr. Duell's company was not even able to pay Miss Gish's salary for two months, but had to give her in part payment his receipted bill for legal services and to ask her for an extension for the balance. . . .

"The wholly unwarranted presumption intimated in the moving picture papers that Mr. Duell hoped to win the favor of

. 267 .

Miss Gish's hand is some indication of the length to which the gentleman is now willing to go in order to coerce her into working for him. There is absolutely no foundation for his presumption that she ever contemplated a matrimonial alliance with him. . . ."

Charles Duell tried to shame me in the press. I went personally to Adolph Ochs of *The New York Times,* Captain Joseph Patterson of the New York *Daily News,* Harry Carr of the *Los Angeles Times,* and William Randolph Hearst and told them in detail, showing them letters and signed papers, what Duell had threatened to do to me. All their papers followed the case closely but without the sensation and scandal Duell sought to inject.

The case was brought to court. My lawyers hired Max D. Steuer to represent me. I wanted to tell my side of the story to the court, but Mr. Steuer felt my testimony was not needed to win the case.

As the trial continued, the newspapers covered it in detail. The New York *Herald Tribune* reported on February 14, 1925:

> . . . Max D. Steuer characterized Duell as a "deep-eyed scoundrel" for whom the actress would never work again even if it meant giving up her screen career. . . .
>
> . . . Steuer declared that Miss Gish's contract was "grossly one-sided." . . .
>
> Miss Gish appeared in court with her mother and listened intently to her lawyer's argument. Holland S. Duell, brother of the plaintiff, testified in support of the producer's complaint, declaring Miss Gish had already been starred in two successful pictures under the terms of the agreement which she wished to cancel. Steuer asserted that by five modifications of the contract, Miss Gish was defrauded of $120,000 by Duell. . . .

The suit went on, leaving me worn and bewildered, the victim of a diabolical man. Certainly I knew about evil, but this episode was my first contact with hatred directed against me, a hatred so strong that it was willing to risk self-destruction in a battle to destroy me. It was a horrible experience, made more so by the worry it was causing my mother and sister. I finally persuaded them to leave New York; it was not their doing, so why, I reasoned, should they be punished for it.

It was at that time that I became known as a vegetarian. Because I was nervous during the hearings, I took carrots with me to nibble on. The carrot fad thus began in the United States, with resulting world-wide publicity. Some friends took me to the Grand Street Follies to see a young actress impersonating me on the stage and eating a carrot.

Finally, on April 2, 1925, extras were on the streets at noon carrying this headline: "Duell Held as Perjurer; Lillian Gish Wins Suit."

On the previous day Mr. Steuer had proved by Duell's own admission that Duell had tried to borrow $50,000 on my contract with Inspiration Pictures, which would not turn the contract over to him finally until he persuaded me to release Inspiration—and that Duell had guaranteed to obtain my signature to an agreement to give up my salary from September until the end of November, as well as other concessions, in return for which Inspiration would let him personally have my contract.

The next morning, when the court opened, Judge Mack said, "In twenty-two years of judicial experience, it has not been my fortune or misfortune to have had before me, with possibly one exception, any case of more flagrant, outrageous breach of trust and overreaching than has been shown on the plaintiff's [Duell's] own testimony, and with the exception of one other civil case there has never been more downright perjury committed than on the part of Charles H. Duell in affidavits and testimony."

"Miss Gish," the New York *American* reported, "sat with wide eyes fixed on the judge in astonishment, for even she had no intimation of the triumphant victory. Not a muscle in Duell's body moved as Judge Mack concluded, 'I hold the witness Duell to bail in $10,000 to answer the charge of perjury.' "

The *American* continued:

> It was Steuer who forced the promoter in the long series
> of contradictions of his own testimony that paved the way for

dismissal of the suit. . . . The fact that Miss Gish won the suit solely on the testimony of Duell's own witnesses and without putting on a single witness of her own was conceded a tribute to Steuer's generalship and skill.

Miss Gish, under the decision, is now free of Duell and the Inspiration Company with the court's assurance that they smashed their contract with her, not she with them.

Charles Duell lost all his money on the lawsuits he brought against me; he was disbarred from practicing law. I was told by lawyers that I could have had him put in prison for a year. But I did not want revenge, only freedom from contact with such a man, which I finally gained. I might point out that Duell died in 1954 and is not to be confused with the other persons named Charles Duell who have achieved prominence in other fields.

I needed someone to catch up with the mail, which was accumulating by the sackful. It consisted mostly of fan letters, and I liked to send each writer a little note or photograph, but it took a long time. And the publicity on the trial, which was then taking place, was adding to the mail load.

A friend of Senator Johnson's knew Phyllis Moir and had great respect for her ability. He suggested that she get in touch with me, explaining that I had just returned from Italy and was innocently embroiled in a lawsuit and in desperate need not only of a good secretary but also of someone who would understand my situation and work closely with me.

Phyllis wrote to me. Later she confessed that she hadn't expected an answer. But I asked her to see me at the Ambassador Hotel, where I was then living. Phyllis wondered what she was getting into. She had never seen a movie star in her life. She was an English girl who had not been in this country long, and she had worked mostly with embassies.

But she appeared at the Ambassador at the appointed hour. Reba, Mother's maid, let her in and asked her to wait, as I was expected soon. In the next room, Phyllis told me later, somebody seemed to be practicing operatic scales in a harsh, unlikely voice. It turned out to be John, my parrot—who was misnamed, as I discovered when he laid an egg.

Phyllis waited patiently for the kind of movie star who would be, as she put it, "very flossy and gay."

"And here came this little figure in a soft blue suit," Phyllis said later, "a Chanel, I believe, and a little pink hat and looking demure and terribly pale and upset. She said immediately, 'I'm sorry you had to wait, but you see I'm having my first lawsuit.'"

Phyllis agreed to come to work for me. She had been working for the famous Mrs. O. H. P. Belmont, whose daughter became the Duchess of Marlborough. Mrs. Belmont had left Phyllis in charge of her estate, as she was usually abroad. Phyllis had become bored with the whole business and had decided that a movie star couldn't be all that bad after the formidable Mrs. Belmont.

After the contract with Duell was voided, I received offers, it seemed to me, from every company in the business. I finally accepted one from Metro-Goldwyn-Mayer and made preparations for returning to Hollywood.

I asked Phyllis, who was faithfully answering the mail, if she would come with me. I told her that life would be more interesting when I was making pictures. She accepted the offer to come live with Mother and me in a comfortable bungalow at the Beverly Hills Hotel.

❧ 21 ❧

Before I left to start my new contract with M.G.M., I had promised to spend a weekend with Joseph and Dorothy Hergesheimer at their lovely stone house in West Chester, Pennsylvania. I had met Joseph Hergesheimer through Dick Barthelmess, who had filmed several of his stories.

On the train to Philadelphia a man approached and introduced himself to me. He was about five feet eight, handsome, delicate, with dark curly hair and a charming manner. He was George Jean Nathan, he told me, and he too was going to visit the Hergesheimers.

Mr. Nathan was the last person I cared to meet, as he had just written a most flattering piece about me in *Vanity Fair,* and I was afraid that after meeting me he would regret it. He had written: "That she is one of the few real actresses that the films have brought forth, either here or abroad, is pretty well agreed upon by the majority of critics. . . . The girl is superior to her medium. . . . The particular genius of Lillian Gish lies in making the definite charmingly indefinite. . . . The whole secret of the young woman's remarkably effective acting rests, as I have observed, in her carefully devised and skillfully negotiated technique of playing, always, as it were, behind a veil of silver chiffon. . . ." We sat and talked for the hour-and-three-quarter trip, during the course of which I found out that Mr. Nathan hated the movies.

It was a delightful weekend, with charming people and good conversation, but I was not comfortable with Mr. Nathan. Later, in New York, he would telephone, and if I answered I would disguise my voice and say that Miss Gish was not in.

Finally, Mother said: "Lillian, you cannot allow Duell to make you a recluse. All men are not like that. If you let him destroy your faith in people, then he has done you the worst kind of harm." I knew that she was right, and I began to accept George's calls.

George took me to several Broadway openings. He introduced me to Henry L. Mencken, his co-editor on *The American Mercury*. I immediately felt at home with Mencken, whom I found a charming and stimulating man. The first time we three had lunch together, I sat between them. I thanked them for printing an article that Joseph Hergesheimer had written about me. Then, to my surprise, they both started talking at once, neither listening to the other, each keeping up a barrage of observations and witticisms. I found out at subsequent lunches that it was their customary way of communicating with each other. Scott and Zelda Fitzgerald often joined us, drinking their whiskey as if it were water with seemingly no effect. I had always enjoyed the company of writers and newspapermen, and this was a thrilling new world to me. When I had to take the train for the Coast, I was sorry to leave.

My contract with Metro-Goldwyn-Mayer called for six pictures in two years, for which I would be paid, I believe, a million dollars. It was the last of the fifty-two-weeks-a-year contracts. After that players were awarded contracts for forty weeks a year.

Although I had been to Hollywood for the premiere of *Romola,* it seemed to me that the movie colony had mushroomed in the short time since my visit. It was a complex of studio cities, each sprawling across many acres.

Friends took me to see the old Triangle Studio, where I had worked for several years. I remembered it as being far from town; now all around it were new buildings. I saw a shabby green fence, in back of which *The Birth of a Nation, Intolerance,* and other fine films had been made. It was there that Douglas Fairbanks had started his movie career and Sir Herbert Beerbohm Tree had made his production of *Macbeth*. When I saw that fence, I knew I was looking at what had been my film home.

The whole structure of film making had changed. Unions had been formed. Everybody's job was circumscribed. Actors could not move a prop. Most of the time they had nothing to say about the choice of costumes. Most astonishing of all, some of the directors were merely part of the machine, doing mechanical jobs. The director no longer searched for a story, cast it, planned sequences, and supervised every detail of his picture until its release. He was simply handed a finished script and ordered to film it, scene by scene, line by line. A small army of assistants (from a dozen departments that had never before existed, including set designers, wardrobe managers, hairdressers, makeup artists, and script writers) were responsible for the work that Mr. Griffith had handled alone for each of his films.

Money was abundant. Luxury was everywhere. Shoeshine boys and cab drivers played the stock market. And in Hollywood indigent young actors were getting used to traveling in limousines and drawing rooms on the Super Chief. Leading players were manicured, made up, and dressed. High-salaried masseurs soothed away the muscle aches of a long day on location, even though doubles, stand-ins, and stunt men did much of the work that the old Biograph players had once performed without question.

Films had become big business.

At that time I made a new friend, Madame Frederick de Grésac. Madame was a Frenchwoman, the godchild of Victorien Sardou and the wife of Victor Maurel, the great French opera singer. She was a distinguished dramatist, who had written plays for Réjane, Marie Tempest, even Duse. She told us that she had been the veiled woman who visited Captain Dreyfus at Devil's Island after his sensational trial. One of the great figures of the post-World War I era, she opened a new world to me. I had first met her before my ill-fated contract with the Frohman enterprise. She was small, thin, animated, with red hair to match her sparkle. She always had two cigarettes lit, one in each hand, her two emerald rings sparkling as she gestured. Madame Freddie had made and lost three or four fortunes, but it didn't seem to disturb her. She loved to cook, and her meals, prepared with skill and love on a two-burner gas stove, were as delicious as if she had commanded an elaborate kitchen. She was a true friend, who always told me what she thought. Once, when I was preparing to play Lizzie Borden on the stage, she said: "How dare you run across the stage as if you were playing the Empress Eugénie. You are playing a New England peasant woman!" I quickly corrected my mistake.

Madame Freddie's candor sometimes shocked Mother. Once at dinner she said to me: "My dear, the Chinese are the best lovers, because the Chinese women are so cold and hard to arouse."

Like all of us Madame Freddie owned real estate in California. When the crash came, we were all to be caught in it, and Madame was for a time jobless and in debt. During our real-estate speculations, Madame came to dinner one night, and Mother happened to tell her about a piece of real estate she was considering buying. Early the next morning Madame Freddie bought it. Mother was outraged and said that she would not have Madame in the house again.

"Mother, the French are like that about money," I said. "But, if any of us were sick, she'd spend weeks nursing us."

George Jean Nathan was enchanted with Madame. They would go off chattering in rapid French when they didn't want me to know what they were talking about.

She was a great romantic, and she had a marvelous mind. Her interests were broad, and she never gossiped about trivia. Her stories were fabulous. During World War II she was in Paris when the Germans entered the city. She escaped with only the clothes she had on and came back to America with nothing. She was living on the West Side of New York in a small room, but she asked me to dinner. She had somehow gotten hold of some wonderful beans and made us the most marvelous meal.

She never told me how she escaped, but I remember her saying that she had been very close to death. I have never forgotten what she said that evening: "What a great adventure it will be to die.

I'm really looking forward to it. My life's been full of adventure, and I am sure it will be that way when I go over."

I had an arrangement with Madame's husband, Victor Maurel, to pose for him in return for voice lessons. He was a painter as well as a singer—and a great teacher. He would leave me in a darkened room, go into an adjoining one, and then tell me to paint a picture of my feelings in *Way Down East* with my voice, as I had painted them with face and body for the screen.

Metro-Goldwyn-Mayer had welcomed me with great banners strung across the streets of Culver City, proclaiming that Lillian Gish was now an M.G.M. star. Looking at them, I had said a silent prayer that they would be equally warm in farewell.

Then I discovered that no preparations had been made for me, no stories (not even ideas), no directors—nothing. I had been signed in the East by Nick Schenck and the business office. As I learned later, there was a struggle going on for power across those 3,000 miles. I was drawing a big salary meantime, and that troubled me. I would have preferred a percentage of the gross so that if the film made money then I would too. I wanted first of all to make fine films; I was sure that rewards would then follow.

In Paris I had met Gustave Charpentier, the composer of the opera *Louise*. I wanted to make a film of the opera, but its subject, free love, was a touchy one, and he was not amenable to any changes. So I brought out my little chest of stories, among which was *La Bohème*. I was confident that Madame Freddie, being French, was the one to adapt Henri Murger's novel *Life in the Latin Quarter,* on which Puccini had based his opera, for the screen. She came west and we worked together on the script.

Dorothy, meanwhile, was making pictures for Henry Wilcox in England and living in London with Charlotte Rennie, Jim's sister, while Jim was acting in the states. Mother shuttled between London and Hollywood, trying to help both her children with their new responsibilities.

Irving Thalberg asked whom I would like for my director. As I had been in Italy for two years, I had seen few recent films, and he ran some of M.G.M.'s latest ones for me. Among them were two reels of an unfinished picture that I found so good that I asked Irving for its director and the entire cast. It was *The Big Parade*. Irving agreed. I wanted Hendrick Sartov as photographer, and Irving said that I could have him too. By then Sartov had invented the soft focus lens, which he named the "Lillian Gish lens." He never let it out of his sight; he used to carry it around in his pocket.

When I suggested to Irving that we use panchromatic film, the new, highly sensitive stock that we had tried on the exteriors of *The White Sister* and had used exclusively on *Romola,* he hesitated.

"We can't handle it in our laboratories," Irving objected, "because we know nothing about it."

"It's the film of the future," I said. "You'll have to use it eventually. Why not let the man whom we took to Italy handle it?"

He reluctantly agreed. When the company saw the results, they tore out all the old equipment and rebuilt their laboratory to handle only panchromatic film in the future. I also persuaded them to build better miniature sets, so that the cameraman and director could plan scenes and lighting before filming and thus save time and money.

When I heard that Erté, a top designer of the time, had been brought over from Paris to do the costumes, I was pleased. I thought he would know just how Mimi should look. But at the first fitting, I found that all the costumes looked like brand-new dresses. I explained that Mimi was being put out of her attic because she could not pay her rent.

"Don't you know that this is made of calico that costs only five cents a yard?" he said, pointing to one dress.

"Yes, but on the screen it will look like a nice new dress," I objected. "Old worn silk would look poorer and move better. This stiff material won't act."

He became very angry with me and refused to cooperate, so I went to our wardrobe mistress, Mother Coulter, with reproductions of paintings, and we redesigned Mimi's clothes. I tried without success to persuade Renée Adorée to do the same. I thought that her costumes in the film destroyed the delicate French beauty that she could have brought to Musetta. Erté released absurd stories to the press, claiming that I refused to wear anything but silk, even when playing a poor girl. (I never learned what he thought of the film, because he never spoke to me again.)

I objected to the sets for the same reasons. "These are poor Bohemians," I protested. "They can't live in a big beautiful house."

"How are we to get exhibitors to pay big prices for your pictures if they don't see production values?" the front office demanded.

The executives finally agreed to let Mimi live in a "big" attic. I couldn't accustom myself to their strange set of values. But I was very happy with King Vidor, the director, and the cast—the romantic-looking John Gilbert, Renée Adorée, Karl Dane, Roy D'Arcy, Frank Currier, George Hassell, and Edward Everett Horton. King owned a large percentage of the gross of *The Big Parade,* which I begged him to keep, but he gave it up in favor of another contract. *The Big Parade* made a fortune.

I was unhappy with the Hollywood style of rehearsal. Before Mr. Griffith would begin filming any production, he would rehearse the entire film from beginning to end. Other directors, I discovered, simply rehearsed each individual scene before it was filmed. I wanted full rehearsals on *La Bohème;* I had never worked without them. Through them an actor could develop his character, grow used to his partners, time his scenes, and set his tempo. This approach wasn't known at M.G.M., nor was my method of rehearsing. It didn't take me long to see that the other players were greatly amused by my actions—opening doors that weren't there, going up and down stairs that didn't exist. When they tried to imitate my actions, they simply became embarrassed. I could not impose my kind of rehearsal on the others, nor could I object when they wanted music for their scenes. I had never had music before, and I simply had to close my ears and continue working. The music was fine, of course, when I wasn't trying to concentrate on a scene.

Madame de Grésac, who was a great help with the French characterizations, objected fiercely to some of the actors who were playing Bohemians, declaring that they did not look convincing, and to the choice of an artist's model, who—she said—looked like a Roman senator instead of the dainty little French girl whom artists would paint in the nude.

I also had original ideas about the love scenes between Mimi and Rodolphe. It seemed to me that, if we avoided showing the lovers in a physical embrace, the scenes would build up suppressed emotion and be much more effective. But I reckoned without the exploitation M.G.M. had given John Gilbert as the "Great Lover." King Vidor agreed with me, but the front office demanded that we include love scenes.

"What I remember most about the filming of *La Bohème*," Phyllis later told a friend, "was that both King Vidor and John Gilbert fell in love with Lillian. For two or three days, when they rehearsed love scenes, Lillian would say with a sigh, 'Oh, dear, I've got to go through another day of kissing John Gilbert.'

"Gilbert soon went from fantasy to reality. He fell in love with Lillian. He started writing her love letters and quarrelling with King Vidor. Lillian wouldn't go out in public with Gilbert. She did not want it to get into the papers, and after Duell, the thought of even innocent gossip was enough to frighten her."

After the opening I received a most discreet proposal of marriage from my leading man.

During the filming of *La Bohème,* I went swimming at 5:00 each morning. Phyllis disapproved. "Those great big waves," she said later, "and nobody on the beach to help if you'd been carried out by the current, which is terrible there. And all through January and February."

Phyllis considered me very Spartan. But I had to keep fit for my pictures. I also went once or twice a week to exercise classes, and I watched carefully what I ate and drank, as I still do. And, as always, tried to set aside some time for myself, for I believe that it is the mind most of all that keeps one youthful and healthy.

To prepare for Mimi's deathbed scene, I went to a hospital to observe the progress of tuberculosis in its terminal stages. Phyllis feared that I would not live through the scene. "Lillian was so tragic in that death scene that the effect was shattering," she said. "Everyone on the set was aware of it; the appalling awareness that Mimi must die hung over the set." King Vidor admitted that he worried that, if they did not hurry to take the deathbed scene, we would never be able to finish the picture. He himself could not watch it. He told Hendrick Sartov to photograph it and let him know when it was over.

Later, in his book *A Tree Is a Tree,* King Vidor wrote of that period, "The movies have never known a more dedicated artist than Lillian Gish."

Actually, the most trying sequence was the one in which Mimi runs through the streets of Paris trying to reach Rodolphe's room. Jostled by the crowds, Mimi grabs a chain on a cart and is dragged on the cobblestones. Finally she jumps on the back step of a bus drawn by horses. At the end I was scratched and bruised and dirty, and a moment after the scene was completed the rear wheel of the vehicle broke away. Had I still been sitting there, my legs would have been crushed.

During the making of *La Bohème,* I was vaguely aware of the strange behavior of everyone at my house. The Irish chauffeur disappeared, and a new man took his place. This change didn't particularly disturb me, for our house seemed to be a way station for servants, but I noticed that, whenever I was ready to go out, Nellie, my personal maid, would be fussing with the canary. Although Phyllis didn't tell me, I suspected what was happening. Someone had threatened to kidnap me. The new chauffeur, I found out, had a gun in a holster under his coat.

"It started with a threat over the telephone," Phyllis told me later. "I didn't want to frighten you so I went directly to L. B. Mayer. It was very difficult to see him. And he had a secretary who was one of the most formidable women I've ever seen in my life. She virtually ran Hollywood.

"Well, I told her I'd like to see Mr. Mayer. She looked at me doubtfully, so I said, 'It concerns the safety of Miss Gish, and, since you're paying her money and she's under contract to you, I should think Mr. Mayer would be interested.' Eventually I got in to see him, and, after I told him of the telephone call, I could see his face change.

He was plainly thinking of the money that was tied up in Miss Gish. So he said he'd have a detective put on the job, watching the house from the outside any time day or night you were home. When you went out, we were supposed to put the bird cage in the window."

Phyllis reminded me recently of the evening when we went to the preview of *La Bohème*. Afterward, we came home and went into the kitchen, where I poured myself a glass of milk.

"Oh, dear," I said. "How I wish I were a cook and didn't have to please so many people."

Phyllis replied, "Here you are one of the most famous movie stars in the world, and that's all you can say!"

La Bohème was first shown at the Embassy Theater in New York on February 24, 1926. The musical compositions were by William Axt, and they were synchronized by David Mendoza and William Axt. George Jean Nathan said that the score was more beautiful than Puccini's.

The New York *Post* said the next day, "The Gish can do no wrong, in the opinion of many who subscribe to the art of motion pictures. . . ."

L. B. Mayer said, after seeing the finished film, that he was proud to have his name on such a picture. It was successful, especially in Germany, where it was called *Mimi* and ran for years.

Two of my good friends in that period were Scott and Zelda Fitzgerald. Phyllis still speaks of her first meeting with them. Mother and I were living in Mrs. Pickford's beach house in Santa Monica. It was Sunday afternoon, and the servants were off. Phyllis answered the knock on the door and saw a handsome young man smiling at her.

"I am a fan of Miss Gish's," he said. "I've come all the way from Milwaukee to see her."

"Oh, I know you," Phyllis said. "You're Scott Fitzgerald."

"Yes," he admitted. Zelda was in the car, and he asked if he might bring her in. They were the most beautiful couple Phyllis had ever seen. They had come to the beach, they explained, to ride the roller coaster at the amusement park in Santa Monica.

I would see Scott and Zelda several times a year. Eventually Zelda's bright spirit dimmed. Scott told me of her illness when we met in Paris. "Zelda is a case," he admitted sadly, "not a person." His voice was calm, as was the upper part of his face, but the lower part was trembling. During his last sojourn in Hollywood, when Zelda was in a sanitarium, he often came to dinner. He would bring young starlets with him, but it was apparent that his interest in them was superficial. I don't think that he ever recovered from the tragedy of Zelda's madness.

In 1937 he sent me a copy of *Tender Is the Night* with a touching inscription:

> For Lillian Gish, My Favorite Actress. On the occasion of her 1st visit to New York of which this book is a practical guide.
> From Her Chattel,
> F. Scott Fitzgerald

❦ 22 ❦

After M.G.M. finished *La Bohème* they still had no story for me. I suggested *The Scarlet Letter*. Mr. Mayer agreed that it was a good story, but, "You can't do it," he said. "It's on the black list."

"How can that be?" I retorted. "It's an American classic, often required reading in the classroom."

"Nevertheless, the church and the women's clubs have banned it," he answered.

I had always wanted to film the story, but I had never been able to find the right actor for the part of the Reverend Mr. Dimmesdale, Hester Prynne's partner in adultery. Mr. Mayer suggested Lars Hanson, a Swedish actor, for the role and arranged for me to see *The Saga of Gösta Berling,* a film he had made with Greta Garbo. When I saw it I thought that he would be the ideal Dimmesdale.

"Would you bring him from Sweden if I get permission to do the story?" I asked. Mr. Mayer agreed.

To the heads of the church and women's organizations, I then wrote that I could not understand why I should not be allowed to bring this fine American story to the screen. They all answered in the affirmative. Having liked my film *The White Sister,* they agreed to lift the ban if I would be personally responsible for this film. So it was put in my hands. Irving Thalberg told me that Frances Marion and I could adapt it.

Irving asked me which director I would like, and I suggested Victor Seastrom. He had come from Sweden a few years earlier, and I had admired his work since seeing his *Stroke at Midnight*. It seemed to me that he had Mr. Griffith's sensitivity to atmosphere.

Both Lars Hanson and Victor Seastrom were perfect for the film. I have always believed that the Scandinavians are closer in feeling to New England Puritans than are present-day Americans. I found Victor Seastrom's direction an education in itself. The Italian school of acting was one of elaboration; the Swedish was one of repression. Lars Hanson played his scenes in Swedish, I in English, neither of us understanding the other. But words did not matter; the drama came through, strong and true.

Henry B. Walthall played the part of Hester's husband, and to my surprise I found that I was now taller than he, in contrast to our early Griffith days. Exercise, fresh air, and good nutrition had added three inches to my height. For some of our scenes he had to stand on a box, which was out of the camera's sight.

He once summed up to me the essence of his acting philosophy as "Think it, feel it, do it."

During the next-to-final week of shooting on the picture, word came from Dorothy that Mother had had a stroke in London. She was not expected to live. Deeply shaken, I cabled Dorothy that I would take the first ship I could from New York. I learned that by leaving Los Angeles in three days I could catch the liner *Majestic* for England.

Irving Thalberg, on hearing the news, said, "We'll work day and night on the scenes you have to do." Victor Seastrom calculated that by working on a twenty-four-hour schedule, we could compress the remaining two weeks' work into three days. During those three days none of us had any sleep.

Phyllis packed our bags and left on the train at Los Angeles. I was driven, still in makeup and costume, to catch the train at Pasadena. Louis B. Mayer, Irving Thalberg, and a number of M.G.M officials came to see me off.

Lillian and screen idol John Gilbert portraying life among the Bohemians in the M.G.M. production of *La Bohème* (1926).

Lillian with Hendrick Sartov, director King Vidor, and Irving Thalberg, the young genius of M.G.M., during the filming of *La Bohème*.

Thalberg and Lillian at M.G.M.; he wanted to arrange a "scandal" for her.

Lars Hansen and Lillian in a scene from the M.G.M. production of *The Scarlet Letter* (1926), one of the American films by the great Swedish director Victor Seastrom.

Lillian as Hester in *The Scarlet Letter*.

Hansen and Lillian at the climax of *The Scarlet Letter*.

Lillian as a Scottish lassie in M.G.M.'s production of *Annie Laurie* (1927).

The trip from Los Angeles to New York took five long days. It was a journey I shall never forget, not only because of my anxiety over Mother's condition but also because of my experiences during the course of it. The newspapers carried the story of Mother's illness and my journey to her side. Wherever the train stopped, hundreds of people were waiting on the platform. At first I wondered why they were there, and the conductor told us that they had all come to see me and express their sympathy and their prayers for her recovery. They pressed upon me their treasured good-luck pieces, holy medals, and prayers written on paper, as well as in their hearts. When I went out on the platform in one city some people told me that they had driven 500 miles to be there. Never before or since have I felt such warmth from so many. One woman held up a baby and asked me to touch it for luck, and they were all still expressing their sympathy and love when the train pulled out.

In London Dorothy was pale with worry and shaking like an aspen leaf. Mother was in a deep coma; she had never regained consciousness, but the doctors thought that there was a slight response when I went to her bedside. In a few days we were sure that she knew I was there.

We had loved the English before, but we now came to adore them. Everyone seemed to share our worries, and the staff of the Savoy seemed personally involved with our heartache. Prayers, kindness, and sympathy seemed to work a miracle. The day before my arrival Mother had not been expected to live; shortly after she seemed definitely improved. But I was then faced with a problem. I had to return to Los Angeles to work—to fulfill my contract—or stay with Mother.

Within three weeks Mother was able to make it clear that she wanted me to take her home.

After arriving in England I had learned what had happened. Dorothy was finishing the film *Nell Gwynn* at the time. Mother was ill with the flu and seemed to be having a difficult recovery. Reba, Dorothy's personal maid, usually went to the studio with Dorothy. But that morning before they left Reba said to Mother, "Mrs. Gish, how are you?"

"Not too well," Mother said, which was unusual for her. She never complained. Reba decided not to go to the studio but to remain with Mother. She stayed until evening.

That evening, Dorothy had a theater date with Petrie Nichols, a young Englishman. She came home right after the performance. She tiptoed into the apartment, so as not to awaken Mother, stepping out of her clothes as she went, leaving them all in little piles as was her habit. She slipped into bed without turning on the light, as Mother's bed was next to hers. She heard Mother's hand fall on the covers— once, twice. The third time she whispered, "Mother?" No answer. She turned on the light and found Mother unable to speak or move.

Reba had been moved to a new room, and the staff could not locate her immediately. Eventually the doctor arrived.

Later, Margot Asquith brought the King's doctor in for consultation. Lord Beaverbrook would stop by, bringing a little paper sack of fresh eggs from his farm. It was during the great strike, when nothing on wheels was moving, but we felt all of London was trying to help us.

Finally Mother had improved sufficiently for us to take her back to Los Angeles. It would be necessary to take the doctor and nurse with us. Dr. Henry Rowan, an Irish nurse, myself, and Mother on a stretcher left by ambulance for Southampton; Phyllis, Jim Rennie, who had come to England when he heard the news, and Dorothy followed by car. Almost as soon as we boarded the liner, the nurse was seasick. Phyllis and I took turns looking after Mother; the doctor helped too. In New York an ambulance was waiting on the pier to take us to the Ambassador, where Mother and I had lived for two years.

It was at that time that Charles Duell started one of the nuisance suits that were to haunt me for the next few years. (He had threatened to sue me again in every state in the union.) In the following weeks whenever I left the hotel it was by the back door.

George Jean Nathan was very kind during those weeks. He presented me with a little dog, a wirehaired terrier, which I named Georgie. He was a dear puppy who cut his teeth on all the best chairs in the drawing room.

Phyllis, meanwhile, was very resourceful in entertaining Dr. Rowan, who, like the nurse, would soon be returning to England. She took him to Coney Island and the theater, and sometimes George Jean Nathan would take all of us uptown to the Cotton Club in Harlem. After three weeks Mother was a bit stronger, and I decided to hire a railroad car to take us to the Coast. It was July and, of course, before the days of air conditioning. Dr. Rowan was concerned that Mother might not be able to stand the heat or the lack of oxygen at the highest altitudes during the journey.

To avoid this hazard we arranged for the private car to be attached to the back of a fast mail train. We had big tubs of ice with fans playing on them for air cooling. But it was hot going through the desert. We brought John the parrot with us, hoping that he would catch Mother's interest.

By the time we arrived in Los Angeles, Mother was still on a stretcher but was able to smile a little and have a pillow under her head. Dr. Rowan and the nurse stayed for a month to ensure that she would be left in safe hands. As the sound of the ocean at our beach house seemed to disturb her, we then moved to a house on a cliff.

Through Mary Pickford, who was familiar with all the employment agencies, we found a fine nurse, Miss Davies, who was devoted to Mother. But, after Dr. Rowan left for England, the new doctor ordered a darkened room and no visitors. By September there was no improvement in Mother's condition—indeed, it seemed to me that it had worsened. On her birthday I disobeyed the doctor's orders; I brought her gifts, opened her windows to sun and air, propped her up in bed, and asked friends in to see her. She improved from that day on.

She did not suffer, although she was still tired. I found that she enjoyed working jigsaw puzzles and saw to it that she had plenty of them.

Duell's harassment followed us out to the Coast. One evening I came home to learn that a man had been trying to serve papers on Mother. Phyllis had been out during the day, but, when she came home before dinner, Percy, the nurse, told her: "I kept him away from Mrs. Gish's room. I told him, 'She's ill, you cannot go up there.' I don't dare tell Miss Gish. It's so frightful!"

Phyllis said that when she told me the news I went quite white. A few minutes later a young man telephoned—someone I had recently met—and he asked if he could take me to a film. Phyllis told me later, "You refused, and I shall never forget the look on your face when you said to me, 'I wish I never had to see another man.' "

I was able to withstand Duell's threats; to have my sick mother subjected to such appalling blackmail gave me the courage to act. I got in touch with William McAdoo, and he arranged for legal protection.

The Scarlet Letter opened in August 1926, at the Embassy. The New York *Sun* commented: "Miss Gish, for the first time . . . plays a mature woman, a woman of depth, of feeling and wisdom and noble spirit. . . . She is not Hawthorne's Hester Prynne, but she is yours and mine, and she makes *The Scarlet Letter* worth a visit."

I had not heard from D. W. in months. My work and Mother's illness had kept me busy. I did not know where he was or what he was doing. Occasional rumors about him made my heart heavy. I heard that he was drinking heavily.

The two films that D. W. had made after *Isn't Life Wonderful* had been undistinguished. The first—*Sally of the Sawdust*—will, however, be remembered for introducing W. C. Fields in his first important screen role. *Sally* was originally a stage comedy, called *Poppy,* which had run for a year on Broadway. D. W. decided that it could be transferred successfully to the screen.

Players who were then working with Mr. Griffith remarked that he seemed to have lost his characteristic drive and vitality. They thought that perhaps he was ill. It is indicative that although Alfred Lunt, that fine actor, played a role in the film, Mr. Griffith seems to have not recognized his talent.

When Mr. Griffith had signed his contract with Paramount, he had neglected to tell them that he owed United Artists one more picture, so that, although it was made at Paramount, *Sally of the Sawdust* was released by United Artists.

Mr. Griffith's next film was *That Royle Girl,* which he claimed he made against his better judgment.

Late in 1925 I had made a brief trip to New York and visited D. W. at the Paramount studios in Astoria. It was a sad meeting. In the past he had always been so proud to show his latest rushes. This time he was embarrassed.

"May I see what you're working on?" I asked.

"I'd rather not let you see it," he said. His voice was hollow, and his eyes reflected despair. "It isn't worth looking at."

The rushes D. W. did not want me to see were from *That Royle Girl.*

As I said goodbye, he reached out and held my arm. "I have fifty bosses now," he said with a faint smile. "But at least I'm paying my debts."

I learned later that he was earning $6,000 a week, plus a percentage of the profits at Paramount, but most of it went to pay off his company's debts. He owed Hendrick Sartov, for instance, $10,000 in back salary. Sartov eventually received every cent of it.

Late in 1926 his third film for Paramount, *The Sorrows of Satan,* was released. Mr. Griffith had made it under protest. D. W. tried to rise above the material, a popular novel of the time, by adding a prologue based on Dante's *Inferno.* One critic who saw the sequences reported that they contained some of Mr. Griffith's best work. But Paramount executives cut the scenes because they thought they were not commercial. Mr. Griffith's ideas were always over their heads. They then re-edited the whole film and made changes in the story until it was no longer a Griffith picture.

Of that film Eileen Bowser has written:

> The financial disaster that resulted marked the end of Griffith's long relationship with Zukor. In what must have been one of his lowest moments, Griffith wrote Zukor a ten page letter recapitulating the difficulties he had encountered in the course of trying to fulfill his contract. The letter makes clear that conflicting instructions from Zukor, Lasky and other execu-

tives made a shambles of the budget and the picture, but the saddest element is its revelation of Griffith's loss of confidence.

My next film, in whose preparations I had not been involved, was *Annie Laurie,* based on the song of that name. John Robinson, who had directed *Sentimental Tommy* so expertly, was in charge. I played opposite Norman Kerry, and, although the reviews were generous when the film opened at the Embassy Theater in New York on May 10, 1927, the heroine lacked the emotional depth and stature of Mimi and Hester. Fans always wrote asking why I didn't smile more in films; I did in *Annie Laurie,* but I can't recall that it helped much.

I found a book by Dorothy Scarborough called *The Wind,* which excited my imagination. Its main character is a wind which constantly blows sand, indoors and out, and finally drives the heroine to madness. It is the story of a gently bred southern girl who goes to Texas, marries a Texan, is violated by a man she has met on the train, murders the man, and finally goes mad. Frances Marion, Victor Seastrom, and Irving Thalberg all shared my enthusiasm for it as did Lars Hanson who was cast for the first time as a cowboy.

As it was to be filmed on the Mojave Desert and spring had already come, we had to work quickly. At first the weather was still reasonably cool, but then the heat burst. Film coating melted from its celluloid base. With temperatures at 120° F., it was impossible to develop the film. Finally the technicians packed it frozen and rushed it to the Culver City laboratories to be thawed out and developed.

Working on *The Wind* was one of my worst experiences in film making. Sand was blown at me by eight airplane propellers and sulphur pots were also used to give the effect of a sandstorm. I was burned and in danger of having my eyes put out. My hair was burned by the hot sun and nearly ruined by the sulphur smoke and sand.

A few days before we finished in the desert, it turned cold. By late afternoon a real sandstorm had arisen with the intensity of a hurricane. The landscape was seen through a veil of sand, and, as they filmed the cowboys and me on our horses, bent forward in the saddle as we made our way back to camp, I wished fervently that Mr. Griffith could be there. How he would have loved to photograph that scene!

The Wind found favor in the eyes of Vladimir Dantchenko, the founder of the Moscow Art Theater. He wrote to me:

> I want once more to tell you of my admiration of your genius. In that picture, the power and expressiveness of your portrayal begat real tragedy. A combination of the greatest sincerity, brilliance and unvarying charm places you in the small circle of the first tragediennes of the world. . . . One feels your great experience and the ripeness of your genius. . . . It is quite possible that I shall write [of it] again to Russia, where you are the object of great interest and admiration by the people.

During the translation of *The Wind* from novel to screen, I was also involved in discussions with Irving Thalberg about *Anna Karenina,* which was to be my next vehicle. Irving did not think that Anna's children should be her own. He thought that they should be adopted, whereas I proposed to follow the Tolstoy original. Otherwise, I believed, we would be laughed out of theaters.

While working for M.G.M., I often saw the young Garbo on the lot. She was then the protégé of the Swedish director Mauritz Stiller. Stiller often left her on my set. He would take her to lunch and then bring her back, and Garbo would sit there, watching. I heard one day that she had lost her only sister, and I sent her flowers and a note. Garbo came to thank me, but she could not speak English. Tears came to her eyes. I couldn't speak Swedish so I put my arms around her and we both cried. I knew how I would feel if I had lost my darling sister and could not get to her from a strange far land.

"She has such a lovely face," I later said to Hendrick Sartov. "Why don't you take some tests of her?" He did, with results that impressed the heads at M.G.M. for the first time.

Garbo's temperament reflected the rain and gloom of the long, dark Swedish winters. She was treated shabbily in her first weeks at

Metro, subjected to all kinds of publicity gimmickry, and she is reputed to have said emphatically that, when she was "beeg like Mees Geesh," she would no longer tolerate it. "No more publicity like this; no more posing in bathing suits!" she vowed.

During my talks with Irving Thalberg over *Anna Karenina* I was suddenly sent for by Mr. Mayer, who had some papers for me to sign. I explained that I had promised my lawyer not to sign anything without his approval. Mr. Mayer grew angry and said I ought to trust him. He explained that he wanted to take me off salary until they had a story ready for me. I had gone off salary while I was in England, but since then there had been ample time for them to prepare a script for me.

"If you don't do as I say, I can ruin you," Mr. Mayer said.

It was the second time I had heard that threat. "I'm sure you can, but I gave my word," I said. "I can't break that; else how could you or anyone else ever trust me again?"

Irving spoke to me about renewing my contract. "We would like to have you stay with us," he said, "but there is something we think would be wise to do."

I knew Irving was my friend, so I listened.

"You see, you are way up there on a pedestal," he explained, "and nobody cares. If you were knocked off the pedestal, everyone would care." He added earnestly, "Let me arrange a scandal for you."

I was startled. The irony of the suggestion made me want to laugh. Charles Duell was in the midst of another one of his attempts to sue me, and I thought of all the time and money I had spent to keep my name clear.

"Thank you for your interest, Irving. But please give me a few days to think about it," I answered.

I had no one to talk it over with. Dorothy was in London; Mother was not strong enough to counsel me, and I did not want her worried. What kind of scandal did Irving want to arrange? I wondered. A romantic scandal, I decided—but for what? To sell pictures? Had the public changed so much? All my life I had been taught to keep my name clean. Mr. Griffith had always maintained that one touch of scandal would finish you in pictures. What had happened to change this? And, after the scandal had died down, they would be obliged to dream up another. Could I be on stage constantly—with a pre-arranged scandal before the release of each new picture?

My answer was a decisive *No.*

I told Irving my decision, knowing that my days at M.G.M. were numbered. I had been happy working with Victor Seastrom, Frances Marion, and Lars Hanson, and I was leaving M.G.M. what I hoped was a good film.

When we saw *The Wind* on the screen, all of us, including Irving Thalberg, thought it was the best film we had ever done. But the months went by, and it was not released. I heard rumors that it was being recut. I was called back to the studio, and Irving explained that eight of the largest exhibitors in the country had seen it and insisted on a change in the ending. Instead of the heroine's disappearing in the storm, she and the hero were to be reconciled in a happy ending.

The heart went out of all of us, but we did what they wanted. Then Mr. Seastrom went back to Sweden, as did Lars Hanson. Frances Marion later told me that it was the last film to which she gave her heart as well as her head.

The script of *Anna Karenina* was finally tailored for Garbo. I understand that the front office even considered changing the title. *Anna Karenina* was a foreign name they thought would surely be confusing to the average movie patron. They tried various one-word titles and decided on *Heat.*

But the prospect of seeing GARBO *in* HEAT on a marquee broke up even the most unimaginative executives. The film was finally en-titled *Love.*

After I made *The Enemy,* which Fred Niblo directed, my two years with M.G.M. were completed. I then considered a number of offers. (During my troubles with Duell I had lost the chance to play the title role of *Peter Pan* on the screen. I was Sir James Barrie's choice for the part, but it was impossible for Jesse Lasky to come to an understanding with Duell.) I finally signed a contract with United Artists for three films at $50,000 a film and 50 per cent of the profits.

I returned once more to New York. I stayed at the Drake with

Mother, who had borne the trip from the Coast quite well. During our stopover in Chicago, the press had brought up the question, "Are you engaged, Miss Gish?"

George Jean Nathan's name and mine had been linked. He had always been known to attend opening nights alone, with only coat, hat, and cane occupying the second seat. But whenever I was in New York during the theatrical season I accompanied him, and columnists had noted it.

I said firmly, "Mr. Nathan is a very brilliant man and my friend."

I saw a good deal of George. He had visited me several times on the Coast, and in spite of Phyllis' qualms about my driving I had taken him sightseeing in my little car. Poor George was very nervous anyway, but he never complained about my ability behind the wheel. Once I took him to a little restaurant on top of a mountain, and Phyllis told me afterward that she and Nurse Percy prayed that we would come back alive.

George's intellectual circle fascinated me. The period after World War I produced the greatest output of creative writing, perhaps the greatest literary period, in our century. Theodore Dreiser, Sinclair Lewis, Sherwood Anderson, James Branch Cabell, Scott Fitzgerald, Eugene O'Neill, Willa Cather, and Joseph Hergesheimer were working then. It was George who exposed me to this milieu, and George's friends seemed to like me. Later I was told that I was the heroine of Joseph Hergesheimer's *Cytherea* and that Queen Helen in James Branch Cabell's *Jurgen* was patterned after me. I believe that if George's friends did like me it was because I kept my mouth shut and was a good listener.

I was especially fond of H. L. Mencken. He had a wonderful gift with words, making three, say, do the work of ten. He did not look at all as his writing would lead one to expect; there was nothing hard-boiled or brittle about him. He had great love and tolerance for the human race.

I remember particularly his kindness to writers. Theodore Dreiser couldn't spell and Mencken read every manuscript Dreiser wrote for spelling errors. Years later, after his stroke, Mencken couldn't remember names easily and it embarrassed him. He was so gallant that he was reluctant to see his women friends because he could no longer pay them his little courtesies.

In the spring of 1927 D. W. wrote to us that he had returned to United Artists, which had not been doing well. The original four partners (including D. W., of course) had not made enough pictures to keep the company alive. United Artists had hired Joseph Schenck, brother of Nick Schenck, New York head of Metro-Goldwyn-Mayer, as production head. Schenck hired D. W., but with the understanding that Griffith would not act as his own front office. Schenck financed the Griffith films through the Art Cinema Corporation, which distributed its films through United Artists.

To D. W., the new Hollywood was a strange land. In the eight years that he had been away, it had grown enormously. One movie had done it all—*The Birth of a Nation*. But the vision he had given it, the dream of a universal language that would enrich and ennoble the world, was seldom seen. Now Hollywood was dominated by a new master, the executive producer, who often oversaw operations from an office in New York.

As hireling for his former company D. W. turned out three pictures—*Drums of Love,* a sex-filled Paolo-and-Francesca story set in nineteenth-century Latin America and obviously aimed for the box office; *The Battle of the Sexes,* a remake of his 1913 film; and *Lady of the Pavements,* a Ruritanian romance that attempted to be daring. *The Battle of the Sexes* had sound effects and a synchronized music track, and in *Lady of the Pavements* Lupe Velez sang a few songs, among them Irving Berlin's "Where Is the Song of Songs for Me?" These three unsuccessful films nearly ended Griffith's career.

Yet, even when frankly trying to make commercial movies, Mr. Griffith found it difficult to follow the formulas. When *Drums of Love* opened, to mixed reviews, at the Liberty Theater on January 24, 1928, Irene Thirer wrote in the New York *Daily News:*

D. W. Griffith Makes Apology in Curtain Speech.
In broken tones he told of having made another film which he supposed wouldn't mean much at the box office.

"I haven't any brains, I guess, as far as that part of the business is concerned. And although I really intended to try and hit public approval with this piece, I went ahead and did something different again. I am glad if you like it."

In 1928, Jack Lloyd, Mr. Griffith's friend, wrote to me hopefully, asking if I would like to make another picture with Mr. Griffith. During a recent screening of *Way Down East* he had suggested this possibility to Mr. Griffith, who seemed greatly interested. Jack felt some enthusiasm on my part would spark the project. He suggested that if I thought it was a good idea I might mention it, without being obvious, in a letter to Schenck.

But nothing came of the scheme.

Lillian and her mother.   PHOTO BY NELL DORR

Lillian in *The Wind* (1928), an M.G.M. production and one of the last of the
outstanding silents.

Lillian in *The Wind*, which was also directed by Seastrom.

Conrad Nagel, Lillian, and Rod La Rocque in *One Romantic Night* (1930), her first talkie.

Uncle Vanya, directed by Jed Harris, marked Lillian's return to the theater in 1930. Left to right: Joanna Roos, Eduardo Cianelli, Lillian, Osgood Perkins.   PHOTO BY VANDAMM STUDIO

Lillian, Mrs. Gish, and Dorothy on the roof of their apartment house after Mrs. Gish's stroke.

𝕴 23 𝕴

When Morris Gest had brought Max Reinhardt's production of *The Miracle* to America in 1923–1924, he had asked me to play the part of the nun. But I was under contract to do *Romola* at the time. My admiration for Max Reinhardt, then the foremost director and producer in Europe, was great, however, and I was happy to sign a three-picture contract with United Artists when I learned that he was to direct them. We hoped that the first would be the story of Theresa Neumann, the peasant girl of Konnersreuth whose stigmata—blood coming from her forehead, hands, feet and sides—had defied scientific explanation. Professor Reinhardt and I thought that her life would make a contemporary miracle play.

While Dorothy was making plans to return to the theater in a play called *Young Love,* I took Mother and her nurse to Germany. It was one of the many European trips we made in search of a cure for her. Because the Germans were so advanced in science and medicine, I hoped that the doctors could help to restore her speech, which she had never regained, as well as the use of her right side.

We arrived in Hamburg at dawn. Professor Reinhardt had sent his secretary, Miss Adler, all the way from Berlin to greet us with flowers. We had thought that members of his staff were the only ones to know of our arrival, but when we arrived in Berlin we found the station jammed with reporters, photographers, and the public, waiting to welcome us.

Although the chief doctor of the Kaiser Wilhelm Institute could do little to effect Mother's recovery, he suggested that she go to Doctor Sinn's sanitorium in Neubabelsburg, near Berlin, where she could have better care. Meanwhile, I was invited to stay at Reinhardt's home, Leopoldskron, outside Salzburg. A castle built in another century, it was as large as a hotel and always filled with candlelight and distinguished guests. Among them was Hugo von Hofmannsthal, the poet, who was to work with us on the story for our picture. Rudolph Kommer was also there. I never quite understood Kommer's official duties for Reinhardt, but he seemed to perform any task that was necessary to ease the director's path. He also arranged Professor Reinhardt's American tours. Madame Reinhardt joined us as soon as her current play closed. She was and is a beautiful actress known to the world as Helene Thimig.

We worked in Leopoldskron for three months. The German theater was at its height then. Reinhardt had five theaters in Berlin and three in Vienna, and the whole town of Salzburg was his stage. I was privileged to watch rehearsals at the Deutsches Theater in Berlin, where Professor Reinhardt was rehearsing *Romeo and Juliet* with the delightful Elisabeth Bergner and a new discovery, Francis Lederer. (I was so impressed with Lederer that I signed him to a contract for three films.) The rehearsals were a model of efficiency; everything was orderly and spotlessly clean. The stagehands were immaculately dressed and took great interest in the actors and the play. I was reminded of the unity of purpose that had marked our own early days in the theater.

I was surprised when Professor Reinhardt asked me to tell Elisabeth Bergner that her puffed sleeves would cut off her face from the audience. I thought it odd that I should be asked to give this perfect actress any suggestion. When I asked Rudolph Kommer why Professor Reinhardt did not speak to her directly, he said: "Don't you know? The Professor can't stand red-haired women."

"But they have worked together successfully many times."

"Ah yes," Kommer said. "The Professor respects her talent."

I noticed that Francis Lederer received most of the Professor's attention; Elisabeth Bergner was allowed to go her own way.

When the play opened, the balcony was too far back, and the crypt scene was played under it too far upstage. On opening night the press complained of the cast's inaudibility. The Professor took another fortnight to restage the play, bringing all the scenes forward. The critics came back for a second appraisal and reported that their Bergner and the new leading man Lederer were the greatest Juliet and Romeo the world had ever seen!

Another production, *The Three Penny Opera,* starring Lotte Lenya, was also a great success.

The artists did me the honor of having a special showing of *La Bohème,* renamed *Mimi,* which was a favorite picture in Germany. Many German singers and musicians performed that night, and nearly every artist in Berlin was in the audience. I wanted so much to tell them how deeply I appreciated the warmth of their welcome, but unfortunately I couldn't speak their language. Professor Reinhardt told me that he didn't remember that in his lifetime anyone in the arts had come to Germany and received a more unanimously favorable press.

I wanted to journey to the village of Konnersreuth to see Theresa Neumann. She was carefully guarded by the Church, and no one was allowed to visit her without special permission. Fortunately, Professor Reinhardt had arranged for letters from the Archbishop of Regensburg granting me permission to see her.

My Austrian maid Josephine came with me. Konnersreuth was hardly a village—only a church and a well surrounded by houses in a circle. We approached the largest of the houses; the door was opened by a little figure in black, who giggled at my poor German and went to fetch the priest. When he read my credentials, he introduced me to the little black figure who was Theresa Neumann. She was pale, shorter and heavier than I was. It was Wednesday afternoon, and she experienced her stigmata only on Fridays. We tried to talk to each other in our own tongues. She said I might come again the following day.

It was my good fortune to find in the village two young priests, one an American who recognized me. They were sympathetic to my need for secrecy. The next day they went with me as interpreters. I thanked Theresa for her prayers for Mother, and she said, "We ought to pray for everybody and especially for those who ask our help and tell us their troubles."

I asked hesitantly to examine her hands, over which she wore little black mitts. The scars on the backs of her hands were the shape and size of quarters; on the palms they were long and narrow. At that time she had been without food for two years and without water for eighteen months. This was verified by the doctors and scientists who sought to analyze the mystery of her condition.

Fortunately, I had been forewarned by the young priests of what to expect on Friday; otherwise I might have fainted when I saw her the following day. It was 8:00 in the morning, and she was in her bed in a tiny room flooded with brilliant sunlight. I stood there, looking at a figure in a blood-soaked nightdress, neither sitting nor lying but seeming to be suspended halfway, with her hands held before her. The Bishop of Lisbon was sitting at the head of her bed. She was in her "passion ecstasy," and the tears of blood had been flowing for eight hours. They had coagulated and pulled down the lower eyelids. The cloth around her head was bloodstained, as were her hands. Her eyes stared intently as she explained with great excitement what was going on. When she was in this ecstasy, she spoke in the languages of the visiting priests—this time it was Portuguese. The week before, one of the young priests told me, her speech had been in English. She had been known to speak in Sanskrit and Aramaic. Yet, when she was normal, she couldn't even write her name. Her father and mother were poor hard-working farmers. They were so proud when a young Jewish lad, after witnessing Theresa's passion, decided to become a Catholic and study for the priesthood. During her passion Theresa would lose five pounds, but she would gain them back later.

I cannot help but believe in miracles after what I saw that day in the farmhouse. I returned to Salzburg more convinced than ever that we should do Hofmannsthal's story of this living miracle.

Our days were spent mainly in discussion and work. Evenings, when we were not at the theater, we enjoyed chamber music in the great hall at Leopoldskron. One evening, as I was dressing for dinner, I heard glorious music. On the terrace below was the Vienna Philharmonic Orchestra playing as a surprise for me.

Reinhardt's small dinner parties usually included forty to fifty guests; larger ones brought at least 250. It was a thrilling experience for me to meet fine artists in every medium. Rudolph Kommer took me to every shrine and place of interest.

Joseph Schenck, for whom we were to make the film, arrived. After a rather heavy lunch, Mr. von Hofmannsthal read the lengthy script aloud, while "Uncle Joe," still suffering from the long train journey, quietly snoozed. But at the end of the reading he said that it was fine and that we must come to Hollywood and begin.

The Professor suggested that it would be easier and less expensive to make it in Germany.

"No," Joe Schenck replied, "you need all the modern equipment and assistance we can give you for your first film. You must do it in California."

Mother's doctor believed that she was making progress and should not be moved for another few months. So I left her with her nurse, Miss Davies, and returned alone to New York, where Dorothy had just opened in *Young Love*. After my summer of German culture, I couldn't help wishing that her adult debut in the theater had been in something more distinguished than this slight comedy. When my disappointment in the play reached the press, Dorothy was cross with me. I couldn't blame her.

I was upset at the changes that were taking place in our working world. Talking pictures had been born. Al Jolson, the man whom Mr. Griffith had wanted to bring to films a few years earlier, had sung in *The Jazz Singer*. When I returned to Hollywood, I saw that every studio was being transformed with soundproofing, which made it airtight. Under the hot lights, the poor actors had to wear rubber suits under their costumes to keep them looking dry during the filming. Joe Schenck suggested that Professor Reinhardt turn our film into a talkie. The Professor went to the desert for three weeks to work but he finally gave up. How could one verbalize a story like Theresa Neumann's? The project was abandoned, and he returned to his castle at Salzburg.

I prepared to make another film, *The Swan*, which Gilbert Miller had produced so beautifully in the theater with Eva Le Gallienne. The company also agreed to let me do Eugene O'Neill's *Strange Interlude*, but before we could buy the property, a plagiarism suit was brought against Mr. O'Neill. The woman who sued him lost, but it meant that I had to give up the prospect of filming his play.

One afternoon during the period when we were preparing to film *The Swan*, I stopped in at the United Artists studio. Mr. Griffith was running screen tests in the projection room. When he saw me, he raised his hand and waved me away.

"Don't come near me, Miss Gish," he called out huskily. "I have a bad cold." I sat down a few seats away, but D. W. shifted his chair so that I could barely see him.

"Is it true you're going to do *Abraham Lincoln?*" I asked.

"Yes, I hope so." He added bitterly, "I'll probably have to wheel in a Pulmotor after he's been assassinated and revive him, so we can have a happy ending."

I asked him a few more questions, but he only mumbled in reply. When I left, he didn't rise to see me out. But Harry Carr, his old friend and mine, did.

When we were out of earshot, he said: "The Boss doesn't have a cold. He just didn't want you to smell his breath."

Before long the press announced that D. W. Griffith was to direct his first talking picture, a biography of Abraham Lincoln. I was happy for him, thinking that it was good Griffith material, and I hoped that he had found himself again. But the announcement told only part of the story, which I later learned from Harry Carr.

In disgust over the plots United Artists was giving him, D. W. had searched for a solid story. He found it in a new book, *John Brown's*

Body, by Stephen Vincent Benét, which he read in proofs before publication. The book, which has been called the only American epic poem, won a Pulitzer Prize for Benét in 1929. D. W. was impressed with Benét's talent and brought the book to the policy makers at United Artists.

"D. W., are you crazy?" they said. "You can't film a poem."

"I've done it before—in *Pippa Passes.*"

"Oh, that was back in the Dark Ages, when people would watch anything."

"But Benét is a great writer. *John Brown's Body* won the Pulitzer Prize."

"So, who's Pulitzer? Whoever heard of him? And who the hell is John Brown?"

A few days later, D. W. had come up with another suggestion. If they would not allow him to do *John Brown's Body,* what about doing the life of Lincoln—with Benét as the writer?

Well, they decided, there might be money in that. Griffith directing Lincoln with a couple of big stars—that sounded more like box office. Walter Huston was hired for Lincoln, Una Merkel for Ann Rutledge, and Kay Hammond for Mary Todd Lincoln.

Benét agreed to write the script, with one stipulation. He was to work exclusively with Mr. Griffith, without interference. He had been warned about the Hollywood hierarchy, and he did not want anything to do with the bosses. The executives agreed.

Benét went to work; he finished his script, and Mr. Griffith took it to the front office. Soon the bosses called for a script conference and insisted on Benét's presence.

Benét sat through the long autopsy on his script without saying a word. Then he rose, looked at D. W., sadly shook his head, picked up his hat, and left. He took the next train back to New York. I believe that was the last Hollywood ever saw of him.

The rumors about D. W.'s drinking ceased while he was making *Abraham Lincoln.* Though the finished film lacked the power that Benét might have brought to the dialogue, it did contain much good Griffith work, and it was well received. It turned in a small profit, but after the film he and Schenck, with whom he had had many disagreements on this and the other United Artists films he had directed, agreed to go their separate ways.

The Swan, which was to be retitled *One Romantic Night,* kept me in Hollywood for about three months. Mary Pickford lent me her bungalow on the United Artists lot, and I slept there whenever I had to be on the set early.

Instead of Professor Reinhardt, we had a new director from central Europe, whose work no one seemed to know. He was lacking in all but one of the three "t"'s so necessary in our world—talent, taste, and temerity. One could survive with two, but he had only temerity. The costume department had created lovely clothes, and Marie Dressler was made to look like a queen, but she was ordered to behave like the heroine of *Tillie's Punctured Romance.* The actors were fine—Rod La Roque as the prince, Conrad Nagel as the tutor, and O. P. Heggie—but the picture was slow and dull. I was unhappy about it. Joseph Schenck thought that I was acting unwisely when I asked to be released from my contract. "You're lucky to have a voice that can be used in talking pictures," he said. "You have a whole new career, and we have great plans for you."

But instead I listened to George Jean Nathan, who was so emphatically against movies.

Dorothy meanwhile went to Germany and brought Mother to London, where I joined them. Although Mother was still without speech, she managed to communicate to us that she did not want to travel anymore. She wanted a home.

"Why, Mother," I said, "you know you like to ramble."

Mother shook her head in an emphatic negative. I had planned to take her to Spain, but, in accordance with her wishes, we all came back to the United States and looked for a suitable apartment.

Mother bequeathed us many gifts, among them an appreciation of beauty. Recently I showed a couturier a bit of Mother's workmanship, a slip with tiny, even stitches. "Sometimes we didn't have enough to eat," I said, "but we always had real lace on our underclothes."

"Why not?" he said with understanding. "An artist can do without bread but not without beauty."

We could never persuade Mother to buy clothes for herself, but she did like to live in beautiful surroundings. I rented an apartment on Beekman Place and Fifty-first Street, facing the East River. My friend Paul Chalfin, who had designed and decorated Vizcaya, the James Deering estate in Miami, planned and decorated it. The furniture consisted of pieces I had collected in Paris. Mr. Chalfin chose robin's-egg blue and turquoise for the main colors, with accents of salmon. The draperies, of panne velvet, were of a special weave, with a mother-of-pearl opalescence. The chiffon curtains were painted blue and yellow. Even on dark days, the effect was of waves of sunshine.

For my rooms, Mr. Chalfin used pale gold for rugs, dull gold taffeta for draperies, and beige-and-white wallpaper as a framework for the French Directoire furnishings. My bedroom and private sitting room also faced the river, and when I awakened in the morning water seemed to ripple on the ceiling and walls, giving me the delightful feeling that I was on a ship. It was the most beautiful apartment we had ever had. But the river noises at night disturbed Mother, so eventually we moved.

Our next apartment was on the corner of Sutton Place and Fifty-seventh Street. This time it seemed best to lease two apartments, one for Mother and the penthouse for me. I wanted a place to entertain my friends without disturbing Mother, who could join us if she wished. We were happy there, until the builders decided to put up an apartment house just beyond us toward the river and blocked our view. Before long there was a vacant apartment in the building next to ours, and we moved into it. I still live there today.

The Sutton Place area is home to me. I have lived in the neighborhood since 1929, and it is like a village where everyone knows you. Recently, when I decided to take out an insurance policy, I found that it is not one's health that concerns the company as much as one's character. I was prepared to brief the salesman, but he said, "Miss Gish, we know all about you—who your friends are, your professional and social life, even what you eat for breakfast."

In an effort to please Mother, I bought a Cadillac and hired a cheerful chauffeur. I thought it would do her good to ride out of the city. But she was happier in a promenade by wheelchair up and down Fifth Avenue, where she could look at the windows and stop to visit with the shopkeepers.

The stroke had deadened Mother's speech center, but with great determination she learned after twelve months to articulate three words. They were "I like you." I can't remember one person whom Mother ever met and disliked. She knew that cruelty and ugliness existed, but she always looked for the goodness in people.

Her mind was still sound; she took great interest in the world around her. It was a long and tedious process, but she learned to sign her checks with her left hand. She was always bright and cheerful. By her quiet will she kept the air of sickness out of our apartment. No one who ever saw her felt that he was visiting an invalid. She walked around the apartment with the help of a cane. Once she slipped in the hall, fell, and struck her head. She laughed at her mishap.

In the 1920s Jed Harris was the boy wonder of Broadway. Every play he produced was a great success. I met him indirectly through George Jean Nathan. George introduced me to Ruth Gordon, an actress whom I greatly admired. He invited the two of us to lunch, and we took an immediate liking to each other. We were both Francophiles, and we both liked a special wine, Clos Vougeot. Ruth said that she had a friend, Jed Harris, who shared our taste for this wine, and it was agreed that each of us would try to find a bottle and that whoever found it first would give a dinner and invite Jed Harris. Not long after I met him at dinner in Ruth's apartment.

George Jean Nathan was an articulate man, and I had learned much about the theater from him. He knew the drama better than anyone I had ever met. He could take any given scene and tell you in detail how twenty different dramatists had treated it, so prodigious was his memory. But that night, I was even more enthralled listening to Jed Harris. He glowed with love of the theater. When I said good-night to Ruth, I whispered: "He's wonderful! I'd work for that man for nothing." Three weeks later he called and asked me to play Helena in Anton Chekhov's *Uncle Vanya.*

For *Uncle Vanya* Jed, with his fine instinct, had gathered a superb cast. Walter Connolly was the weary, disillusioned Vanya; Osgood Perkins, father of Tony Perkins, was Astroff, the hard-drinking, disillusioned doctor; Eugene Power played the ailing city professor; Joanna Roos was Sonia, his unhappy daughter; Kate Mayhew was Nurse Marina; and Isabel Irving, Eduardo Ciannelli, and Harold Johnsrud played the other roles. Rose Caylor—Mrs. Ben Hecht and herself Russian—did the translation, with Jed working on the adaptation.

George read the acts as they were completed. He read the first act and approved of it. He read the second act and was enthusiastic. When he finished the third act, however, he said, "Lillian, you cannot do this play."

We had been in rehearsal for two weeks before the third act was completed. His statement was so contradictory to what he had said before that I was astounded.

"You will have to get out of this play," he repeated.

"How can I? We open in less than two weeks."

"That's immaterial," he persisted. "You get out of it, get sick, go out of town. You can't hold your own against that last great speech they've given Sonia. She will wipe up the floor with you."

"That's too bad," I said, "but I promised to do the play, and I shall do it."

"That doesn't mean a thing; you haven't signed a contract."

"My word is my contract."

"Well, if you don't step out now, you'll never get another job in the theater as long as you live."

His judgment, which I valued, made me dread opening night.

Worthington Miner, Jed's assistant, was in charge of many rehearsals, but neither he nor Jed gave me much direction. When my scenes came up, Jed would say: "You've directed a movie. Take this scene, and do it as you would in films." I was too frightened to protest, only hurt that he helped everyone but me, who needed it most. My character represented that quality that all men search for and is always just beyond their reach, and it was not an easy assignment. I wondered if he was sorry that he had chosen me.

I asked him years later why he had neglected me when I had needed guidance so badly.

"I felt that I had a frightened bird in my hand, and if I gave it direction it would fly away," he said.

I never had a contract with him; I had said that I would work for nothing for the chance to make such a distinguished re-entry into the theater, and I meant it. I was surprised when an envelope was handed to me at the end of the first week with a large sum of money. I heard later that Jed's staff was worried for fear that I would walk out. But apparently Jed counted on my professionalism and knew that I would carry on.

In that period there was enmity between films and the theater, and, as I had long acted in films, I was anxious about the critics' reactions. I wanted to slip quietly back into the theater. I asked Jed not to use my name on the marquee. Richard Maney, Jed's press agent, told me afterward that it took him three days to get up the courage to ask me if they could use my name on the road.

When we took *Uncle Vanya* to Boston, Maestro Serge Koussevitsky came to see the play, and later he and his wife had dinner with us at the Ritz. The Maestro had been a friend of Chekhov's; he had seen the first performance of *Uncle Vanya* in Moscow. He related the story of the performance and the audience's reactions, and we sat listening until dawn. Where American audiences laughed, the Russians had wept; their laughter was matched by our tears. He could not have been more flattering to us when he compared the two renditions. We were very taken with the Maestro. His eyes had that look of wonder that is common among children but that most of us lose with maturity. He made us feel personally involved in the Boston Symphony, then a little world of its own, and we were allowed to come to rehearsals, which were always more interesting to us than the finished concerts.

The cast of *Uncle Vanya* was inspiring, particularly Kate Mayhew. Kate was in her eighties and still a joyous woman. To be associated with her was to relive American theatrical history, for she had come to the theater as a child. She had once been the understudy of Lotta Crabtree. She and her sister had no money; they had given all their valuables to their friends before they had grown old.

Some years later, Jed said to me: "Remember Kate Mayhew in *Vanya?* She was so right—the pivot—around her everything else fell into place."

Not wanting to see the bad news in print, I resolved not to read the notices until the play closed. If they said I was terrible I would despair. If they were good I would wonder what I had done that night that was right, looking backward instead of forward.

Later I read that Percy Hammond of the *Herald Tribune* had written, "In the future when I am told that association with the films is a destructive influence, I shall cite Miss Gish's appearance in *Uncle Vanya* to prove the contention wrong."

24

The night that *Uncle Vanya* ended its engagement at the Biltmore on November 29, 1930, D. W. Griffith came backstage to congratulate me. I hadn't seen him in quite some time. It was more than eighteen years since that midsummer day when Mother, Dorothy, and I had entered the old Biograph Studio. He made no mention of his plans; his departure from the payroll of United Artists had made his future a question mark. He talked mainly about the D. W. Griffith Corporation, which had been set up in his name in 1920 to sell stock to the public. He told me: "These are people who saw and loved my pictures and because they believed in them, they have invested all their savings. Hard-working men. Widows with children. How can I let them down? It keeps me awake at night, trying to figure out which story will make money."

In March 1931, when Dorothy was playing in Shaw's *Getting Married,* she received a note by messenger.

"Dear Dorothy," she read, "I bet you won't do this. I bet you won't come over and have supper with me at the Astor Hotel after your performance."

It was signed "D. W. Griffith."

Dorothy thought that it was some kind of college prank. Nevertheless, after the show she went to the Astor. D. W. was in an alcoholic stupor; he had probably been drinking when he sent the note. There was a nurse in the room trying to take care of him.

It made Dorothy ill to see what was happening to this great man. It seemed that there was no longer any place for him. He could not make movies the Hollywood way, which meant that he could not make movies at all anymore. The enforced leisure, to say nothing of the blow to his pride, must have been unbearable for a man who had worked so hard all his life.

Then D. W. seemed to regain control of himself for a while. He came to our apartment for dinner one night in the spring. With his usual secretiveness, he spoke guardedly of a film that he was planning, another talkie. From what we could tell, it seemed to be concerned with the problems of alcoholism. We made the logical deduction that it drew on his own experiences and did not pry. Actually, the story was based on a novel by Émile Zola, *The Drunkard*. D. W. did not tell us where he was getting the money, but evidently he had been awarded a fair-sized tax refund two years earlier, and the company treasurer had invested it in stock. In spite of the Depression, the stocks made money and that, plus a small bank loan, was enough to finance a low-budget picture.

Paramount agreed to let him use one of its sound studios. A small cast was assembled, and rehearsals began. But at the last minute the dealings with Paramount fell through. Mr. Griffith scouted frantically for a place to work and finally rented the studio in the Bronx where in 1913 he had shot the interiors for *Judith of Bethulia*. I heard that he was working with second-rate equipment, forced to shoot some scenes outdoors, where the primitive sound equipment could not pick up the actors' voices. He labored through the film. *The Struggle* opened at the Rivoli in New York on December 10, 1931, and the reviews were dreadful. One trade paper bypassed a review out of respect for Mr. Griffith's former stature. He hid in his hotel room and refused to see anyone. *The Struggle* ran for one week, and then United Artists withdrew it from general release.

It was the last film D. W. Griffith ever made.

The Film Library of the Museum of Modern Art ran it recently for Anita Loos and me. Anita, who wrote the script with her husband John Emerson, had wanted to treat the story humorously, with Jimmy Durante in the leading role. It seemed to her the only way that the film could turn out well. D. W. seemed to give her suggestion serious thought, but in the end he filmed it as a drama, with Hal Skelly in the lead and Zita Johann as his wife. Except for a certain vividness in the factory sequences, where Mr. Griffith showed his usual skill with documentary scenes, I was disappointed with the film and saddened by his attempt to copy himself.

When D. W. Griffith stopped making movies, the purpose went out of his life. He was the hardest-working man I have ever known. During the years I worked for him, he spent sixteen hours a day and sometimes more on the job, with never a vacation. Intense, driving work insulated him from the world. In the beginning, his creative talent was nourished by exposure to the people in his company. But success and fame put him on a pedestal. He became surrounded by men who bowed to his orders when what he needed was the friction of independent minds. It is a sad fact that one must suspect those who say, "You're wonderful." It seems to me that one should count all one's critics as friends.

He also lost touch with the common man, whom he had loved and with whom, particularly in his early years, he had felt a close kinship. He isolated himself in a remote studio. He built his own little world of work at Orienta Point and left it only for increasingly unpleasant trips into the other world, either to find money or to fight censorship. He stayed at his studio all day and then watched rushes until 1:00 or 2:00 in the morning. He lived in a small house on the estate and ate his meals in the commissary. Once his chauffeur said to Agnes Wiener: "What is the matter with the Boss? Has he no family to see?" Sadly, although he helped to support many members of his family, he had none.

When he had to go to work for other people to obtain money, his films suffered. He needed artistic control to make successful pictures. He failed completely whenever he deliberately set out to make a commercial movie; he did not understand what audiences of the time required and could not believe in the films he was doing.

His good friend Herb Sterne once said to me, "D. W. made the virginal the vogue, and it reigned until Volstead, gin, and F. Scott Fitzgerald gave birth to the flapper." His concept of woman was shaped by his inheritance and environment. The line of demarcation was sharp between the good girl and the girl whose morals were elastic. I remember when we reported to Mr. Griffith that Marguerite Clark, in her first film, *Wildflower*, had taken off her stockings right before the viewer. He was shocked.

"Doing such things before the camera!" he exclaimed. "How can I compete with that?"

He was also shocked when in *Joan, the Woman*, made before Joan of Arc was canonized, Cecil B. De Mille added love scenes to her story. And he was appalled at the way that the Bible was transferred to the screen. "I'll never use the Bible as a chance to undress a woman!" he said.

He saw himself as similar to a newspaper editor, in a position to affect not only his country but also the world. He regarded his films as the news, editorial pages, features, human interest, comics—and he took an editor's responsibility for his point of view.

Some of his strengths were also his failings. He believed that he was the heart, mind, and soul of his movies. He was right about the director's role, but being right did not always bring commercial success. He made a serious mistake in not capitalizing on the success of the players he created. He believed that whom he used in a film did not matter as much as the story itself and how it was told. He seemed confident always that if he lost one fine actor he would discover another equally good. Yet often, in the midst of production, he would suddenly regret the loss of a favorite player. "Why did I ever let Dick go?" he would say. "He would have been perfect in this!"

Some time after the failure of *The Struggle,* the D. W. Griffith Corporation went into bankruptcy. At the auction that followed, D. W. was the highest bidder for the rights to twenty-one of his films. He bought them for $500.

During my first adult season in the theater, I learned that I had more control over my body than over my voice. Having been told that Margaret Carrington, Walter Huston's extremely intelligent sister, was the finest voice teacher in New York, I sought her out. She said that I did not look strong enough for her system of voice training. But I had seen many strong men collapse while I kept on working, so I asked if I could go to her doctor and have him report to her on my physical condition. After a lengthy examination, he found that I had strained my heart, perhaps from having worked steadily for nine years without a vacation. He suggested that a visit to the spa in Bad Nauheim might make me fit again. The results were so good that I returned to the spa a year later; indeed, whenever I have a vacation, I try to spend it at a health resort. Over the years I have visited at least twenty of them.

I returned to New York, hoping that Mrs. Carrington would work with me. She agreed to take me on as a pupil. She taught only as long as a pupil held her interest, she told me, and she would take no fee.

As far as I know, Mrs. Carrington's system for building control, strength, and color in the voice has never been equaled in America. She had an extraordinary effect on her pupils. She had prepared John Barrymore with ten weeks of rugged work for his *Hamlet*. Dorothy told me of having lunch with Mr. Barrymore a few months before his death. She said that he was acting silly until she mentioned Margaret Carrington; then he became serious. Everything he had done that was worthwhile, he said, was because of Margaret Carrington. He talked for a half-hour about what a great woman she was. Without her, he claimed, he would have been a fifth-rate actor.

Soon after I started working with her, Mrs. Carrington telephoned me late one evening. She asked me how I would like to play Camille in America's second oldest theater, the Central City Opera House in the mountains above Denver. Central City was a ghost town, and its opera house, closed for fifty years, was to be reopened in grand style. The governors from adjoining states and their staffs would come in private trains and would travel the last few miles in stagecoaches. Everyone would be dressed in the costumes of the period of our play. Seats would cost $100 apiece and would be available only to those whose ancestors had come west in covered wagons. As the town was two miles above sea level, she added, we would be obliged to go to Denver for three weeks of rehearsal in order to become acclimated. Central City had once been a miners' capital, and it was planned to hold a grand ball in the Teller House next to the Opera House, the same ballroom where General Ulysses Grant had once been entertained. I was captivated by everything she said and agreed to go.

Everything Margaret promised came true. The production was underwritten by Delos Chappell and a group of leading citizens in Colorado. Edna James—Delos' wife—did the translation of the play. Robert Edmond Jones, the director and producer, found in his research that the play had originally been presented in Paris at the time when Chinese art came into vogue. The first Camille was patterned after a little Ming figurine, and her appeal to men was a virginal quality that made each one feel that he was the first in her arms. We strove to attain this quality. Later, when the play was presented in New York at the Morosco Theater, an announcement in the program reminded the audience:

> In viewing this presentation of Camille, the audience is asked to recall and bear in mind the fact that Dumas's great heroine, Marguerite Gautier, was intended by him to be a young woman. His "Camille" was based on the life of Marie Duplessis, one of the most famous of all Parisian courtesans—who died and was deeply mourned at the age of twenty-four. Dumas's Marguerite was no middle-aged sophisticate, taking quick profit of her life. Instead she was a young girl who, governed solely by her great heart, rose at last to spiritual heights which have immortalized her.

When H. T. Parker, critic for the Boston *Transcript,* reviewed the play, he said that *Camille* was being seen as it was originally meant to be done probably for the first time in our country.

Bobby Jones, in addition to directing the play, designed the costumes and sets, many of which he painted himself, with the help of a man who had toured as a carpenter in a play with me when I was seven years old. The total cost of the women's costumes was only

Lillian as Camille (1932) in the production for which Robert Edmond Jones looted the most elegant houses in Denver of props.

Lillian and Dorothy in the 1930s.   PHOTOGRAPH BY NELL DORR

Lillian and Max Reinhardt at his castle in Salzburg, Austria.

Lillian photographed by Ben Pinchot.

George Jean Nathan in his rooms at the Royalton Hotel in New York.

$500. Bobby went to Hearn's Basement on Fourteenth Street and picked up fine fabrics and trimmings. With his imagination he transformed them into elegant clothes.

For the furniture and props, all the great homes of Denver were open to Bobby. From one he selected a beautiful crystal chandelier, from another fine furniture, from a third a rare rug. Many old families lent their jewels for the production. The jewels were so valuable that a policeman and a detective were hired to guard them. I remember the detective sitting in the wings, a big fellow weighing about 300 pounds, with a gun in each hand. Toward the end of the play tears would be rolling down his cheeks. I couldn't look at him without losing my concentration.

As Central City was a ghost town then, we could have bought houses there for $10 apiece. Now its theatrical activity has turned it into a national institution, and it is a thriving city.

About that time, Lawrence Langner brought Dorothy, Rollo Peters, Romney Brent, Fania Marinoff, and Armina Marshall together to start a repertory company in a barn in Connecticut, which has since become famous as The Westport Country Playhouse. The players all agreed to work for $30 a week, and the playhouse became the model for dozens of summer theaters throughout the country. Their original idea was to do Shakespeare, Ibsen, and several modern plays. But one old drama, *The Streets of New York*, threw the schedule off balance by proving a great hit.

We heard that D. W. was drinking again. He avoided old friends and was obviously uncomfortable, though not ungracious, when he met them by chance. A few business associates kept track of him. Periodically he seemed to gain control of himself, only to go overboard in another direction. He bought clothes with abandon, as if they might restore his reputation. He wrote a long letter to Lord Beaverbrook, seeking a commission for a movie, but Beaverbrook politely hedged. Rumors cropped up in movie columns: He would be made head of R.K.O.; he was going to stage a play about the American Revolution.

His wife Linda Arvidson suddenly broke her long silence. Where were her alimony payments? Their separation agreement had granted her 15 per cent of his weekly earnings, with a minimum guarantee of $400 a week. With each new rumor of a comeback, he received another dunning letter from her.

In 1933 he returned to Hollywood for a series of radio shows, in which he reminisced about the early days of movie making, but he received no movie offers. It had taken a few years for the Depression to catch up with Hollywood, but it finally hit with a vengeance. Many studios were in trouble. For United Artists the future looked dark. The company wanted to rid itself of a partner who drew dividends without producing profits. D. W. sold his interest in the company for $300,000. He did not realize it then, but he had closed off his last avenue of return.

We heard from friends that D. W. had gone home to Kentucky. A true southerner, he had maintained his legal residence there all those years. He told friends that he meant to live at La Grange, where his brother Will and his family had lived, but actually, after a few brief visits, he set up quarters in Louisville's Brown Hotel, where he was soon a familiar figure at the bar in the Bluegrass Room. He replied to inquisitive reporters that he was resting: "I want to back off from the studio merry-go-round."

He apparently continued to indulge in sudden shopping tours, buying clothes extravagantly and without any real purpose. Once, we heard, he arrived at Churchill Downs wearing a gray suit, a purple tie and hat, and driving a purple Mercedes. Money for this extravagance came from the sale of his United Artists stock, from occasional returns on reruns of his films, and, oddly enough, from his own carelessness.

He told Boyd Martin, a Louisville friend and theater critic for the Louisville *Courier-Journal,* that a bank in New Orleans, which was being rebuilt, had come across a safety-deposit box of his containing $100,000 in cash. And in 1933 Federal receivers went through the bankrupt Alexandria Hotel, where D. W. had stayed in the early Hollywood days, and found an envelope addressed to him containing $20,000 in bills. Sadly enough, D. W. had never known what to do with money, if it was not money he needed to make his films.

One of the plays I acted in at that time was *9 Pine Street,* the story of Lizzie Borden, who was accused of the ax murders of her father and stepmother. To prepare for the part, I asked the help of the great criminologist, Edmund Pearson, who had written much about her. At our first meeting he said, "You can't play Lizzie Borden; she was a very homely woman."

Nevertheless, he helped me enormously. He came to the dress rehearsal, and, afterward, in my dressing room, he said, "You know —on the stage you look just like Lizzie."

I asked him how he had happened to make criminology his life work.

"One morning before school, at breakfast," he said, "I heard my mother and father talking of a woman called Lizzie Borden."

I wanted D. W. to do a film of the play and arranged a meeting for him at the Roosevelt Hotel in New York with Laura Wilk, an agent, and a French financier who was willing to underwrite the film.

Suddenly D. W. said, "Whatever gave you people the idea that I wanted to make another film?"

I don't know why he changed his mind. Perhaps it was pride; perhaps his self-confidence was at a low ebb.

I worked with Bobby Jones again in the Philip Barry play, *The Joyous Season.* Bobby designed superb costumes and a set to frame every mood of the play without intruding. Then he left for the Coast to do a film. Had he stayed until we opened and lighted the play, we would have had a success. It was a delightful comedy, but it couldn't be enjoyed in the dark. Onstage we looked like characters out of Gorky's *Lower Depths.* I couldn't see into the eyes of Moffat Johnson, that fine actor, when we played a scene together.

When I complained to Arthur Hopkins, the producer, that outwardly gentle little man said, "You mind your business, which is acting, and I'll mind mine."

He had no eyes for the stage, only perfect ears. This production

. 321 .

was his first without visual assistance, so the amusing side of the play failed to cross the footlights, and we lost the audience's interest.

George Jean Nathan considered Sean O'Casey and Eugene O'Neill the greatest playwrights in the world. George wrote a great deal about O'Casey and was disappointed when his play *Within the Gates* closed after a week's run in London. But he helped to bring the play over to the United States. I was grateful to George for doing this, although he was not responsible for my getting the role of the Young Whore in the production.

O'Casey came to this country for the rehearsals. During the first few months of production, he spent most of his time in my dressing room. "I can't stay out there," he would say, gesturing toward the lobby, his eyes twinkling behind their heavy glasses. "They keep asking me what my play is about, and I don't know what to tell them."

George arranged for him to stay at the Royalton Hotel, his own headquarters. O'Casey brought so few possessions—a few shirts, socks, and underwear—that he would put one sock in one drawer and its partner in another drawer. He seemed to own only the brown suit and cap that he wore. He spoke with an Irish lilt, and it was a joy to listen to the poetry in his speech. He was fascinated by electric gadgets, amazed by the different ways in which one could switch on a light—push, pull, twist, turn. He would go about, trying them all like a child.

His poetic turn of mind evidently appealed to our audiences, for the play ran in New York for six months. When we left to go on tour, word came to us in Philadelphia that the play had been banned in Boston. A short time later O'Casey wrote me:

> The last performance must have been a strange experience and I should have given a lot to be there, though not so much as I should have given to be present when the ban was declared in Boston. I got a whole pile of correspondence about it, and a lot of press-cuttings, but these couldn't give the thrill I'd have got from standing and hitting out in the center of the fight. Though the ban caused some excitement and a lot of

talk, I should have preferred the tour and it is a pity that the Jesuits of Boston were able to stop it.

He added:

> Let me thank you, Lillian, for a grand and a great performance; for your gentle patience throughout the rehearsals, and for the grand way you dived into the long and strenuous part of "The Young Whore."

The beautifully bound copy of *Within the Gates* that rests in my library has this inscription:

In Remembrance of Things Past,
of this play's production and performance
When we all, at least, battled
together for the return of some
of the great things that belong to Drama
A bad thing well done can never feel success;
A good thing well done can never feel failure.
      With love,
          Sean O'Casey

Although Dorothy and Jim had separated some time after her return to the stage, she had not filed for divorce until 1935. She almost didn't obtain her divorce, because she refused to testify against Jim. "He's a wonderful man," she told her lawyer, "and I will have nothing said against him." When she went to court the judge asked her in exasperation, "Do you want this divorce, or don't you?" Finally Dorothy volunteered that Jim had driven her into a fit of hiccoughs for six days, and the divorce was granted.

It was not long after that she began to suffer from stomach pains. "It's my gall bladder," she told her doctor. He said that there were no signs of gallstones and that he did not consider an operation necessary. It turned out that she had a stomach ulcer.

Almost from the time she was born, Dorothy had been nervous and apprehensive. She was a colicky baby, Mother said, and stomach spasms continued to dog her all her life. "Miss Apprehension," we dubbed her. She was hounded by self-doubts. Whenever she planned to do something for anyone, she would say pessimistically, "It won't turn out right anyway." I remember her as a young film star, standing before her mirror, the doors of her closets open, as she tried on and discarded one dress after another.

"Do I look all right, Reba?"

"You look beautiful."

"Lillian, does this look good?"

"It looks lovely on you."

Everything that was mine, from a new frock to a new role, seemed to her superior to what she had. She worried over every part she ever played in the theater. She would fret incessantly over the script, wondering if her judgment had been right. "Can I play the part?" she would ask herself. "Will I be any good? Will they be disappointed in me? What will Mother and Lillian think?"

"But remember all your successes," we would say. Nothing helped. She would be unable to sleep and to eat.

"Just one bite," Reba would coax. "One little bite."

"I can't swallow it, Reba, it won't go down."

She always kept her problems to herself. She played a series of major roles in successful plays with outer composure and inner anguish. At rehearsals she would be her usual gay self, and the cast would never guess at her ordeal. But, before the curtain went up on opening night, Dorothy was often ready for the hospital.

"Dorothy, why don't you have a glass of beer?" friends would ask. "It will help you to relax." But any alcohol was anathema to her. Whenever Jim had taken one Scotch and soda, she had been convinced he was tight.

She refused to seek professional help for her problems. When friends urged her to see a psychiatrist, she would reply lightly, "I have enough friends who will listen, without paying them twenty-five dollars an hour."

Fortunately, she had been blessed with an iron constitution. Mother always said, "Dorothy is twice as strong as Lillian." She could work all day in a film, or all evening in a play, and then go out to dine and dance until dawn, without showing the slightest sign of fatigue. But she was careless with her health. All her life she waged an unrealistic struggle against her weight. Once she simply stopped eating. When she was down to eighty pounds and looked like a skeleton she thought herself lovely. She kept Reba busy taking in seams or letting them out. She would often subsist on a diet of pretzels, potato chips, and ice cream. I'm sure that her eating habits contributed to her stomach problems later on.

She always seemed to be cold. "Reba, feel my hands. Feel my feet. They're like ice."

Reba, massaging her hands and feet, would say, "It's your circulation."

"No, I'm cold inside me, Reba."

One night in 1935, when I was living in New York, I was awakened by the telephone. It was 3:00 in the morning.

"Miss Lillian Gish?"

"Yes."

"One moment, please. I have an overseas call from London."

"Lillian, Lillian! Why did you leave me? Why aren't you here? Nobody can do this except you." It was D. W.

I don't know whether or not he had been drinking. He was incoherent. He had gone to England to remake *Broken Blossoms,* but he couldn't find a suitable Lucy. He kept saying: "You must come over and play Lucy! I can't make the film without you." This appeal wasn't in character. In the nine years I had been with him, he had never expressed a particular need for me or any other player.

"That's not true," I answered. "But why don't you make something else? You have better ideas than that. You don't need to make your old films again."

But he kept repeating that he needed me, that he couldn't make the movie otherwise. Not knowing what to say, I protested feebly. Then there was a click, and the telephone went dead.

I awakened Dorothy and asked her what she thought we should do. She suggested that we cable the producer, Herbert Wilcox. He cabled back that D. W. was all right, not drunk, but that the plans for *Broken Blossoms* had fallen through and D. W. was returning home.

I learned later that he had sold the rights to *Broken Blossoms* to an English firm, the Twickenham Film Company, for $15,000 and had agreed to direct the remake.

Dolly Haas, a beautiful and sensitive actress, was signed for the part of Lucy. But on his arrival in London D. W. had spotted a French girl, Ariane Borg, and had decided that she was perfect for the role. When his new bosses heard of it, they naturally said no. Dolly Haas was already under contract; they couldn't afford to pay two actresses for one part. One afternoon D. W. and Miss Borg burst in on the producer and several executives and without a word of explanation began to act out the scene in which Battling Burrows finds Lucy in the Chinaman's room and beats her brutally. The men were absolutely aghast. They were convinced that they had hired a madman.

That night D. W. telephoned me.

I was taking another heart cure at Bad Nauheim when I read in a foreign newspaper that D. W. Griffith had married a young woman called Evelyn Baldwin on March 2, 1936. He had earlier obtained his divorce from Linda Arvidson. Evelyn and her mother had come to Louisville, and he and Evelyn were married there at the Brown Hotel. A witness at the wedding said that he was as ardent as an eighteen-year-old youth.

Evelyn Baldwin was about thirteen when she first met D. W. Her mother had taken her to an afternoon benefit at the Astor Hotel, and among the guests she noticed a tall, distinguished man watching her. When they were introduced, he pointed his forefinger at her and said in a deep voice, "You are Little Nell."

"No, sir, I'm Evelyn Baldwin," she said politely.

"You are Little Nell," he repeated. He then explained that he was preparing to make a film of *The Old Curiosity Shop* and was looking for a girl who approximated Dickens' Little Nell. Evelyn, small-boned and fair, with blonde curls, seemed ideal.

Later she told me that D. W. had given her a copy of *The Old Curiosity Shop* and that she had read it dutifully. From then on he frequently asked her, her mother, and her two older sisters to dinner, and afterward he would rehearse Evelyn in the role of Little Nell. Billy Bitzer took her first test in 1925. She admitted later that she had been bewildered, for she knew nothing of acting.

D. W. dropped his plans for the Dickens film when he heard that an English studio had already completed a version of the book. But he continued to see the Baldwins. Evelyn's father had died, and he often visited her, her mother, and her sisters at their home in Bellaire, Long Island. Probably the warmth of the family unit appealed to him. He kept in touch with them even when he went to California. On his return to New York, he would take them out to dinner, perhaps to Coney Island or a Manhattan restaurant, followed by a round of night clubs. When Evelyn was nineteen she was assigned a small role in *The Struggle,* which was to be his final picture; she married him three years later.

Instead of coming east, the couple went to the Coast three days after the wedding. There, at the Eighth Annual Presentation of Awards by the Academy of Motion Picture Arts and Sciences, D. W. was awarded an Oscar. The special citation praised his "innovations, upon which the industry has built much of its success" and spoke of "a spontaneous desire to pay a tribute of sincere respect and regard for his genius."

He and his new wife remained in the film capital for several weeks. He visited W. S. Van Dyke, one of his former assistants, who was then directing the film *San Francisco,* and directed one of the crowd scenes in the film "just for fun." There was a rumor that he would be hired for a remake of *Way Down East,* but nothing came of it.

On one of their return trips east, D. W. let us know that he was coming as far as Newark and wanted to see us. He dared not come into New York; his first wife claimed that his divorce was illegal and was threatening him with suit for bigamy. He believed, however, that her main interest was financial. Her process servers were waiting to hand him papers demanding $50,000 in back alimony payments. (For years, D. W. remained in exile from New York, but eventually Linda Arvidson caught up with him and brought him into court. He claimed that he had paid her more than $1 million over the years and that it was sufficient. After a series of legal fights, his defense was upheld. She drifted out of his life again and died a year after his death.)

Mother, Dorothy, and I drove to New Jersey to meet D. W.'s bride. We found a slight, endearing girl with soft eyes and a child-like smile. Her mother, who was staying with them, was equally gentle.

The great surprise was D. W. himself. He seemed not to have changed at all. His hair had thinned a bit, and he was somewhat thicker in the waist, but that afternoon we were listening again to the man who had burst into arias and boomed commands in the Biograph studio twenty-five years before. He spoke excitedly of the films he was planning and the writing he hoped to do when they returned to Louisville to live.

"We are so happy," Evelyn whispered as we left. "Just pray that he gets back into pictures soon."

But jobs did not materialize. His family expenses were heavy; his relatives needed help with houses and cars. His sister Ruth was ill, and the doctor bills were high. Yet for the most part his life for the next three years was pleasant and active. He built a new wing on the house in La Grange, and in the summer he and Evelyn lived there. In the winter they moved to the Brown Hotel or traveled, living for periods in Philadelphia, Newark, and Miami, with many trips to the West Coast. Every morning when he was living in Kentucky, he strolled down to the Sweet Shoppe in the center of town and treated the customers to coffee. Then he went home to work. Evelyn had learned shorthand, and every day she took down reams of material for films, for plays, and for his eventual autobiography, which he intended to title *D. W. and the Wolf*. ("The wolf," he explained, "is poverty.") When the flow of words was too much for her, he hired a secretary to work in shifts with her. According to Evelyn, his ideas for films came by the hundreds, and, though they needed the testing and experimentation of rehearsals, during which he always honed his stories, they were all good.

During that period, according to Evelyn, he also wrote very sensitive poetry. He could not believe that films alone were his destiny.

He had to write something great before he died. Long before Evelyn knew him, she said, he had begun work on a project called *The Treadmill,* which he said he would probably complete on his eightieth birthday. It was the story of humanity from the beginning of time. He would work on it for a couple of years and then put it away.

Boyd Martin, the Louisville critic and also the director of The Players, an amateur theatrical group, once asked D. W. to take the part of Lord Porteous in Somerset Maugham's *The Circle,* a part that John Drew had played on Broadway. "You're perfect for it," Martin urged.

"I couldn't," D. W. replied. "People would look at me, and I'd get as flustered as an ingenue."

"Well, why don't I play Lord Porteous then and you direct the play?"

"Don't do that," D. W. said. "Don't ever let anyone take over your theater."

Evelyn said of D. W. later, "I think he was probably the most complex personality I've ever known. . . . He had a great love of art and music. He had many fine things and he also had the contrary side of him. He lacked many of the gayer sides of life—things that had nothing to do with art."

She agreed with all who knew and loved him that he was a great lover of people. He never really bore hatred for anyone. He might be angry or annoyed, but the emotion never lasted. He never appeared bitter because he could not find work. Though directly and indirectly he had helped hundreds of people get their starts, he never made a comment about ingratitude. Instead, he was almost embarrassed or apologetic for having risen so high and then so obviously declined.

Once Boyd Martin asked him how he felt when he looked back and considered the careers of so many people whom he had started on the road to success.

"Let's not talk about it, do you mind?" D. W. said and then laughed. "I'm more interested in whether the plumber will be at the place in La Grange in the morning."

Several months after meeting D. W.'s wife, I had a visit from Miss Iris Barry, an attractive young woman who worked for the Museum of Modern Art in New York City. She explained that she was the curator of a small branch called the Film Library. I had never heard of it.

"We've only started," she said. "The public is just beginning to realize that the motion pictures are a unique art form. The Museum wants to obtain representative prints which will show the growth of films from their early days. Plans are under way for a new building on West Fifty-third Street, which will have a complete theater and office space for the collection."

Surprised and delighted with this news, I asked how I could be of help.

"Well, our hardest job is to get important films." Nobody in Hollywood was interested. But if Griffith contributed his films, then others would follow suit. In any case, she said, without *The Birth of a Nation* and *Intolerance,* their collection would not mean much. They needed all the Griffith films they could get.

"Could you speak to him for us?" she asked.

I said that I would try.

Miss Barry added that it was important to obtain his films as soon as possible. Many early pictures had already been ruined. "The old type of film disintegrates after a few years. We want to make new copies before the old prints turn to dust."

I wrote D. W. immediately, and he replied that he had copies of most of his films. Some were in a vault in Kentucky; others in a New York warehouse. The expense of storage was high. He added that he could not afford to pay the tax that Kentucky was going to levy against his films. I suggested that the Film Library might be the ideal place for them. They would take care to preserve the negatives, and there people would be able to see them and learn from them. He agreed to donate not only the films but some of his personal files as well.

The material included more than 250,000 feet of early films, correspondence, business papers, and his press book—a record of his career as a director and producer from 1913 to 1924.

The New York Times reported that "the contribution is regarded as one of the most valuable single acquisitions that the Film Library has received, since it is expected to reveal many interesting details of Griffith's work during the years of his great creativeness."

John E. Abbott, director of the Film Library and Iris Barry's husband, said that several months would be required to assort and catalogue the material, which Eileen Bowser has since done so carefully.

After D. W.'s gift, many other directors and stars gave their pictures to the Film Library, which today has the finest collection of early films in the world.

🌿 25 🌿

I went to England to do *The Old Maid*, which Guthrie McClintic had directed in New York with Judith Anderson and Helen Mencken. We rehearsed in London and toured the provinces for eight weeks. The English company brought together by Hugh Beaumont was a most distinguished one. But I couldn't please the woman director from Germany. She criticized everything I did, especially the way I delivered lines. It was my first experience working in the English theater, and at first I thought, "Well, maybe that is how they do things over here."

I would say to her, "Do you want me to run across the stage here?" and she would answer before the entire company, "We will see if you know how to run across a stage." I would think, Well, I may not know how to use my voice to suit her, but at least my body is well trained.

She continued to single me out for criticism, and the company became increasingly outraged. The cast got together without telling me and sent a telegram to Binky Beaumont, informing him that something was wrong and asking him to come up. When he arrived, the members complained about the way this woman was treating me. Is it any wonder that I love actors? They just would not tolerate this woman's abuse of me, which, incidentally, I don't believe I had provoked. Guthrie McClintic was summoned to take her place, but he didn't like the costumes, the sets, and some of the players, so we decided not to bring the production to London.

Irene Vanbrugh, a member of our cast, and I went to spend a weekend at the castle of Sir Ian Malcolm, who had represented the British government in the Suez Canal. He was married to a famous English beauty, and they had four beautiful children. His eleventh-century castle was occupied by his children, and he and his wife lived in a modern castle—only 150 years old. Sir Ian raised prize cattle and sheep, and specimen flowers in his greenhouses as well as asparagus, peaches, and other fruits. An airplane brought oysters and other delicacies from France. My room was enormous, and the bed was as large as the average room. The castle was bigger than a Hollywood set.

Sir Ian was the first man I had ever seen in full evening kilts. At dinner we would hear the bagpipes in the distance and soon the pipers would come down the great hall, and march into the dining area and around the table. Then we would all lift our glasses—the pipers too—and after drinking to Scotland they would all break their glasses.

Before I left, Sir Ian told me that he also raised terriers and asked me if I would like one. I went out to the kennels to make my choice, expecting to see four or five puppies. Instead there were about eighty dogs, all prize West Highland white terriers. I had never seen West Highlands before, and I thought they were adorable. As I stood there uncertainly, one of them came up to me and tried to catch my skirt.

"I don't think I have to make a choice," I said. "This one has already picked me."

"Did you say you knew nothing about these?" Sir Ian said, smiling. "You've picked the best one in my kennel."

I named him Malcolm and left him with his mother until I finished my tour and could send for him. He came to London—he was five months old by that time—and we sailed for home. For the next sixteen years we lived happily together. He trained me well. I was the one who jumped through the hoop, who ran for the ball and brought it back to him. He rarely left my side.

Judith Anderson as Queen Gertrude and Lillian as Ophelia in Guthrie
McClintic's 1936 production of *Hamlet*.   PHOTO BY VANDAMM STUDIO

Lillian as Ophelia and John Gielgud as Hamlet.

Lillian and Burgess Meredith in *The Star Wagon*. They had five minutes to change from sixty-five-year-olds to a couple of eighteen.

Lillian with Percy Waram in the 1941 Chicago production of *Life with Father*.

Lillian with Griffith and his wife Evelyn in their West Coast home.

Sir Ian Malcolm, who presented Lillian with Malcolm, her West Highland white terrier.

Lillian with Malcolm.

Lillian and Lionel Barrymore in *Duel in the Sun* (1946). Lillian and Lionel had acted together in early Griffith films.

Through Guthrie McClintic, I was asked to play Ophelia to John Gielgud's Hamlet. Judith Anderson was to play the Queen. Neither of us had ever played Shakespeare before and were extremely nervous at the prospect of playing with England's greatest classical actor. Judith Anderson told me, "I'm too frightened to open my mouth."

"I look at the word 'no' and I can't pronounce it," I answered.

Then Guthrie McClintic said to us, "How do you think I feel directing a man who has acted in *Hamlet* and directed it twice?"

Later, at rehearsal, McClintic, to ease our tension, started to climb a rope that was dangling on the empty stage. Everyone laughed at his monkey antics, and our embarrassment dissolved. When rehearsal resumed, the play began to come alive.

This 1936 production of *Hamlet* had sets by Jo Mielziner, who had also designed the sets for *Uncle Vanya*.

McClintic's conception of Ophelia was strikingly original. Instead of a sweet, pathetic little girl he wanted a lewd Ophelia. I wore a costume of bright yellow, with a red stocking pulled over one arm and its partner tied around my neck. McClintic got the idea for the stocking on the arm as he was walking down Broadway one evening and saw a demented woman mumbling to herself. She was wearing stockings on her hands instead of gloves.

Dorothy was so nervous at the opening that she became violently ill. She thought that John Gielgud played his first scene with such emotional impact that he would not be able to top it. Neither she nor anyone else was yet aware of the enormous emotional power of this actor. He played on his voice of almost three octaves as if it were an organ, and with such feeling that those of us backstage were always in tears.

During our run John Emery, who played Laertes, left to accept a Hollywood contract. The actor who replaced him became nervous during the dueling scene at his first matinee, and John's face was suddenly streaming blood. We all thought that his eye was damaged, but instead of thinking of himself he said to the actor after the curtain came down: "Perhaps we should come in before the performance tonight and rehearse the duel. Don't worry about this little scratch; it will be healed by then."

We had all adored John from the first rehearsal. From the way he took direction, one would have thought that he had never before heard of *Hamlet,* let alone produced it twice himself. All the other actors would stand backstage watching him perform when they were not changing costumes. I have never seen that compliment paid to any other actor. His talent, intelligence, and craftsmanship were all impeccable, as were his manners.

When I complained to Arthur Hopkins, the producer, that we were about to close while still playing to standees (John Gielgud had a six-month contract), he said, "My dear, don't you know that a fine *Hamlet* will always wear out its Hamlet before it does its audience?"

Earlier Tyrone Guthrie had asked me to come to the Old Vic to do *Within the Gates,* with himself as director "for the ear" and Michel St. Denis "for the eye." But I hesitated, recalling that the play had already opened and closed in London within a week. I did not believe that my playing one character would make the difference. It was cowardly of me, and I have since regretted missing the chance to work with two great directors.

I was also asked to play Belle Watling in *Gone With the Wind,* but I was committed to Guthrie McClintic for September rehearsals of a Maxwell Anderson play, *The Star Wagon.*

Meanwhile Peggy Ashcroft, the great English actress, was in New York, playing with Burgess Meredith in Anderson's *High Tor.* Max Reinhardt was also in New York at that time, and we all had long sessions of good theater talk in my penthouse. One evening Eleanora Mendelssohn and I decided to give a supper party. Eleanora was a fascinating woman, very honest, very forthright. She loved Professor Reinhardt.

A great pianist was to play, for the first time in this country, at our party. My baby grand was too small, so I had the problem of getting a concert grand up to the seventeenth floor for the evening. But it was worth all the trouble to have Rudolf Serkin play for us. The terrace and living room were still crowded when I retired at 5:30 in the morning to get a little sleep before the matinee performance of *Hamlet.*

In the fall I played in *The Star Wagon* with Burgess Meredith. Burgess and I had five minutes to change from a man and woman of sixty-five to an eighteen-year-old couple. I went to a Russian artist, an expert in character makeup, and she taught me how to make the transition with my hair and face in three minutes.

I was nine years old when I fell in love for the first time. The boy was tall, with curly, reddish-blond hair and blue eyes; he had a lovely voice, and he sang in the play we were acting in. I don't remember his name, which is just as well, for he never paid me the slightest attention. But from the age of nine I was always falling in and out of love.

But marriage is a twenty-four-hour-a-day job, and I have always been much too busy to make a good wife. Older women used to say to me, "Whatever you do, don't get married." All their troubles seemed to be caused by their husbands. Besides, my mother had not been able to succeed in marriage, and I doubted that I could succeed where she, who was wise and perfect, had failed.

"My films are my children," I once said to Helen Hayes, and she replied, "The pain of having a child is nothing compared to the pain of creating a character."

I had been seeing George Jean Nathan for several years. In that time he had asked me repeatedly to marry him.

Once when he came to visit me on the Coast, I was eager for him and D. W. to meet. George liked D. W., but D. W., oddly enough, did not want me to continue seeing him. Madame de Grésac had been very fond of him until once, during Prohibition, he had had a case of whiskey sent to my house so that it would be there when he wanted it—and then charged it to me. The bill was $200, and Madame was outraged, but I found it amusing.

George could be charming, and things that might have disturbed other men never seemed to bother him. For instance, he never complained about having to wait for me. "I like going out with a girl who looks as though she has taken three hours to dress," he would say. His pet name for me was Potato. He liked potatoes, especially potatoes Anna at the Colony.

I often considered marrying him, but his possessiveness disturbed me. Once, when we were having dinner in a restaurant, a gentleman came over and asked, "May I have permission to speak with Miss Gish?"

George stood up. "Certainly not," he replied icily.

But what bothered me most—and the main reason that I hesitated—was his attitude toward Mother and Dorothy. He seemed to resent my love for them.

George, however, was so confident that he could persuade me that he told Brooks Atkinson we were to be married. George and Mr. Atkinson had gone to visit Eugene and Carlotta O'Neill on the night of O'Neill's fiftieth birthday, and afterward the two men stopped by the Golden Cockerel, a speak-easy, where George confided in Mr. Atkinson.

When I finally rejected George's proposal, his pride was wounded. When he couldn't reach me, he would call Dorothy and scare her half to death by threatening to commit suicide or to harm me in some way. "I'll ruin you," he vowed to me. "Where Duell didn't succeed I will, because I've got the writing talent."

After persuading him what a terrible wife I would make, I went off to Europe and avoided making an enemy of him. Luckily for George, he later married Julie Haydon.

He would not allow me to see him later when he was desperately ill from a series of small strokes. Brooks Atkinson used to visit him once a week, and I called Mr. Atkinson once to ask if George was in financial need. Julie Haydon, who looked after him tenderly during that long illness, would telephone me and say that he needed round-the-clock nursing, but that she did not have access to his money. Mr. Atkinson and George's lawyer went to the Hanover Bank to ask permission to open his safety-deposit box. The lawyers and the bank officials found a stack of bonds and cash. One lawyer remarked, "If this had been handled properly, it could have been a great fortune."

I was and always will be grateful to George for sharing his knowledge of drama, good food, and good wine with me. Through him I came to know all the interesting writers and artists of the twenties and thirties. It was a rare and great privilege to listen to the most exciting minds of our time. And I will always be glad that I didn't marry him and spoil his life.

In going through my books the other day, I found these inscriptions in two of George's first editions:

> To Lillian Gish, my dearest, who in the seventh year of our love remains still the one person in whom, gifted as I am in the art, I find utterly nothing to criticize.
> With the present and enduring devotion of
> George Jean Nathan

And two years later:

> For Lillian, my dearest, in this, the ninth year of us; for the Lillian whose sweetness and very great loveliness of mind and heart have understood my deep deep love for her and have quietly tolerated its sometimes awkward and irritating expression; for Lillian, the only girl I have ever seen in this world with whom I should wish to live out my days.
> George

❧ 26 ❧

In 1939 D. W. moved back to the Coast, this time to stay. He wrote us the good news: He had been hired by the Hal Roach Studios and was working on a film called *One Million B.C.* For the leads he had picked two bit players—Victor Mature and Carole Landis.

But the final outcome was dismal. D. W. simply could not work in harness. When a difference of opinion arose between him and Hal Roach, he ordered Roach off the producer's own set. That ended his comeback.

"I used my six months with the Hal Roach studio to good advantage—studying the so-called new technique," he wrote to me. "I was interested to see that many of the best directors, Frank Capra and Lewis Milestone in particular, are getting back to the old silent technique, merely using dialogue to heighten the effect. More and more they are getting away from the 'talkie talkie' pictures and a very good thing in my humble opinion. If you saw *Gone With the Wind* you surely must have noticed that it was pretty much the technique of our day, heightened by the use of dialogue and color."

He mentioned the fact that a recent physical examination had proved him in excellent physical health, "perfect for a man of thirty-five." (He was sixty-four.) He added that it was a much better examination than one twenty years earlier, when he was being insured for a half-million dollars. "The Doctors seemed agreed that with ordinary care I should live to be a hundred. I am not so much interested in this from selfish reasons, but because I feel I have so much work yet to do, and am happy to find that physically I am promised many years in which to accomplish this work."

He added a description of an amusing incident in which he had been bitten by a dog and concluded, "After this sad and harrowing experience, I don't even trust Malcolm and decline to send him my love, or at least very much love."

He signed his letter "David."

In all the years I had known him and worked with him, I had always called him Mr. Griffith. It took me a while to grow accustomed to calling him by his first name.

I embarked on a lecture tour across the country. Naturally Malcolm came along. Traveling with a dog was not simple in those days. Once I had to stay with him in the baggage car. Another time I hid him under my cape and looked very pregnant. But Malcolm was an asset on the platform. Whenever he decided that I had talked long enough, he would grab my skirt in his teeth and pull me off the stage, so that I was always sure of at least one laugh.

Dorothy and I went to see the New York production of *Life With Father*, starring Howard Lindsay and Dorothy Stickney. After the performance I said: "This is the play we've been waiting for to take through America. This is the play for all the people who've seen us in films."

My sister introduced me to Mr. Lindsay backstage. "I'd like the first company that goes on the road for me," I told him, "and the second for my sister. And I'd like the movie rights for Mary Pickford."

I hadn't consulted Mary, of course, but I was sure that she would want to do it. Mr. Lindsay and Russel Crouse, his collaborator on the play, laughed. It had been open only a few days, and they didn't yet know whether or not it would be a success.

As I went out, I thought, "Well, they think I'm pretty quaint."

But in about a month they called me up and asked, "Were you serious?"

"Certainly," I replied.

It was agreed that I would tour with the second company and that Dorothy would go with another unit. Howard and Russel said to us, "Don't sign a long-term contract, because we have a play for the two of you together."

"That's wonderful," I said. "Could we read it?"

"It isn't finished yet," Howard said.

"Well, what's it about?"

"It's a comedy about murder and insanity."

"Murder and insanity!" Dorothy exclaimed. "That's a comedy?"

Thinking that it didn't sound very promising, we signed run-of-the-play contracts, which kept me busy for eighteen months and Dorothy for two years. Lindsay and Crouse could not wait for us, and *Arsenic and Old Lace* was produced on Broadway with Jean Adair and Josephine Hull.

When *Life With Father* opened in Chicago in 1940, I thought it would play there a few months and that we would then slowly tour west. Instead, we remained in Chicago for sixty-six weeks, and people toured to see us. In all that time I never missed a performance as Mrs. Day.

I enjoyed doing this endearing comedy of warm family life, but it was a rugged role. I had little time between scenes to do anything but attend to my seven costume changes. On matinee days I ran up and down the stairs of the set a total of fifty-eight times, so that by the end of the week I was quite tired.

I shared with Malcolm a comfortable suite of rooms facing Lake Michigan at the Blackstone Hotel, which had been suffering a decline in business for some years. The reopening of the Blackstone Theater with a hit seemed to restore business in that section of the city. Frequently Carl Sandburg was my guide for a tour of the city, particularly the Chicago Art Institute. I had a special cab driver, whose beat was the Blackstone Hotel. If I wanted to go out, Mr.

Marks would drop me at my destination and then, with Malcolm in the front seat beside him, pick up other fares until it was time to call for me.

That winter Clifton Webb, Helen Hayes, and I were all playing in various theaters in Chicago, and we decided to join forces and give a party. It was a skating and dancing party held at a rink. Ernie Byfield, the manager of the Ambassador Hotel, catered it, and we served everything from hot dogs to caviar, from cokes to champagne. People came as they chose, wearing slacks or evening dress. Our guests, the youngest of which was a six-year-old from our company, told us it was the best party they had been to in years. It went on till dawn, with the help of very little alcohol.

The Republican National Convention was held in Chicago that year. Paul Patterson of *The Baltimore Sun* was at the Blackstone with H. L. Mencken, and they thought I should see how a convention was run. As the press box was restricted to the working press, I needed an admission badge. Fortunately, a Mr. Bone from *The Manchester Guardian* had missed his boat in Southampton, so I was Mr. Bone by day, and Dorothy, who came to Chicago for the event, was Mr. Bone by night. Our greatest pleasure was in watching the workings of the press. I understood for the first time why Mencken was so renowned and admired. He would sit at a typewriter in his shirt sleeves because of the heat, a cigar in his mouth, a green eyeshade to protect him from the glare, pounding out his report on the speaker of the moment. When he missed something that was said, he called out, without looking up, and a dozen notes were placed before him by eager hands, which he read as he continued typing. Paul Patterson said that Mencken rarely rewrote; his first copy usually went unchanged to press.

When we knew that *Life With Father* was closing, I received an offer to do a film of *Ladies in Retirement* if I could begin work by May 15. Ruth Gordon offered to play my part of Mrs. Day for the last two weeks, which would certainly have given the play a glorious boost. But Oscar Serlin could not release me. So I lost the movie role and the $85,000 that went with it.

Dorothy's intestinal problems had worsened in the previous few years. During the two years that she was touring in *Life With Father,* she was in constant pain. Finally, in the middle of her tour, she was rushed to the hospital. She was so ill that she could not even keep water down.

The Chicago company of *Life With Father* had closed, so I took over for her. When she felt better, she went back to the company, but the pain continued, and eventually an operation was necessary.

I returned to films after an absence of ten years to make *The Commandos Strike at Dawn,* a drama about Nazi-occupied Norway. Playing the same role for a year and a half had drained me; I had reached the point where I would look at the actors and say to myself, "Who are they?" For about nine months an actor can find new and imaginative things to do with his role, and it is interesting to see the reactions of different audiences to the lines. But after that it becomes increasingly difficult to keep one's characterization fresh.

Working in films at that time, however, was much less exciting than it had been twenty years earlier. Before I had been responsible for my films; I had involved myself in various facets of production. Now acting in films was largely a matter of doing as you were told and collecting your salary.

Jean Renoir, who had left occupied France to make films in Hollywood, approached me about working with him in his first Hollywood film. I agreed eagerly. But when he saw the script he brought it to me and said, "I've been told that I can't change a movement, a word, a comma of this script. We are two creative people; we wouldn't be happy working like this, unable to do what we wanted and believed in. Do you still want to do it?" I told him no, I would prefer to work with a less creative director if I had to work that way. After I saw the movie, *Swamp Water,* I was glad I had refused. The story and setting were the most unlikely imaginable for a Frenchman like Renoir. Considering his unfamiliarity with the background, it is remarkable that the film was as good as it was.

I wanted to get David Wark Griffith's story told on celluloid, where it belonged. I hoped to interest someone in doing a Great Americans series, beginning with the story of David, father of films, then going on to Thomas Edison, father of light, to Henry Ford, father of the motor car, and so on. I wrote a short outline, which George Davis bought and published in *Harper's Bazaar*. Jesse Lasky of United Artists was most enthusiastic about the idea. He and Mary Pickford were planning to do films together and were looking for their first story. Up to that time very few screen biographies had been made and no story of a living person. Lasky was willing to take a chance on this theme, but for some reason Mary was against it.

I had known Mary for too long to jeopardize our friendship by approaching her about it, so I turned to other producers, among them an executive at R.K.O. I did not tell David of Mary's decision, and in a letter to me he wrote, "Personally, I believe the United Artists release would give us a much better opportunity of realizing profits despite the fact that the late Douglas Fairbanks told me that they had robbed me of a million dollars by selling *Way Down East* with other pictures. . . ." What he was referring to was the block system. Whenever the company had a successful picture, it would lump that film with several weak ones and sell the group as a block. Each film would earn the same amount of money.

D. W. added that, if Gianninni, a banker, would advance us a half-million dollars, he was confident that he could persuade Sol Lesser or some other producer to join us. He believed that, in spite of increasing production costs, he could make a big picture for that sum. He mentioned that his *Abraham Lincoln* had cost considerably less and had contained spectacular war scenes.

> But I made proper preparation before we started shooting and made the whole thing in twenty-seven days. . . .
> I am absolutely certain there never has been a better chance for me to make another fortune than this very day. All I need is financial backing. . . . If one Lillian Gish is smart enough to get Gianninni to put up half a million, then the aforesaid Lillian Gish with D. W. Griffith can clean up. . . . Write what you think of the idea of approaching some of the United Artists producers. . . . The studios need producing companies to help

. 346 .

pay their overhead, so if Lillian Gish and D. W. Griffith approach them with $500,000 in their pocket, you may rest assured the Welcome Mat will be outside the door.

I was determined to see the idea of his biography realized; I was convinced that it could be a success. I hired Russell Birdwell to do publicity. He arranged for us to meet down at the old Triangle lot for photographs and interviews.

But I should have been forewarned by Hedda Hopper, who knew her Hollywood. In her column she wrote, "Lillian is continuing the fight to sell the life story of D. W. Griffith to the screen, which I know she won't do, 'cause if our producers are going to glorify anybody then it's going to be themselves. They've practically forgotten the man who started their fortunes—D. W. Griffith."

At first I did not believe her. I spoke to a number of studios, all of which said they were interested and wanted to do it. We would get our hopes up, and then suddenly they would change their minds, for one reason or another. It was almost a conspiracy of indifference. Perhaps D. W. had achieved too much fame, and the reigning powers were afraid that he would run away with the picture industry again. For him it was no doubt a deep disappointment and a bitter experience.

D. W. would never let his feelings show if he could help it, and he passed the failure of our plans off as a joke. "Well, I always thought she had brains," he would say, meaning me, "but apparently I was wrong. She thought she could sell this idea about the old man, but she didn't have sense enough to know that no one out here is interested in the old man." And then he would laugh.

During the early years of World War II, David and Evelyn lived at the Roosevelt in Hollywood, but the owners decided to break up their suite into single rooms to meet the sudden demand for living space, and it was necessary for them to find a place to live. Property values were high, but they bought a small house on Peck Drive on the south side of Beverly Hills. Situated on a tricorner, perched high above the city, it provided no privacy. It was finished in Spanish stucco, which David loathed. He said that he was going to Americanize the property by putting a fence around it, so that they could sit in the garden without being exposed.

When I first entered the house, I was startled to see the Victrola and the furniture from *Way Down East*. He probably had had these pieces in storage after the closing of his Mamaroneck studio.

David seemed to be out of place in his new surroundings. I had never seen him as domesticated. But, if domesticity embarrassed him, the happiness Evelyn brought to his life more than made up for it.

He still owned a ranch at San Fernando, which he had bought around 1920. It was about seventy acres, with orange, lemon, and avocado trees and a house where the caretaker and his wife lived. There was a large, open-air screened room furnished with wicker pieces and a grill. It was this room that David used when he went to visit the range.

Many Sundays he would go out there with Evelyn and some of his friends, including Herb Sterne, the writer; Dudley Nichols, the director; and associates from earlier days, among them W. S. Van Dyke, Marshall Neilan, and Del Henderson. The talk would be stimulating and gay.

The first time I went to the ranch I wanted to climb the trees for fruit, so I wore slacks. David laughed, but Herb exclaimed: "I don't want to see Anna Moore [the heroine in *Way Down East*] in trousers. It's a terrible sight."

"But I can't climb in a skirt," I protested.

We would often spend an entire day out there, a quiet, out-of-doors day that we all loved. Evelyn and I would bring food, and we would all go on a picnic. Sometimes David would bring a book, and we would read Shakespeare or Dickens. And Herb still recalls the evening when we read *Cyrano de Bergerac,* with David giving Richard Mansfield's interpretation of the title role and me reading Roxanne. Another day, on the way home after a picnic at his ranch, he pointed out to us the sites for the battle scenes of *The Birth of a Nation*.

He loved the ranch, and he had reached a point in his life when the land really meant something to him. He would look it over with pride, inspecting the fruit, much of which was marketed. He might have built out there, but it was still far away, and the roads were not as good as they are now. Today the land is very valuable, but it was less so when he finally sold it. When he had bought it, the oil rights had been reserved by the seller, so it was not easy to dispose of.

He seemed destined never to have money. Perhaps it was a character trait, because even when he had the chance to make money he spoiled it. He would always say: "If I'd only bought this! Look what happened. But if I had bought it, it wouldn't have happened. I'd have put a jinx on it."

Sometimes he screened old films that he hadn't seen in years—*The Avenging Conscience, Judith of Bethulia, Home Sweet Home,* and *The White Rose*—and when he didn't like a scene he would say, "I want to reshoot that." Some of his old films drove him out of the room, and he wouldn't return until they were over.

He had retained his interest in people. Sometimes when we went for a walk, he would follow a character around for an afternoon, observing how he walked and the gestures and mannerisms that revealed the core of his character. He was interested in the world around him and always had an opinion on what was happening.

One night at about 10:00 David telephoned me in great excitement. A friend of my cousin's from Ohio was with me, helping me with secretarial chores and driving, while I was working in a film. "You and Virginia get right down here," he exclaimed. "I've just seen a great movie. We'll wait for you and see it again."

The picture was *The Miracle of Morgan's Creek*. After we had seen it, we all walked up and down the sidewalk, talking about it. "It restores my faith in talking pictures," David said. "Who is this Preston Sturges? I must meet him."

Not long afterward Preston Sturges, who had produced and directed the film, Dudley Nichols, and David came to the house I had rented on Lenora Drive and, after dinner, talked far into the night. That was the beginning of a series of dinner parties and a warm friendship between David and Sturges.

About that time Greta Garbo said to me: "I've always wanted to meet D. W. Griffith. He is the only man in California I haven't met that I would like to meet."

"Well, that's wonderful," I said. "It will please him immensely. What would you like to do—go out for lunch or dinner?"

"It would be nice to have dinner at your house," she said. So I telephoned David while she was there. The invitation pleased him immensely.

"How shall I dress?" he asked.

"Well," I said, "wear your ribbons and bows and look your prettiest."

And he and Evelyn came all dressed up that night. It was a midsummer evening, very warm at our little house, and we had dinner outdoors. I think Greta was eager to meet him because she had been told he very much resembled Mauritz Stiller, the director who had first discovered her and had brought her to this country. She said as much, and it deeply hurt David's vanity; he had thought she wanted to meet him for himself.

At that time we started the Hollywood Great Books discussion group around our dining room table, with two students from The University of Chicago leading the discussions. (I had attended Robert Hutchins and Dr. Mortimer Adler's Sunday-night group when I was in Chicago.) David and Evelyn joined us, as did many others in the film world. When I went east again, there were more people wanting to join than teachers to oblige.

David came to my home in Beverly Hills often for dinner. I remember one happy evening when we celebrated his and Herb Sterne's birthdays with a screening of *Way Down East*. Richard Barthelmess and his wife, Mary Pickford and her husband Buddy Rogers, and Buddy's mother were there.

In the summer of 1945 David was awarded an honorary doctorate of literature for his contributions to the development of the motion-picture art. He wrote to me that he could not go to the University of Louisville to accept the degree because he was working on a scenario for George Cukor of M.G.M. The script was one of his own, *The Twilight Revelers*, about a troupe of actors touring the old West.

But, like his other projects, it fell through. Cukor, a perceptive man, had great respect for David and his contribution to the industry. He wanted the heads of M.G.M. to put David on salary as a creative consultant, not only to save his pride but also to tap the still-rich resources of his mind. The industry had done as much for Max Reinhardt, paying him a salary of $50,000 a year, yet Reinhardt, although he had contributed enormously to the theater, had given little to films. But the executives refused.

I had agreed to do *Duel in the Sun* for David Selznick. D. W. didn't approve. "Don't do films," he said. "You know what bad lighting and photography can do. They will only photograph you badly to enhance their lady loves."

His words proved prophetic. On one film that I did, the cameraman told the star, "Now stay out of Miss Gish's light or you'll look forty years older." They did work to make one look worse, unlike Griffith, who had always striven to make his character actors look beautiful.

When I repeated this incident to D. W., he consoled me: "Any actress can look good at any age, if she is good enough and still holds interest, whereas mere beauty fades and grows dull. I'll bet on you to survive no matter how badly they photograph you."

The day I arrived in Hollywood to work on *Duel in the Sun,* he was there to greet me. I hadn't unpacked before a string of bellhops marched in bearing boxes of orchids from Selznick. As I opened them, I said, "I believe Mr. Selznick thinks he has signed Hope Hampton." D. W. found this remark highly amusing.

But no one could have been kinder to me than David Selznick, both while I was making *Duel in the Sun* and a few years later, when I worked with him and his wife Jennifer Jones in *Portrait of Jennie.*

In the winter of 1947 I prepared to play with John Gielgud again in *Crime and Punishment.* When I told John that I thought I was too old for the part of Sonia, he said, "If you are too old to play Sonia, then I am too old to play Raskolnikov." But I was eager to play Katerina, which I knew Edith Evans had done in London and which she had said was the most difficult role she had ever had up to that time. John agreed to let me try Katerina, and Dolly Haas played Sonia.

We opened in a great blizzard. The critics were kind to us. I enjoyed working not only with John but also in a Russian play. The Russians think I look Russian, and they have used my films for teaching actors.

One afternoon when I was free I took Mother's nurse, Miss Fairbairn, to see Tennessee Williams' *A Streetcar Named Desire*. Afterward, we went backstage to see the star, Jessica Tandy, and I told her how lovely I thought she was in the play. "Yes," she said, "and I have you to thank for this."

Her words startled me, and I gave some foolish answer. Outside I said to Miss Fairbairn, "I wish I could think of lovely things like that to say when actresses come to my dressing room."

That night I was at 21 having supper with John Gielgud when Jessica and Hume Cronyn, her husband, came by our table. I said to John in their presence, "Jessica was gracious enough to thank me for her role in *Streetcar*."

A few minutes later, Hume Cronyn came back and said to me: "Jessica wasn't being gracious. Don't you remember, a few years ago, we brought you a play from an unknown playwright—which he'd written for you. He wanted you to do it out west. But you couldn't because your mother was ill. Jessica went west and played it and when he saw it on the stage, he decided to withdraw it and lengthen it. *Streetcar* is the same play; it's the same character—only the story's longer. If you don't believe it, get his book and you'll see that it's dedicated to you." And it was true; *Portrait of a Madonna* had become *A Streetcar Named Desire*. Had I gone west to do the original one-act play, I could have played it on Broadway.

In the East, I had heard rumors that David and Evelyn had separated. I telephoned Herb Sterne, who confirmed them. David had been very difficult in recent days; he had insulted most of his friends. He resented domestic routine and railed unjustly at Evelyn and the bonds of marriage.

Evelyn's mother left for the East, but conditions did not improve. David went to several sanitariums, but none of them was of permanent help. For months Evelyn struggled to help him. At last she could take no more and sued for divorce. David supported her plea, saying that he was "a bachelor at heart," and the divorce was granted in November 1947. Madame Sul-Te-Wan, his friend since the days of *The Birth,* offered to take their three cats, adding wryly that, as the animals resembled her more than anyone else in the family, she wanted to raise them.

I telephoned Evelyn, who told me that David had given her no choice. He moved to the Knickerbocker Hotel, back again to an impersonal hotel suite, a lonely, tragic figure.

David's idea of womanhood was that of the child wife—frail, delicate, compliant, loving. When he married he dreamed of a snug cottage, fresh curtains, spring flowers—even grace before meals. But the dream was in conflict with reality. He idealized womanhood on the screen, but when he had to live with it he could not make the adjustment.

I have always had the feeling that, if the two of them had left Hollywood, gone to strange countries, and discovered the wonders of the world together, his enjoyment of life would have been prolonged.

❧ 27 ❧

After David moved to the Knickerbocker, he went into seclusion. He stayed in his room, and at night he roamed the streets of Los Angeles, unrecognized. He didn't accept telephone calls, and his mailbox was crammed with uncollected letters. One day Ezra Goodman, a reporter for the New York newspaper *PM,* did manage to get an interview with him. On a trunk in the room lay David's floppy brimmed hat and cane. In the kitchen, gathering dust, were two cans of film, containing a print of *Orphans of the Storm.*

David spoke as he pleased. "I am seventy-three years old and I can say anything I like about this movie business." Yet he directed no blast at the industry. He mentioned the monotony of the West Coast climate and said wistfully that he would like to be in New York again. He commented on the movies of the time: "Today they have forgotten movement in the moving picture—it is all still and stale. The moving picture is beautiful; the moving wind in the trees is more beautiful than a painting. Too much today depends on the voice. I love talking pictures properly done . . . [but] we have taken beauty and exchanged it for stilted voices. . . . In my arrogant belief, we have lost beauty."

I was in Boston about to open in Sir James Barrie's *Legend of Leonora,* when the telephone rang in my room at the Ritz Hotel. It was a call from Lloyd Wright, David's attorney on the Coast. "He's dead, Lillian. He died this morning of a stroke."

The day before, David had been stricken suddenly with a cerebral hemorrhage at the Knickerbocker. Somehow he had managed to stumble downstairs and into the lobby. The hotel physician was called, and David was rushed to Temple Hospital. He was in a coma by the time he arrived, and he never regained consciousness. He died the following morning, on July 23, 1948. At his bedside were his niece and nephew, Ruth and Willard Griffith.

Because of contract commitments, neither Dorothy nor I could attend his funeral. Later Mae Marsh wrote to me that she and director John Ford had visited the funeral parlor where David lay in state to pay their last respects. An attendant told them that only four other people had been there, one of them Cecil B. De Mille.

But on July 28, when reporters and photographers were on hand at the Masonic Hall (David had been a Mason) to cover the funeral, Hollywood's top names turned out. Outside the Hall, the bobby-soxers, autograph seekers, and amateur photographers swarmed, treating the sad moment as if it were a premiere.

Inside, producers, actors, and actresses filed past David's coffin with solemn faces. Toward the end of the line came Madame Sul-Te-Wan, who had been waiting outside the hospital room when he died. As she reached the coffin, she burst into tears.

"God bless you," she said, weeping. "God bless you."

As the service began, Herb Sterne kept to the rear. "I was an honorary pallbearer," he wrote me, "but I didn't want to sit with the others. Many of them could have given Griffith work—and didn't."

As the pallbearers filed to their seats of honor in the front, one of Hollywood's most famous personalities whispered to Herb: "See how pale those old men look. They could have helped D. W. Now they realize how selfish they were, and they're afraid."

In two beautiful eulogies Donald Crisp, acting president of the Academy of Motion Picture Arts and Sciences, and Charles Brackett,

Academy vice-president, summed up what was for many people "the tragedy of his later years."

"Difficult as it might have been," Crisp said, "for him to have played a subordinate role, I do not believe that the fault was entirely his own. I cannot help feeling that there should always have been a place for him and his talent in the motion-picture field. It is hard to believe that the industry could not have found use for his great gift."

Charles Brackett added: "It was the fate of David Wark Griffith to have a success unknown in the entertainment world until his day, and to suffer the agonies which only a success of that magnitude can engender when it is past. Even the Academy's presentation of an Oscar in 1936 did little to ease Griffith's heartache. There was no solution for Griffith but a kind of frenzied beating on the barred doors of one day after another. Unfortunately, when he is dead, a man's career has but one tense. The laurels are fresh on the triumphant brow. He lies here, the embittered years forgotten—David Wark Griffith—the Great."

Among the survivors was Albert Griffith, his brother, who was known as Albert Grey during the years he served as D. W.'s manager. And there was Evelyn, his former wife. The honorary pall-bearers and friends who attended the services included Monte Blue, Charles Chaplin, Cecil B. De Mille, Samuel Goldwyn, Will Hays, Joseph Henabery (Abraham Lincoln in *The Birth*), Del Henderson, Theodore Huff, Blanche Sweet, Rex Ingram, Jesse Lasky, Arthur Ungar, Erich von Stroheim, Raoul Walsh, Lloyd Wright, S. Earl Wright, George Bagnall, Hedda Hopper, Emmet Lavery, Mae Marsh, Conrad Nagel, David O. Selznick, Preston Sturges, Laura La Plante, Walter Wanger, William Wyler, Gabe Yorke, J. Searle Dawley, Frank Borzage, Tom Wilson, Walter Lang, and Louis B. Mayer.

After the ceremony David's body was flown to La Grange and buried in the family plot at Mount Tabor Cemetery, near the old frame church where he had attended Sunday school. Two years later he was laid to rest in a new grave, surrounded by old rails removed from the Griffith farm and marked with a new stone given by the Screen Directors Guild.

Mary Pickford, Richard Barthelmess, Evelyn Baldwin Griffith, and I attended the services. The Reverend Lloyd Moody of Shelbyville, who had preached David's funeral sermon, said the prayers, and Albert S. Rogell, vice-president of the Screen Directors Guild spoke: "Dear friends, we are gathered here today in the presence of the Almighty Supreme Director of the universe to pay tribute to the master mortal director, David Wark Griffith. He rightfully has been called The Father of the Motion Picture Industry. Some of his blessed children stand beside me. . . ."

I glanced up at the crowd that had collected and looked into the faces of the young. They were bewildered by the reactions of the older people, who were pressing handkerchiefs to their eyes. How I wished then that they could someday know the beauty and faith that David Wark Griffith had bequeathed to them.

Afterward, I dropped a rose on his grave, not from a little chariot pulled by white doves, but by tender hands expressing what was in a sad, grateful heart.

The day he died I wrote:

Dear David,

Did you leave with a heavy heart? I know how deeply you believed in the goodness of the human family. But so did another man in a loincloth, who was shot to death in this same, sad year. You were bound together by your deep desires to bring peace to a confused and tortured world. If Gandhi left his life and teachings as our inheritance, you found the way to take them to the remotest corners of the globe—you taught us, as children, that we were taking the first tiny steps in a new glorious medium that had been predicted in The Bible and called the Universal Language. That when it could be brought to its full power, it would bring about the millennium. Since it broke down the barriers that many languages create, you knew that properly used, it could bring peace to the world. So you wrote on celluloid a new formula that would cure the world's ills. Your record of this new medium is there for all to see in the films you made from 1908 to 1912. It is strange that you who loved the written and spoken word so dearly should have created a new art form which spoke so clearly without ever putting a word on paper. I can still hear your indignant cry when you read that your film, *The Birth of a Nation,* was full of prejudice. You said these critics hadn't seen your picture or else they would know that the black man when bad was made so by the white. That you had been raised by Negroes and loved and understood them as only you could—and in that moment, the idea for your favorite film *Intolerance* was born. As I look again at the film, I wonder how its four intricate stories, with all their detail, could have been kept so clearly in the head of one man, without the help of a single note. This film was your answer to those critics of your *Birth of a Nation.* Whether you were doing little poems like *Romance of Happy Valley, True Heart Susie, Broken Blossoms, The Great Love, The Greatest Thing in Life, Hearts of the World, Way Down East, Orphans of the Storm* or *Isn't Life Wonderful*—they are all monuments you have left to point the way for others who will care enough to fight to make their dreams articulate on celluloid. May their prayers of thankfulness to a loving, patient mentor reach you and cheer you on your way. No century that has given the world a Dante—an Edison—a Griffith can be wholly bad. Had they joined forces peace would reign again upon our earth. Then unto you our farewell love, dear David. Thou art well loved, dear David. We shall not look upon your like again.

Lillian Gish

In *The Screen Writer* of August 1948, some of those who were close to David paid him tribute. Among them was Lionel Barrymore, who wrote: "D. W. Griffith is dead and there is wailing and gnashing of teeth. Yes, but a trifle belatedly.

"He moved quietly, a silent and rather sorrowful figure in this film capital for the last ten years. . . . I feel honored to have been associated with him in the smallest way, although, bless him, he always tried to make one feel his contribution was great even though it might have been piffle. He was my dear friend and I salute him with all my heart."

Frank Capra, the brilliant director, said: "Since Griffith, there's been no major improvement in the art of film direction. . . . He was indeed the poor man's Shakespeare."

When Cecil B. De Mille received the Screen Producers' Milestone Award in 1956 he said: "People used to flatter me by saying that

D. W. Griffith and I were rivals. Griffith had no rivals. He was the teacher of us all."

But to me the most moving tribute was James Agee's eulogy, written shortly after D. W.'s death. Agee wrote:

> He achieved what no other known man has ever achieved. To watch his work is like being witness to the beginning of melody, or the first conscious use of the lever or the wheel; the emergence, coordination, and first eloquence of language; the birth of an art; and to realize that this is all the work of one man. . . .
>
> One crude but unquestionable indication of his greatness was his power to create permanent images. All through his work there are images which are as impossible to forget, once you have seen them, as some of the grandest and simplest passages in music or poetry. . . .
>
> Even in Griffith's best work there is enough that is poor, or foolish, or merely old-fashioned, so that one has to understand, if by no means forgive, those who laugh indiscriminately at his good work and his bad. . . . But even his poorest work was never just bad. Whatever may be wrong with it, there is in every instant . . . the unique purity and vitality of birth or of a creature just born and first exerting its unprecedented, incredible strength; and there are, besides, Griffith's overwhelming innocence and magnanimity of spirit; his moral and poetic earnestness; his joy in his work; and his splendid intuitiveness, directness, common sense, daring, and skill as an inventor and as an artist. Aside from his talent or genius as an inventor and artist, he was all heart; and ruinous as his excesses sometimes were in that respect, they were inseparable from his virtues, and small beside them. . . .
>
> Hollywood and, to a great extent, movies in general, grew down from him rather than up past him; audiences, and the whole eye and feeling of the world, have suffered the same degeneration; he didn't have it in him to be amenable, even if he'd tried; and that was the end of him. . . .
>
> There is not a man working in movies, or a man who cares for them, who does not owe Griffith more than he owes anybody else.

Lillian and friend in the play *The Curious Savage* (1950).

Lillian and Dorothy arriving at Palm Beach to appear in *The Chalk Garden*. With them is Rover, Dorothy's Pekingese.

PHOTO BY BERT AND RICHARD MORGAN

Lillian with famed primitive artist Grandma Moses, whose life Lillian portrayed on television.

Lillian and Paul Ford as the "good" Americans in Peter Glenville's M.G.M. film of *The Comedians* (1967).

Hal Holbrook and Lillian in the Broadway production of Robert Anderson's 1967 play, *I Never Sang for My Father*.

PHOTOGRAPH BY MARTHA SWOPE

Lillian and Helen Hayes playing the pixilated sisters in the ABC-TV production of *Arsenic and Old Lace* (1968).

✲ 28 ✲

In the fall of 1948 Professor Glenn Hughes had his play, *Mrs. Carlyle,* ready for rehearsal in Seattle. I had not wanted to go so far west, but as he had written it for me I accepted, and went off to work with a delightful group of talented people. After three weeks I got a telephone call from Dorothy. "Mother is ill," she said. "The doctors think it's appendicitis and want to operate."

"Should I fly home?" I asked her.

"No," she answered, "they believe they have everything under control."

The operation was "successful," but Mother died suddenly on September 16. I flew back immediately. I was stunned and unbelieving; we had kept her well and happy for over twenty years. Professor Hughes asked me to return, as they could find no one to replace me in such a short time. We opened quickly for a five-week run. It was not easy to leave Dorothy in those grief-filled days.

The following winter there were offers from a new source. A gifted young man, Fred Coe, who was in charge of Philco Playhouse, sent me a script, *The Late Christopher Bean.* I have always been eager to try something new so I agreed to meet him, and soon I was playing in a vital new medium very much like the early movies. The main difference was that the performance was "live"; you had only one chance, and no one could prompt or help you. My enthusiasm and excitement persuaded Dorothy to do a play she had previously acted in, *The Story of Mary Surratt,* for Fred Coe. When John Patrick, the author of that sad, beautiful play, saw it on television, he told Dorothy that he thought it was better than the theater version.

I shall always be grateful to Fred for helping me to finally realize my dream of doing D. W. Griffith's life story. Fred produced for television a biography of D. W. combining a dramatic narrative of his life with excerpts from his films. I helped with the script. The program was called *Silver Glory* (the title was my invention) and starred John Newland as D. W.

One of the most distinguished shows that Fred produced was Horton Foote's *A Trip to Bountiful.* The play, about a woman searching for her lost spirit, was a bold step forward. After it was shown, the president of C.B.S. called the president of N.B.C. and congratulated him on the broadcast. "Tonight," he said, "television came of age."

A Trip to Bountiful was the first television film that the Museum of Modern Art requested for its archives. It was so successful that it was later produced on the stage with the original cast (with the exceptions of Eileen Heckart and John Beal).

The night *A Trip to Bountiful* opened, I received a treasured telegram from Robert Sherwood who, back in the early days of films, had been a movie reviewer on a newspaper. Bob, I recall, was the only film critic that Mr. Griffith took seriously. I wrote him and thanked him for the telegram. He answered:

Dearest Lillian,

I had a real jolt when I received a letter from you saying, "A thousand thanks for remembering me on opening night . . ."

Remembering you. My God, Lillian, do you imagine I could ever forget you. You were the most transcendent of stars when I was a $25 a week movie critic and I was thrilled when I had the honor of meeting you and D. W. Griffith and Dick Barthelmess one day at lunch at the Biltmore. Since then, you have proved yourself to be not only a great, divinely inspired actress but one of the finest, most essentially honest and decent persons I have ever known. So—if ever I miss an opening night telegram sometimes—don't ever imagine that I fail to remember you, with love—

Bob Sherwood

Eva Marie Saint was acting in the play at the time that Elia Kazan was looking for a girl for *On the Waterfront*. When he saw her in *Bountiful* he cast her for his movie. All the time that she was playing in *Bountiful* she was also making the movie, yet she never missed a performance. She would say, "This is what got me my job in the first place." Finally Fred Coe insisted that she not play matinees; the pace was too hard on her.

William Faulkner's *The Sound and the Fury* was the last television play that I did with Fred. Later, I acted in his stage production of *All the Way Home*, a beautiful drama based on James Agee's *A Death in the Family*, which won the Pulitzer Prize for the 1960–1961 season.

Fred Coe, who developed so many gifted directors, writers, and players in the early days of television, has always seemed to me to deserve the designation of "father of the medium." I suspect that he and Burr Tillstrom, the creator of Kukla, Fran and Ollie, are responsible for selling more television sets than any other two people. But I could never persuade Fred to use a trademark—a triangle in which would be inscribed "A Coe Show"—so that everyone would recognize and appreciate his talent. He was not interested in publicity for himself; he felt that only those who worked with him mattered.

One of the highlights of those early television years for me was my meeting with the great primitive artist Grandma Moses, whose life I portrayed on television. Grandma Moses was pure spirit. She may have had little knowledge in the worldly sense, but she possessed great intuitive wisdom. She was all affirmation. After the production she gave me one of her paintings, which hangs to the left of my living room fireplace alongside another Grandma Moses, a treasured gift from Helen Hayes.

In 1954, when Charles Laughton was about to direct his first movie, *Night of the Hunter,* he and James Agee, who wrote the script, ran and reran D. W.'s films at the Museum of Modern Art. Mr. Laughton wanted to capture some of the excitement of a Griffith film in his own picture. "Griffith's pictures made you sit up straight in your chair in anticipation of what was coming," he said. "All the surprise has gone out of modern films."

I played in the movie, which was about the battle between good and evil. Parts of the film were excellent, but it was not fully sustained because Mr. Laughton did not want to "ruin" Robert Mitchum's image by having him play a thoroughly wicked man. In the earlier days of films, it would have been considered a triumph to play evil convincingly.

The next film I worked in was *The Cobweb,* which Vincente Minnelli directed. One night he invited Ina Claire and me to his house for dinner. Liza was eight or nine years old then and completely star-struck. "As soon as you leave the house," Mr. Minnelli warned us, "she'll be giving an imitation of both of you. She's fascinated with actresses." Liza, I think, has developed into a fine performer, the true daughter of her gifted parents.

The following summer Dorothy and I were offered the leading roles in *The Chalk Garden,* Enid Bagnold's play. Our producers were two charming men—Richard Barr, who does Edward Albee's plays today, and Charles Bowden, who has produced Tennessee Williams. At first we were going to alternate the roles, but, as we had only three weeks before opening, we thought it best to concentrate on one. Dorothy chose the grandmother's role, and I played that of the governess. It was the first time that we had acted together on a stage since our childhood.

I had been concerned about Dorothy during rehearsals. Opening night in Toronto was worse than I had feared. Dorothy had not been eating or sleeping, so of course could not remember her lines. She wanted to refund the money to the audience. But the next night she recovered and gave a good performance, and we went on to a successful summer tour.

Yet there was a subtle but disturbing change in Dorothy after that. She stopped going out; she would not see people.

"If we can only get Dorothy working again, everything will be all right," Vincent Donahue said, voicing all our hopes. Vinnie was the sensitive young director of *Sunrise at Campobello* and *The Sound of Music* in the theater, and a devoted friend. "When she gets a play and returns to the theater, she'll be better," he predicted.

He took it upon himself to find the right script for her. But her old self-doubt reasserted itself with even greater vehemence.

"I can't. I can't do it!" she would say.

"Of course you can," Reba would repeat the litany. "All you need do is make up your mind that you will."

And Dorothy would protest, "Nobody wants me to do what I want to do." That was her everlasting complaint, particularly to Reba.

The truth is that she did not know what she really wanted to do. She had always had trouble making decisions and assuming responsibilities. In some ways she had never grown up.

Her room was always a ragbag of discarded dresses, hats, shoes, and bags after she finished dressing. She never settled for the first dress she put on. When she came home, her progress from door to bedroom was marked by a trail of garments, which she began to shed as soon as she opened the door. It was not that Dorothy was deliberately untidy. She just did not seem to know what was expected of her.

"Dorothy needs five people to take care of her," Mother would say with a sigh. We finally accepted the fact and picked up after her. She was such a witty and enchanting child that we enjoyed indulging her. First Mother and I spoiled her and later Reba, her friends, and her husband Jim. Reba called Dorothy "Baby," and so did Jim. With the best intentions in the world, we all helped to keep her a child.

I remember trying to teach her to be tidy. She had exquisite handkerchiefs and gloves, but her dresser drawers were always in a state of confusion. Her best handkerchiefs were lost; there were more single gloves than pairs. "Let's start with your glove drawer and try

. 365 .

to keep it tidy," I suggested. But my suggestion didn't work. Later, because of her disorderliness, I could not share an apartment with her.

When they were married Jim had run the apartment in New York, counted the linens, and sent her clothes to the cleaners—all with good humor. He neglected his work to help her whenever she needed him.

One year while she was making a picture in England, she decided to rent a house. She had been living there three months when one morning she met a strange woman on the stairs. It was the cook. Dorothy made a joke of the fact that she had lived there so long without knowing what her cook looked like.

She was forever losing things. Once, when we were in steamship offices in Stockholm buying tickets for a North Cape cruise, Dorothy left her tickets and money on the counter and walked away. Fortunately, we discovered the loss and returned to the office, where tickets and money were waiting for us. Another time she left my address book at Gristede's. Why she should have taken it from my apartment to the grocer's is something I could never discover.

She was also accident-prone. On the birthday of our friend, Berry Smith, we were invited to a party at her home. We took a taxi across Central Park to the Dakota. As Dorothy stepped out of the cab, she slammed the door on her thumb and crushed it.

Another time, we were leaving the apartment of Elizabeth and Tommy Noyes. The house elevators were being converted to self-service, so we took the back entrance. As we descended the winding staircase, she suddenly slipped and fell backward down the stairs, landing on her head. We dared not move her in case there was a spinal injury. It was not easy to find a doctor on a Sunday afternoon in midsummer, but finally her own doctor had us bring her to Columbia Presbyterian Hospital, where she remained five days for tests. Fortunately, she had been wearing her long hair high on her head, which was also protected by a hat, and she had only a small cut on the head to show for the fall.

But her worst accident occurred when she was run over by an automobile. It was while Mr. Griffith was directing *The Birth of a*

Nation. It was Thanksgiving Day, and we were all working. At that time we did not have a commissary at the studio, so we ate in a small restaurant about two blocks away. I ate lunch early and went back to the studio, but Mae Marsh, Miriam Cooper, Mr. Griffith, and Dorothy stayed behind. On the way back to the studio, as Mae and Dorothy stepped off the curb to cross the street, a car sped toward them. They avoided it but did not see a second car directly behind it. Dorothy pushed Mae out of its path. The car hit Dorothy; she was knocked down and dragged nearly forty feet. Her foot was injured.

Mr. Griffith carried her to a doctor's house. She later remembered how kind he was. Dorothy had great character; she did not cry. She grabbed his ears in her pain as they cut the shoe off, all the while saying, "Don't tell my mother; don't tell my sister!"

The tip of her toe was amputated, and she was taken home. While she was convalescing, Mr. Griffith sent over a small projector and film, and Mack Sennett, although he did not know her, also sent pictures to amuse her.

They were filming the great battle scenes in *The Birth* at the time, and Dorothy was furious at having to miss them. But Mr. Griffith made certain that she saw them all, as well as the film that she had been working on at the time—*How Hazel Got Even.*

"It's funny about my being in an automobile accident," Dorothy said during her convalescence. "I went to a fortune teller a month ago and was warned to be careful about automobiles. The woman told me I was to be hurt by one within a short time. And really, I have tried to be careful ever since, but that didn't save me."

I was asked by the U.S. State Department to do two plays at the opening of Congress Hall in Berlin. One was Tennessee Williams' *Portrait of a Madonna,* the original one-acter from which *A Streetcar Named Desire* had evolved. The other was a short play, *The Wreck of the 5:25,* by Thornton Wilder, a playwright I greatly admire.

I have been very fortunate in being able to act in the works of many of the greatest playwrights—European and American, classical and modern. I have always said that I am rather snobbish about my playwrights. But Shakespeare, of course, remains my favorite. When the American Shakespeare Festival Theater produced *Romeo and Juliet* at Stratford, Connecticut, I was delighted to play the Nurse.

In August of 1965 I reported to the Disney Studios to film *Follow Me, Boys!* and then came east to start rehearsals for the musical *Anya. Anya* was my first musical and my third attempt to work with George Abbott. Once was for *Boy Meets Girl,* a spoof on the movies, and the second time was for *The Nightingale,* which was, I believe, a poetic Chinese play written by an American. But each time something intervened.

It was a privilege to work for George. He has no duplicity. He does not flatter. He says what he means. It was a special joy to work in *Anya,* which was based on the play *Anastasia,* about the mystery woman who claimed to be the youngest daughter of the last Czar of Russia. All the time that I was in my dressing room getting ready for my role as the Empress, I could hear the lovely voices of the cast tuning up. But the play closed suddenly. The actors, singers, and dancers were heartbroken; everyone wept. We were all in love with the play. I still believe that one day it will reopen and be a success, because of its combination of Rachmaninoff's music with the most fascinating mystery of the first half of our century.

Dorothy was living at the Villa Chiara in Rapallo, that beautiful resort on the Italian Riviera. I was staying with her after finishing a film, *Warning Shot,* for Paramount in California, when I heard from the gifted English director Peter Glenville. Peter had directed me in 1950 in a stage comedy by John Patrick called *The Curious Savage.* Peter was planning to film *The Comedians,* the novel by Graham Greene, and asked me to play the role of Mrs. Smith, a well-meaning but naïve American visitor to Haiti. I accepted the offer. I would be working in Africa and Nice, which was a short motor trip from Rapallo.

The Comedians is about a group of people living in Haiti, but, because it shows conditions under "Papa" Duvalier's dictatorship, we could not film there. Location shots were filmed in Cotonou, Dahomey, on the coast of Africa. The cast included Elizabeth Taylor,

Richard Burton, Sir Alec Guinness, Paul Ford, and Peter Ustinov. The government of Dahomey treated us graciously, housing us in three comfortable cottages that had been built for officials who come to the country for conferences. Fortunately, we had air conditioning in our rooms.

It was a splendid company to work with, all professionals and particularly interested in the film because, as Peter Glenville said, "It will be the first feature film ever made of a live and extremely controversial political situation."

We spent two months in Dahomey and then went to Nice for additional scenes. I was in my room at the Hotel Negresco on the morning of Easter Saturday when the telephone rang. Princess Grace's lady in waiting was speaking. Would I come to dinner Sunday night?

After I had accepted, I realized that I had brought no dress suitable for the occasion. My costumes for the film had not turned out right, and I was using old clothes that I keep for such roles.

I telephoned Richard Hanley, Elizabeth Taylor's assistant, for help. "What a pity I didn't know sooner," he said. "Elizabeth had ordered several dresses sent from Paris, but they didn't please her, so I've just returned them. I'm certain one would have fitted you. Let me call Elizabeth."

Shortly after, a package arrived. With characteristic thoughtfulness, Elizabeth had sent over a lovely Dior dress and a full-length white mink. The coat was perfect, but the dress, unfortunately, was too small over the diaphragm.

By then it was 4:00 in the afternoon, but the concierge suggested that I visit the shop of Marie-Thérèse, whose clothes have great style. There I found a frock in pale green, but it required taking in. As time was short, the seamstress hurriedly basted it, and that was how I wore it, careful all the while not to take a deep breath.

I truly looked forward to seeing Princess Grace again. It would be our third meeting. The first had been when Fred Coe was planning the television production of *Silver Glory*. He had asked me to interview three girls for the role of Lillian Gish. One was Grace Kelly, an aspiring young actress. Several years later while I was making a film for M.G.M., I was having lunch in the commissary one day when Howard Strickling, head of M.G.M.'s press department, brought over a lovely girl and introduced her to me. "Yes, I know Miss Gish," Grace Kelly said. "I was sent to her for a part, but she didn't give me the job."

When Howard left for a moment and Grace Kelly and I were alone, I explained the reason to her. She had arrived at my apartment looking so poised and beautiful; I had thought of the young Lillian, whom I remember as gauche and frightened, and I had asked myself, How can this radiant creature interpret that girl? I told her I hoped that she understood.

Sir Alec and Lady Guinness called for me, and we drove to the palace together. The Burtons were there, as well as Peter Glenville. When I met Princess Grace, it was apparent to me that she fit beautifully into her new milieu. Grace Kelly, like me, had played the part of the princess in *The Swan,* and it was a singularly appropriate film for her. Her interest in those around her was genuine; her grace and kindness put everyone at ease. Her mother, Mrs. John Kelly, was also present, and it was clear where Princess Grace had acquired her beauty and graciousness.

Since Dorothy and I had been asked to do *Arsenic and Old Lace* on Broadway, a good many years had passed. In Rapallo, I heard from Thérèse Lewis, the television producer, that Helen Hayes was to play in Hubbell Robinson's television production of the play and had suggested me for the part of the other sister. I have known Helen since 1930 and am godmother to her son James and to his son, but I had never worked with her. I accepted with pleasure.

In February 1968 I was playing in *I Never Sang for My Father,* Robert Anderson's moving memoir, and I had to play matinees and nightly performances while working in *Arsenic and Old Lace.* We were allowed a month for rehearsals and the taping of the television play.

During the first three weeks of *Arsenic* rehearsals, we were expected at the studio at 10:00 in the morning, so that I had to get up before 8:00. I would rehearse until 6:00 P.M., have a quick dinner, and arrive at the theater by 7:00. By the time I came home from the theater and took my makeup off, it would be nearing 1:00. We also rehearsed on Sundays, which meant that I worked every day of the week.

Because commuting from the studio to the theater and back left me so little time I thought that I would have a cot put into one of the rooms at the studio and live there. But there were no rooms with windows, so I went back to sleeping in my apartment each night.

The last week of a television production is always the most hectic, and by the time that we began to tape *Arsenic and Old Lace* I had to be up at 5:00 in order to be in the makeup chair by 7:00 in the morning. During that week Lois Wilson went on for me twice in the Anderson play, once when we worked beyond the time that I had to leave for the theater. The other performances I managed.

It was a pleasure working in this production of *Arsenic and Old Lace*. The men in the cast were hilarious. Fred Wynn, who played the original Boris Karloff role, would go out for lunch in full makeup and scare the wits out of children who saw him on the street. He had to do it though; it took him two or three hours to put the makeup on.

It was great fun watching rehearsals of scenes I was not in. But, of course, when one is working acting is serious business. In television, especially, an actor has about one-tenth the time he should have to make other people laugh.

In developing my characterization I concentrated on the fact that my character's life centered on who was coming in that door. Her greatest excitement was when the doorbell rang. I thought that she should be played as a slap-happy child.

One night, not long after *I Never Sang for My Father* closed, I received a summons from Rapallo and was on a trans-Atlantic flight three hours later. Dorothy, stricken with bronchial pneumonia, died a few days after I reached her bedside.

Dorothy and I had been much closer than most sisters. We had always been concerned with each other's welfare. I remember what she said after her automobile accident: "I'm so glad it didn't happen to my sister. That's what I'm grateful for this Thanksgiving—even if I didn't get a mouthful of turkey because of it."

Even when our work separated us, there was a kind of extra-sensory perception that bound us together. I think of the first words that Hal Holbrook uttered in *I Never Sang for My Father*—out of context, perhaps, but with a special meaning for me: "Death ends a life, but not a relationship."

Within the last few years, Rollins College and Mount Holyoke College have awarded me honorary degrees. In each case, as I sat among the dignitaries, I thought of the meaning of a diploma for many people who receive education but are not truly educated. In my early years I used to feel inferior around my cousins; most of them had gone to college, and I thought that they knew a great deal more than I did. Now I realize that, although I never went much to school or received a diploma, I have kept right on learning. I never wanted to own anything but books, and I have always been curious and had the energy to pursue my interests.

I have learned the responsibility of my work and also its joys—the feeling of wonder that I am in a profession in which every day is a new challenge to the player who responds and appreciates it. Once I read that in order to do something one must be somebody, and therein, I suspect, lies the secret of a happy life. Christopher Morley once described a happy life as one spent in learning, earning, and yearning.

It seems to me that a happy life should be in balance, that one must live equally in the mind, body, and spirit. Those who are lacking in one of these three attributes cannot be totally happy. It is only by keeping all three nourished through the rich resources at our call that we can tap the true source of our strength.

I carry with me one of D. W.'s favorite quotations: "What you get is a living. What you give is life."

A Gallery of Portraits of Lillian
by Nell Dorr.